EX CULTU ROBUR

This book offers a major reassessment of the philosophy of Peter Abelard (1079–1142) which argues that he was not, as usually presented, a predominantly critical thinker but a constructive one. By way of evidence the author offers new analyses of frequently discussed topics in Abelard's philosophy, and examines other areas such as the nature of substances and accidents, cognition, the definition of 'good' and 'evil', virtues and merit, and practical ethics in detail for the first time.

Part I discusses Abelard's life and works, and considers problems of chronology and canon (including the question of the authenticity of the correspondence with Heloise). Part II analyses Abelard's ontology, epistemology and semantics, showing how he tried to reconstruct the ideas he had learned from Aristotle, Porphyry and Boethius to fit his presumption that there is nothing which is not a particular. Part III analyses Abelard's ethical theory, showing that it is far wider and more sophisticated than has been believed.

'. . . he has produced not only an outstanding exposition of Abelard's philosophy, but a work that opens up for specialists and non-specialists the world of twelfth-century thought.'
William J. Courtenay in *The Times Literary Supplement*

'John Marenbon has buried himself in Abelard's writings and in the writings of his contemporaries, and produced what must be the most scholarly account to date of Abelard's ideas.'
Roger Scruton in *The Times*

The philosophy of
PETER ABELARD

John Marenbon
Trinity College, Cambridge

Published by the Press Syndicate of the University of Cambridge
The Pitt Building, Trumpington Street, Cambridge CB2 1RP
40 West 20th Street, New York, NY 10011-4211, USA
10 Stamford Road, Oakleigh, Melbourne 3166, Australia

First published 1997
First paperback edition 1999

Printed in the United Kingdom at the University Press, Cambridge

A catalogue record for this book is available from the British Library

Library of Congress cataloguing in publication data

Marenbon, John.
The philosophy of Peter Abelard/John Marenbon.
p. cm.
Includes bibliographical references (p. 350) and index.
ISBN 0 521 55397 0 (hc)
1. Abelard, Peter, 1079–1142. I. Title.
B765. A24M37 1997
189'. 4–dc20 96–11872 CIP

ISBN 0 521 55397 0 hardback
ISBN 0 521 66399 7 paperback

WV

Suae specialiter suus singulariter

Contents

Preface

Like almost everything I have written, this book attempts to bridge the gulf between what, from the backgrounds of their exponents, may be described as 'philosophical' and 'historical' approaches to writing about medieval philosophy. I look at Abelard's arguments and positions, and I ask what sense we can make of them and whether they cohere with one another. But I do so within an historical framework, which is intended to take account both of Abelard's development as a thinker and the general presuppositions and aims of his work. Such a method runs the risk of producing a book that will interest no one. Whether I have avoided it, others must judge.

Indeed, there is just one aspect of this book where *I* insist on being the sole arbiter: the extent of my debts, in writing it, both to institutions and to individuals. I have for a long time had the good fortune to belong to Trinity College, Cambridge, which has provided stability and support for my work; and in Anne Barton, Eric Griffiths, Jeremy Maule and Adrian Poole I have had colleagues there who have shown extraordinary tolerance and warmth to someone with academic interests so very different to their own. I should not, however, have undertaken so ambitious a project were it not for my especial good luck in having been given a British Academy Research Readership for the academic years 1991–2 and 1992–3.

Nor do I think I could have completed my project without the help and advice of the many colleagues, who have discussed problems with me, provided material or read drafts of chapters or the whole book: Charles Burnett, Michael Clanchy (who also kindly showed me some of his forthcoming book on Abelard), Yukio Iwakuma, Edouard Jeauneau, Jean Jolivet, Max de Gaynesford, Arthur Gibson, Bodil Holst, Christopher Kirwan, Simo Knuuttila, Christopher Martin, Constant Mews, Richard Sorabji (and the members of the Warburg Institute seminar run by him and Charles Burnett), Padmush Thuraisingham, Alan Weir.

I owe a very special debt to Peter Dronke and David Luscombe for their encouragement, perceptive criticism and generous help from the earliest stages of my project onwards; and to Anthony Kenny and Neema Sofaer, who showed me, at a time when I thought my book was almost ready, that I still had *much* more work to do.

In William Davies I have had the best of editors. Laura Pieters Cordy has worked unstintingly, combining thoroughness, intelligence and kindness, to transform diskettes liable to give a computer indigestion into ones to delight a publisher. Jean Field smoothed the process of copy-editing with her combination of scrupulous care and intelligent tact.

An author's closest family usually looks to the end of the acknowledgements for its more than well-deserved commemoration; but mine, which deserves it yet more, must look elsewhere: Sheila to the dedication, and Maximus – guess!

Abbreviations

Abbreviations for Abelard's works, the logical textbooks of Aristotle and Porphyry and Boethius' commentaries on them are listed in the Note on the reference system on pages xvi–xx.

Abélard en son temps	J. Jolivet (ed.), *Abélard en son temps. Actes du 9e centenaire de la naissance de Pierre Abélard (14–19 Mai 1979)* (Paris, 1981)
AHDLMA	*Archives d'histoire doctrinale et littéraire du moyen âge*
Akademieabhandlungen	M. Grabmann, *Gesammelte Akademieabhandlungen* (Paderborn/Munich/Vienna/Zurich, 1979)
AL	*Aristoteles Latinus*
Bautier	R.-H. Bautier, 'Paris au temps d'Abélard' in *Abélard en son temps*, pp. 21–77
BGPMA	Beiträge zur Geschichte der Philosophie des Mittelalters, Texte und Untersuchungen
Busse	Porphyry *Isagoge*, ed. A. Busse in *Commentaria in Aristotelem graeca* IV, 1 (1887)
CC [cm]	Corpus christianorum [continuatio mediaeualis]
Checklist	J. Barrow, C. Burnett, D. Luscombe, 'A checklist of the manuscripts containing the writings of Peter Abelard and Heloise and other works closely associated with Abelard and his school', *Revue d'histoire des textes* (1984–5), 14–15, 183–302
CIMAGL	*Cahiers de l'Institut du moyen-âge grec et latin*

Commentaries and glosses	J. Marenbon, 'Medieval Latin commentaries and glosses on Aristotelian logical texts before *c.* 1150 AD' in C. Burnett (ed.), *Glosses and commentaries on Aristotelian logical texts* (Warburg Institute Surveys and Texts 23) (London, 1993), pp. 77–127
Cousin I, II	V. Cousin (ed., with the assistance of C. Jourdain and E. Dupois), *Petri Abaelardi opera hactenus seorsim edita* I (Paris, 1849); V. Cousin (ed., with assistance of C. Jourdain), *Petri Abaelardi opera hactenus seorsim edita* II (Paris, 1859)
CSEL	Corpus scriptorum ecclesiasticorum latinorum
D'Amboise/Duchesne	F. d'Amboise, *Petri Abaelardi Filosofi et Theologi, abbatis Ruyensis, et Heloisae conjugis ejus, Primae paracletensis abbatissae opera* (Paris, 1616) (see appendix, n. 11)
Dict.HGE	*Dictionnaire d'histoire et de géographie ecclésiastique*
Lottin	O. Lottin, *Psychologie et morale au XIIe et XIIIe siècles* V (Gembloux, 1959)
Mews	Introductions by C. Mews in *Op. Th.* III, pp. 15–81, 203–308
MGH	Monumenta Germaniae Historica
MPL	J.-P. Migne, *Patrologia latina*
MS	*Mediaeval Studies*
Op. Th. I–III	E. Buytaert (I, II), E. Buytaert and C. Mews (III) (eds.), *Petri Abaelardi opera theologica* (Turnhout, 1969/1987) (CC [cm] 11–13)
Ouvrages inédits	V. Cousin (ed.), *Ouvrages inédits d'Abélard, pour servir à l'histoire de la philosophie scolastique en France* (Paris, 1836)
Peter Abelard	E. Buytaert, *Peter Abelard: proceedings of the international conference, Louvain, May 10–12, 1971* (Louvain/The Hague, 1974) (Mediaevalia Lovaniensia, ser. I, studia II)
Petrus Abaelardus	R. Thomas (ed.), *Petrus Abaelardus (1079–1142): Person, Werk und Wirkung* (Trier, 1980) (Trier theologische Studien 38)

Phil. Schr.	B. Geyer (ed.), *Peter Abaelards philosophische Schriften* (Münster, 1919–31) (BGPMA 21)
Pierre Abélard	*Pierre Abélard, Pierre le Vénérable* (Paris, 1975) (Colloques internationaux du Centre national de la recherche scientifique 546)
RB	*Revue bénédictine*
RTAM	*Recherches de théologie ancienne et médiévale*
Scritti	M. dal Pra (ed.), *Pietro Abelardo. Scritti di logica* (2nd edn, Florence, 1969)

Note on the reference system

In the case of most works cited, details are given in the footnotes. Full details are given at the first mention, authors' names and shortened titles only at subsequent mentions. All primary sources, and all secondary works mentioned twice or more, are also listed in the bibliography. For the works of Abelard himself, the logical textbooks of Aristotle and Porphyry, and Boethius' commentaries on them, details are usually given in brackets within the text, using as necessary the abbreviations explained below.

In my quotations, I follow the reading and orthography of the edition cited, except that: (1) I adjust editorial punctuation where necessary to bring out the meaning of the passage; (2) where I give a reference to a manuscript as well as a printed source, I follow the manuscript reading; (3) in citations from the *Sententie Abaelardi* I follow the (as yet unpublished) Luscombe edition.

THE WORKS OF ABELARD

The following list includes all Abelard's known surviving works and direct reports of his teaching, and cites the best edition of each. (Questions of authenticity are discussed in chapters 2 and 3 below.) References in the text and notes are to the pages and lines of the editions listed and use, where necessary, the abbreviations given in the left-hand column.

Apologia	Ed. in *Op. Th.* I, pp. 359–68
Carmen	*Carmen ad Astralabium*: J. Rubingh-Bosscher (ed.), *Peter Abelard. Carmen ad Astralabium. A critical edition* (Groningen, 1987)
Carmen figuratum	E. Ernst, 'Ein unbeachtetes "Carmen figuratum" des Petrus Abaelardus', *Mittellateinisches Jahrbuch* 21 (1986), 125–46

Cat.frag.	Fragment of commentary on *Categories*: in *Scritti*
Coll.	*Collationes*: R. Thomas (ed.), *Petrus Abaelardus. Dialogus inter Philosophum, Iudaeum et Christianum* (Stuttgart/Bad Cannstatt, 1970)
Comm.Rom.	Commentary on Romans: in *Op. Th.* I
Comm.Cant.	Commentary on the Pauline Epistles by an anonymous pupil of Abelard, with material reported from Abelard's lectures: ed. A. Landgraf, *Commentarius cantabrigiensis* (Notre Dame, 1937–45)
Conf. fid. Hel.	*Confessio fidei ad Heloissam*: ed. in C. Burnett, '"Confessio fidei ad Heloisam" – Abelard's last letter to Heloise? A discussion and critical edition of the Latin and medieval French versions' *Mittellateinisches Jahrbuch* 21 (1986), 147–55
Conf. fid. 'Universis'	*Confessio fidei 'Universis'*: ed. in C. Burnett, 'Peter Abelard: a critical edition of Abelard's reply to accusations of heresy', *Mediaeval Studies* 48 (1986) 111–38
De int.	*De intellectibus*: ed. in L. Urbani Ulivi, *La psicologia di Abelardo e il 'Tractatus de intellectibus'* (Rome, 1976)
Dial.	*Dialectica*: L. de Rijk (ed.), *Petrus Abaelardus. Dialectica* (2nd edn, Assen, 1970)
ed.Por./ed.Per./ed.Div.	Literal glosses on the *Isagoge*, *De interpretatione* and *De divisione*: in *Scritti*
Ep. 2–14 etc.	Letters 2–14: 2–5, and 6–7, ed. J. Muckle, *MS* 15 (1953), 47–94 and 17 (1955), 240–81; 8, ed. T. McLaughlin, *MS* 18 (1956), 241–92; 9–14, E. Smits (ed.), *Peter Abelard. Letters IX–XIV* (Groningen, 1983). The Letter to his *socii* (unnumbered) is ed. in R. Klibansky, 'Peter Abailard and Bernard of Clairvaux', *Mediaeval and Renaissance Studies* 5 (1961), 1–27 at pp. 6–7 (see also chapter 3, n. 62).
Exp. Hex.	Commentary on the Hexaemeron: in *MPL* 178 (but quotes are taken, as indicated, from Avranches, Bib. mun., 135); references to the final section, missing in this edition, are to E.

	Buytaert, 'Abelard's Expositio in Hexaemeron', *Antonianum* 43 (1968), 163–94; they are prefixed by 'Buy.'
Exp. Or. Dom./Symb. Ap./Symb. Ath.	C. Burnett (ed.), 'The Expositio Orationis Dominicae "Multorum legimus orationes": Abelard's exposition of the Lord's Prayer', *RB* 95 (1985), 60–72; *Expositio Symboli Apostolorum* and *Expositio Symboli S. Athanasii*: in *MPL* 178
Glossulae	Commentary on *Isagoge* (incip. 'Nostrorum petitioni sociorum'): in *Phil. Schr.*
Gl.sec.voc.	*Glossae secundum vocales* (on the *Isagoge*): C. Ottaviano (ed.), in *Fontes Ambrosiani* III (Florence, 1933)
HC	*Historia Calamitatum*: J. Monfrin (ed.), *Pierre Abélard. Historia calamitatum*, (4th edn, Paris, 1979)
Hymn.Par.	*Hymnarius Paraclitensis*: *Hymn collections from the Paraclete* (Gethsemani Abbey, Trappist, Kentucky, 1989) (Cistercian liturgy series 8–9)
Planctus	1, 4 and 6 in P. Dronke, *Poetic individuality in the Middle Ages* (Oxford, 1970) at pp. 148, 119–23, 203–9; 3 in W. von den Steinen, 'Die Planctus Abaelards – Jephthas Tochter', *Mittellateinisches Jahrbuch* 4 (1967), 122–44, at pp. 142–4. For 2 and 5 the complete edition in W. Meyer, *Gesammelte Abhandlungen zur mittellateinischen Rythmik* I (Berlin, 1905), pp. 347–52, 366–74 must still be used
Problemata	*Problemata Heloissae*: in *MPL* 178 (but quotes are taken, as indicated, from Paris BN, lat. 14511)
Reportatio	Marginalia reporting Abelard's teaching in London, British Library, Cotton Faustina A X (unpublished)
Sc.	*Scito teipsum*: D. Luscombe (ed.), *Peter Abelard's 'Ethics'* (Oxford, 1971)
Secundum Mag. Petrum	*Secundum Magistrum Petrum sententie*: in L. Minio-Paluello (ed.), *Twelfth-century logic* II: *Abaelardiana inedita* (Rome, 1958)
Sent.	*Sententie Abaelardi*: quoted (by his kind permission) from the unpublished edition of

	David Luscombe. References are to the paragraphs of this edition, and also (Bu.) to the edition by S. Buzzetti (ed.), *Sententie magistri Petri Abaelardi (Sententie Hermanni)* (Florence, 1983)
Sent.Flor.	*Sententie Florianenses*: ed. H. Ostlender in *Florilegium Patristicum* 19 (Bonn, 1929)
Sent.Par.	*Sententie Parisienses*: in A. Landgraf (ed.), *Ecrits théologiques de l'école d'Abélard* (Louvain, 1934)
Sententie Magistri Petri	Ed. in Mews, '*Sententie*', pp. 177–83
Serm. 1–33, etc.	Sermons 1–33: in *MPL* 178; and see chapter 3, n. 80, for supplementary material
SN	*Sic et non*: B. Boyer and R. McKeon (eds.), *Peter Abailard. Sic et non* (Chicago/London, 1976–7); q. 117 in J. Barrow, 'Tractatus Magistri Petri Abaelardi de Sacramento Altaris', *Traditio* 40 (1984), 328–36
Soliloquium	C. Burnett, 'Peter Abelard "Soliloquium". A critical edition', *Studi Medievali* 25, 2 (1984) 857–94
sup.Por./sup.Pred./ sup.Per.	Commentaries from the *Logica* on the *Isagoge*, *Categories* and *De interpretatione*: in *Phil.Schr.,* the authentic last section of *sup.Per.* is ed. in Minio-Paluello *Abaelardiana inedita* (*sup.Per. (M)*)
sup.Top.	Commentary on *De differentiis topicis* from the *Logica*: in *Scritti*
TChr	*Theologia Christiana*: in *Op. Th.* II
tsch	Early drafts of *Theologia Scholarium*: in *Op. Th.* II
TSch	*Theologia Scholarium*: in *Op. Th.* III
TSum	*Theologia Summi Boni*: in *Op. Th.* III

THE WORKS OF ARISTOTLE AND PORPHYRY

References are given in brackets within the text, first to the standard numbering of Aristotle's works (based on Becker's edition) or, for the *Isagoge*, to the pages and lines of *Busse*, then to the pages and lines of the edition of the Latin text used by Abelard in *AL* (L. Minio-Paluello (ed.), *AL* I, 1–

5, *Categoriae vel Praedicamenta* (Bruges/Paris, 1961); L. Minio-Paluello (ed.), *AL* II, 1–2, *De interpretatione vel Periermenias* (Bruges/Paris, 1965); L. Minio-Paluello (ed.), *AL* I, 6–7, *Categoriarum supplementa* (Bruges/Paris, 1966).

THE LOGICAL WORKS OF BOETHIUS

References are given in brackets within the text to *MPL* 64, except for the commentaries on the *Isagoge* (*1inIs.*, *2inIs.*) where the references are to the edition by S. Brandt (Vienna/Leipzig, 1906) (CSEL 48) and those on *De interpretatione* (*1inDeIn.*, *2inDeIn.*) where the references are to the edition by C. Meiser, 2 vols. (Leipzig, 1877, 1880).

ANONYMOUS TWELFTH-CENTURY (AND EARLIER) COMMENTARIES ON ARISTOTELIAN LOGIC

These are referred to according to the numbers of the Catalogue in *Commentaries and glosses* (e.g. P14, C16).

Bibliographical note for the paperback edition

Aside from the present note and the correction of some typographical errors, this paperback edition is an unaltered reprint of the hardback edition, published two years ago. My purpose here is to draw readers' attention to two important books – one published, one about to appear – which alter our understanding of Abelard. They are both concerned mainly with Abelard as a person, and his relations with Heloise, rather than with his philosophy or theology, and so they have close links with Part I, rather than Parts II or III, of my book.

The originality and importance of Michael Clanchy's *Abelard. A Medieval Life* (Oxford/Malden, Mass., 1997) does not lie in any additions or alterations to the chronology and external details of Abelard's life, as reconstructed by modern scholars and presented below in Chapter 1. Clanchy's achievement consists, rather, in putting flesh on these bare bones and presenting a credible and vivid picture of Abelard's personality, aims and decisions. Clanchy also looks at Abelard's relationship with Heloise in a way which links interestingly with the discussion below (especially Excursus 2 and Chapter 14). There I (following on ideas proposed by Peter Dronke) question the old assumption that any intellectual influence must have been *from* Abelard *to* Heloise. Why not vice versa? Chanchy goes far further in the range and importance of what he believes Abelard learned from Heloise. He makes a convincing case that Heloise was not a teenager when she first met Abelard, but a lady in her twenties, far better read in the ancient classics than Abelard himself, who had specialized in logic. From her, Clanchy claims, Abelard learned to admire the wisdom and virtuous lives of the pagan philosophers, and later, when she was an abbess and Abelard a monk, Heloise's letters transformed him from a rather conventional anti-feminist to one of the outstanding medieval exponents of the abilities and achievements of women. Both these ideas are plausible, although the argument for the first is somewhat speculative because it depends on taking Abelard's account in the *Historia Calamitatum* of what Heloise said fifteen years earlier as substantially accurate.

Clanchy does not contribute to the debate as such on the authorship of the love letters (see below, Excursus 1): he believes that other recent scholars have made an overwhelming case for their authenticity. But his analysis of the letters does help, indirectly, to bear out the view that they are authentic, by showing better than ever before, and without a trace of anachronism, how they are psychologically plausible. Constant Mews's *The Lost Love Letters of Heloise and Abelard: Perceptions of Dialogue in Twelfth-Century France* (New York, forthcoming, probably in 1999) also contributes to the question of Abelard and Heloise's letters in an unusual way. Mews argues that a late-medieval manuscript records long excerpts from a correspondence exchanged by Abelard and Heloise at the time they were lovers. Although the modern editor of these letters raised the possibility that they might be Abelard's and Heloise's, the idea was not taken seriously. Mews now supports it with detailed stylistic and contextual arguments. He also examines the contrasting attitudes towards love held by the two parties, as well as looking at the wider phenomenon of male–female exchanges in the early twelfth century. Not until scholars have had the chance to consider Mews's detailed evidence and arguments will it become clear whether these new love letters will be generally accepted as authentic. Whatever the verdict, Mews's book – both by its presentation of the new letters, and through its wider treatment of twelfth-century women – will certainly help to shape discussions about Abelard and Heloise in the coming years.

John Marenbon
January 1999

Introduction

Unlike most of his contemporaries, Peter Abelard is a well-known thinker. General histories of philosophy give at least a passing mention to his theory of universals and, sometimes, to his ethics; whilst in surveys of the Middle Ages Abelard usually figures as the lover of Heloise and opponent of St Bernard, the representative of a new restlessness in intellectual life at the beginning of the twelfth century. Specialist work, too, has not been lacking. Almost every aspect of Abelard's work and life has been the subject of detailed study, from his logical and theological theories to his personal correspondence and the accusations of heresy made against him. Abelard is, none the less, a thinker who stands in need of a re-evaluation – and one which goes beyond the mere effort to compose a coherent picture from the mass of detailed research now available, or to provide a partial reinterpretation. For a single, underlying view has dominated discussion of Abelard's thought from the early seventeenth century, when a collection of his writings was first printed, until the present day.

This claim may seem surprising. Abelard was controversial in his lifetime and remained so after his death. The judgements of his work by historians seem, at first sight, sharply conflicting: some have seen him as superficial and misguided, whereas others have given him a hero's role in the development of philosophy. But, behind these differences, there emerges a remarkable agreement between his admirers and antagonists about the nature of Abelard's thought. Even his severest detractors have recognized the sophistication and ingenuity of his reasoning; even his eulogists have been ready to admit that he cannot be numbered among the great, original philosophers. His strength, both sides agree, lay in argument and criticism, not in constructing any coherent and wide-ranging system of thought. The judgements of two scholars, both leading experts on Abelard, show this common, underlying view very clearly – its development is studied in more detail below, in the appendix. Charles de Rémusat, writing his biography of Abelard in the mid-nineteenth century, explained that Abelard was a thinker 'fecund in details, comments, arguments, but not rich in broad perspectives ... a critic of the first class, but mediocre in invention'.[1] Over a hundred years later, Jean Jolivet (whose analyses have done so much to improve modern understanding of Abelard) writes in similar vein

> Abelard is neither a giant of thought, nor an author of the second-rank. His is a lively but limited mind, both helped and hindered by his character and historical circumstances ... [H]e is not responsible for any leap of genius, of the sort which goes beyond, and yet expresses, its age ... In a word, neither in his life nor in his thought was Abelard an *inventor*.[2]

Moreover, the work of recent historians, which has done so much to free our understanding of his work from anachronism, has also tended to give added force to the impression of Abelard as brilliant but neither profound nor truly innovative. Earlier writers were inclined to describe Abelard, whether by way of praise or blame, as a rationalist, and to attribute to him a set of characteristic, unorthodox views on central areas of Christian doctrine. Modern scholarship, by contrast, has shown that Abelard was far from rationalism in any sort of eighteenth or nineteenth-century sense, and many scholars have argued that, on most questions of doctrine, Abelard was much closer to the thought (predominantly Augustinian) of his contemporaries than was once believed. Outside quite technical matters of logic, it is implied, Abelard must be seen as important only in matters of detail and method – an attitude strengthened by an idea which has been taken up by more recent historians but goes back at least to the fifteenth-century historian Trithemius: that Abelard's theology is characterized by its application of the methods of logic to discussing Christian doctrine.[3]

The aim of this book is to show that this view of Abelard as a mainly critical thinker is inaccurate and unjust. His was more than a fleeting, superficial brilliance. He was a constructive and, at times, systematic philosopher; and, although it is certainly true that he (like many of his contemporaries) used the methods of logic in treating Christian doctrine, his theology is remarkable for much more than its method. Abelard's writings do not, however, form a single, coherent system. Abelard's interests and achievements fall into two roughly chronological phases. As a logician, he worked within the structure provided by the ancient texts which made up the logical curriculum. He provided cogent and often original answers

[1] *Abélard* (Paris, 1845) II, p. 547
[2] *Abélard ou la philosophie dans le langage* (Paris, 1969), pp. 95–6.
[3] See appendix (below, pp. 344–5).

to the philosophical questions which this study raised, but he did not pursue them systematically. He developed a sophisticated account of the semantics of universal words, but he did not resolve an underlying tension which runs through his ontology. As a writer on Christian doctrine, by contrast, Abelard strove to create his own theological system. Although he used methods and concepts he had developed within his logic, they were incidental to his main suppositions and aims. The bearing of Abelard's theological system was predominantly ethical: in the course of developing it, he elaborated a coherent, systematic and wide-ranging moral theory.

This book considers Abelard primarily not as a theologian or a logician, but as a philosopher. Since, however, his ethics is intimately bound up with the doctrinal questions he explored, Abelard's theology cannot be ignored, although his views on the various controversial questions about the faith are not its central concern. And since Abelard's consideration of ontology, semantics and epistemology is conducted in the course of logical commentary, technical questions of logic cannot be avoided, although they will not be pursued for their own sake.

The plan is simple. Part I gives a general account of Abelard as a whole: his life, his writings and teaching and the overall shape and growth of his thought. Part II looks at the mainly coherent, but unsystematic philosophy which he developed in close connection with his study of logic. Part III examines the ethical system which binds together his theology.

Part I

Chapter 1

A life

The main source for all except the last decade of Abelard's life is his own *Historia calamitatum*. Recently, some scholars have queried this work's authenticity, but their arguments are unconvincing (see excursus).[1] Although it is Abelard's own composition, the *Historia* must, none the less, be used with care. Abelard wrote with particular literary and didactic aims in view, exercising a careful control, which was not that of the dispassionate biographer, over what he included, what he emphasized and what he passed over in silence.[2] A range of other evidence can be used to fill in and correct the account in the *Historia* and throw light on Abelard's last years – contemporary letters and poetry, charters, chronicles and hagiographies. Above all, the wider political and ecclesiastical history of the period helps to put the details of Abelard's life into perspective.[3]

LE PALLET

Peter Abelard[4] was born in 1079 and grew up at Le Pallet, on the very edge of the Duchy of Brittany, only a few miles west of the boundary with Anjou and north of that with Poitou, in easy reach of the towns of the

[1] See below, pp. 82–93.

[2] On the genre and aims of the *Historia*, see below, pp. 73–4.

[3] Two particularly valuable studies from this point of view are: R.-H. Bautier, 'Paris au temps d'Abélard' in *Abélard en son temps*, pp. 21–77 (*Bautier*) and D. Luscombe, 'From Paris to the Paraclete: the correspondence of Abelard and Heloise', *Proceedings of the British Academy* 74 (1988), 247–83. A succinct but detailed account of Abelard's life is included in C. Mews, *Peter Abelard* (Aldershot, 1995) (Authors of the Middle Ages 5. Historical and religious writers of the Latin West), pp. 9–20.

[4] The correct form is almost certainly pentasyllabic: 'A|ba|e|lar|dus': cf. C. Mews, 'In search of a name and its significance: a twelfth century anecdote about Thierry and Peter Abaelard', *Traditio* 44 (1988), 171–200, at pp. 171–9, 196–200. 'Abelard' will, however, be used in this book since it is the accepted English version of his name.

Loire where learning flourished. It is not certain whether Abelard spoke Breton,[5] or whether his family was even Breton in origin.[6] His parents belonged to the minor nobility. Berengar, his father, may have been the castellan of Le Pallet or, more probably, one of the knights who guarded the castle and the castellan in return for small landholdings.

Peter was the eldest son and could have expected to follow his father as a knight and landholder. But Berengar had received a rudimentary literary education before he learned knightly pursuits and he saw to it that his sons too would be educated (*HC* 62: 13–17).[7] Abelard explains that the more he learned, the fonder he grew of study, until he decided to give up 'the pomp of military glory along with his inheritance and the privileges of the eldest son' (*HC* 63: 22–3). Choosing the 'arms' of dialectical reasoning and preferring the 'conflict of disputations to the trophies of battle [Abelard] ... wandered disputing from place to place – wherever [he] heard that the art of dialectic flourished' (*HC* 63: 25 – 64: 30). He could hardly be vaguer in the *Historia* about exactly where he studied, except to suggest that it was at more than one place. Here he seems to have made a deliberate omission. The young Abelard was taught at Loches and Tours 'for a long time' by one of the most famous logic masters of the time, Roscelin – as Roscelin himself reveals in a letter written over twenty years later.[8] Although Roscelin was not, as some nineteenth-century historians made him, a heretic, free-thinker and martyr for intellectual liberty, even stripped of his legend

[5] At *HC* 98: 1244 where Abelard says that he could not understand the language of the monks of St Gildas (cf. Mews, 'In search', p. 194); but Peter Dronke has pointed out to me that Abelard may have been saying, not that he was ignorant of Breton, but that he could not understand the dialect of Breton spoken in the Vannetais, the area of St Gildas.

[6] According to an epitaph cited by Richard of Poitiers (*Chronicon*, MGH Scriptores 26, p. 81: 26; quoted in Mews, *Peter Abelard*, p. 9) Abelard's father was Poitevin, his mother Breton. Mews ('In search', pp. 193–5) points out that the name 'Abaelardus' was shared by a contemporary, the son of Humphrey, the Norman count of Apulia, and he goes on to suggest that Abelard's own family was Norman. This may be correct, but the evidence for the supporting argument Mews adduces – that there was 'an ethnic divide' between Bretons and Normans at the court of the count of Nantes – is very shaky.

[7] Such literacy in a knight was by no means extraordinary: see M. Clanchy, *From memory to written record* (2nd edn, London, 1993), pp. 224–52.

[8] *Epistola ad Abaelardum*, ed. in J. Reiners, *Der Nominalismus in der Frühscholastik* (Münster, 1910) (BGPMA 8, 5), pp. 63–80; cf. p. 65: 26–7: 'Turonensis ecclesia vel Locensis, ubi ad pedes meos magistri tui discipulorum minimus tam diu resedisti.' Abelard's time as Roscelin's pupil is also mentioned in a rather garbled note copied into the first folio of a twelfth-century manuscript, Munich Bayerische Staatsbibliothek, clm 14160 (ed. in L. Hödl, *Die Geschichte der scholastischen Literatur und der Theologie der Schlüsselgewalt* (Münster, 1960) (BGPMA 38, 4), p. 78 and in Mews, 'In search', pp. 172–3 (with translation)).

he remains a controversial figure.[9] By the time he taught Abelard, he had already developed a trinitarian theology which provoked attacks from Anselm of Canterbury and, many years later, from Abelard himself.[10] But theological matters were not, at this stage, Abelard's concern. He may well, however, have learned from Roscelin a rather special way of interpreting the ancient logical texts as discussions about words, not about things – although later he came to regard Roscelin's logic, no less than his theology, with utter contempt.[11] Little wonder that he had no wish to reveal that he had once sat at Roscelin's feet!

PARIS

'At length', Abelard arrived at Paris. He was drawn, not by the political or intellectual eminence of the town – in 1100 Paris was fairly unimportant, both politically and scholastically – but by the master there, William of Champeaux, 'who was at that time outstanding in the teaching of this subject [logic (*dialectica*)] both in reputation and reality' (*HC* 64: 33–4). Surviving sources allow a glimpse – no more than that – of William's work as a teacher of the arts. As well as the logical *Introductions*, commentaries by him on two rhetorical works are known, as well as reports of his logical doctrines, which show that he had distinctive ideas about many areas, including topical argument, division, signification and modal logic.[12]

In the *Historia calamitatum*, Abelard casts William in the villain's role. His account of the years from *c.* 1100 to *c.* 1117 is the story of William's moves and machinations against his young pupil, and Abelard's counter-attacks, checks and final victory. William's initial approval of him vanished,

[9] For a critique of the legend, and a reconstruction of his biography, see F. Picavet, *Roscelin philosophe et théologien d'après la légende et d'après l'histoire* (Paris, 1911).

[10] Roscelin had to defend his views on the Trinity at a council held in Soissons in 1092, after which he went to England and then, perhaps, Rome (Picavet, *Roscelin*, pp. 50–2). Whether he taught Abelard in the period immediately before 1092 (until Abelard was about thirteen) or later in the 1090s, or at both periods, is not certain.

[11] See below, p. 109 (on Roscelin's method of reading logical texts); pp. 57–8 (on Abelard's contempt for him).

[12] See K. Fredborg, 'The commentaries on Cicero's De inventione and Rhetorica ad Herennium by William of Champeaux', *CIMAGL* 17 (1976), 1–39; 'William of Champeaux on Boethius' Topics according to Orléans bibl. mun. 266', *CIMAGL* 13 (1974) (= *Studia in honorem Henrici Roos septuagenarii*), 13–30; L. Reilly ((ed.) *Petrus Helias. 'Summa super Priscianum'* (Toronto, 1993) (Studies and texts 113), pp. 22–6) has argued that William also wrote the *Glosule* to Priscian, but his view has not gained general acceptance. On William's *Introductiones*, see below, p. 38, n. 3. On William's life, see J. Châtillon, 'De Guillaume de Champeaux à Thomas Gallus', *Revue du moyen âge latin* 8 (1952), 139–62, 247–72.

he says, in the face of his tendency to question and his success in disputation (*HC* 64: 34–8); and his older fellow pupils became envious of his abilities. Abelard decided to set up his own school and – since Paris was at this time still a straightforward cathedral school, with a single master – he chose Melun, the favoured residence of the king. William tried to prevent a rival school being set up so near, but with the help of some of William's powerful rivals Abelard had his way (*HC* 64: 45–57). He taught at Melun probably between *c.* 1102 and *c.* 1104 – and perhaps it was there, teaching close to the royal court, that he acquired the epithet 'Palatinus', which plays on his town of origin (Palatium) and the word's usual meaning, 'courtly'. Abelard's fame as a teacher of logic grew, he says; that of his fellow pupils and even of William himself disappeared. Abelard decided he could now move nearer to Paris, and transferred his school to the location of another royal palace, Corbeil. But after only a little time there, he became ill, he explains, from overwork and had to leave France for Brittany (*c.* 1105), although even there he was sought out by some enthusiastic pupils (*HC* 64: 58 – 65: 69).

By the time he returned to Paris, probably about 1108, William had given up his archdeaconry and moved with a few disciples to St Victor, a hermitage on a deserted site on the left bank of the Seine. There he followed the Rule of St Augustine, living the life of a regular canon, but continuing all the same to teach publicly.[13] Abelard decided that he would once more follow William's teaching, this time on rhetoric. Among various disputations with him, Abelard attacked William's view about universals and compelled him to abandon it for another (*HC* 65: 80 – 66: 100).[14] As a result of this victory, William's keenest students deserted him for Abelard, and the pupil whom William had appointed as his successor at the school of Notre Dame gave his position up to Abelard and became his student (*HC* 66: 101–8). But Abelard was not allowed to teach at Notre Dame for long. 'After I had been in charge of teaching logic there for a few days', says Abelard, 'my master began to grow pale with such envy, to burn with such anger as words cannot easily express.' William managed to have his original appointee as successor (who had handed over teaching to Abelard) removed entirely from the school, accused of grave wrongdoings, and in his place he put a rival of Abelard's (*HC* 66: 108–16). Abelard then set up his school once more at Melun. Not long afterwards (*c.* 1111) William moved away from the outskirts of Paris to the countryside, spurred

[13] *HC* 65: 71–80. Cf. J.-P. Willesme, 'Saint-Victor au temps d'Abélard' in *Abélard en son temps*, pp. 95–105 and Châtillon, 'De Guillaume de Champeaux', pp. 145–6.

[14] For William's view about universals and Abelard's criticisms, see below, pp. 113–14.

(according to Abelard) by rumours that his conversion to the religious life was incomplete. Abelard took the chance to move back to Paris but, since Notre Dame already had a master (William's new appointee), he set up his school on the Mont Ste Geneviève. William promptly returned and reopened his school at St Victor, but the effect of this was to attract away the pupils from his appointee at Notre Dame, who was thus forced to give up teaching altogether (*HC* 66: 116 – 67: 144). From about 1110 to 1112, the two schools of logic, William's at St Victor, Abelard's on the Mont Ste Geneviève, existed together, and their pupils and masters engaged each other in disputations.[15] Abelard, by his account, was victorious.[16] He was called back to Brittany by his mother, who had decided to enter monastic life (as her husband had already done). By his return to France in 1113, William had already been made bishop of Châlons, and Abelard decided to go Laon to study *divinitas* (see below) (*HC* 67: 155–63). After his brief stay there, he returned to Paris and from about 1113 to 1117 he was at last able peacefully to be the master at Notre Dame (*HC* 70: 241–51).

So runs Abelard's own account. But there was another, political dimension to these events of which he says very little.[17] William of Champeaux was not only a distinguished teacher; he was also an important figure in public life – 'almost the chief adviser to the king', as a student reported of him at the time just before he gave up his archdeaconry.[18] Through him Abelard was dragged into the pattern of rivalries and alliances which formed round Philip I and his successor, Louis VI. William was closely associated with Ivo, bishop of Chartres, a leading exponent of the Gregorian reform in France. William's greatest rival was also an archdeacon of Notre Dame: Stephen, a member of the influential de Garlande family, who at various times between 1101 and 1137 was chancellor and seneschal to the

[15] St Goswin's hagiographer describes what may well have been such a dispute, in which, accompanied by a group of friends, the young Goswin – at that time a student of logic – goes up the Mont Ste Geneviève, interrupts Abelard's class, challenges what he has said and (it is claimed) has the better of the argument: see the *uita prima* of St Goswin in R. Gibbon (ed.), *Beati Goswini vita ... a duobus diversis eiusdem coenobij Monachis separatim exarata* (Douai, 1620), pp. 14–17.

[16] *HC* 67: 144–54. D. Robertson (*Abelard and Heloise* (New York, 1972), p. 112) argues that the Ovidian quotation through which Abelard makes this point is being used ironically; there is a fine discussion of the whole question in M. Clanchy, 'Abelard – knight (*miles*), courtier (*palatinus*) and man of war (*vir bellator*)', in S. Church and R. Harvey, *Medieval knighthood* V (Woodbridge, 1995), pp. 101–18, at pp. 102–3.

[17] It has been reconstructed in *Bautier*, pp. 58–67.

[18] P. Jaffé, *Monumenta Bambergensia* (Berlin, 1869) (Bibliotheca rerum germanicarum 5), §160, p. 286, cited in Luscombe, 'From Paris to the Paraclete', p. 251, n. 29.

king. It seems clear that Stephen de Garlande was the chief of the powerful rivals of William (cf. *HC* 64: 54–5) who helped Abelard to set up his first school in Melun (where the king, at that time their ally, was residing); and that Abelard's move from Melun to Corbeil was dictated by the king's break with the de Garlande family.[19] Abelard's period of sickness in Brittany (*c*. 1105–8) corresponds to a time when the de Garlande family was out of favour; whilst William's retreat to St Victor, and Abelard's return to the schools of Paris, coincides with its rehabilitation, and the Mont Ste Geneviève may have recommended itself to Abelard because Stephen de Garlande had been appointed dean there.[20] The period from 1113 when Abelard was at last able to teach at Notre Dame was also a time when the de Garlande family was at its most powerful, and when the bishop of Paris was the man who had handed over the school of Notre Dame to Abelard in 1109, much to William of Champeaux's anger.[21]

This political dimension, rather than intellectual differences, may explain why the hostility between Abelard and William was so intense. Although Abelard certainly attacked William's views on universals, at no point in the *Historia* does he slight his master's intellectual abilities. In his logical writings, Abelard on occasion mentions a view as William's, and sometimes disagrees with it; but never contemptuously, in the manner he treats Roscelin's opinions. In the *Dialectica*, Abelard reports a view about the analysis of certain problematic statements of existence as 'his master's' – by which he almost certainly means here William's – and then goes on to explain how 'in order to defend his master's view' he would argue in a particular way.[22] This suggests a considerable degree of intellectual partnership between Abelard and his master.

There was less common ground, however, between Abelard and William's own master, Anselm, whose school at Laon Abelard attended to study *divinitas*. For Anselm – as Abelard's account (*HC* 68: 164 – 70: 240) makes clear – *divinitas* consisted of glossing the Bible. Abelard was not impressed by Anselm, calling him a fire which produces smoke not light, a leafy tree without fruit. He attended Anselm's classes less and less frequently and then, despite his lack of experience, made his fellow students the offer that he himself would comment on an obscure part of scripture – the prophecy of Ezechiel. By the third of his lectures, he reports, the students were all

[19] *Bautier*, pp. 54, 61–2.
[20] *Ibid*., p. 63.
[21] *Ibid*., pp. 63–4.
[22] *Dial*. 136: 19–20: 'Sed ad hoc, memini, ut Magistri nostri sententiam defenderem, respondere solebam'; cf. p. 135: 29–32 for William's view.

struggling to attend and anxious to copy down what he said. Anselm – stirred up, Abelard says, by two of his senior students, Alberic of Rheims and Lotulf of Novara – forbade Abelard from continuing his classes of biblical commentary in Laon, using the rather desperate pretext that, if Abelard made any errors, he might be blamed for them. In his description, Abelard goes out of his way to make clear that he did not set out deliberately to challenge or undermine Anselm. Rather, he began his classes in answer to a challenge from his fellow students – albeit one provoked by his own comment that a special training in biblical exegesis was unnecessary. But was Abelard, who had already competed successfully against an established teacher, really so passive as he suggests?

Abelard returned to Paris and, at last in charge of the school of Notre Dame, he enjoyed 'several years' (from 1113 to *c.* 1116) of untroubled teaching (*HC* 73: 243–51). Abelard's position now seemed secure; his fame spread, the number of his pupils (and so his wealth) increased. This was the moment when Abelard's future seemed most promising. But, as Abelard comments (*HC* 70: 252), 'prosperity always puffs up fools': there soon followed the romance with Heloise, and its disastrous ending.

HELOISE

The account of Abelard's passionate affair with Heloise found in the *Historia calamitatum* is at once privileged and compromised. No one knew what happened better than Abelard himself; no one, perhaps, had better reason to include some details and leave out others. It has already become clear how, in telling about the events of the previous two decades, Abelard shaped his narrative by careful omissions and choices of emphasis. Would he here, recounting a more intimate story, reveal all (or even, fifteen years after the events, be able to disentangle past motives and feelings from his retrospective assessment of them)? There are other accounts of the romance and its consequences, although each is unreliable or unclear in its own way: the sarcastic letter written to Abelard in 1118 by Fulk, prior of Deuil, who probably owed loyalty to Heloise's family;[23] Roscelin's letter to Abelard, sent at a time (*c.* 1120) when the men were exchanging counter-

[23] *MPL* 178, 371B–376B; a missing section is edited in D. van den Eynde, 'Détails biographiques sur Pierre Abélard', *Antonianum* 38 (1963), 217–23 at p. 219 (where – pp. 219–20 – a date before the end of 1118 is established). On Fulk and his motives, see Luscombe, 'From Paris to the Paraclete', pp. 255–6.

accusations;[24] Heloise's corrections to Abelard's report of her views, written nearly twenty years after the events (*Epp.* 2 and 4); and some enigmatic snatches of apparently contemporary verse.[25] From the evidence, taken together, there emerges a broad outline of events which is fairly certain.[26]

Abelard was living in the house of Fulbert, a canon of Notre Dame, in the cathedral close near to his school. Fulbert was the maternal uncle and guardian of Heloise, a girl of sixteen or seventeen, who was probably related on her father's side to the Montmorency or the Beaumont family and who had been brought up at the nunnery of Argenteuil.[27] Heloise's intellectual talents were probably stimulated by the atmosphere of the cathedral and its school; and she may also have become accustomed there to the idea of women living with clerics, faithful but outside the ties of Christian marriage.[28] Fulbert encouraged his talented niece's interest in learning and made Abelard her private tutor. He soon became her lover. All this took place probably late in 1115 or early in 1116.[29] Abelard himself insists that this was his first amorous or sexual experience: previously he had been well known for his chastity (*HC* 71: 272–5; 72: 331; 73: 369). Fulk of Deuil suggests that, on the contrary, Abelard was known for his affairs with women.[30] But Fulk is hardly a trustworthy witness, since his letter is

[24] *Epistola ad Abaelardum* 78: 3–80: 9; on the circumstances of this letter, cf. below, pp. 14–15.

[25] Edited by P. Dronke in J. Benton, P. Dronke, E. Pellegrin, 'Abaelardiana', *AHDLMA* 49 (1982), 273–91, at pp. 278–81; the rest of this article contains further discussion of the poems and the manuscript in which they appear.

[26] H. Silvestre makes a reconstruction along very similar lines in 'Die Liebesgeschichte zwischen Abaelard und Heloise: der Anteil des Romans' in *Fälschungen im Mittelalter* V (MGH Schriften 33, 5) (Hanover, 1988), pp. 121–65 at pp. 124–5 (= an extended version, in translation of 'L'idylle d'Abélard et Héloïse: la part du roman', *Académie royale de Belgique, Bulletin de la classe des lettres et des sciences morales et politiques*, 5th series, 71 (1985), 157–200). Silvestre, however, believes that *only* what is attested outside *HC* and the personal letters can be trusted, because he considers *HC* a thirteenth-century forgery (see below, pp. 83–6).

[27] See *Bautier*, pp. 75–7.

[28] See C. Brooke, *The medieval idea of marriage* (Oxford, 1989), pp. 89–92.

[29] These dates have been established with some certainty in *Bautier*, p. 56, n. 1. Bautier draws attention to the disappearance of Fulbert's name from the list of canons of Notre Dame in 1117 (later to be restored).

[30] Fulk refers to Abelard as a fornicator and frequenter of prostitutes (*Letter to Abelard*, 372D–373A) and later (374D) mentions sarcastically the weeping of women at his castration *propter te militem suum, quem amiserant* and offers (373C) the ironic consolation that Abelard can now be received as a guest without his host fearing that he will cuckold him. On the tone and object of this letter (which some scholars have taken as offering sincere praise and condolence), see Luscombe, 'From Paris to the Paraclete', pp. 255–6. On the question of Abelard's sexual conduct, see F. Chatillon, 'Notes Abélardiennes' III: 'Inconduite

intended to slight Abelard. Nor, however, can Abelard's own account be trusted: if he did have a reputation for promiscuity, he may well have chosen to cover it up in the *Historia*.

After a while, Fulbert discovered about the liaison and Heloise found that she was pregnant. Abelard snatched her from her uncle's house and left her in Brittany, under his sister's care. He made his peace with Fulbert, not only by apologizing and pleading the power of love to overcome the greatest men, but also by promising that he would marry Heloise – on condition that the marriage should remain secret (*HC* 74: 391 – 75: 424). According both to the *Historia* (75: 425 – 78: 551) and her own letter of many year's later (*Ep.* 2), Heloise argued vehemently against the marriage, but she did not prevail. She gave birth to a son, Petrus Astralabius, and she married Abelard. Abelard describes how, in order to maintain the secret of the wedding, the couple saw each other rarely, but how Fulbert and his followers, despite their promise, began to spread news of the marriage. Heloise in turn insisted on denying that it had taken place. To protect her from her uncle's angry reaction, Abelard took her to the nunnery of Argenteuil, where she was clothed as a nun although not veiled (*HC* 78: 551–79: 578). In her second letter, Heloise confirms that she spent this period at Argenteuil, where she shared the life of the nuns (*Ep.* 4, 79).

Not long afterwards, in 1117, Fulbert and his relations plotted against Abelard: a party of men entered Abelard's room at night and castrated him – an act which was recognized as illegal, since the two men who were caught were themselves castrated and blinded, and Fulbert suffered a temporary disgrace and confiscation of property.[31] Abelard gives a very clear explanation in the *Historia* of why Fulbert arranged the attack on him. When Fulbert and his relations heard that Heloise was at Argenteuil they thought that Abelard had tricked them (with the secret marriage) and that, wanting to be rid of Heloise, he had made her become a nun.[32] This is a plausible story, and it is difficult to see why Abelard would have invented it were it not true.

Abelard describes his reaction to castration as shame – both about his past conduct and his present status as a eunuch – combined with the feeling that God had justly punished him. In his 'wretchedness and contrition' he

d'Abélard avant la rencontre d'Héloise', *Revue du moyen âge latin* 20 (1964), 318–34 and Silvestre, 'Die Liebesgeschichte', pp. 139–40.

31 *HC* 79: 578–91; for Fulbert's disgrace, see n. 29 above; cf. J. Verger, 'Abélard et les milieux sociaux de son temps' in *Abélard en son temps*, pp. 107–31 at p. 120.

32 *HC* 79: 578–81: 'avunculus et consanguinei seu affines ejus opinati sunt me nunc sibi plurimum illusisse, et ab ea moniali facta me sic facile velle expedire'.

chose to become a monk, he says, in the confusion of his shame rather than from devotion to monastic life. He asked Heloise to become a nun even before he entered his monastery, and she willingly obeyed his command (*HC* 80: 592 – 81: 627). There were, perhaps, social assumptions and pressures which may have made such a drastic choice, for himself and Heloise, seem almost inevitable to Abelard.[33]

ST DENIS AND THE COUNCIL OF SOISSONS

Abelard did not, however, choose to seclude himself in a remote monastery. He entered St Denis, only a few miles from Paris. One reason for the choice of this rich abbey, closely connected with the French monarchy, may have been that Abelard's patrons enjoyed great influence over the king at this time. Other reasons may have been the abbey's proximity to Heloise at Argenteuil, and to Paris.[34] For Abelard's mode of life was not, in fact, so greatly changed. After a period at St Denis itself, Abelard moved to a house belonging to the abbey and occupied himself there 'in his accustomed manner' as a schoolmaster, attracting crowds of pupils (*HC* 82: 665–7). Abelard explains his behaviour in two (not entirely mutually coherent) ways. He was begged, he says, both by his abbot and by other clerics to continue the teaching he had formerly given in order to win praise and money, but now to do it for the love of God and for the benefit of the poor (*HC* 81: 642–54). And, he adds, he made himself unpopular by criticizing the degenerate life of his abbot and fellow monks, so that they were keen to remove him from their midst (*HC* 81: 654 – 82: 662). But Roscelin says nothing of Abelard's being driven out of St Denis (although this might have suited his critical purposes). He suggests that the abbot and monks went to great lengths to meet Abelard's wishes, and when the first house to which he went did not meet his requirements, allowed him another one in which to set up his school. Roscelin insists that he continued to earn money from his teaching and to take this money personally to Heloise.[35]

Abelard was quickly afflicted by new troubles. His theological teaching had already been criticized by his old master, Roscelin, before he wrote it

[33] Y. Ferroul ('Bienheureuse castration. Sexualité et vie intellectuelle à l'époque d'Abélard', *Bien dire et bien aprandre* 4 (1986), 1–28) is one of the few historians to explore these questions. He shows convincingly that various courses of action were in principle open, but his suggestion that Abelard chose monastic life in order to realize his full intellectual potentialities is not well supported – and certainly not by *HC*!

[34] As Luscombe suggests in *Peter Abelard* (London, 1979), p. 13.

[35] *Epistola ad Abaelardum*, p. 79: 12–35.

up as the treatise now known as *Theologia Summi Boni*.[36] But it was not Roscelin, it seems, but rather two pupils of Anselm of Laon, Alberic of Rheims and Lotulf of Novara, now masters of the school at Rheims (*HC* 83: 710–12), who instigated the proceedings which would lead to the work's condemnation at the Council of Soissons.[37] Abelard plausibly ascribes their hostility to their wish to be thought the sole heirs of Anselm and William. A competent expositor of scripture, Alberic was unequal to the subtleties of more speculative theology.[38] But he and Lotulf were very skilled when it came to political manipulation. They saw to it that Abelard was summoned, in March 1121, to a council at Soissons, in the province of their own archbishop (of Rheims), to be held in the presence of the papal legate, Cono of Palestrina. Cono was a leading exponent of the Gregorian reform and had worked closely with William of Champeaux.[39] He might well be expected to be hostile towards Abelard. Abelard says (*HC* 84: 736–9) that the council was able to find nothing heretical in his book. Abelard's case was championed at the council by Geoffrey, bishop of Chartres (and, it seems, ally of Abelard's patron, Stephen de Garlande).[40] Geoffrey first proposed (*HC* 86: 809–12) that Abelard should be allowed freely to defend his doctrine against whatever objections were made to it. When this was not accepted, he suggested a compromise. Abelard should return to St Denis and a larger council should meet there to examine his case (*HC* 86: 823–32). The legate, says Abelard, accepted this suggestion, but Alberic and Lotulf realized that they would be unlikely to succeed against Abelard

[36] See below, pp. 54–8.

[37] The only primary sources for the Council are Abelard's own account (*HC* 83: 714–89: 909) and a brief one in Otto of Freising's *Gesta Friderici* (ed. G. Waitz and B. von Simson (3rd edn, Hanover/Leipzig, 1912, MGH Scrip.rer.ger. in usu scholarum), 69: 27–34; cf. *Mews*, pp. 54–7, and also J. Miethke, 'Theologenprozesse in der ersten Phasen ihrer institutionellen Ausbildung: die Verfahren gegen Peter Abaelard und Gilbert von Poitiers', *Viator* 6 (1975), 87–116, at pp. 92–5 and J. van Laarhoven, 'Magisterium en theologie in de 12e eeuw', *Tijdschrift voor Theologie* 21 (1981), 109–31, at pp. 110–15. On Alberic, Lotulf and the school of Rheims, see J. Williams, 'The cathedral school of Reims in the time of Master Alberic, 1118–1136', *Traditio* 20 (1964), 93–114, esp. pp. 94–6.

[38] Abelard *TChr* 301: 1128–302: 1146 (cf. *TSch* 440: 1003–14); *HC* 84: 751–85: 777; cf. Williams, 'The school of Reims', pp. 97–9, 104–5.

[39] See T. Schieffer, *Die päpstlichen Legaten in Frankreich* (Berlin, 1935) (Historische Studien 263), pp. 198–212; art. Conon de Préneste by C. Dereine in *Dict.HGE* XIII, cols. 461–71. Abelard suggests in *HC* (87: 845; cf. 89: 932–4) that the legate was not himself in favour of the condemnation. The fact remains, however, that Cono allowed himself to be persuaded to a solution which, if in a sense a compromise, was one far less favourable than Abelard might reasonably have hoped.

[40] *Bautier*, p. 68.

outside their own diocese (St Denis was in the ecclesiastical province of Sens, where the archbishop, Henry Sanglier, was a cousin of Stephen de Garlande).[41] They needed to persuade the archbishop and the papal legate, and they chose carefully the argument which they would put to each. To the archbishop they said that it would be very shameful to him if this case were transferred to another set of judges, and also that it would be dangerous if Abelard were allowed to escape in this way. To the legate they argued that it was reason enough for condemnation that Abelard had read the book publicly and allowed it to be transcribed without the approval of the Pope or ecclesiastical authority (*HC* 87: 838–52). The legate, says Abelard, was 'less well educated than he should have been' and relied greatly on the archbishop's advice; and the archbishop, in his turn, relied on that of Alberic and Lotulf. Cono was thus brought, unwillingly, to change his mind and condemn the book without enquiry (*HC* 87: 855–7, 838–46). Abelard was forced to suffer all the indignity of a condemnation: himself to cast his work into the flames, and to recite a confession of faith, not in his own words, but those of the Athanasian creed, 'which any boy could do'. To increase Abelard's humiliation, he was handed the text of the creed 'in case he should say that he did not know it' (*HC* 88: 902–4). He was also to be confined perpetually in a monastery other than his own (*HC* 87: 847–8). Yet this end to the proceedings at Soissons was less disastrous for Abelard than it might appear. The legate seems to have agreed (or at least indicated) in advance to Bishop Geoffrey (who had told Abelard) that he would revoke the sentence of imprisonment almost immediately (*HC* 87: 857–67). Abelard was sent to St Médard, a monastery to which (according to its prior's hagiographer) unlearned monks were entrusted, 'so that they might be educated; dissolute ones, to be corrected; headstrong ones, to be tamed'.[42] Goswin, who was prior there, had already tussled with Abelard when he had been a student, and Abelard a teacher, of logic. If his hagiographer is to be trusted, he handled this second encounter with a patronizing kindness, which he was quick to exchange for threats of physical punishment when Abelard gave a sarcastic reply.[43] After a short while, the legate released Abelard, as promised, and he was sent back to his own monastery.

He did not remain there long. A quarrel arose between Abelard and the monastery about whether their founder, St Denis, had been bishop of

[41] *Ibid.*

[42] *Beati Goswini vita*, p. 78; cf. J. Miethke, 'Abaelards Stellung zur Kirchenreform. Eine biographische Studie', *Francia* 1 (1973), 158–92, at p. 162.

[43] *Beati Goswini vita*, pp. 78–80.

Athens (as the ninth-century abbot, Hilduin, held) or Corinth (Bede's view, which Abelard held to be weightier). Abelard was accused, not merely of insulting the monastery, but the very kingdom of France (*HC* 90: 962 – 91: 981). It was under these circumstances, Abelard says, that one night he left St Denis secretly and made his way to the territory of Count Theobald, which is where his *cella* had been previously. This time he stayed at St Ayoul of Provins (a house belonging to the monastery of Moutier-la-Celle) where his friend Radulphus was prior (*HC* 91: 987 – 95).[44]

THE PARACLETE AND ST GILDAS

Once Abelard had set himself up at the priory of St Ayoul in Provins, he probably intended to run a school there; but neither he nor the prior nor Count Theobald could persuade Adam, the abbot of St Denis, to absolve him and to give him permission to live as a monk wherever he chose (*HC* 91: 981–1016). Adam died shortly afterwards and was succeeded by Suger.[45] At first, Suger was equally deaf to Abelard's requests, despite the support of the bishop of Meaux. Abelard called on his powerful supporter Stephen de Garlande and managed to obtain from Suger an agreement – confirmed in the presence of the king – that he could go 'to whatever solitary place he wished' provided he did not place himself under the obedience of any other abbot (*HC* 92: 1018–37).

Abelard was given a small piece of land in the parish of Quincey, near Nogent-sur-Seine, in the county of Champagne. There he built an oratory in mud and wattle, which he dedicated – with a defiant reference to his condemnation at Soissons – to the Holy Trinity (*HC* 1037–42).[46] He did not remain alone, but came to run what was both a school and a sort of monastery. His own account emphasizes the monastic or eremitical aspect. Abelard explains that he was forced to set up as a schoolmaster by 'intolerable poverty', and that his pupils were able to take over the running of the

[44] See Miethke, 'Abaelards Stellung', p. 163. Abelard's Letter 11, to the abbot monks of St Denis, may be a retraction (though one which in fact gives way little in principle) demanded by Abbot Adam – see E. Jeauneau, '"Pierre Abélard à Saint-Denis"' in *Abélard en son temps*, pp. 161–73 at pp. 168–72 and Smits, *Abelard. Letters IX–XIV*, pp. 139–53. It remains possible, however, that in *HC* Abelard exaggerates the seriousness of the affair. There is no indication that, after the Council of Soissons, Abelard would have been allowed by the monastery, as before, to continue teaching: was this the real reason for his flight?

[45] On Suger, see L. Grodecki, 'Abélard et Suger' in *Pierre Abélard*, pp. 279–86; J. Benton, 'Suger's life and personality' and G. Constable, 'Suger's monastic administration' in P. Gerson (ed.), *Abbot Suger and Saint-Denis* (New York, 1986), pp. 3–15, 17–32.

[46] See Miethke, 'Abaelards Stellung', p. 165.

establishment, leaving him free for his studies; and that, in any case, those who had deserted the comforts of the towns for the austerities of the wilderness were less like students than hermits (*HC* 94: 1109–19; 92: 1046–50; 94: 1092–3). In fact, Abelard's new school seems to have been a great success. The original oratory was replaced by a larger construction in wood and stone, which Abelard rededicated to the Paraclete, the Comforter (*HC* 94: 1116 – 95: 1124). Although Abelard by no means conceals his success in attracting students, his account in the *Historia* quickly passes on to the envy and detraction which this aroused. But the time at the Paraclete was in fact one of Abelard's longer periods of uninterrupted teaching, beginning in 1122 and probably lasting until 1127.

The opposition to Abelard did not come this time directly from the schoolmasters, but from a couple of what Abelard sarcastically calls 'new apostles', stirred up against him by his rivals (*HC* 97: 1200–2). One ('whose boast was that he restored monastic life') has traditionally been identified as St Bernard; the other ('whose boast was that he had restored the life of regular canons') as St Norbert of Xanten, whom Abelard makes clear elsewhere that he regarded as fraudulent.[47] Some scholars have questioned whether Bernard is meant here; but the identification is very plausible, especially since at this time Bernard was conducting a wider campaign, mainly through Suger, against the de Garlande family and their associates.[48] According to Abelard, these new apostles preached against him, casting aspersions on both his faith and his manner of life and turning some of his powerful supporters against him (*HC* 97: 1204–10). Abelard says that he entertained the idea of fleeing his persecutors by exiling himself from Christian lands entirely to 'live a Christian life among the enemies of Christ' (*HC* 97: 1221 – 98: 1228).

[47] See his description of Norbert's unsuccessful attempt to raise people from the dead in *Serm.* 33, 605C. On Abelard and Norbert, see also W. Grauwen, 'Het getuigenis van Abaelard over Norbert van Gennep', *Analecta praemonstratensia* 63 (1987), 5–25 and 'Nogmaals over Abaelard, Bernard en Norbert', *Analecta praemonstratensia* 65 (1989), 162–5.

[48] A. Borst ('Abälard und Bernhard', *Historische Zeitschrift* 186 (1958), 497–526, at pp. 501–3) argues that by 'the restorer of the monastic life' Abelard meant, not Bernard, but Norbert, and by 'the restorer of the regular canons', Abelard was referring to Norbert's companion, Hugo Farsitus. But Miethke ('Abaelards Stellung', pp. 167–9) puts a strong case for the traditional identification. A detailed account of different scholars' arguments is given in E. Little, 'Relations between St Bernard and Abelard before 1139' in M. Pennington (ed.), *Saint Bernard of Clairvaux* (Kalamazoo, 1977), pp. 155–68. For Suger's part cf. *Bautier*, p. 69 and Benton 'Suger's life', p. 5 and n. 22 (where he describes Bautier's case as 'reasonable but not proven').

In fact, sometime between 1126 and 1128,[49] he left France and returned to his native Brittany, when he accepted election to the abbacy of St Gildas, a remote monastery in the Breton-speaking part of the region, on the Rhuys peninsula not far from Vannes. Abelard presents his time at St Gildas as a type of exile and, in an aside, he makes clear that he would not have sought the abbacy voluntarily.[50] Suger's consent was easily obtained for Abelard to attach himself to another monastery (*HC* 98: 1238–9). Perhaps Suger saw this as a chance to remove Abelard from the kingdom; perhaps as a way of bringing reform to a particularly corrupt monastery. For St Gildas, it seems, displayed all the vices of unreformed Benedictinism. Instead of living a communal, celibate life, without any goods of their own, the monks kept their concubines and children from their own pockets; and a local magnate had taken over much of the monastery's land and exacted heavy taxes from the monks (*HC* 99: 1262–71). Abelard may, in his early years as a monk, have been less outspoken and enthusiastic a reformer than his self-portrayal in the *Historia* would suggest; but his writings from the mid and late 1120s indicate that, by the time he went to St Gildas, the ideal of an austere, self-denying, collective monastic life had become one of the themes dominating his thought.[51] Abelard regarded it as his duty to try to reform the monks of St Gildas, impossible though this might be: 'I knew for sure that, if I tried to compel them to follow the rule to which they were sworn, I would not escape with my life; and that if I did not do this so far as I could, I would be damned' (*HC* 99: 1259–62). He seems to have begun by trying to improve his monks through preaching, but with little success.[52] His charges merely tried, he says, to murder him (*HC* 106: 1497–1511).

[49] Miethke, 'Abaelards Stellung', p. 170, n. 72, observes that Abelard must have been at St Gildas by 15 March 1128 (the date of the charter cited in n. 56 below). *Serm.* 33 helps to indicate the date more exactly because (cf. Miethke, 'Abaelards Stellung', nn. 72 and 114 and C. Mews, 'On dating the works of Peter Abelard', *AHDLMA* 52 (1985), 73–134, at p. 124) the sermon makes (595A, 603A) veiled, but unmistakeable, references to Norbert's elevation to the episcopacy, which took place in late June or early July 1126 (cf. W. Grauwen, *Norbertus Aartsbisschop van Magdenburg (1126–1134)* (Brussels, 1978) (Verhandelingen van de k. ac. v. Wetenshapen . . ., Kl. d. Letteren 40), pp. 49–172). The sermon is, from its contents, clearly directed to a community of unreformed monks; and it must have been preached soon after Abelard became abbot, before his attempts to impose reform led to the breakdown of relations between him and his monks. The feast of John the Baptist, 24 June 1127 is then, as Mews suggests, the most probable date for the sermon.

[50] Cf. *HC* 107: 1558–9: 'ut nostro etiam exemplo eorum qui id sponte appetunt ambitio refrenetur' (*HC* 107: 1558–9): *pace* Bautier (*Bautier*, p. 66), Abelard is clearly making a contrast between himself and those who, unlike him, actually desire such things as abbacies.

[51] See below, pp. 306–7.

[52] See his *Serm.* 33 (cf. n. 49 above); cf. Miethke, 'Abaelards Stellung', pp. 177–81.

Later, using the threat of excommunication, he succeeded in making some of the worst troublemakers swear that they would leave the monastery. Although they tried to break this oath, Abelard had his sentence enforced by a council which included the count, the papal legate and bishops. But the monks who remained, he says, turned out to be even worse than those he had forced to go (*HC* 107: 1534–49). Eventually, Abelard took to living outside the monastery itself, in one or another of its *cellae*, with a few companions (*HC* 106: 1525–6).

Despite these dismal circumstances, as an abbot Abelard was a figure of some importance in the area and even more widely. He is listed, for instance, among the dignitaries who are witnesses to the restoration of a chapel to the nuns of Ronceray by Count Conan III on 15 March 1128;[53] and when the Count was sick, he visited him at Nantes (*HC* 106: 1511–12). The Chronicle of Morigny lists Abelard, 'a monk and abbot, a pious man and director of the most excellent schools to which people came from almost all the Latin world', among those dignitaries, including St Bernard and many bishops, who attended the consecration of an altar at Morigny by Pope Innocent II on 20 January 1131.[54] None of this altered the fact that his life, very understandably, appeared to him not merely unpleasant (as it had often been) but wasted. He had given up his students but he was able to achieve nothing in the way of spiritual teaching or reformation with his monks (*HC* 99: 1283–9). Indeed, Abelard's years at St Gildas (five at least) were by far the longest period in his adult life when he did not teach as a schoolmaster.

The one consolation to Abelard in this period arose from apparently unpropitious circumstances. Since Abelard's castration, Heloise had been a nun at Argenteuil, where she had become prioress. In 1129 Suger succeeded in having the nuns expelled and, by bringing forward forged documents to prove his case, making Argenteuil into a possession of St Denis. The nuns were accused of depraved conduct; but there is good reason to regard this as a pretext (perhaps without foundation in fact) for an action which increased the wealth of St Denis.[55] Abelard was able to rescue Heloise and some of the nuns from Argenteuil by giving them the oratory of the Para-

[53] See *Checklist* §383.

[54] L. Mirot (ed.), *La Chronique de Morigny (1095–1152)* (Paris, 1909), pp. 53–4.

[55] See T. Waldman, 'Abbot Suger and the nuns of Argenteuil', *Traditio* 45 (1985), 239–72; *Bautier*, pp. 71, 75; Constable, 'Suger's administration', pp. 20–1; Miethke, 'Abaelards Stellung', p. 182 and n. 143. Waldman and Constable give some credence to the reports of the nuns' irregularities.

clete which he had abandoned – a gift eventually confirmed by the Pope (*HC* 100: 1310–20).[56] Abelard preached in order to raise money for the new nunnery (*Serm.* 30) and visited the Paraclete from time to time. The nuns seemed to him a safe haven in his stormy life as an abbot of unruly monks (*HC* 101: 1341–5; 105: 1476–81). Although he made sure to avoid any chance for intimate discussion with Heloise, these visits to the Paraclete were the subject of malicious rumours – even despite, Abelard complains, his castration (*HC* 101: 1345 – 105: 1463).

THE SECOND PARIS PERIOD

There is no firm evidence of the exact date when Abelard set himself up again as a master in Paris. John of Salisbury attended his lectures in 1136, but – given the amount of material which is based on his lectures in this period – he had almost certainly been teaching for a few years before then. He cannot have yet abandoned his abbacy and returned to Paris in March 1131, when the chronicler of Morigny (writing not long afterwards) describes him as 'a monk and abbot';[57] and, from the evidence of the correspondence with Heloise, a date early in 1133 would seem most plausible.[58] If Abelard's original decision to accept the offer of a remote abbacy was not an unconstrained choice, but a response to the overwhelming pressure of his enemies in France, it is probable that a change in political circumstances was necessary before he could resume teaching in Paris. Late in 1132 Stephen de Garlande, Abelard's patron, who had been out of royal favour since 1127 or 1128, regained his influence and his position as chancellor.[59] Was it the change in his fortunes which made Abelard's last Parisian period of teaching possible?[60] Certainly, it was on the Mont Ste Geneviève – on land, that is, belonging to the abbey of which Stephen was dean – that

[56] The papal privilege confirming the donation is printed in *D'Amboise/Duchesne*, pp. 346–7 and C. Lalore (ed.), *Collection des principaux cartulaires du diocèse de Troyes* II (Paris, 1878), pp. 1–3 (*Checklist* §416).

[57] See above, n. 54. The mention of Innocent II's privilege, issued 28 November 1131, confirming Heloise and her nuns' possession of the Paraclete in *HC* (100: 1317–20) confirms this, since *HC* finishes before Abelard has begun teaching in Paris.

[58] See below, pp. 75–6.

[59] A reconciliation between Stephen and the king may have taken place as early as April 1129; but, according to Bautier, it is only after his resumption of the chancellory that Stephen can be said to have returned to grace – cf. *Bautier*, p. 70, n. 1.

[60] As Bautier (*Bautier*, p. 77) suggests.

Abelard chose to place his new school. He probably lodged in the monastery of St Hilaire.[61]

The Paris to which Abelard had returned was a very different town for a schoolmaster from the Paris he had left. Masters and their schools had proliferated, and Paris had become a great centre for the study of theology, as well as logic and the other liberal arts.[62] Abelard had been away from the city for about fifteen years, and for the preceding five years or so he had not been teaching at all. Yet he seems quickly to have drawn students and disciples to himself. Even Abelard's opponents had no doubt about the popularity and influence of his teaching and work,[63] whilst his pupil, John of Salisbury, describes Abelard as 'famous' as well as learned and 'admired by all'. When, after Abelard's departure from Mont Ste Geneviève, John became the student of Alberic, he describes his new master as 'the best of *the other* logicians': John, at least, held Abelard supreme even over his most able opponent and the most influential logician of the 1140s.[64]

Most of Abelard's time as a teacher in and around Paris before 1117 had been shaped by his bitter conflict with William of Champeaux. That there were, in the 1130s, sharp intellectual differences between Abelard and other logical masters (especially Alberic) is clear from the comments reported by

[61] Cf. John of Salisbury, *Historia Pontificalis* (ed. and transl. M. Chibnall (London etc., 1956), p. 63 (where John is discussing Arnold of Brescia): 'apud sanctum Hylarium, ubi iam dictus Petrus fuerat hospitatus'). Some writers (e.g. J. Sikes, *Peter Abailard* (Cambridge, 1932), p. 26; *Mews*, p. 22) suggest that Abelard resided at St Hilaire sometime between 1137 and 1140, rather than earlier, but John of Salisbury's words do not imply this.

[62] See R. Southern, 'The schools of Paris and the School of Chartres' in R. Benson and G. Constable (eds.), *Renaissance and renewal in the twelfth century* (Oxford, 1982), pp. 113–37, esp. pp. 128–33. There are good documentary sources giving lists of important masters teaching in Paris in the period immediately after Abelard's departure: John of Salisbury's account of his education in *Metalogicon* II, 10 (on which cf. K. Keats-Rohan, 'John of Salisbury and education in twelfth century Paris from the account of his *Metalogicon*', *History of Universities* 6 (1986–7), 1–45); William of Tyre, *Historia* XIX, 12 (edited and discussed in R. Huygens, 'Guillaume de Tyr étudiant: un chapitre (XIX, 12) de son "Histoire" retrouvé', *Latomus* 21 (1962), 811–29). Although the number of masters in Paris was probably greater by the mid-1140s than it had been a decade earlier, there is no reason to think that there was a *sudden* increase after the time of Abelard's departure.

[63] Bernard of Clairvaux writes (*Ep.* 191 in J. Leclercq and H. Rochais (eds.), *Sancti Bernardi opera* VIII (Rome, 1977), p. 42: 13–14):' homo ille [*sc.* Abaelardus] multitudinem trahit post se et populum qui sibi credat habet' (all subsequent references to St Bernard's letters are to this edition). Luscombe (*The School of Peter Abelard* (Cambridge, 1969) (Cambridge studies in medieval life and thought, 2nd series, 14), pp. 3–5) assembles the evidence for Abelard's popularity as a teacher: much of it refers to the period after 1132.

[64] J. Hall (assisted by K. Keats-Rohan), (ed.) John of Salisbury, *Metalogicon* (Turnhout, 1991) (CC [cm] 98), p. 71: 10–11; cf. p. 20: 13–15. See, however, below, pp. 52–3.

pupils.[65] But there is no sign during this period of personal hostility to Abelard among his fellow masters. When the distinguished theologian Walter of Mortagne heard Abelard's pupils claiming that their master had reached a complete understanding of the Trinity, and found passages in a draft of Abelard's *Theologia* which suggested that this was really his view, he wrote to him with friendliness and respect.[66] He firmly rejects the view he attributes to Abelard: indeed, he can hardly believe, whatever the apparent evidence, that Abelard *does* hold a view so contrary to scriptural authority.[67] Yet he avers, without irony, that Abelard 'is pre-eminent above others in [the study of] Holy Scripture'.[68] The respect was shared, since Abelard modified his draft directly in response to Walter's criticisms.[69] And one passage in Walter's letter mentions a theological discussion in which he and Abelard had recently engaged – a rare glimpse of the intellectual exchanges which were possible with colleagues, as well as with his pupils.[70] The attack on Abelard would come, this time, not from his fellow masters, but from theologians outside the schools: William of St Thierry, Thomas of Morigny, Bernard of Clairvaux.

John of Salisbury reports that Abelard left the Mont Ste Geneviève 'all too soon' after his own arrival there in 1136.[71] Yet from the letters of St Bernard it is clear that Abelard was teaching, presumably in Paris, almost up to the time of the Council of Sens, in June 1140.[72] If Abelard resumed his lectures on the Mont after a break, it is odd that John does not mention it. Most likely, therefore, Abelard (perhaps after a time away) resumed teaching elsewhere in Paris, possibly devoting himself exclusively to theology (with the result that enthusiastic pupils like John of Salisbury had to continue their instruction in logic with other teachers). Abelard's later period as a master in Paris was therefore in all probability the longest

[65] On Alberic, see below, pp. 52–3.

[66] The letter is ed. in H. Ostlender, *Sententiae Florianenses* (Bonn, 1929) (Florilegium patristicum 19), pp. 34–40; see below, p. 59.

[67] Letter, pp. 36: 27–37: 1.

[68] Letter, p. 40: 5–6.

[69] See *Mews*, p. 217.

[70] *Letter*, p. 40: 12–14: 'Quod, si bene memini, audivi vos fateri, quando novissime invicem contulimus de quibusdam sententiis. Praeterea apud nos ventilatum est vestram affirmare sapientiam, quod . . .'

[71] *Metalogicon*, pp. 70: 1–71: 12.

[72] See e.g. Bernard of Clairvaux, Letter 331 (pp. 269: 18 – 270: 3): 'Rudes et novellos auditores ab uberibus dialecticae separatos . . . ad mysterium Sanctae Trinitatis . . . introducit'; Letter 336 (ibid., p. 276: 1): 'Scribit, docet et contendit verbis ad subversionem audientium.' For the date of the Council of Sens, see below, n. 100.

stretch in his life of hardly broken activity as a teacher, stretching perhaps from early in 1133 to 1140.

THE COUNCIL OF SENS

The events which led to Abelard's appearance at the Council of Sens in 1140 and to the end of his teaching are no doubt closely connected to the political tensions and changes of the period, both in France and Rome. But it is very difficult to be sure about the exact nature of these links, except that they were almost certainly more complex than scholars have usually believed. On 1 August 1137, King Louis VI died and Stephen de Garlande was once again removed from the chancellorship. The cessation of Abelard's lectures on the Mont Ste Geneviève and even his eventual condemnation have been linked to Stephen's fall.[73] Yet Stephen was still Dean of Ste Geneviève in April 1138.[74] In the first years of the new king's reign, it was not perhaps as clear as it would become in retrospect that the de Garlande family had lost its influence. Stephen's friend, Algrin, was chancellor from 1137 until 1139 or 1140;[75] and only in 1140 did Stephen de Garlande retire to St Victor.[76] In Rome, St Bernard's influence was great, since he had been a powerful advocate for Pope Innocent II during the period from 1130 to 1139 when his election was disputed; but Abelard, too, had strong supporters there, including Guy of Castello, Cardinal priest of St Mark and later Pope Celestine II, who had been loyal to Innocent from the start.[77]

William of St Thierry happened, by chance he says, to come across a book of Abelard's called his 'Theologia': or rather, as he explains, two books 'containing almost the same thing, except that in one there was more, in

[73] *Bautier*, p. 77; *Mews*, p. 22.

[74] See Charter 19 (between 3 April and 31 July 1138) in A. Luchaire, *Etudes sur les actes de Louis VII* (Paris, 1885), p. 105.

[75] Luchaire, *Etudes*, p. 52; on Algrin's friendship with Stephen of Garlande, see *Bautier*, pp. 70, n. 1, 71, n. 4.

[76] *Bautier*, p. 77.

[77] See F. Schmale, *Studien zum Schisma des Jahres 1130* (Cologne/Graz, 1961) (Forschungen zur kirchlichen Rechtsgeschichte und zum Kirchenrecht 3), pp. 55–6 and cf. Luscombe, *The school*, pp. 20–2. On the political allegiances of another supporter of Abelard's, Hyacinthus Boboni, later Pope Celestine III, see P. Zerbi, 'San Bernardo di Chiaravalle e il concilio di Sens' in *Studi su S. Bernardo di Chiaravalle nell'otto centenario della canonizzazione* (Rome, 1975) (Bibliotheca Cisterciensis 6), pp. 49–73, at p. 65, but cf. Luscombe, *The school*, pp. 22–3 and Verger, 'Milieux sociaux', p. 112.

the other rather less'.[78] One of these books was Abelard's *Theologia Scholarium*; the other was almost certainly the work which St Bernard and others would refer to as his *liber sententiarum*.[79] William had been a friend of Abelard's, but he could not continue friendship with a man whose teaching, he thought, corrupted the faith and endangered the Church.[80] He therefore drew up a *Disputatio adversus Petrum Abaelardum*, which quoted the offending passages from Abelard's work and gave patristic testimony to contradict them.[81] In the Lent of 1140,[82] William sent his treatise, with a letter and the two books by Abelard, to Geoffrey, bishop of Chartres and to St Bernard. Bernard replied to William, saying that he approved of his concern, but that in such great matters he would not act precipitately. He and William should meet, but that could not be until after Easter. He added that 'many of the things [which William reported] – almost all of them indeed' had been unknown to him up until then.[83]

The supposed heresies which William now imputed to Abelard were, therefore, news to Bernard, but it seems most probable that there had been covert dislike, if not open hostility, for some years.[84] Bernard was probably one of the two 'new apostles' who, Abelard believed, were persecuting him during his days at the Paraclete.[85] Although this does not necessarily mean that Bernard did in fact attack Abelard, directly or indirectly, or even that he knew anything much about him or his work, Abelard is unlikely to have imagined the hostility without some basis. Moreover, a letter survives from *c.* 1125 in which Bernard replies to Hugh of St Victor's reports of the

78 On William, see P. Zerbi, 'Guillaume de Saint-Thierry et son différend avec Abélard' in M. Bur (ed.), *Saint-Thierry, une abbaye du VIe au XXe siècle* (Saint-Thierry, 1979), pp. 395–412.

79 William explains this in his letter to Bernard and Geoffrey of Chartres (ed. in J. Leclercq, 'Les lettres de Guillaume de Saint-Thierry à Saint Bernard', *RB* 79 (1969), 375–91) at pp. 377–8: see p. 377: 26–30. On the *liber sententiarum*, see below, pp. 62–3.

80 Letter to St Bernard and Geoffrey, 378: 67–9: 'Dilexi et ego eum, et diligere vellem, Deus testis est; sed in causa hac nemo umquam proximus erit vel amicus.' About the nature and length of this friendship, there is disagreement: cf. Zerbi, 'Guillaume', p. 398, n. 10.

81 *MPL* 180, 249–82.

82 The date of 1140 is accepted by Leclercq and Rochais (*Sancti Bernardi opera* VIII, p. 263, n. 1) and Mews ('The lists of heresies imputed to Peter Abelard', *RB* 95 (1985), 73–110, at p. 82) although Zerbi ('San Bernardo di Chiaravalle', p. 49 and 'Guillaume', p. 396) suggests 1139. But 1139 seems very unlikely because there is no suggestion in any of the accounts of as much as a year's delay.

83 *Ep.* 327, p. 263: 14–15.

84 For the opposite view, Borst, 'Abälard und Bernhard', pp. 500–9 and E. Little, 'Relations between St Bernard and Abelard before 1139' in M. Pennington (ed.), *St Bernard of Clairvaux* (Kalamazoo, 1977). See also Smits, *Abelard. Letters IX–XIV*, pp. 120–36 on *Ep.* 10.

85 See above, p. 20.

teachings on baptism of a theologian whom, he says, Hugh leaves unnamed.[86] The doctrines, severely criticized by Bernard, are close to Abelard's.[87] Abelard may well have been the anonymous theologian, and despite his denials, Bernard may well have known that Abelard was meant, but thought it most prudent not to name him.[88] This remains conjecture. What is certain, however, is that Bernard was a – perhaps the – central figure in the reforming party which had been consistently hostile to Stephen de Garlande and to Abelard himself. Bernard need not have done anything directly against Abelard for Abelard to regard him, and with good cause, as an adversary.

William of St Thierry was not the only person to attack Abelard's doctrines at about this time. Thomas of Morigny (like William, once a friend of Abelard himself, and an ardent admirer of St Bernard's) who came in mid-Lent 1140 to live at the monastery of Saint-Martin-des-Champs in Paris, has now been tentatively identified as the author of the *Capitula haeresum xiv*, a list of fourteen heresies supposedly perpetrated by Abelard, with quotations from the same works cited by William, and brief counter-arguments.[89] Thomas may have acted independently, in the hope perhaps of winning Bernard's favour; or at the instigation of Bernard himself. Bernard would use the works of William and Thomas in producing his own compositions directed against Abelard. From William's *Disputatio* (and perhaps also the *Capitula haeresum xiv*) he would take much of the material for his own letter-treatise against Abelard, sent to Pope Innocent II;[90] from

[86] The so-called *De baptismo*: *MPL* 182, 1031–46; cf. Ott, *Untersuchungen zur theologischen Briefliteratur der Frühscholastik* (Münster, 1937), (BGPMA 34), pp. 495–548.

[87] The closeness to Abelard's of the doctrines criticized by Bernard has been recognized by scholars since Deutsch (*Abälard*, pp. 466–72), including Ott, Luscombe (*The school*, p. 196) and Miethke ('Die Stellung', pp. 168–9). Arguments by Sikes (*Abailard*, pp. 214–15) and Little ('Relations', pp. 165–6) that Abelard's doctrine of baptism was very different from the anonymous theologian's are unconvincing.

[88] Ott (*Untersuchungen*, p. 497) is certain that Bernard knew Abelard was meant, but Borst ('Abälard und Bernhard', pp. 500–1) doubts it. For Little ('Relations', p. 166), if the theologian was Abelard and if Bernard knew this, then the choice not to name him indicates that at this stage Bernard's relations with him were 'very correct'.

[89] See Mews, 'The lists', 77–110. Mews (pp. 102 and 106) suggests that Bernard may have sent him the books of Abelard's he had received from William, and that Thomas acted as 'Bernard's aide throughout the affair'.

[90] The letter-treatise is Bernard's Letter 190 (pp. 17–38). On manuscripts and revisions of this letter, see J. Leclercq, 'Les formes successives de la lettre-traité de Saint Bernard contre Abélard', *RB* 78 (1968), 87–105 and the important corrections made to Leclercq's views in Mews, 'The lists'. On Bernard's use of William's and, possibly, Thomas's work, see *Mews*, pp. 279–80.

the *Capitula haeresum xiv* especially, but also from William's *Disputatio*, would be drawn the list of nineteen heresies (*Capitula haeresum xix*).[91] When the *Capitula haeresum xix* were appended to the letter-treatise, the whole work formed a succinct but comprehensive statement of Bernard's case against Abelard.

The abbot of Clairvaux did not, however, proceed immediately to request a public condemnation of Abelard. According both to his secretary and hagiographer, Geoffrey of Auxerre, and to the French bishops in their account of events to the Pope, Bernard arranged a private meeting (the bishops say two, the first one to one, the second involving 'two or three' witnesses) at which he admonished Abelard to correct his books and prevent those who listened to his teaching from drawing theological errors from it.[92] Bernard was going through the procedure laid out in the gospel for correcting a fellow Christian who had erred: first speaking to him alone, then with the aid of two or three witnesses and then, if he will not listen, proclaiming his error to the Church.[93] Geoffrey of Auxerre, always keen to show the efficacy of his master's words, reports that Abelard did agree to correct everything as Bernard wished; but his testimony is not supported by the French bishops in their letter.[94]

Whether or not some agreement was reached, there is no suggestion in the sources that there was a period of time after his meeting with Bernard during which Abelard was supposed to correct his teaching and eventually failed to do so.[95] Geoffrey of Auxerre says that, once he left Bernard, Abelard changed his mind, 'guided by bad advice'.[96] But it emerges both from a letter of Abelard's, and from the French bishops' letter to the Pope, that Bernard was preaching against Abelard to the students of Paris, and

[91] The genesis of these *Capitula* is carefully studied in Mews, 'The lists'. He shows that Leclercq ('Formes successives') is wrong to claim that the nineteen *Capitula* were not drawn up until the Council of Sens.

[92] See Letter from the bishops of France to Pope Innocent II (traditionally printed as St Bernard's Letter 337) (ed. J. Leclercq, 'Autour de la correspondance de S. Bernard' in *Sapientiae doctrina. Mélanges de théologie et de littérature médiévales offerts à Dom Hildebrand Bascour O.S.B* (Louvain, 1980) (RTAM numéro spécial, 1), pp. 185–98, at p. 188: 41–5) and cf. Geoffrey of Auxerre, *S. Bernardi vita prima*, *MPL* 185, 225–466, 311A.

[93] See Matthew 18: 15, as cited and discussed by L. Kolmer, 'Abaelard und Bernhard von Clairvaux in Sens', *Zeitschrift der Savigny-Stiftung für Rechtsgeschichte*, kanonistische Abt. 67 (1981), 121–47, at p. 127; and cf. Zerbi, 'San Bernardo di Chiaravalle', p. 56.

[94] *S. Bernardi vita prima* 311A. On Geoffrey's way of portraying Bernard, cf. Zerbi, 'San Bernardo di Chiaravalle', p. 56.

[95] As hypothesized by, for instance, Borst, 'Abälard', pp. 508–9.

[96] *S. Bernardi vita prima*, 311AB.

that he also spoke against him at Sens, in the presence of the archbishop.[97] Bernard seems to have concentrated his efforts especially on denouncing Abelard to the highest authority of all in the Church. Bernard sent his letter-treatise (Letter 190) against Abelard to Pope Innocent with the list of nineteen heresies appended to it. Knowing that Abelard had influential followers in Rome, Bernard also wrote letters to various important figures in the Curia, warning them of Abelard's errors.[98] It was, he believed, for the Church authorities, in particular, the highest authority at Rome, to proceed against the heretic: he, Bernard, had done what he could.[99]

From Bernard's point of view, Abelard was a heretic, whom he had dutifully denounced to the Church. But from Abelard's point of view, Bernard was a slanderer, who had cast unjust aspersions on his teachings, even among the students of Paris. Abelard tried to ensure that others would see the case from his perspective, and he sought redress against Bernard. He asked the archbishop of Sens, who was due to hold the next large Church council, to tell Bernard either to withdraw his accusations or to attend the council, on the octave of Pentecost (2 June 1140),[100] when Abelard would defend whatever in his teaching the abbot of Clairvaux criticized.[101] Abelard's wish that Bernard should, in person and in public, accuse him, and that he should have the chance to answer the accusations, not only threatened to make the subject of argument questions which the abbot of Clairvaux considered to be matters of faith: it also cast Bernard himself in the role of accuser – and, should the defence against his charges prove convincing, of false accuser.[102] Little wonder that a note of rancour enters

[97] Letter of the bishops of France, pp. 188: 45–189: 57; Abelard's letter to his *socii* (ed. in R. Klibansky, 'Peter Abailard and Bernard of Clairvaux', *Mediaeval and Renaissance Studies* 5 (1961) 1–27 (edition on pp. 6–7), p. 7: 23–7: 'Sciatis autem quod ... me iam audisse ... quanta ille Datianus meus [*sc.* Bernardus] in me veneni sui probra vomuerit: primo quod Senonis in praesentia domini archiepiscopi et multorum amicorum meorum, quod deinde Parisius de profundo nequitiae suae coram vobis vel aliis eructuaverit.' Whether or not Bernard's attack on Abelard to the Parisian students should be identified with his sermon *De conversione ad clericos* (*MPL* 182, 833–56) is disputed: see Borst 'Abälard und Berhard', pp. 512–13 (for identification); Zerbi, 'San Bernardo di Chiaravalle', p. 57 (against).

[98] Most likely letters 188, 331–2, 336 (and 338, written at this time but probably not sent until after the Council of Sens: cf. Borst, 'Abälard und Bernhard' p. 511, n. 8).

[99] See especially letter 188, to the bishops and cardinals of the Curia (pp. 10: 13–14, 10: 18–11: 1).

[100] Almost all scholars are now agreed on 1140 as the year of the Council of Sens, rather than 1141 as had sometimes been suggested: cf. P. Zerbi, 'Remarques sur l'epistola 98 de Pierre le Vénérable', in *Pierre Abélard*, pp. 215–32 at p. 215, n. 1.

[101] See *S. Bernardi vita prima*, 311AB; Abelard, Letter to his *socii*, p. 7: 28–30.

[102] Cf. Kolmer, 'Abaelard', pp. 131–3.

Bernard's account of events when he records that Archbishop Henry acceded to Abelard's request, or that the French bishops (writing after the Council, when Bernard's party had prevailed) describe the incident defensively.[103]

Bernard's reluctance to attend the Council, stressed afterwards both by himself and by the bishops of France, was probably genuine – to go there, it seemed, would be to accept Abelard's view of the position; yet, since Abelard had ensured that the meeting he demanded was widely known about, to be absent would be an admission that he was in the wrong.[104] Yet, in the event, Bernard turned the situation to his own advantage. He arrived in Sens on 1 June and persuaded the bishops to attend a private meeting that evening.[105] Although he was attacked by Hyacinthus Boboni, one of Abelard's influential Roman supporters, he managed to prevail over the assembled company (which included the metropolitans of Sens and Rheims and almost all their bishops).[106] Probably Bernard read out the supposedly heretical propositions one by one and invited the bishops to condemn each proposition by adding after it: *Damnamus*.[107] When the council met the next morning, Abelard was no longer, as he had planned, in the position of a man defending himself against a slanderer. He was confronted with Bernard's list of his propositions, which the bishops had already agreed to condemn as heresies. He was given the choice of denying they were his, defending their truth or correcting them. Instead, he appealed to the Pope's judgement and left the assembly with his followers.[108] Geoffrey

103 St Bernard, Letter 189, p. 14: 15–17; Letter of the bishops of France, pp. 188: 48 – 189: 54.

104 St Bernard, Letter 189, p. 14: 18–15: 1; Letter of the bishops of France, p. 189: 57–69.

105 Reconstructions of the events of 1–2 June 1140 (similar except for points of detail) are found in Borst, 'Abälard', pp. 515–20; Zerbi, 'San Bernardo di Chiaravalle', pp. 65–72; Kolmer, 'Abaelard', pp. 134–9. The most direct evidence for the evening meeting is the Letter of the bishops of France, p. 190: 106: '[sententias pravi dogmatis eius] pridie ante factam ad vos appelationem damnavimus'; see also the exaggerated, satirical account in the *Apologia* by Abelard's follower, Berengar of Poitiers (in R. Thomson (ed.), 'The satirical works of Berengar of Poitiers: an edition with introduction', *Mediaeval Studies* 42 (1980), 89–138, at pp. 112–14), and John of Salisbury, *Historia Pontificalis* (ed. and transl. M. Chibnall (London, 1956)) pp. 17–18, for an account of a similar stratagem employed by Bernard against Gilbert of Poitiers at the Council of Rheims.

106 Letter of the bishops of France, p. 189: 78–82.

107 Cf. Kolmer, 'Abaelard', p. 135.

108 Bernard (Letter 189, p. 15: 8) says that Abelard made his appeal and left whilst the supposedly heretical propositions were being read out. Neither the account in the letter of the French bishops (p. 190: 90–1: 'visus est diffidere magister Petrus Abaelardus et subterfugere, respondere noluit'), nor that of the archbishop of Rheims (printed with the letters of St Bernard, no. 191: Leclercq and Rochais, *S. Bernardi opera* VIII, p. 42: 8–9) is incompatible with this: only Geoffrey of Auxerre's account (cited in the note below),

of Auxerre presents Abelard's failure to reply as a sign that his reason had been overcome; but it seems, on the contrary, that Abelard acted very rationally, countering Bernard's stratagem and saving himself from immediate condemnation.[109]

Although the bishops would observe to the Pope that they doubted the legality of Abelard's appeal, they decided that they had to accept it, at least to the extent of allowing Abelard himself to go free.[110] But what about Abelard's supposedly heretical teaching – the nineteen *Capitula* which, the night before, the bishops had agreed to condemn? In the individual letters to Innocent II which they despatched directly after the Council, Bernard, the French bishops and the archbishop of Rheims all state clearly that the offending doctrines had been condemned by them: the Pope is requested to confirm the condemnation and make it everlasting, and to act against Abelard himself, imposing on him silence, a ban from writing, as well as condemning his books.[111] Yet the letter from the French bishops says explicitly that it was on the evening before that they had condemned Abelard's heretical propositions: it mentions nothing about the condemnation's being reiterated at the full meeting of the Council. Bernard's letter, and more decisively the letter from the archbishop of Rheims, *do* give the impression that it was at the full Council on 2 June that the propositions were condemned.[112] But since both of them studiously omit any mention of the gathering on 1 June, they could hardly do otherwise. It is possible, then, that the Council of Sens broke up without reiterating the condemnation of Abelard's doctrines made by the bishops the previous night.[113]

written later and in the context of a hagiography, contradicts it. For a different view, see C. Jaeger, 'Peter Abelard's silence at the Council of Sens', *Res publica litterarum* 3 (1980), 31–54.

109 See *S. Bernardi vita prima*, 311C; cf. Kolmer, 'Abaelard', pp. 137–8; Zerbi, 'San Bernardo di Chiaravalle', pp. 67–8.

110 Letter of the bishops of France, p. 190: 96–8.

111 Letter of the bishops of France, p. 190: 99–116; Letter of the archbishop of Rheims, pp. 42: 10 – 43: 1; St Bernard, Letter 189, pp. 15: 9 – 16: 6.

112 Bernard himself mentions Abelard's appeal to the Pope at the meeting on the 3rd and then writes, 'Porro capitula, iudicio omnium examinata, inventa sunt fidei adversantia, contraria veritati' (p. 15: 9–10): the impression is given of chronological succession, but this is not definitely stated; the archbishop of Rheims writes, 'Episcopi autem, qui propter hoc in unum convenerant, vestrae reverentiae deferentes, nihil in personam eius egerunt, sed tantummodo capitula librorum eius ... medicinali necessitate abiudicaverunt', giving the clear impression that the condemnation was made after Abelard's appeal (p. 42: 10–13).

113 Zerbi ('San Bernardo di Chiaravalle', pp. 70–1) and Kolmer ('Abaelard', pp. 138–9) are certain that the condemnation was reiterated; Mews (*Mews*, p. 292) states forcefully, but without giving evidence, that it was not.

CLUNY

As Bernard, hoping to influence the papal judgement, sent off another series of letters to Rome,[114] Abelard probably began his own journey there. He stopped on his way at the great monastery of Cluny, probably aware that its abbot, Peter the Venerable, although a friend of Bernard's, differed sharply from the abbot of Clairvaux on many issues. As Peter the Venerable explained in a letter he sent to the Pope,[115] Abelard told him the purpose of his journey. Peter reassured him: the Pope's justice would not fail him. While Abelard was at Cluny, Abbot Rainard of Cîteaux visited the monastery and tried to arrange for peace to be made between Abelard and Bernard. Peter joined in urging Abelard to go with Rainard and meet Bernard. He also advised Abelard that if there was anything he had written or said which offended the ears of the faithful he should, as Bernard and other good and wise men urged, remove it from his speech and delete it from his writings. 'And thus', says Peter, 'it happened.' Abelard returned to Cluny, his peace made with Bernard.[116] The letter goes on to add that, in the meanwhile, Abelard had also agreed to make Cluny his home for ever and abandon teaching. Peter is writing to Innocent because he fears that 'at the insistence of some' Abelard will be forced out of Cluny 'like a swallow from his home or a dove from the nest he rejoices to have found': will the Pope please order Abelard to spend his remaining days at Cluny?

When, and under what circumstances, was this letter written? Abelard's plea to the Pope was unsuccessful. On 16 July, very probably of 1140 rather than 1141, Innocent despatched two letters, both addressed to the archbishops of Rheims and Sens and to St Bernard.[117] In one of them, after a couple of prefatory paragraphs on heresies in general, Innocent thanks its recipients for standing in the way of Abelard's heresies and, after noting that he has acted with the advice of his bishops and cardinals, condemns not only the *capitula* he had been sent but all of Abelard's 'perverse doctrine', and Abelard himself, on whom as a heretic he imposes perpetual silence. Abelard's followers and defenders are to be excommunicated.[118] The other

[114] As well as Letter 189, probably 192–3 and 330 and 333–5.

[115] Letter 98, in G. Constable (ed.), *The letters of Peter the Venerable* I (Harvard, 1967) (Harvard historical studies 78), pp. 258–9.

[116] On this meeting, see also below, p. 71.

[117] See Zerbi, 'San Bernardo di Chiaravalle', pp. 46–7, *Mews*, p. 285, n. 137 and Zerbi, 'Remarques sur l'epistola 98', pp. 230–2 and n. 28 for arguments for 1140 as opposed to 1141.

[118] Printed with St Bernard's letters, no. 194.

is a brief note, to the same three people, ordering Abelard and Arnold of Brescia to be confined separately in religious houses ('where it seems to you best') and for their books to be burnt.[119] Although Peter the Venerable may have written his letter as a preventative measure, before he heard of this condemnation,[120] it is simpler to suppose that it is a response to it. Peter does not ask Innocent to set aside his sentence, but slightly to change its terms. Instead of being confined separately in a religious house chosen by St Bernard and the archbishops of Sens and Rheims, Abelard should be ordered by the Pope to remain at Cluny for the rest of his days and be allowed to form part of the community there. The imposition of silence on him is unnecessary, Peter suggests, since he has already given up the schools of his own choice. The news of the reconciliation with Bernard is designed to influence Innocent in Abelard's favour and the reported conversation with which the letter begins is designed to achieve the same object, this time through a reproach, respectful because merely implied: has the Pope been just to condemn Abelard without hearing his side of the case? If anyone could sway the Pope, it was Peter who, like Bernard, had been one of Innocent's firm and important supporters in the years when he struggled to establish his legitimacy. Indeed, Abelard's choice of Cluny as a stopping-place may not have been fortuitous. Did Abelard, directing his steps towards Rome perhaps with more resolution than confidence, hope that in some way an encounter with Peter the Venerable might save him?

For so it did. Abelard was not forced from his new-found nest, although after a while Peter sent him to the Cluniac priory near Chalon-sur-Saône, where the climate would better suit his failing health.[121] Already, in his letter to the Pope, Peter had observed that Abelard's remaining days 'perhaps were not many'.[122] He was over sixty years old and possibly suffering from a form of cancer.[123] In a famous letter to Heloise, Peter tells her about

119 Printed from an early MS in Leclercq, 'Les lettres de Guillaume', p. 379. In some editions (e.g. *MPL* 182, 350, n. 493) there is a note appended, ordering that it should not be shown to anyone until 'these letters' (presumably the two of them) are presented to the archbishops at their meeting in Paris, soon to take place; but the note is not found in this manuscript.

120 So Pietro Zerbi has argued: see '"In Cluniaco vestra sibi perpetuam mansionem elegit" (Petri Venerabilis *Epistola* 98). Un momento decisivo nella vita di Abelardo dopo il concilio di Sens' in P. Zerbi, *Tra Milano e Cluny* (Rome, 1978) (Italia Sacra 28), pp. 373–95 (= *Storiografia e storia. Studi in onore di Eugenio Dupré Theseider* II (Rome, 1974), pp. 627–44); cf. also Zerbi's earlier study of Letter 98, 'Remarques sur l'epistola 98'.

121 See Peter the Venerable, Letter 115 (I, p. 307); for the identification of the priory, see Constable, *The letters* II, p. 178.

122 Letter 98 (I, p. 259).

123 See Constable, *The letters* II, p. 178.

the last months of her husband's life. Exactly how much of this description is based on accounts Peter had received, how much is merely an idealized portrait of a good man's death, is not easy to decide. Peter says (and presumably would not have lied about the matter) that he had managed to persuade the Pope to lift the sentence of excommunication from him, so that he was able to receive the eucharist frequently. He describes Abelard's comportment as of the humblest, his time spent in prayer, reading and what writing his health allowed.[124]

Abelard was already ill when he came to Cluny and, despite his move to Chalon-sur-Saône, his condition deteriorated. Less than two years passed between Abelard's arrival at Cluny in late June or early July 1140 and his death on 21 April 1142. He was brought to his death-bed, where he made his final confession, took communion and commended his body and soul to God. And so, as the abbot of Cluny records, 'Master Peter, who was reputed throughout nearly all the world for his unique mastery of learning, and was known of everywhere, ended his days as the pupil of him who said, "Learn from me, because I am meek and humble in heart." '[125] In an epitaph, Peter the Venerable developed this theme. Abelard, our Aristotle, who could overcome all things by the force of his reason and the skill of his words, had the better conquered all things by becoming a monk of Cluny and turning to the true *philosophia Christi*.[126] For Peter, Abelard had transformed himself from *Peripateticus Palatinus* to philosopher of Christ; for Abelard himself, the two roles had been complementary.

[124] On what writing was done at Cluny and Chalon-sur-Saône, see below, pp. 70–1.

[125] Peter the Venerable, Letter 115 (I, p. 307).

[126] See C. Mews and C. Burnett, 'Les épitaphes d'Abélard et d'Héloïse au Paraclet et au prieuré de Saint-Marcel, à Chalon-sur-Saône', published as an appendix (pp. 61–7) of C. Mews, 'La bibliothèque du Paraclet du XIIIe siècle à la Révolution', *Studia monastica* 27 (1985), 31–67, where the epitaph is edited and Peter's authorship of it confirmed.

Chapter 2

Teaching and writings on logic

During the course of his life Abelard played many parts: the ambitious young man, the lover, the monk, the reforming abbot, the heretic. But – as the last chapter has made clear – one role remained constant through all these vicissitudes. Abelard was, above all, a teacher. From the time when, in about 1100, hardly more than a teenager, Abelard set up a school in rivalry to William of Champeaux, until about 1140 – apart from his period of illness as a young man (*c.* 1105–8) and his years at St Gildas (*c.* 1127–32) – his principal activity was that of teaching his band of enthusiastic pupils. Even his relationship with Heloise ended, as it had ostensibly begun, as a didactic one – with Abelard producing a succession of works in the 1130s for her and her nuns. Much of Abelard's writing is therefore closely related to his activity as a teacher. Rather like that of a teacher or lecturer today, Abelard's work as a master involved both repetition and change. In the *Historia* (73: 353–4), he remarks revealingly that, while his energies were taken by the affair with Heloise, his lectures (*lectio*) became careless and lukewarm: instead of using his inventive intelligence (*ingenium*), he was content to repeat what he had previously discovered. Clearly, then, Abelard covered much the same material from year to year in his teaching in a given area but, when he was not distracted by romance, he was always thinking afresh. Abelard's thought was, therefore, in a state of constant evolution. This process provides the context – often half-concealed – within which the relationship of his surviving writings can be grasped. The written works are not, however, related to Abelard's teaching in a simple or uniform way. They range from those (the early logical commentaries, for instance, or the late theological *Reportatio*) which are direct but incomplete records of lectures, through texts written up or adapted from his teaching in various ways to those which were conceived as independent literary texts from the start, but are none the less linked to the framework of his thought as it developed in his teaching.

Moreover, Abelard's thought does not trace a straightforward, linear pattern of development. Like many of his contemporaries (for instance, Roscelin and William of Champeaux, Gilbert of Poitiers and Walter of Mortagne) he taught in two different main areas: logic and what would now be called (in the broadest sense) theology. It might appear that for the greater part of his career – from 1113, when he began commenting on Ezechiel in challenge to Anselm of Laon, until at least 1136 – he exercised these two functions jointly and equally. But, as will emerge, his writings tell a different story; and it is more than a mere convenience of presentation to begin by considering Abelard the logician.

THE EARLY COMMENTARIES

Study of logic in the early twelfth century centred on a small number of ancient logical texts.[1] Abelard lists them in his *Dialectica* (146: 10–17): 'just two' by Aristotle himself – the *Categories* and the *De interpretatione,* Porphyry's *Isagoge* (these three all in Latin translation), and four books by Boethius – the *De differentiis topicis*, *De divisione* and his treatises on categorical and hypothetical syllogisms.[2] Teachers of logic, like William of Champeaux and probably Abelard himself, might also write independent *Introductions* to logic, but these were elementary textbooks, not the sophisticated

[1] For general background to twelfth-century logical commentaries, see *Commentaries and glosses*, esp. pp. 85–97.

[2] The *Categories* was usually read in a translation based on the lemmata to Boethius' commentary – the 'composite' Boethian version (in L. Minio-Paluello (ed.), *AL* I, 1–5, *Categoriae vel Praedicamenta* (Bruges/Paris, 1961), pp. 47–79; cf. *Commentaries and glosses*, p. 78, n. 5); the *De interpretatione* and the *Isagoge* were known in Boethius' translations (in L. Minio-Paluello (ed.), *AL* II, 1–2 *De interpretatione vel Periermenias* (Bruges/Paris, 1965), pp. 5–38) and *AL* I, 6–7 *Categoriarum supplementa* (Bruges/Paris, 1966), pp. 5–31. *De topicis differentiis* is found in *MPL* 64, 1173–216 (no modern edition exists, but there is an excellent English translation, with explanatory notes and essays: E. Stump, *Boethius' 'De topicis differentiis'* (Ithaca/London, 1978)), *De syllogismo categorico* at *MPL* 64, 793–83 and *De divisione* at *MPL* 64, 875–92. *De syllogismo hypothetico* has been critically edited by L. Obertello (Brescia, 1969) (Logicalia 1). Sometimes *De diffinitione*, a work by Marius Victorinus but usually attributed at the time to Boethius (ed. T. Stangl, *Tulliana et Mario-Victoriniana* (Munich, 1888) (Programm des K. Luitpold-Gymnasiums in München), pp. 17–78, reprinted in P. Hadot, *Marius Victorinus. Recherches sur sa vie et ses œuvres* (Paris, 1971), pp. 331–62) was added to the curriculum; the assortment of other texts which had been widely used for studying logic in the ninth and tenth centuries (Alcuin's *De dialectica*, Book IV of Martianus Capella's *De nuptiis Philologiae et Mercurii*, Apuleius' *Peri hermeneias*, Augustine's *De dialectica* and the pseudo-Augustinian *Categoriae decem*) was no longer in favour, although the *Categoriae decem*, at least, continued to be used: see *Commentaries and glosses*, pp. 78–9.

treatises of later in the century.[3] The principal way of learning about logic was to work carefully through the ancient texts, pondering over the interpretation of each passage, analysing the structure of Aristotle's, Porphyry's and Boethius' arguments and sometimes delving into the problems they raised. Serious work on logic took the form of commentary on the ancient texts or, at least, was closely linked to it.

Not surprisingly, then, the earliest records of Abelard's logical teaching are in the form of commentaries – to Porphyry's *Isagoge*, Aristotle's *De interpretatione* and Boethius' *De divisione*.[4] In one manuscript (Paris, Bibliothèque nationale, lat. 13368) these works are found with titles attributing them explicitly to Abelard (a mark of the special esteem in which he was held, since almost all early twelfth-century logical commentaries are anonymous). Another manuscript (Munich, Bayerische Staatsbibliothek, clm 14779) contains unattributed commentaries on the *Isagoge* and *De interpretatione* which are closely related to the Paris manuscript's texts of Abelard.[5] The Paris text of the *Isagoge* commentary is considerably longer than that found in the Munich manuscript; whereas, in the case of the *De interpretatione* commentary, it is the Munich version which is the more extended. Scholars have differed over the relationship between the texts in the two manuscripts.[6] But, on a close comparison, it seems most probable either that

[3] On William of Champeaux's *Introductiones*, see L. de Rijk, *Logica modernorum* II, 1 (Assen, 1967), pp. 130–46 and Iwakuma, 'William of Champeaux and the *Introductiones*' (forthcoming in the Acts of the 10th European Symposium on medieval logic and semantics, ed. H. Braakhuis and C. Kneepkens). William's *Introductiones* are ed. by Y. Iwakuma, 'The *Introductiones dialecticae secundum Wilgelmum* and *secundum G. Paganellum*', *CIMAGL* 63 (1993), 45–114. As Constant Mews ('On dating', pp. 74–5) has persuasively argued, the *Introductiones parvulorum* which Abelard mentions in the *Dialectica* (174: 1, 232: 10–12, 269: 1, 329: 4) is an independent introductory textbook to logic and not, as some scholars have believed, a name for Abelard's early commentaries.

[4] Edited from the Paris manuscript in *Scritti*, pp. 3–42, 70–203 (= *ed.Por.*, *ed.Per.*, *ed.Div*; see *Checklist* §292). The very final sections of *ed.Por.* and *ed.Per.* are missing. (Here and elsewhere, details will be given only of the most recent editions of each of Abelard's works, to which the references in the course of this book are made. Details of earlier editions will be found in *Checklist*.)

[5] The *Isagoge* commentary is edited in Y. Iwakuma, '"Vocales", or early nominalists', *Traditio* 47 (1992), 37–111 at pp. 74–100; the *De interpretatione* commentary is unedited, but there are extracts from it in J. Marenbon, 'Glosses and commentaries on the *Categories* and *De interpretatione* before Abelard', Appendix, in J. Fried (ed.), *Dialektik und Rhetorik im früheren und hohen Mittelalter* (Munich, 1966), pp. 21–49.

[6] The Munich *Isagoge* commentary has been mentioned by various scholars since Georg Scheppss first noted it in 1893: see Iwakuma, 'Vocales', p. 58, n. 76. In *Peter Abelard and his school* (King's College Cambridge Fellowship dissertation, 1962), pp. 225–34, David

the two *Isagoge* commentaries are each records of Abelard's lectures, or that they are both based on a common fund of straightforward, literal exegetical material, to which Abelard added the extra, more discursive sections found only in the Paris version. In the case of the *De interpretatione* commentary, there is strong reason to believe that both versions are taken from Abelard's lectures, but that the text in the Munich manuscript (as yet unpublished) represents Abelard's teaching most fully and accurately.[7]

These three commentaries, which very probably date from *c.* 1102 to 1104, Abelard's earliest years as a teacher,[8] exemplify an approach to exegesis probably learned from Roscelin, where the *Isagoge* and the *De divisione* are read as being entirely about words, not things.[9] Their form is also unusual. The commentaries consist, for the most part, of literal, word-by-word exegesis. Abelard concentrates on explaining Aristotle's argument and showing how it is constructed (often by recourse to the theory of topics). A personal view quite often emerges, but it appears in shortish asides, or in the choice of wording. Longer interpretative discussions are infrequent – although they are less rare in the *De interpretatione* commentary (especially in the Munich version).[10] By contrast, most commentaries of the very early twelfth century contain not only close analysis of the text but also lengthy digressions on matters of logical importance or controversy raised by it, usually derived (often verbatim) from Boethius' commentaries.[11] Abelard has simply omitted the discursive and derivative element.

The Paris manuscript also contains a fragment of a commentary on the *Categories* (just the end of the section on substance and part of the discussion

Luscombe argues that it is the work of a pupil of Abelard's, adapted from the text as preserved in the Paris manuscript. (I am very grateful to David Luscombe for having allowed me to consult this unpublished work). In 'Vocales', pp. 58–60, Yukio Iwakuma suggests that the Munich manuscript preserves the source (which he attributes to Roscelin) of the commentary by Abelard on the *Isagoge* in the Paris manuscript. The Munich *De interpretatione* commentary has been little discussed, but Iwakuma ('Vocales', p. 61) suggests that it too is by Roscelin and was used by Abelard as his source.

7 See my 'Glosses and commentaries', Appendix; I intend to discuss this text more fully in an article in preparation ('Exegesis, universals and ontology: Abelard and the approaches to logic at the turn of the twelfth century').

8 See Mews, 'On dating', p. 75; *Scritti*, p. xv. If *Cat.frag.* is later, but still before *c.* 1110, then this would argue for a date very early in the twelfth century for these commentaries.

9 See below, pp. 108–10.

10 There is, for instance, an extended discussion of future contingents and necessity: see Marenbon, 'Glosses and commentaries', pp. 42–3.

11 See *Commentaries and glosses*, p. 86.

of quantity).[12] Although there is no attribution in the manuscript, there are many extended parallels with passages from Abelard's *Logica*, which point to his authorship.[13] But the fragment, although it employs the same method of verbal exegesis, seems not to be a companion piece to the other three commentaries by Abelard in the manuscript. Moreover, the form of the fragment has more in common with Abelard's other, later logical works, where detailed analysis of the text is combined with discursive treatment of problems raised by it; and (by contrast with the literal commentaries) the problems discussed correspond to a large extent to those raised in the *Dialectica* and the *Logica*,[14] and the solutions often proceed along the same lines. Could it be from just a little later in Abelard's earliest period (*c.* 1105 or *c.* 1108)?

THE 'DIALECTICA'

These early works show that Abelard was a highly proficient – and, in turn-of-the-twelfth-century terms, very fashionable – logician. It is the *Dialectica*, however, which was Abelard's first (and so far as pure logic goes, perhaps his greatest) masterpiece.[15] But, almost all scholars until the recent work of Constant Mews have considered this large textbook of logic, at least in its final form, as one of Abelard's later works.[16] Since its dating is central to an understanding of Abelard's intellectual development, it is

[12] Edited in *Scritti*, pp. 43–67. (= *Cat.frag.*; *Checklist* §292). Dal Pra and other scholars have always considered *Cat.frag.* to belong to the group of literal commentaries.

[13] The parallels are listed in *Scritti*, pp. xxiii–xxvi.

[14] For the individual commentaries which make up the *Logica* (usually referred to by scholars as the *Logica Ingredientibus*), see below, pp. 46–7. For evidence that *Cat.frag.* is not much later than the *ed.sup.Por.*, *ed.Per.* and *ed.Div.*, see below, p. 110.

[15] Edited by L. de Rijk, *Petrus Abaelardus. Dialectica* (2nd edn, Assen, 1970) (= *Dial.*; *Checklist* §274).

[16] Cousin, the work's first editor, dated it tentatively to Abelard's final years at Cluny (*Ouvrages inédits*, p. xxxv). This dating was widely accepted. Geyer (*Phil. Schr.*, pp. 605–9) dated it to *c.* 1133 to 1136/7; J. Cottiaux ('La conception de la théologie chez Abélard' (Part 1), *Revue d'histoire ecclésiastique* 28 (1932), 247–95 at pp. 263–7) argued that it was composed in stages, between 1121 and 1134; L. Nicolau d'Olwer ('Sur la date de la *dialectica* d'Abélard', *Revue du moyen âge latin* 1 (1945), 375–90) argued that it was originally written in *c.* 1118 but revised in 1121–3 and again in 1135–7. His conclusions were taken as authoritative until Mews ('On dating', pp. 78–89) argued for a date in the period from 1117 to 1120, but before the *Logica*. De Rijk ('Peter Abelard's semantics and his doctrine of being', *Vivarium* 24 (1986), 85–128, at pp. 103–8) has accepted Mews's dates but believes that the *Dialectica* is roughly contemporaneous with the *Logica*. Most recently, Mews (*Peter Abelard*, p. 28) has suggested that Treatise I of *Dial.* (which is in great part lost) may have been written before the rest of the work, 'perhaps before 1113'.

important to pause for a moment to consider the arguments about its chronology.[17]

The strongest arguments for dating the *Dialectica* emerge from comparison with the *Logica*, Abelard's set of long commentaries on Aristotle, Boethius and Porphyry which, as will be explained, cannot have been written after 1121. In many cases, the doctrines of the two works are the same. Where they differ, the exposition in the *Logica* is always the one which it makes best sense to see as the later. Three of the most striking instances are a passage on sophisms, where the *Logica* shows a knowledge of Aristotle's *De sophisticis elenchis* missing in the *Dialectica*;[18] the analysis in the *Logica* (absent in the *Dialectica*) of impersonal statements;[19] and the rejection in the *Logica* of a 'common opinion' about the nature of time which, in the *Dialectica*, Abelard accepts as his own view without comment.[20] But there are many more.[21] This relative chronology is supported by some independent evidence for dating the *Dialectica* even to before 1117, when Abelard became a monk. In a prefatory passage (469: 7–9), Abelard mentions critics who attack him for devoting himself to logic, saying that 'a Christian should not treat of things which do not pertain to the faith'. If Abelard had already been a monk, it is difficult to see why they did not make (and how Abelard could have avoided answering) what, to a twelfth-century reader, would have been a far more telling and obvious criticism – that a *monk* should

[17] I will give a more detailed discussion of this issue in an article in preparation (provisional title: 'Dating Abelard's *Dialectica*'), where further details and arguments to support the position taken here will be found.

[18] Compare *sup.Per.* 399: 2 – 400: 37 with *Dial.* 181: 17 – 183: 17; on Abelard and the *De sophisticis elenchis*, see below, pp. 52–3.

[19] See K. Jacobi, 'Diskussionen über unpersönliche aussagen in Peter Abaelards Kommentar zu *Peri Hermeneias*' in E. Bos (ed.), *Mediaeval semantics and metaphysics* (Nijmegen, 1985) (Artistarium supplementa 2), pp. 1–63, who, supposing *Dial.* to be later than the *Logica*, remarks (p. 2): 'It is astonishing that this discussion ... is not taken up again in the *Dialectica*.'

[20] Compare *sup.Pred.* 184: 38–186: 14 with *Dial.* 62: 17–31; see below, pp. 146–7.

[21] Mews gives a long list ('On dating', pp. 82–7); although in some cases de Rijk ('Peter Abelard's semantics', pp. 104–7) discovers weaknesses in Mews's arguments, many of them remain convincing. One of de Rijk's most carefully developed arguments (pp. 106–22) against dating the *Dialectica* altogether earlier than the *Logica* is that the *Dialectica* has a more developed view of the meaning of 'est'. In fact, the two-part theory of predication which is the distinctive feature of the account in the *Dialectica* is found in Garlandus' *Dialectica* (ed. L. de Rijk (Assen, 1959) (Wijsgerige teksten en studies 3)) p. 46: 4–8; the work was written probably just after 1100, and Abelard may well have taken it from there: cf. Iwakuma, 'Vocales', pp. 52–3; for the identification of Garlandus and the date of his *Dialectica*, see pp. 47–54 of the same article.

not give himself over to such secular pursuits.[22] It is also unlikely that, as a monk and after the scandal of his affair with Heloise, Abelard would have chosen as logical examples phrases like 'May my girl-friend kiss me' and 'Peter loves his girl'.[23]

By contrast, most of the positive arguments made by earlier scholars for a dating, or a revision, of the *Dialectica* in the 1130s or later are very weak and have been ably answered by Mews.[24] But there is one piece of evidence for a late date or revision which is, at first sight, impressive. Towards the end of the *Dialectica* (558: 18–559: 14), Abelard criticizes those who identify the Platonic World Soul with the Holy Spirit. Exactly this identification is made in all three version of Abelard's *Theologia*.[25] What can Abelard be doing here but taking back his earlier, radical views, most probably in response to the criticisms which would lead (or had led) to his appearance at the Council of Sens? So scholars from Cousin to Nicolau have argued. There is, indeed, no doubt about the anti-Platonic tone of the passage.[26] Abelard describes Plato's doctrine of the World Soul as a 'fiction (*figmentum*) utterly removed from the truth' and leading to the conclusion that there must be two souls in each man. And, in order to show how wrong Plato could be, he adds that Plato also believed in the pre-existence of souls. But what separates the two treatments is not a difference in attitude to Christianity, but a difference in approach to Plato. In the *Dialectica*, Abelard takes what Plato says at face value and consequently rejects it as false. In the *Theologia Summi Boni* and the subsequent versions of the *Theologia*, he argues in detail that Plato should not be read literally here – if Plato had meant what he said literally, he would have been the greatest of fools, not the greatest philosopher[27] – and he explains the Christian truth which is

22 As Nicolau ('Sur la date', p. 378) argues. Mews ('On dating', p. 96) uses this passage as evidence for a date *after* 1117, saying that the criticism is the same as that levelled against Abelard (*HC* 82: 683–4) in the period 1118–21, when he was teaching as a monk at a *cella* of St Denis. But, in fact, then the criticism was directed against Abelard specifically as a monk.

23 Again, Nicolau ('Sur la date', pp. 378–9) made this point, which Mews ('On dating', p. 97) rejects.

24 'On dating', pp. 95–6.

25 *TSum* 99: 355 – 106: 572; *TChr* (100: 897 – 124: 41); *TSch* (368: 1411 – 397: 2232).

26 Mews ('On dating', pp. 98–9) argues rather unconvincingly that there is no contradiction between the view of the World Soul in the *Dialectica* and that in the *Theologia* (although there is some development).

27 *TSum* 101: 428–31: 'Ex hac itaque Macrobii traditione clarum est ea que a philosophis de anima mundi dicuntur, per inuolucrum accipienda esse. Alioquin summum philosophorum Platonem summum stultorum esse deprehenderemus' = *TChr* 116: 63–6; *TSch* 386: 1920–23.

carefully and deliberately hidden from the unworthy by Plato's *involucrum*.[28] If the passage in *Dialectica* is taken as a later rejection of his earlier views, Abelard must be supposed simply to have passed over in silence the distinctions he had previously drawn to make Plato compatible with Christian faith. Everything is explained simply, however, if the passage in the *Dialectica* was written by Abelard *before* he had come to the sophisticated understanding of Plato evident in the *Theologia Summi Boni* and the later versions of the *Theologia*.

Unlike most of Abelard's other logical works, the *Dialectica* – which survives in a single manuscript, from which about the first tenth has been lost – is not in outward form a set of commentaries, but an independent treatise. This appearance of independence is, however, an illusion. Even Abelard himself, immediately after boasting that his contributions to 'peripatetic eloquence' will be no fewer or slighter than those of the most celebrated authorities known in Latin, goes on to add that there is no less work or value in the 'exposition of the words [of authoritative texts]' than in 'devising theories' (*inventio sententiarum*), and to express the hope that his *Dialectica* will provide a *summa* of the ancient logical texts and make them available for readers (146: 2–20). The structure of the *Dialectica* (like that of Garlandus' *Dialectica*, written ten or fifteen year earlier)[29] follows the accepted logical curriculum. Treatise I deals, Abelard explains (142: 15–16), with the 'parts of a sentence' (*partes orationis*) – the blocks from which statements and then arguments are built. This involves treating the material normally covered in the *Isagoge*, the standard introductory book in the logical curriculum (the section is missing, but its subject-matter is evident from cross-references); in the *Categories*, the next book in the canon; and finally treating the questions about signification which usually arose in connection with the opening chapters of the next work of the canon, the *De interpretatione*. In Treatise II he brings together discussion of categorical statements (based on the remaining parts of *De interpretatione*) and the categorical syllogisms made up from them (based on Boethius' treatise). Treatise III is concerned with topical reasoning, based on Boethius' exposition in his *De topicis differentiis*. In Treatise IV Abelard deals with hypothetical statements and syllogisms (the subject-matter of Boethius' *De hypotheticis syllogismis*). Finally, Treatise V covers the material treated in the two remaining short works of the logical curriculum, Boethius' *De divisione*

[28] See also below, pp. 56–7.

[29] Garlandus' *Dialectica* is a little less comprehensive, since it lacks sections on definition and division.

(which provides Abelard with the chance to discuss parts and wholes)[30] and Marius Victorinus' *De diffinitione*. Abelard's only change to the accepted ordering is to treat the material on equivocal and univocal words from the beginning of the *Categories* in the final treatise, and the subjects covered by Aristotle in this text after the ten Categories themselves in Treatise III on topics. But Abelard gives the whole work a strange appearance by choosing what he must have believed were impressively Aristotelian titles for the five treatises: *Book of parts*, *Prior analytics*, *Topics*, *Posterior analytics*, *Divisions*.[31] Not only does the *Dialectica* follow the order of the usual logical curriculum, it is also clearly based on his lectures on the individual ancient texts – as its closeness in many parts to the *Logica* (and, in the relevant section, to the *Categories* fragment) indicates. Sometimes he seems to have refashioned his lecture notes, but sometimes he copied them closely, abbreviating here and there: there are inconsistencies which cannot easily be explained except on the assumption that Abelard is copying, over-hastily, from material which had previously been differently arranged and more extensive,[32] and some passages give in a form terse to the point of incomprehensibility objections and counter-objections of the sort which would have occurred in schoolroom discussion.[33]

Although the *Dialectica* (or at least Treatise II of it) is addressed by Abelard to his brother, Dagobert, for the education of 'nephews' (*Dial.* 146: 23–5), it is anything but a simplified or introductory work. Mainly in the sections dealing with the subject-matter of the *Categories* and *De interpretatione*, Abelard develops his distinctive and subtle ontology – his account of substances, forms, their interrelation and the links between them, language and thought. This aspect of the *Dialectica* will be examined in detail in Part II. But, important though these discussions are, it is not to them that Abelard gives the greatest emphasis. His main aim is to study and distinguish different types of valid argument. He considers, though rather briefly, the traditional Aristotelian moods of the categorical syllogism, but

[30] On Abelard's mereology, see D. Henry, *Medieval mereology* (Amsterdam/Philadelphia, 1991) (Bochumer Studien zur Philosophie 16), pp. 64–180.

[31] Both Geyer (*Phil. Schr.*, p. 605) and de Rijk (*Dialectica*, p. XXX; cf. p. XXXII) have rejected the titles of Treatises II–V as later additions. But it is most unlikely that anyone would have added them, as they believe, once the contents of Aristotle's *Analytics* were better known, whilst they make perfect sense as Abelard's own, part boastful, part witty flourish.

[32] See e.g. the reference at 377: 26 to a position 'mentioned above' (*ut supra meminimus*), when there has in fact been no allusion to this position before then; and the reference at 379: 7–8 to indirect and direct contraries (*contraria . . . sive mediata sint sive immediata*) as if the distinction had been explained, which it is not until later (380: 4 ff.).

[33] E.g. 209: 12–210: 28, 373: 28–374: 19.

his strongest interest is in 'consequences' or, as they would now be called, conditionals or entailment statements (such as, 'if Socrates is a man, he is an animal'). He examines them in the long treatise (IV) on hypothetical syllogisms and in the even longer treatise (III) on topics (together treatises III and IV occupy half of the surviving text). Recently, Christopher Martin has shown just how boldly innovative is Abelard's treatment here of topical reasoning.[34] The ancient theory of topics, as transmitted by Boethius' *De topicis differentiis*, had been concerned with finding rhetorically convincing rather than irrefragable arguments. Abelard wishes, rather, to use the theory to explore the conditions for logically valid reasoning. Some topics on which Boethius had based arguments (such as the topic from authority: 'what the authority of wise men confirms is so') are to be rejected entirely. But Abelard goes further: the requirement that it is impossible for the antecedent to be true when the consequent is false – the modern definition of strict implication – is enough to ensure a correct argument, but it is a necessary, not a sufficient condition for the truth of a conditional. To be true, a conditional must have an antecedent which 'of itself requires' the consequent (284: 1–4). When conditionalized, the moods of the categorical and hypothetical syllogism satisfy this criterion. They are perfect entailments, in Abelard's view, because they are true by virtue of their form, whatever terms are used. Conditionals like 'if Socrates is a man, he is an animal' are not true by virtue of their form (substitute for instance 'donkey' for 'animal', and it becomes false). Such a conditional depends on the relation between 'man' and 'animal' and on the principle (*maxima propositio*) of topical reasoning that whatever belongs to a species belongs to the genus of that species. Abelard describes an entailment of this sort as 'imperfect' (*imperfecta inferentia*) (see *Dial.* 256: 25 – 257: 23). Abelard also clearly distinguishes between what is needed for the truth of a conditional and what is required for the validity of an argument: an argument is valid so long as it is impossible for its premisses to be true and its conclusion false.

A little before he wrote the *Dialectica*, Abelard may also have composed a treatise on sophisms (fallacious arguments), which he refers to as the *libri Fantasiarum* (*Dial.* 448: 3–4). The work does not survive, but a discussion of sophisms found in Orléans, Bibliothèque municipale 266 under the

[34] See his 'Embarrassing arguments and surprising conclusions in the development of theories of the conditional in the twelfth century' in J. Jolivet and A. de Libera (eds.), *Gilbert de Poitiers et ses contemporains* (Naples, 1987) (History of Logic 5), pp. 377–400 at pp. 385–93 and 'The logic of the *Nominales*', *Vivarium* 30 (1992), 110–26 at pp. 113–22. The rest of this paragraph summarizes Martin's views. See also E. Stump, *Dialectic and its place in the development of medieval logic* (Ithaca/London, 1989), pp. 87–109.

heading '*Secundum M<agistrum> Petrum sententie*' may well be a fragment from it.[35]

THE 'LOGICA'

Not long after he had finished the *Dialectica*, Abelard was busy preparing another comprehensive logical work – this time in the form of commentaries – based on similar material. The *Dialectica*, it has been argued, was probably written up before 1117 (although a date *c.* 1118–19 cannot be definitely excluded) and so probably based on the lectures he was giving at Paris around 1115 to 1116, shortly before or at the beginning of his affair with Heloise. When Abelard took up teaching logic again a little while after he entered St Denis, he probably used much the same material as he had done in Paris, but with some revision and development. This was probably what he wrote up, between about 1118 and 1120, for his new work. The *Logica* survives in rather less complete form than the *Dialectica*, and what remains must be reconstructed from three different manuscripts.[36] One manuscript (Milan, Biblioteca Ambrosiana, M 63 sup.) contains commentaries on the *Isagoge*, *Categories* and *De interpretatione*, each explicitly attributed to Abelard. But, in fact, the final section (490: 20 – 503: 26) of the *De interpretatione* commentary is not Abelard's work at all, but that of a logician with opposing views.[37] In Berlin, Deutsche Staatsbibliothek, lat. fol. 624, however, there is found, anonymously, another text of this commen-

[35] The *Secundum M<agistrum> Petrum sententie* (*Checklist* §301) is edited by L. Minio-Paluello, *Twelfth-century logic. Texts and studies* II, *Abaelardiana inedita* (Rome, 1958), pp. 111–21. Its authorship is discussed on pp. xxxix–xli of the introduction; cf. also de Rijk, *Logica modernorum: a contribution to the history of early terminist logic* I (Assen, 1962), pp. 110–12 and R. van der Lecq, 'The *Sententie secundum Magistrum Petrum*' in Jolivet and de Libera, *Gilbert de Poitiers*, pp. 43–56. Henry (*Medieval mereology*, p. 179) casts a doubt on the attribution of the work to Abelard.

[36] The commentaries on the *Isagoge* (= *sup.Por.*), *Categories* (= *sup.Pred.*) and *De interpretatione* (= *sup.Per.*) – from the Milan manuscript only, with the inauthentic ending, are edited in *Phil. Schr.*, 1–3 (Münster, 1919–27) (BGPMA 21). The authentic ending of the *De interpretatione* commentary (*sup.Per* (M)) is edited in Minio-Paluello, *Twelfth-century logic*, pp. 3–108 (all these are *Checklist* §294). The *De differentiis topicis* commentary (= *sup.Top.*; *Checklist* §307) is edited in dal Pra, *Scritti*, pp. 205–330. Most scholars describe this set of commentaries as his *Logica Ingredientibus* (from the opening: 'Ingredientibus nobis logicam . . .') in order to distinguish it from his later commentary on Porphyry, which they call the *Logica Nostrorum Petitioni Sociorum*. But since, as I shall argue, it is more accurate to call this later work the *Glossulae*, the simple title *Logica* will be used here without danger of confusion.

[37] As demonstrated by Minio-Paluello, *Abaelardiana*, pp. XVII–XX.

tary by Abelard, but with the authentic conclusion. And, in Paris, Bibliothèque nationale, lat. 7493 there is the beginning of a commentary on *De topicis differentiis*, attributed in its title to Abelard, which from cross-references can be seen to belong to the same collection as the other three.[38] Cross-references also indicate that the *Logica* contained a commentary on Boethius' treatise on hypothetical syllogisms (so far undiscovered).[39]

Despite this messy transmission, there is every reason to consider the *Logica* an integral work, conceived as a whole (though showing some small developments in thought during its course).[40] Abelard has reworked his lectures carefully. His language is well chosen and usually elegant; and he is more selective here than in the *Dialectica*, excluding discussions of secondary importance in order to set out the main issues clearly. The surviving parts of it may give a slightly misleading impression of the *Logica*. From the length of the opening portion, the commentary on *De topicis differentiis* seems as though it would have been very long. If the rest of it and the commentary on *De syllogismis hypotheticis* had not been lost, the emphasis of the *Logica* might seem much the same as that of the *Dialectica*. All the same, there is no denying that Abelard's interest in the wider philosophical questions raised by logic is deeper here than in the earlier work. His ontology, although the same in most respects, is explored with more detail and sophistication.[41] Abelard now also elaborates a theory of cognition and of the relation between thought and language.[42] He treats the problem of future contingents, God's prescience and human freedom more thoroughly,[43]

[38] See dal Pra, *Scritti di logica*, pp. XXXII–IV, who convincingly corrects the view of Cousin (*Ouvrages inédits*, pp. ix–x) and Geyer (*Phil. Schr.*, p. 592) that this commentary belongs with the early literal ones.

[39] At *sup.Pred.* 291: 24–6; *sup.Per.* 389: 7; cf. Geyer, *Phil. Schr.* p. 598.

[40] See *Phil. Schr.*, p. VIII. Mews ('On dating', pp. 76–7) does not agree that we can speak of *sup.Por.*, *sup.Pred.*, *sup.Per.* and *sup.Top.* as forming parts of a single work. But he arrives at this view by taking the various past and future tense cross-references from one commentary to another as being real pasts and futures, rather than – as seems more likely – the pasts and futures of authorial cross-reference ('I have said above', 'I shall say below'). More recently, Mews ('Aspects of the evolution of Peter Abaelard's thought on signification and predication' in Jolivet and de Libera, *Gilbert de Poitiers*, pp. 15–41 at p. 39, n. 68) has argued – in my view, unconvincingly – that *sup.Per.* and *sup.Top.* were written several years later than *sup.Por* and *sup.Pred.*, towards the mid-1120s: I shall discuss this point in my 'Dating Abelard's *Dialectica*'. For small signs of development between *sup.Por.* and *sup.Per.*, see below, pp. 167–70.

[41] See below, pp. 115 n. 47, 135–6, 144–5.

[42] See below, pp. 165–70.

[43] See below, p. 226.

and his discussion of modal statements, already impressive in the *Dialectica*, has become more sophisticated.[44]

ABELARD'S LATER LOGIC

The reason why the *Logica* can be dated firmly to 1121 or before lies in its relation to Abelard's first version of the *Theologia*, the *Theologia Summi Boni*, which was condemned at the Council of Soissons in March 1121. There, led by his need to explain how God is three and one, Abelard argues that there are more meanings of 'the same' and 'different' than Porphyry had recognized in his *Isagoge*.[45] This development, which involves a big step in Abelard's thought about semantics, is quite absent from the *Logica*. Another commentary on the *Isagoge*, the *Glossulae super Porphyrium* attributed to Abelard in its sole surviving witness (Lunel, Bibliothèque municipale, 6),[46] includes exactly this discussion, in a version more developed than that of the *Theologia Summi Boni*. And there turn out to be three further witnesses to Abelard's teaching on Porphyry after the time of the *Logica*. The same Milan manuscript (Biblioteca Ambrosiana, M 63 sup.) which contains much of the *Logica* also includes an *Isagoge* commentary which is entitled 'Glosse super Porphyrium secundum uocales' – 'according', that is to say, 'to those who take universals to be words', which was Abelard's position.[47] The commentary turns out to consist, with just a few exceptions, of passages often garbled but very close or identical to either the *Logica* or the *Glossulae*. Although the possibility that it is a compilation cannot be ruled out, it is more plausible to think that it derives from Abelard's lectures – though perhaps from more than one account of them.[48] Then there is a fragment entitled 'Positio uocum sententiae' in Orléans, Bibliothèque

[44] This discussion is found in the final section of *sup.Per.*, edited from the Berlin manuscript by Minio-Paluello.

[45] See below, pp. 150–1.

[46] Edited in *Phil. Schr.*, 4 (1933); (= *Glossulae*; *Checklist* §295)

[47] Edited in C. Ottaviano (ed.), *Fontes Ambrosiani III: Testi medioevali inediti* (Florence, 1933), pp. 107–207; Geyer edits a few excerpts in *Phil. Schr.*, pp. 581–8 (= *Gl.sec.voc.*; *Checklist* §327). Ottaviano's edition is marred by misreadings and mispunctuation.

[48] Geyer (*Phil.Schr.*, pp. 610–12) argued that the work is a compilation. Ottaviano (*Fontes Ambrosiani*, pp. 95–6) supported Abelard's authorship, but weakened his position by the extraordinary claim that the (often very corrupt) text in the Milan manuscript is Abelard's autograph. More recently, Constant Mews ('A neglected gloss on the "Isagoge" by Peter Abelard', *Freiburger Zeitschrift für Philosophie und Theologie* 31 (1984), 35–550) has made a powerful case for Abelard's authorship, although the *Checklist* still places it in the category of 'unauthenticated or anonymous writings' giving Abelard's teaching.

municipale, 266, discussing Porphyry's definition of genus which has many parallels with the *Logica*, *Glossulae* and the *Glosse secundum uocales*, and also probably derives from Abelard's teaching, although its ponderous didactic style suggests that it has been reworked by someone else.[49] Most interesting, however, is a little treatise in Avranches, Bibliothèque municipale, 232, which is explicitly attributed to Abelard and given the title *De intellectibus* ('On thoughts').[50] Much of *De intellectibus* is close (though at times notably different in argument) to Abelard's discussion of cognition in the *De interpretatione* commentary of the *Logica*. Other parts of it run parallel to the discussion of universals in the *Glossulae* and, on occasion at least, it gives what is obviously a more complete version of the same passage.[51]

Behind all four texts lies Abelard's teaching. The *Glossulae* are a written-up version of lectures, as their opening (505: 3–5) makes clear: 'At the request of my fellows (*socii*) I have undertaken the labour of writing logic, and in accord with their wishes I shall expound what I have taught about logic.' And the very close parallels with this commentary show that *De intellectibus* must have been written up at about the same time, from the same material. Some divergences in doctrine indicate that the *Glosse secundum uocales* must be a little earlier, probably from the time when Abelard was working on or had just finished the *Theologia Summi Boni* (*c.* 1120–1), and the *Positio uocum sententie* just a little earlier again.[52] But whether the development between the *Positio* and the *Glossulae* reflects

[49] This has been discovered by Yukio Iwakuma: see 'Vocales', pp. 54–7 for discussion of this work, and pp. 66–73 for an edition.

[50] Edited by L. Urbani Ulivi in *La psicologia di Abelardo e il 'Tractatus de intellectibus'* (Rome, 1976), pp. 103–27 (= *De int.*; *Checklist* §311).

[51] Compare *Glossulae* 530: 24 – 531: 19 and *De int.* 123: 22 – 124: 33, where *De int.* 124: 14–27, which have no parallel in the *Glossulae*, answer a question raised in both works but left unanswered in the *Glossulae*. Geyer (*Phil. Schr.*, pp. 613–15) advanced a complicated theory according to which *De int.* was written by a pupil familiar with Abelard's way of thought and using an unknown, lost work of Abelard's, but Ulivi (*La psicologia*) has thoroughly answered his objections to Abelard's authorship. The work is accepted as authentic by the *Checklist*. See also below, pp. 50–1.

[52] In *Gl.sec.voc.* (178) and *TSum* (143: 757–8) Abelard states that to be the same 'in essence' is equivalent to being the same 'by predication', whereas in *TChr* he omits this claim and in the *Glossulae* (558: 17–21) he mentions the position as one which seems to be true but is not (cf. below, p. 150 n. 29); also, *Gl.sec.voc.* and *TSum* still call universals *voces* – a use repudiated in the *Glossulae* (522: 10 – 524: 20) and avoided in *TChr*: see Geyer, *Phil. Schr.*, pp. 600–3; Mews, 'A neglected gloss', pp. 51–5, 'On dating', p. 78; 'Aspects', pp. 26–8. Iwakuma ('Vocales', pp. 55–7) shows that, on a number of points, the doctrine of the 'Positio uocum sententie' must be earlier than that of *Gl.sec.voc.*

changes introduced by Abelard into his oral teaching, or merely Abelard's second thoughts when writing up his lectures, is not certain – indeed, it is not clear whether he lectured on logic at all between the Council of Soissons and his return to Paris in the 1130s.

From these works, it is clear that Abelard's thinking in connection with logic developed in some striking ways between the beginning and the middle of the 1120s. There is an important development in his semantics, and in his ontology with regard to accidents;[53] the theory of universals is revised;[54] the account of perception and knowledge is altered.[55] Yet what remains of Abelard's logic from *c.* 1121 to *c.* 1126 is slight in bulk compared with the impressive surviving testimony to his previous five years of logical teaching. Moreover, the *Glossulae* – so far from being the only remaining part of a comprehensive set of commentaries – give the distinct impression of a project begun ambitiously and concluded very hastily. The work begins in the same manner as the *Logica*, with an expansive prologue followed by detailed exegesis of the very beginning of the *Isagoge*, and then a lengthy discussion of universals, in which the various current theories are criticized and Abelard's own views explained and defended. But at the start of the next section, on Genus (534: 2–4), Abelard says that he has left out exposition of the letter of the text, and after this point, he includes only very occasional passages of literal exposition, and concentrates on examining the problems raised by the text (sometimes cramming in disjointedly at the end of a section extra questions and solutions which might have been generated by discussion of the text at lectures: cf. 540: 10–40; 557: 4–12). Even these discussions are terse by comparison with the *Logica*, and the last two-fifths of Porphyry's text is rushed over in a few pages.

Yet Abelard may well have produced one fairly substantial logical work in this period which has been lost. In both the *Theologia Christiana* (343: 2470–1) and the *Theologia Scholarium* (529: 938–9) Abelard mentions a work he has written called the *Grammatica*. Despite its title, this treatise seems, from Abelard's comments, to have dealt with logical matters – in particular, it contained a rethinking of his ideas about the categories (an area where, from the *Theologia Christiana*, it is clear that he had changed his views).[56]

[53] See below, p. 136.

[54] See below, pp. 178–9, 186–90.

[55] See below, pp. 170–3.

[56] Geyer (*Phil. Schr.*, pp. 616–19) notes these references but does not think they refer to a lost *Grammatica*. Mews ('Aspects', pp. 31–8) argues that they do, and attempts to reconstruct the contents of the work. He notes that the reference in *TChr* to the *Grammatica* is to section of it on the 'reconsideration of the Categories' (*retractatio predicamentorum*), and

It is even possible that the *De intellectibus* may be a section from this missing *Grammatica*. At one point in the *De intellectibus* Abelard refers his readers to a fuller discussion of a point he has mentioned '*in constructionibus*' – that is 'in [the section on] how words are put together into sentences'.[57] There is no such discussion in the *De intellectibus* as it now stands, and a discussion of *constructio* is just what might be expected in a philosophically oriented *Grammatica*.[58]

Even taking into account this lost treatise, it would still be fair to say that by the mid-1120s the main direction of Abelard's interests had moved away from logic – especially since the most striking developments in his logic during this period seem to have been brought about as a result of the thinking suggested by the theological problems he was tackling. This change became far more marked in the fifteen years – the last of Abelard's working life – which followed. Abelard was giving logic lectures as late as 1136,[59] but he does not seem to have written up his logical teaching again, as he had done repeatedly in the earlier period. There does, however, exist some evidence for the content of Abelard's logical teaching in the 1130s. Anonymous logical commentaries and textbooks from the 1130s, 1140s and later mention positions taken by Abelard on a variety of logical questions.[60] Since

suggests that Abelard's other cross-references (*TChr* 286: 687–8, 713–14; 344: 2506) to a *retractatio/discretio predicamentorum* must be to this same part of the *Grammatica*. Mews does not, however, consider whether *De intellectibus* belonged to this lost work.

57 117: 23–4: 'de quo plenius in constructionibus prosequimur'.

58 Two other pieces of evidence support the suggestion that *De int.* is a part of the *Grammatica*: (1) in *TChr* (286: 711–14) Abelard reveals that his treatise 'on the distinction of the Categories' (probably – see note 56 above – part of the *Grammatica*) contains a discussion of *constructio*; (2) if *De int.* is part of the *Grammatica*, then it is likely that other parts of the *Grammatica*, too, would be drawn, like *De int.*, from the same material as is used in the *Glossulae*. In fact, just such a parallel emerges from the brief reference to the *Grammatica* in *TSch*: compare *TSch* 529: 939 – 530: 949 with *Glossulae* 549: 12–20 – cf. Geyer, *Phil. Schr.*, pp. 618–19.

59 See above, p. 25.

60 Of the commentaries, the most important for their mentions of Abelard are those on the *Isagoge* (P 25), *Categories* (C 17) and *De interpretatione* (H 17), *De syllogismis hypotheticis* and *De sophisticis elenchis* in Berlin, 624; the *Isagoge* commentary (P 20) in Vienna, Österreichische Nationalbibliothek, cvp 2486, the *Categories* commentary (C 15) in Padua, Biblioteca universitaria 2087 and the *De interpretatione* commentary (H 15) in Paris, Bibliothèque nationale, lat. 15015. All these are discussed, and many of the remarks about Abelard's teaching printed, in L. de Rijk, 'Some new evidence on twelfth century logic: Alberic and the School of Mont Ste Geneviève (Montani)', *Vivarium* 4 (1966), 1–57, at pp. 23–55; for C 15 see also F. Bottin, 'Quelques discussions sur la transitivité de la prédication dans l'école d'Albéric du Mont' in Jolivet and de Libera, *Gilbert de Poitiers*, pp. 57–72. De Rijk edits the Berlin commentary on *De sophisticis elenchis* in *Logica modernorum* II, 2 (Assen, 1967). Of the treatises, the most important are the *Introductiones montane minores* (ed. in de Rijk,

these texts record, or stem from, the logical teaching and controversies which took place in the Paris schools from the 1130s onwards, it is very probable that, when their authors refer to Abelard's positions, they are basing themselves on his lectures from this period.

Does this mean that the absence of any logical works from the 1130s directly written by Abelard is merely an accident of transmission and that perhaps, by careful research, it might be possible to reconstruct the contents of a whole new phase of Abelard's logical thinking? The material known at present suggests that, on the contrary, there were few exciting new developments, and that Abelard did not write up his teaching in this area again because he had little new to add. Certainly, there are some changes to his doctrine, or additions to it – such as the development of his ideas about statements and their tenses, although this is closely related to his theological discussions in the *Theologia Scholarium*.[61] But mostly the points attributed to Abelard are of minor importance, or else they are ideas already discussed in his *Dialectica*, *Logica* or his theological works (the doctrine that God cannot do more than he does is often brought up – and rejected – by logicians; possibly Abelard brought this into his logical as well as his theological lectures).[62] One of the most telling of the references to Abelard is well known. It reports an exchange with Alberic, the leading logician on the Mont Ste Geneviève in the late 1130s and 1140s and Abelard's fiercest opponent:[63]

Logica modernorum II, 2), the *Introductiones montane maiores* in Paris, Bibliothèque nationale, lat. 15141 (cf. de Rijk, 'New evidence', pp. 12–22), the *Summa Sophisticorum elenchorum* and the *Tractatus de Dissimilitudine argumentorum* (both ed. in de Rijk, *Logica modernorum* I (Assen, 1962) and the *Summa dialetice artis* by William of Lucca, who refers to Abelard as the 'Philosophus' (ed. L. Pozzi (Padua, 1975) (Testi e saggi 7)). This William is taken by his editor to be the William who became Bishop of Lucca and died in 1194; but F. Gastaldelli ('Linguaggio e stile in Guglielmo da Lucca', *Salesianum* 41 (1979), 482–8) has argued that he should be identified with the William of Lucca who wrote a commentary on pseudo-Dionysius' *Divine names*.

[61] See J. Marenbon, 'Vocalism, nominalism and the commentaries on the *Categories* from the earlier twelfth century', *Vivarium* 30 (1992), 51–61 at pp. 58–61. An apparently new distinction between statements which are *multiplex* and those which are *plura* is attributed to Abelard in H 17 (Berlin, 624, f. 91va; cf. *sup.Per.* 382: 8–387: 29).

[62] See H 17 (Berlin 624, f. 95ra) printed in de Rijk, 'New evidence', p. 46; and cf. *Summa Sophisticorum elenchorum* (at de Rijk, *Logica modernorum* I, p. 402: 14 ff.).

[63] On Alberic, see de Rijk, 'New evidence', W. Courtenay, 'Nominales and nominalism in the twelfth century' in J. Jolivet, Z. Kaluza, A. de Libera (eds.), *Lectionum varietates* (Paris, 1991) (Etudes de philosophie médiévale 65), pp. 12–48 at p. 16 and Marenbon, 'Vocalism, nominalism', pp. 54–8.

Master Peter says: 'I have read and re-read the *Elenchi*, but I haven't found a sophism of univocation there.' 'I don't doubt you haven't found it', says Master Alberic, 'because you haven't understood the text.'[64]

Abelard's comment here is exactly the same as what he says about the sophism of univocation in the *Logica*.[65] Since the student who records the dispute between Abelard and Alberic is clearly reporting what the masters on the Mont Ste Geneviève are teaching at the time, it is fairly clear that Abelard was content to repeat, almost verbatim, the view which he had reached about this subject fifteen years before. But the *De sophisticis elenchis* were the newest and leading enthusiasm of the logicians of the 1130s, like Alberic.[66] Abelard was one of the earliest medieval logicians to see this treatise, but never went beyond the fleeting, incidental use he had made of it in the 1120s.[67]

In other areas, too, Abelard's logic seems to have been overtaken by the work of younger men. His theory of the truth conditions for consequences – the same as that he had devised twenty years before in the *Dialectica* – was shown by Alberic to lead to self-contradiction;[68] and Alberic subjected almost every aspect of Abelard's interpretation of the *Isagoge* and the *Categories* (especially his view that universals are not things) to remorseless criticism which, to judge from the surviving commentaries of the time, was widely accepted. Was Abelard, over fifty years old (a considerable age at that time) and worn down by a series of failures and continuing conflicts, past his prime as a thinker by the 1130s and content to live off his intellectual capital? By no means. The final decade of his working life was his most productive and his work at this time perhaps his most original and certainly his boldest. But his energies were now given almost entirely to theology. It is this side of his work which must now be examined.

64 H 17 (Berlin 624, f. 92ra) printed in de Rijk, *Logica modernorum* I, p. 620: 27–9, where the close parallel with *sup.Per.* is noted.

65 *Sup.Per.* 400: 32–6: 'Memini tamen quendam libellum vidisse et diligenter relegisse, qui sub nomine Aristotelis de sophisticis elenchis intitulatus erat, et cum inter cetera sophismatum genera de univocatione requirerem, nil de ea scriptum inveni.'

66 See de Rijk, *Logica Modernorum* I.

67 As Mews ('On dating', p. 129) perceptively observes: 'in the 1130's Abelard was no longer at the forefront in the teaching of logic, having written his major works on the subject well over ten years earlier, before the new texts of Aristotle had become widely known'.

68 Alberic's argument against Abelard has been reconstructed from the *Introductiones montane maiores* by Christopher Martin, in 'William's machine', *Journal of Philosophy* 83 (1986), 567–72, 'Embarrassing arguments', pp. 394–400 and in 'The logic', pp. 122–4.

Chapter 3

Abelard's theological project

From 1113, when he started to expound Ezechiel in response to a challenge from his fellow pupils in the school of Anselm of Laon, Abelard taught sacred doctrine as well as logic. Nothing survives of this early teaching, however, and it was perhaps no more than a chance for Abelard to show off his brilliance to an uncritical audience.[1] His attitude to theology changed sharply after he entered St Denis. Certainly, in his first years as a monk, he still gave a great deal of time to logic, not only giving logical lectures but writing up his *Logica*. But soon he was already engaged on a part of the theological project which would, in one form or another, increasingly dominate his intellectual life and his writing.

THE 'THEOLOGIA'

The first surviving record of this new area of Abelard's activity is the treatise usually known as the *Theologia Summi Boni*, although it was probably entitled simply *De Trinitate*.[2] As Abelard explains in his *Historia*, his pupils

> asked for human and philosophical reasons and insisted that it was not enough for something just to be said – it had to be understood (*plus que intelligi quam que dici possent efflagitabant*). Indeed, they said that it was vain to utter words if they were not then understood, nor could anything be believed in unless it was first understood, and that it was ridiculous for someone to preach to others what neither he nor those he taught could grasp with their intellects, for then (as Christ complained) the blind lead the blind. (83: 693–701)

[1] Note Abelard's phrasing in *HC* 70: 247–8: 'ut me non minorem gratiam in sacra lectione adeptum jam *crederent* quam in philosophica *viderant*'.

[2] *Op. Th.* III, pp. 85–201 (= *TSum*; *Checklist* §310). On the title, see *Mews*, pp. 17–18 (but, for the opposite view, cf. H. Ostlender, *Peter Abaelards Theologia 'Summi Boni'* (Münster, 1939) (BGPMA 35, 2/3), pp. XXI–XXII).

These words express the rationale behind Abelard's enterprise in the clearest and most uncompromising terms (more uncompromising than Abelard might have been willing to put into his own mouth). The *Theologia Summi Boni* begins by addressing the very problem they raise boldly and directly. 'For God to be three persons – Father, Son and Holy Spirit – is', he explains, 'as if we were to say that the divine substance is powerful, wise and benign, or rather that it is power itself, wisdom itself, benignity itself' (87: 21–4). And, as Abelard shows in the next paragraph, power, wisdom and benignity are that in which the highest perfection consists, and without any one of them a being would be far from perfect, whereas 'that being in which these three things come together – that he can fulfil what he wishes, and being benign he wishes well and he does not overstep the limit of reason by lacking reason – he is indeed considered to be truly good and perfect in all things' (87: 34–7). The implications of this position are radical, but need to be stated carefully. Abelard does not, of course, deny that God can be correctly described as being the three persons, Father, Son and Holy Spirit, of orthodox Christian teaching. Nor does he think that this distinction between the divine persons is merely verbal: indeed, much of his detailed logical discussion in the *Theologia Summi Boni* (which, later, he would further elaborate) is intended to clarify the exact nature of this distinction. None the less, Abelard does clearly make the claim that in using the terms 'Father', 'Son' and 'Holy Spirit', we are saying that God is power, wisdom and benignity, and that it is precisely these attributes which rational reflection tells us we must attribute in their highest form to a being who is perfect. There may seem to be an inconsistency here, since to make a more than verbal distinction between the divine persons involves a stronger claim than differentiating three different attributes of God. Abelard might reply, however, that his analysis of difference later in the treatise is intended to show just how God's real triunity is explicable in terms of a special relation between him and his attributes. Abelard also protects himself by making an additional claim, on which he insists later in the treatise (120: 155 – 122: 216), using pagan philosophical as well as Christian testimony, that God is beyond human speech and understanding. Yet, although he is careful to avoid implying that our knowledge of the Trinity is exhaustive. Abelard concentrates not on its limitations, but rather on its extent and accuracy. In a very important way, he is willing to argue that the divinity is comprehensible.[3]

[3] On Abelard's approach to theology, see J. Cottiaux, 'La conception de la théologie chez Abélard' (Parts 2 and 3), *Revue d'histoire ecclésiastique* 28 (1932), 533–51, 788–828 and W.

Moreover, since for God to be the Trinity is for him to be powerful, wise and benign, and these are the attributes which any intelligent person gives to a perfect being, no one, Jew or Gentile, is without faith in the Trinity. What St Paul says of the pagans, 'What is known of God has been shown to them' (Romans 1: 19), means: 'what pertains to the divinity they perceived by reason, because reason naturally teaches each man these things' (200: 1338 – 201: 1347). Abelard's view of the Trinity as (in this respect at least) rationally evident thus leads him to another of the important features of this *Theologia* and its later versions: the extensive use of pagan philosophical sources as witnesses to the doctrine of the Trinity. The chief among them is Plato. No longer taking the words of the *Timaeus* literally, but as an *involucrum*, an extended metaphor, Abelard is able to read the passage on the World Soul – which he had rejected as a misleading figment when he wrote the *Dialectica* – as a prophecy of the Holy Spirit.[4] Abelard even finds a way of resolving the apparent contradiction between the Christian belief that the Holy Spirit is coeternal with the two other persons of the Trinity, and Plato's view, as he understood it, that the World Soul had a beginning in time – a contradiction which would prevent the identification of the World Soul with the Holy Spirit. When the Holy Spirit is called the

Simonis, *Trinität und Vernunft* (Frankfurt, 1972) (Frankfurter Theologische Studien 12), pp. 35–65. Throughout his account, and especially in considering the changes Abelard makes in the later versions of the *Theologia*, Cottiaux tends to exaggerate Abelard's orthodoxy and underestimate the extent to which he thought a rational understanding of the Trinity was possible. Simonis convincingly (and with ample documentation) corrects this view.

[4] See above, pp. 42–3. There seems to be some connection between William of Conches' commentary on Macrobius and Abelard's interpretation of Plato's *involucrum* – as pointed out by Edouard Jeauneau in his edition of William's *Glosae super Platonem* (Paris, 1965) (Textes philosophiques du moyen âge 15), p. 145, note (c), where he prints the relevant extracts. The dating of the Macrobius commentary is uncertain, although it is probably roughly contemporary with *TSum*. Given that William refers to the view that the World Soul is the Holy Spirit as that 'held by some' and that he is briefer and far more tentative than Abelard, it is less likely that he influenced Abelard than that William has Abelard himself in mind or that they are both influenced by a common source. See also E. Jeauneau, 'Note critique sur une récente édition de la *Theologia 'Summi Boni'* et de la *Theologia 'Scholarium'* d'Abélard', *Revue des études augustiniennes* 37 (1991), 151–8, at pp. 157–8. On twelfth-century interpretations of the World Soul, see also T. Gregory, *Anima Mundi* (Florence, 1955). On *integumentum/inuolucrum* in twelfth-century use, see E. Jeauneau, 'L'usage de la notion d'integumentum à travers les gloses de Guillaume de Conches', *AHDLMA* 24 (1957), 66–84 (= E. Jeauneau, *Lectio philosophorum* (Amsterdam, 1973), pp. 158–76); P. Dronke, *Fabula: explorations into the uses of myth in medieval Platonism* (Leiden/Cologne, 1974), pp. 1–67; W. Wetherbee, 'Philosophy, cosmology and the twelfth-century renaissance' in Dronke, *A history of twelfth-century western philosophy* (Cambridge, 1988), pp. 21–53, esp. pp. 35–9.

World Soul, Abelard says, this name derives from its function of animating or vivifying; but before anything other than God existed, there was nothing for it to animate. Therefore, although the Holy Spirit always existed, it was not always the World Soul and, in this sense, the World Soul did have a beginning in time.[5] As well as Plato, Abelard also cites other pagan prophets of the Trinity, such as Mercurius Trismegistus and the Sibyl.[6]

The *Theologia Summi Boni* does not, however, continue as the calm exposition of a rational faith in the Trinity found in Book I. Books II and III are presented as a defence of the doctrine that God is both three and one against the arguments of those pseudo-dialecticians, who use supposedly philosophical arguments to attack the doctrine of the faith.[7] Their tone is aggressive and personal, and at one point (140: 680–1) Abelard speaks (in the singular) to a certain dialectician 'or rather dissimulating sophist': 'Reply to me, you clever logician...' There is little doubt that this 'sophist' is Roscelin, Abelard's teacher many years before. What seems to have happened is that Roscelin heard about Abelard's oral teaching and criticized him for suggesting that the divine substance is singular (a criticism which might be made about the theory of the Trinity as power, wisdom and benignity, which could easily be misinterpreted as meaning that the divine persons are merely different descriptions of the same thing). Abelard, in his turn, attacked by writing a letter to the canons of Tours (who included Roscelin himself) and Roscelin replied with a vicious letter to Abelard.[8] Books II and III of the *Theologia Summi Boni* were Abelard's counter-blast. Roscelin had, earlier in his life, been brought to trial for discussing the Trinity in a way which might suggest it consists of three separate Gods. His approach is the same in his exchange with Abelard, who tries, by contrast, to show that the tools of logic, used properly, can give an adequate

[5] *TSum* 198: 1265 – 200: 1334. The idea is repeated in the later revisions of the work: *TChr* 337: 2287 – 341: 2397; *TSch* 492: 2520 – 495: 2623.

[6] 98: 334–48, 108: 634–110: 667. See P. Dronke, *Hermes and the Sibyls: continuation and creation* (Cambridge, 1990) (= *Intellectuals and poets*, pp. 219–41).

[7] 114: 3 – 115: 35, 201: 1352 – 67; cf. *Mews*, p. 42.

[8] This is the most plausible reconstruction of what lies behind Roscelin's letter to Abelard (ed. in Reiners, *Nominalismus* (pp. 63–80) and Abelard's Letter 14. Scholars, however, from Stölzle, *TSum*'s first editor (*Abaelards 1121 zu Soissons verurteilter Tractatus de unitate et trinitate divina* (Freiburg, 1891)) to Ostlender, *Abaelards Theologia 'Summi Boni'* and Mews (*Mews*, pp. 42–6) have tended to present Abelard as the initial aggressor – even though there is no good evidence that Roscelin was still teaching *c.* 1120 – and, ignoring the difference in tone between Book I and Books II and III, to present the whole of *TSum* as having been conceived as an attack on Roscelin. On the chronology of the dispute, see also Smits, *Letters*, pp. 192–202.

(though necessarily limited) account of how God can be both three and one.

When Abelard was forced, at the Council of Soissons, to commit his *Theologia Summi Boni* to the flames with his own hands, his reaction was not to give up the project he had begun, nor even to modify or soften his approach. Within four or five years he had produced a new *Theologia*, boldly entitled *Theologia Christiana*, which incorporated about nine-tenths of the *Theologia Summi Boni* into a treatise nearly three times its size.[9] Abelard quotes more patristic authority in this revised treatise, but he also amplifies his account of pagan prophecies of the Trinity. His underlying view of the Trinity as power, wisdom and benignity is unaltered, but in one respect developed. Abelard now says (73: 51–2) that to call God Father, Son and Holy Spirit is a way of referring to 'the power *which generates*, the wisdom *which is generated* and the benignity *which proceeds*'. Since he makes clear that this knowledge is naturally available to all (345: 2535–9), Abelard is suggesting that not only the persons of the Trinity but their interrelations are, to some extent at least, discoverable through reason – a position in accord with his investigation of the logic of triunity. These logical arguments retain the same basic structure as before, but are now greatly refined and extended.[10] The criticisms directed at Roscelin remain, but Abelard adds to them invective against other leading theologians of his time.[11] As well as amplifying his earlier position, Abelard extends his discussion into two largely new areas. Responding to criticism of his use of pagans as authorities on the Trinity, he devotes most of Book II to an extended eulogy of ancient Greece and Rome, the austere lives of their philosophers and the uprightness of their citizens. Many of the so-called pagans were, Abelard insists, Christians before the coming of Christ, and the ancient city-states

[9] *Op. Th.* II, pp. 71–372(= *TChr*; *Checklist* §308). The best witness to the *Theologia Christiana* as Abelard conceived it is Vatican, Biblioteca apostolica, Reg. lat. 159, which contains some minor revisions of the version of which Book I only is preserved in Durham Cathedral, A.IV.5. See *Op. Th.* II, pp. 30–1 and C. Mews 'Peter Abelard's (Theologia Christiana) and (Theologia 'Scholarium') re-examined', *RTAM* 52 (1985), 109–58, at p. 154. Two further manuscripts preserve a text with changes and marginalia introduced – as Constant Mews has shown – by Abelard in the process of transforming *TChr* into *TSch*: see below, p. 59 n. 16. On the date, see Mews, 'Abelard's Theologia re-examined', pp. 151–4: Mews argues for 1122 to 1125 and shows the implausibility of Buytaert's suggestion (*Op. Th.* II, pp. 50–2) that, whilst the version in the Durham manuscript dates from 1123–5, that in the Vatican one was not composed until much later (1134–5).

[10] See below, p. 151–4.

[11] 300: 1102 – 303: 1174: on the identity of the masters, see Cottiaux, 'La conception', pp. 257–9; *Op. Th.* II, pp. 47–9 and Mews, 'Abelard's Theologia re-examined', p. 153 – whose scepticism about many of the identifications which have been made is justified.

and their inhabitants provide an example which should put the monks of Abelard's own time to shame.[12] This remarkable, golden picture of antiquity underlines Abelard's advocacy of the ancients which is already evident in his treatment of Platonism in the *Theologia Summi Boni* and which would provide one of the roots of his ethical thinking and become integral to his theological system.[13] In Book V, Abelard sets about examining the threefold nature of God in the way which his doctrine of the Trinity implies: God as power, wisdom and benignity. But Abelard breaks off after he has treated divine omnipotence.[14] The *Theologia Christiana* remained unfinished and, to judge from the few remaining manuscripts, it was not a work Abelard ever intended for wide circulation.

The definitive, final version of the *Theologia*, the *Theologia Scholarium*, uses parts of the *Theologia Christiana*, but cuts out many others, rewrites some sections and adds new material and arguments.[15] A number of manuscripts survive bearing witness to this process of revision, which Abelard probably began immediately after his return to teaching in Paris, if not before.[16] Even once he had published a full version of the work – probably in the mid-1130s – Abelard twice made changes and additions in response to the criticisms which led to his appearance at the Council of Sens, and

[12] See below, pp. 305–7.

[13] On Abelard's Platonism, see T. Gregory, 'Abélard et Platon', *Studi Medievali* 3a ser. 13 (1972), 539–62 (= *Peter Abelard*, pp. 38–64) and L. Moonan, 'Abelard's use of the *Timaeus*', *AHDLMA* 56 (1989), 7–90.

[14] The description of Book V in the *capitula* at the beginning of *TChr* (71: 32–4) seems to be an attempt, by Abelard or someone else, to make the best of its failure to realize its plan by describing its theme as God's immutability, which is indeed what is most stressed in the discussion of his omnipotence.

[15] *Op. Th.* III, pp. 313–549 (*TSch*; *Checklist* §309).

[16] The steps by which Abelard turned *TChr* into *TSch* have been very carefully investigated by Constant Mews (in 'Abelard's Theologia re-examined', pp. 124–58 and in *Mews*, pp. 210–21). Mews shows convincingly that the version of *TChr* witnessed by Monte Cassino, Archivio della Bada, 174 and Tours, Bibliothèque municipale, 85 is not (as Buytaert, the editor of *TChr*, believed) a new recension of the treatise but rather a working copy of the text with additions and abridgements to be incorporated into *TSch*; and that the 'shorter versions of *TSch*', printed separately by Buytaert (*Op. Th.* II, pp. 401–51) are drafts of new or substantially revised material for *TSch*. Mews's own theory, however, calls for certain qualifications and refinements: I shall suggest some of these in 'Abelard and his pupils at work' (in preparation). It is certain that some of this process of revision took place after Abelard took up teaching again, because Walter of Mortagne's letter criticizing points in one of the drafts (see above, p. 25) makes it clear that Abelard is once more a schoolmaster (see e.g. pp. 34: 9–10, 14; 37: 9; 40: 29–30; and cf. Mews, 'Abelard's Theologia re-examined', p. 155, n. 104).

the latest version (preserved in one manuscript only, Oxford, Balliol College, 296) also has a final section which is missing elsewhere.[17]

The *Theologia Scholarium* is designed to realize the project which Abelard had set himself when he began the teaching which led to his first *Theologia*, but from which he had been partly diverted, first by his quarrel with Roscelin and then by the need to answer the attacks made against the *Theologia Summi Boni*. In Book I he develops one aspect of his view of the Trinity, by giving the Old Testament and then, at great length, the pagan prophecies of the Trinity. Here he uses his *Theologia Christiana* directly, although he adds more material. Book II is devoted mainly to the logical analysis of triunity. It is far briefer than the corresponding part (Books III and IV) of the *Theologia Christiana*, and without much of the invective. Abelard is now willing to pass over some of the fine distinctions he laboured to make in the earlier work, in order to present his argument here more clearly and directly.[18] Book III carries the investigation of God as power, wisdom and benignity much further than the final book of the *Theologia Christiana* had done. The treatment of omnipotence is completely revised, more assured and more sophisticated.[19] A section on God's wisdom is now included,[20] and the themes to be covered in considering his benignity are sketched out before the work, in its longest version, comes to its abrupt end, leaving out just the very final part of the planned discussion.

In the *Theologia Scholarium*, but not the earlier versions of the *Theologia*, Abelard precedes his presentation of the Trinity as power, wisdom and benignity with a statement of orthodox faith about the Trinity – the Father, who is not born but exists from himself and not from any other; the Son, who is born from the Father alone and the Holy Spirit who proceeds from the Father and the Son (326: 219 – 329: 306). This, like the preface to the work (313: 1 – 316: 100), an exercise in preventive exculpation – Abelard is writing at the insistent request of his students; he is putting his philosophical talents to the best possible use; he will accept correction and, should he proffer erroneous doctrine, he should not be thought a heretic, since he does not wish to persist in error – is a sign of a new-found, and as it turned out, fruitless, caution on Abelard's part. Abelard's approach to the doctrine of the Trinity, however, has not altered. Once he comes to explaining what is meant by the divine persons (330: 336 – 331: 354), even more clearly than

[17] On the dating of this final version, see below, pp. 70–1.

[18] Cf. *Mews*, p. 207.

[19] See below, pp. 218–19.

[20] See below, pp. 228–32.

in the earlier versions of the *Theologia*, Abelard treats 'Father', 'Son' and 'Holy Spirit' as being words which express God's power, wisdom and benignity.

The *Theologia Scholarium* begins quite differently from any of the previous versions of the work. Instead of launching into his discussion of the Trinity, Abelard announces (318: 1–2) that 'the totality (*summa*) of human salvation consists in three things: faith, charity and the sacraments', and he goes on to give definitions of each of the three. What this introduction does is to outline a comprehensive plan of Christian doctrine for investigation – a plan in which discussion of the Trinity forms merely one part in the first of three main divisions. There is, however, no reason to assume that Abelard envisaged extending the *Theologia Scholarium* to cover the rest of this large area.[21] Rather, he is placing his present subject in context: it is no longer the whole of his theological project but a part of a wider scheme.

THE 'SIC ET NON' AND THE 'SENTENTIE'

There is indeed evidence that, more than a decade before he wrote the *Theologia Scholarium*, Abelard already thought that discussion of God as triune power, wisdom and benignity was only part of his theological project. It is provided by one of Abelard's most often mentioned, though rarely read or rightly understood productions: *Sic et non*.[22] The short preface apart, *Sic et non* consists entirely of quotations from authoritative writers, in most cases the Church Fathers. It differs from earlier systematic collections like the canonist Ivo of Chartres' *Panormia* or the *Deus summe*, which were used by Abelard in making his compilation,[23] by explicitly arranging the

[21] This was the theory, influential for many years, of Heinrich Denifle: 'Die Sentenzen Abaelards und die Bearbeitungen seiner Theologia vor Mitte des 12. Jhs.', *Archiv f. Litteratur- und Kirchengeschichte* 1 (1885), 402–69, 584–624: cf. *Mews*, p. 222.

[22] *Sic et non*: B. Boyer and R. McKeon (eds.), *Peter Abailard. Sic et non* (Chicago/London, 1976–7); q. 117 in J. Barrow, 'Tractatus Magistri Petri Abaelardi de Sacramento Altaris', *Traditio* 40 (1984), 328–36 (= *SN*; *Checklist* §305).

[23] For parallels between Ivo and *SN*, see Boyer and McKeon, *Sic et non*, pp. 635–45; on the probable use of *Deus summe*, see N. Haring, 'The *Sententiae Magistri A.* (Vat. Ms. lat. 4361) and the School of Laon', *Medieval Studies* 17 (1955), 1–45, at pp. 3–4. H. Reinhardt ('Die identität der Sententiae Magistri A. mit der Compilationes Ailmeri und die Frage nach dem Autor dieser frühscholastischen Sentenzsammlung', *Theologie und Philosophie* 50 (1975), 381–403) argues that the collection was put together by Elmer, an English Benedictine monk and pupil of Anselm of Canterbury's. But it is questionable whether the manuscript (Cambridge, University Library, Ii.4.19) which contains the ascription 'Compilaciones Ailmeri' represents an independent English tradition, as Reinhardt believes, since the notes

quotations to give opposing answers – the 'yes' and 'no' of the title – to a series of discrete questions (for example: 'That God is not a substance and against this' (no. 9), 'That the Son has no beginning and against this' (no. 14)). The purpose behind this arrangement is not to undermine authority – in his preface, indeed, Abelard suggests a whole variety of ways in which the apparent contradictions between his sources can be reconciled – but to order the material which he wishes to use in his theological investigations. Abelard seems to have regarded *Sic et non* as a type of notebook, to which he often turned for groups of quotations to illustrate a certain point of view, and to which he added new material as he came across it. Even in the earliest and shortest version, compiled a little after the Council of Soissons, Abelard includes not only questions on God as three in one, but a long, composite question on Christology.[24] In the next version, from the early to mid-1120s, Abelard includes material on almost the whole range of subjects included in the programme outlined at the beginning of the *Theologia Scholarium*, although not in exactly the same order.[25]

It is in the teaching recorded in the collections of *Sententie* that he explores this programme systematically. Three main collections of Abelardian *Sententie* are known: the *Sententie Abaelardi* (or, as they will usually be called here for brevity, simply the *Sententie*; some scholars refer to them as the *Sententie Hermanni*);[26] the *Sententie Florianenses*[27] and the *Sententie Parisienses*.[28] The *Sententie Abaelardi* were printed nearly two centuries ago, but doubts about their authenticity have prevented many scholars from realizing their true value as a witness to Abelard's comprehensive theological system. It has been thought that they were based at second-hand on a lost, much extended version of the *Theologia Scholarium*;[29] or, more recently, that they,

which immediately follow *Deus summe* include two Sentences (*Lottin* §§36 and 68) by Anselm of Laon.

24 This is made up of what will be separated as eight different questions (66, 64, 75, 67, 42, 41, 70, 71) in the final version.

25 Mews ('The *Sententie* of Peter Abelard', *RTAM* 53 (1986), 130–83, at p. 164) says that the main order *is* the same, but this is hard to accept, since the questions on the sacraments are sandwiched within the discussion of sin and charity. The two later versions of *SN* make the ordering even more different from that set out in *TSch*.

26 *Sententie Abaelardi*: quoted (by his kind permission) from the unpublished edition of David Luscombe. References are to the paragraphs of this edition, and also (Bu.) to the less reliable edition by S. Buzzetti (ed.), *Sententie magistri Petri Abaelardi (Sententie Hermanni)* (Florence, 1983) (= *Sent.*; *Checklist* §334).

27 Ed. in Ostlender, *Sententiae Florianenses* (= *Sent.Flor.*; *Checklist* §330).

28 Ed. in A. Landgraf, *Ecrits théologiques de l'école d'Abélard* (Louvain, 1934) (Spicilegium sacrum lovaniense. Etudes et documents 14), pp. 3–60 (= *Sent.Par.*; Checklist §332).

29 Denifle, 'Die Sentenzen'.

and also the *Sententie Florianenses* and *Sententie Parisienses*, were all derived from the (now lost) *Liber sententiarum*, mentioned by St Bernard, which itself was taken from Abelard's oral teaching.[30] Constant Mews, however, has now demonstrated that, except for a revised version of the *Sententie Abaelardi*, all three collections date back to the period (*c.* 1132–5) when Abelard was still working to produce the first full version of his *Theologia Scholarium*, and that they give a direct and accurate account of his teaching.[31] The *Liber sententiarum* mentioned by St Bernard is a different, later report of Abelard's teaching.[32] According to Mews, the *Sententie Abaelardi* are an official *reportatio* of Abelard's lectures, corrected and revised by Abelard himself, whilst the other two collections are unofficial accounts of his oral teaching. Perhaps this is, to some extent, an oversimplification;[33] but there is little doubt that the *Sententie Abaelardi* give an accurate digest of Abelard's teaching, whilst parts of the *Sententie Parisienses* preserve the give and take of discussion in Abelard's classes.

A number of systematic theological works survive which probably have at their basis the teaching which went on in Paris and elsewhere from the 1120s to the 1140s.[34] Abelard, then, was probably not alone in teaching

[30] H. Ostlender, 'Die Sentenzbücher der Schule Abaelards', *Theologische Quartalschrift* 117 (1936), 208–52. For Bernard's references to the *Liber sententiarum*, see *Ep.* 188 and 190, pp. 11: 15, 40: 9–10). William of St Thierry mentions what seems to be this work, without naming it, in his letter to Bernard (p. 377: 28–9). Abelard, however, writes in *Conf. fid. 'Universis'*, 138: 5: 'nusquam liber aliquis qui sententiarum dicatur a me scriptus repperiatur'; cf. *Apologia* 360: 34 – 361: 43.

[31] 'The *Sententie*'. The modern editor of the *Sententie*, S. Buzzetti had argued (pp. 4–6), independently from Mews, that the *Sententie* must be attributed to Abelard, but he gives the evidence only a very cursory consideration.

[32] Mews edits the fragments of this *Liber sententiarum* (which are retrievable from quotations) as the '*Sententie Magistri Petri*' in '*Sententie*', pp. 177–83 (*Checklist* §329).

[33] I shall discuss this in 'Abelard and his pupils at work'; Mews does not perhaps take sufficient account of Abelard's denial (see above, n. 30) that he ever wrote a 'liber sententiarum'. David Luscombe ('The school of Peter Abelard revisited', *Vivarium* 30 (1992), 127–38, at p. 128) arrives at a judicious formulation: 'Clearly this collection of sentences [the *Sententie Abaelardi*] represents the teaching given by Abelard to students as reported or copied, perhaps by some of those students. This is a well written work; it is far from being a set of loose *reportationes*.'

[34] One of the most important is Hugh of St Victor's *De sacramentis* (*MPL* 176, 173–618). On the relation between this work and Hugh's oral teaching, see B. Bischoff, 'Aus der Schule Hugos von St. Viktor' in *Aus der Geisteswelt des Mittelalters* (Münster, 1935) (BGPMA Supplementband 3, 1), pp. 246–50; on Hugh's teaching and Abelard, see Luscombe, *The school*, pp. 183–97. It is probable that a number of the Sentence collections usually attributed to 'The School of Laon' are, in fact, based on theology lectures from the 1130s and later. One case in point is *Principium et causa omnium* (ed. in F. Bliemetzrieder, *Anselms von Laon systematische Sentenzen* (Münster, 1919) (BGPMA 18, 2–3), pp. 47–153) (which was

sacred doctrine systematically and argumentatively, in the way indicated by the collections of *Sententie*, although he may well have been among the pioneers. Moreover, his arrangement of material was peculiar to him and his followers.[35] Instead of ordering his discussion according to the plan of sacred history, Abelard chose the plan which allowed him best to set out his coherent and rational view of Christian doctrine. The study of faith has two main parts for him: first, the investigation of God as a Trinity of power, wisdom and benignity, and the exploration of the questions about God's ordering of things which arise in connection with each of these attributes;[36] then a consideration of God's benefits to mankind – especially the incarnation, the reasons behind it and its effects. For Abelard, this involved especially emphasizing the Passion as an example of supreme, self-sacrificing love, by following which we are enabled to love God properly.[37] To study charity is, for Abelard, to study the ethics of human actions – what is virtue and vice, what is merit and sin. To the sacraments rather less attention is given and the emphasis here too is often ethical.[38] Theology comes to be focused on the examination of a Trinity graspable, in most respects, by reason; the setting forth of Abelard's bold, morally based view of why God became incarnate and suffered death on the Cross; and the development of a detailed theory of human morality in relation to this conception of God and his work.

THE COMMENTARY ON ROMANS AND THE ETHICAL TREATISES

Abelard's theological project grew from his view of the Trinity as power, wisdom and benignity, and it was this area of it which Abelard explored most repeatedly and in the greatest detail. But the other parts of the scheme set out as a whole in the *Sententie* were also the subjects of more detailed study by Abelard in individual works.

originally published as the Sentences of Anselm of Laon himself) which Yves Lefèvre has shown ('Le *De conditione angelica et humana* et les *Sententie Anselmi*', *AHDLMA* 26 (1959), 249–75, at pp. 251–5) must derive from lectures which, because of the teachings by Abelard to which it refers, cannot have taken place before the mid-1130s. On the 'School of Laon', see V. Flint, 'The "School of Laon": a reconsideration', *RTAM* 43 (1976), 89–110 and M. Colish, 'Another look at the School of Laon', *AHDLMA* 53 (1986), 7–22.

35 See Mews, '*Sententie*', pp. 167–8.

36 See below, pp. 216–17.

37 See below, pp. 321–3.

38 Cf. Mews, '*Sententie*', pp. 151–2, 158.

Abelard's detailed treatment of God's benefits to mankind is found in the commentary on St Paul's letter to the Romans, which he wrote early in his last period of teaching at Paris.[39] Indeed, Abelard may well have been drawn to comment on this text precisely because more than any other book of the Bible it gave him the chance to develop his ideas on grace and on redemption. Although he interprets Paul's letter thoroughly, verse by verse, Abelard puts his greatest energies into lengthy discussions of the controversial questions raised by the text on these themes (for instance – how is it that we are redeemed through Christ's death?[40] What is original sin and by what justice can children be punished for the sins of their parents?[41]) as well as on ethical problems concerning sin, will and the nature of love. After he had completed the written text of this commentary, Abelard went on lecturing on the letter to the Romans, and also on most of the other Pauline epistles (which gave further opportunities to discuss grace and works, as well as raising questions about, for instance, the sacraments of baptism and the eucharist). No full text of these later lectures survives, but fragments of them can be found in a commentary on the Pauline epistles written in the 1140s by a disciple of Abelard's.[42] Not only is the commentator greatly influenced in all he writes by Abelard's teaching and writing, he also has to hand notes of Abelard's own lectures, from which he frequently quotes, calling his master, as William of Lucca also did in the *Summa dialetice artis*, the *Philosophus*. Although often (in the

[39] Ed. in *Op. Th.* I, pp. 41–340 (= *Comm.Rom.*; *Checklist* §271). A cross-reference to 'Book II of the *Theologia*' in connection with the analogy between a bronze statue and the Trinity (*Comm.Rom.* 70: 816 – 71: 817; cf. *TChr* 306: 1285 – 307: 1329, *TSch* 462: 1645 – 464: 1703) shows that Abelard must already have transformed the five-book *TChr* into the three-book *TSch*; but other cross-references to the *Theologia* suggest (cf. *Mews* 226–7, against Buytaert, *Opera theologica* I, pp. 27–33) that the *TSch* had not yet reached its first full version. Shortly after the work was issued (as represented by Angers, Bibliothèque. municipale, 68), Abelard probably made minor revisions to about the first quarter of it, which are found in the two other surviving manuscripts and *D'Amboise/Duchesne* (based on a lost manuscript): see the evidence presented by Buytaert at *Opera theologica*, I, pp. 20–4, although Buytaert himself draws a different conclusion.

[40] See below, pp. 322–3.

[41] See below, p. 325.

[42] Ed. A. Landgraf, *Commentarius cantabrigiensis in epistolas Pauli e schola Petri Abaelardi* (4 vols.) (Notre Dame, 1937–45) (University of Notre Dame, Publications in mediaeval studies 2) (= *Comm.Cant.*; *Checklist* §326). Landgraf's introduction and notes show in detail the relation of the commentary to Abelard's teaching, which is analysed by Luscombe (*The school*, pp. 145–53). Abelard also wrote brief expositions of the Lord's Prayer (ed. C. Burnett, 'The Expositio Orationis Dominicae "Multorum legimus orationes": Abelard's exposition of the Lord's Prayer', *RB* 95 (1985), 60–72) and of the Apostles' Creed (*MPL* 178, 617–30) and the Athanasian Creed (*MPL* 178, 629–32).

section on Romans) these quotations correspond closely to the arguments put forward in the written commentary, in a few cases they express ideas which Abelard did not develop until later in the 1130s.[43]

Abelard began his detailed thinking about the ethics of human acts – the main topic discussed under 'charity' in his theological scheme – when he was eulogizing the lives of the ancients in the second book of the *Theologia Christiana*. He developed his thought on this subject in a remarkable pair of dialogues or *Collationes*, which were very probably written late in the 1120s, when he was at St Gildas, away from his pupils and the schools.[44] Abelard had already tried his hand at the dialogue form in a brief, internal dialogue between 'A.P.' and 'P.A.' (Abaelardus Petrus and Petrus Abaelardus), which has aptly been named the *Soliloquium* and explores the links between the worship of Christ (Wisdom or the Word), philosophers (lovers of wisdom) and logicians (who follow the Word).[45] The *Collationes* are far more ambitious, involving three figures – a Jew, a Gentile Philosopher 'content with natural law' (41: 8),[46] and a Christian – as well as Abelard himself, who is to act as judge, although the work finishes before he delivers any final judgement. It is tempting to think that, deprived of

[43] At I, p. 4, the *Philosophus* puts forward a view of love more developed than that in *Comm.Rom.*; and the quote at I, p. 179, on ignorance and good intentions, is very close to *Sc.* 54: 1–25 and *TSch* 547: 1536–4, but to none of the earlier writings.

[44] Ed. Thomas, *Petrus Abaelardus* (= Coll.; *Checklist* §270). Giovanni Orlandi and I are collaborating on a new edition with English translation for Oxford Medieval Texts: on the deficiencies of Thomas's edition, see G. Orlandi, 'Per una nuova edizione del *Dialogus* di Abelardo', *Rivista critica di storia della filosofia* 24 (1979), 474–94. London, British Library, Royal XI.A.5 (incomplete) and Oxford, Balliol, 296 give a slightly revised version of the text found in Vienna, Österreichische Nationalbibliothek, cvp 819: see E. Buytaert, 'Abelard's Collationes', *Antonianum* 44 (1969), 18–39 and Orlandi, 'Per una nuova edizione'. On the date, see Mews, 'On dating', pp. 104–26. There he presents very strong arguments against earlier scholars' datings to the mid-1130s or to the 1140s, and suggests 1125 to 1126; but Mews is now inclined (personal communication) to favour 1126 to 31. At any rate, the treatment of circumcision provides very strong grounds for dating *Coll.* earlier than *Comm.Rom.* (cf. Mews, 'On dating', pp. 112–13).

[45] Ed. by C. Burnett, 'Peter Abelard "Soliloquium". A critical edition', *Studi Medievali* 3a serie, 25, 2 (1984), 857–94 (= *Soliloquium*; *Checklist* §306). Burnett suggests that, since for further information on the virtues of the philosophers it refers not to *TChr* itself but to a lost *Exhortatio ad fratres et commonachos*, *Soliloquium* may have been written before *TChr*.

[46] J. Jolivet, 'Abélard et le Philosophe', *Revue de l'histoire des religions* 164 (1963), 181–9 and 'Doctrines et figures de philosophes chez Abélard', in *Petrus Abaelardus*, pp. 103–20 at p. 114 and n. 79, has argued for the Philosopher's origins in Islamic lands; cf. also R. Thomas, *Der philosophische-theologische Erkenntnisweg Peter Abaelards im Dialogus inter Philosophum, Judaeum et Christianum* (Bonn, 1966) (Untersuchungen zur allgemeinen Religionsgeschichte n.f. 6), pp. 166–83.

pupils with whom to argue and test out his ideas, Abelard resorted to the dialogue form as a way of exploring his thoughts, allowing each of his characters, the Jew and the Philosopher, as well as the Christian, to develop to the full the implications of their positions.

The *Collationes* draw on a familiar literary genre, but transform it in accord with Abelard's characteristic ideas. Literary debates between Christians and non-Christians were common in Abelard's time. Jewish–Christian disputations had a very long history, but there are also at least two dialogues by pupils of Anselm of Canterbury in which the Christian debates with a complete unbeliever.[47] Abelard, however, has his Jew debate, not with a Christian but with the Philosopher, who argues powerfully that there is nothing of value contained in the Old Law followed by the Jew which is not also to be found in natural law which the Philosopher knows by reason and follows. When, in the second dialogue, the Christian debates with the Philosopher, he treats him not as an ignoramus or even as someone to be won over to Christianity, but as an intellectual equal with whom he can engage in a constructive discussion about the Highest Good (a discussion which ranges over many of the central issues of ethics: the nature of the virtues, the definitions of good and evil, the relation between acts and intentions). Although, at times, the Philosopher is shown to err, Abelard lays great emphasis on the large area of agreement between him and the Christian. If, by the end of the work, the Philosopher has become a somewhat passive interlocutor, this seems to be merely because the Christian is the better, more rationally convincing arguer.

Abelard continued to develop his ethical thought for the rest of his life. The commentary on Romans developed the ideas in the *Collationes* about sin and intention, the *Sententie* added new elements to the moral theory, and even in the late 1130s Abelard was still clarifying and refining his ethical arguments and terminology. By 1139, he had brought his latest ideas together in a treatise he sometimes called his 'Ethics' but for which he

[47] See A. Funkenstein, 'Basic types of Christian anti-Jewish polemic', *Viator* 2 (1971), 373–7; A. Abulafia, 'Jewish–Christian disputations and the twelfth-century renaissance', *Journal of Medieval History* 15 (1989), 105–25; and C. Gale, 'From dialogue to disputation: St Anselm and his students on disbelief', *Tjurunga* 44 (1993), 71–86. The two disputations with unbelievers are Gilbert of Crispin's *Disputatio Christiani cum gentili* (in A. Abulafia and G. Evans (eds.), *The works of Gilbert Crispin, Abbot of Westminster* (London, 1986)) and the *Libellus de nesciente et sciente* by Ralph, abbot of Battle (unedited; see R. Southern, 'St Anselm and his English pupils', *Mediaeval and Renaissance Studies* 1 (1941), 3–34, at pp. 15–17 and Gale, 'From dialogue to disputation', p. 78).

decided, challengingly, to use as a title the Socratic maxim 'Know thyself': *Scito teipsum* (*Sc.*).[48] Abelard planned a treatise in two books, the first dealing with vice, sin and penitence, the second with virtue and merit. All but one of the surviving manuscripts, however, break off shortly before the end of the first book; Oxford, Balliol, 296 preserves the end of Book I and the opening of a second book.[49] In *Scito teipsum*, Abelard presents his ideas in a way which is at once clear, orderly, concise and yet vivid. The memorable or shocking examples (the woman who accidentally smothers her child, Christ and his – for Abelard – guiltless executioners) which Abelard uses to develop his argument give an idea of what made his lectures so popular and, to his opponents, so disturbing. For there is definite evidence that at least parts of *Scito teipsum* belonged to Abelard's oral teaching before he polished them for his written treatise. It is provided by a set of marginal notes in an Anglo-Saxon manuscript (London, British Library, Cotton Faustina A X) which record comments and answers to questions given by 'Master Peter Abelard'.[50] Many of the notes deal with the matters which Abelard discusses in *Scito teipsum*. The doctrine (including the notion of consent, which Abelard developed only in his last years) is the same,[51] and some of the illustrations famous from *Scito teipsum* are here already, although less carefully presented.[52] Not all of the discussions in the London *Reportatio*

[48] Ed. (with parallel English translation) by D. Luscombe, *Peter Abelard's Ethics* (Oxford, 1971) (= *Sc.*; *Checklist* §285). Abelard refers to the work as his *Ethica* in the prospective cross-references in *Comm.Rom.* (126: 138–41; 293: 245–6; 307: 348) and, at the beginning of the second book, he refers back to the previous part as 'the above little book of our Ethics' (128: 2); but *Scito teipsum* is the title given in the manuscripts. On the date, see Luscombe, *Ethics*, p. xxx.

[49] On this manuscript and the material it alone preserves, see below, p. 71.

[50] The existence of these marginalia was first noted by N. Ker, *Catalogue of manuscripts containing Anglo-Saxon* (Oxford, 1957), pp. 194–6 and reported in *Checklist* §328 (= *Reportatio*); cf. p. 201. They are discussed briefly in Luscombe, 'The school revisited', p. 129. The authors of the *Checklist* have announced their intention to publish them. I am grateful to Charles Burnett for letting me use his transcript of them, although I have also consulted the manuscript.

[51] See below, pp. 259–60.

[52] For instance, compare *Reportatio* (London, British Library, Cotton Faustina A X, f. 107r): 'Sicut si aliqua mater filium suum in lecto suo secum ponat ex caritate et dilectione, ea scilicet intentione quod non habeat pannorum unde sibi et filio sufficienter prouidere possit, et cum ipsa angula non sit, uelit nolit dormiet, et dormiens filius opprimetur' and *Sc.* 38: 13–18: 'Ecce enim pauper aliqua mulier infantulum habet lactentem nec tantum indumentorum habet ut et paruulo in cunis et sibi sufficere possit. Miseratione itaque infantuli commota, eum sibi apponit ut propriis insuper foueat pannis, et tandem infirmitate eius ui naturae superata, opprimere cogitur.' Some interesting ethical examples are not taken over in *Sc.*: for instance (f.108r), the motif – which appears in Shakespeare's *Measure*

correspond to topics considered in *Scito teipsum*. Subjects broached include the salvation of unbelievers and of the unbaptized (ff. 109v–110r), which Abelard discusses in his commentary on Romans; and whether, 'since God cannot do other than he does, he could punish a sinner more than he in fact does' (f. 110r) – a question relating to ideas about God's omnipotence discussed at length in the *Theologia Christiana* and *Theologia Scholarium*. Are the notes in the London manuscript gathered, then, from a number of different sets of lectures (perhaps on the Hexaemeron and on the letter to the Romans)? Or do they represent the sort of questions and answers which would have accompanied a systematic course covering the ground set out in the *Sententie*? Unless further evidence comes to light, these questions must remain open.

BEFORE AND AFTER SENS

Shortly after he wrote *Scito teipsum*, Abelard was overtaken by the series of events which led to his appearance at the Council of Sens. The list of his 'heresies' compiled by Bernard and his associates was neither entirely fair, nor a complete distortion of his system.[53] It combined statements taken out of their context or without the qualifications Abelard gave them, with some (for example: that God can do only what he does, how he does and when he does it, or that we do not inherit guilt but only punishment from Adam) which very accurately represented Abelard's views. Abelard turned from teaching and developing his system to answering these accusations against him. His most detailed attempt, probably dating from just before the Council, is the *Apologia* directed to Bernard, in which he planned to consider each of the nineteen supposed heresies in turn.[54] To judge from what survives (only the beginning and a few fragments), Abelard's manner is not so much combative as pedagogic. He explains at considerable length why those who draw heretical implications from what he has said

for Measure – of the wife who secretly substitutes herself for the woman with whom her husband has decided to commit adultery.

53 See above, pp. 28–9.

54 The fragments of the work are edited in *Op. Th.* I, pp. 359–68 (*Checklist* §268). They consist of the beginning portion and quotations made by Thomas of Morigny in his *Disputatio catholicorum patrum* (ed. by M. Carra de Vaux St Cyr in *Revue des sciences philosophiques et théologiques* 47 (1963), 205–20) which was written in reply to it. Buytaert (pp. 352–5) argues convincingly for a dating of Thomas's *Disputatio*, and therefore also the *Apologia*, before the Council on the grounds that it would otherwise be inexplicable that Thomas does not mention it.

misunderstand his line of thought and the logical principles on which it is based. Abelard's stance towards the accusations is similar in a far more intimate document which he probably wrote at much the same time as the *Apologia*, the Confession of Faith addressed to Heloise, which is known only because it is quoted by Abelard's follower, Berengar of Poitiers.[55] Although Abelard makes an absolutely orthodox profession of his faith, he does not renounce anything he has said and maintains that any accusations against him are based on a distortion of what he has taught. Abelard's other confession of faith, the *Confessio fidei 'Universis'* is very different, not just because it is addressed to the Church as a whole, but because in one important respect it shows a far more submissive attitude.[56] Although Abelard is keen here, as elsewhere, to justify himself and cast Bernard into the role of an unjust accuser, he does not – as in the confession to Heloise and the *Apologia* – combine this self-justification with a reassertion of his characteristic views. After a preface which has some close parallels with the beginning of his *Apologia*, Abelard considers each of the doctrines on which he has been accused of heresy and either explicitly rejects them or makes a straightforward profession of orthodox faith. Where, in the *Apologia* and confession to Heloise, he disowns only what he considers to be misrepresentations of his views, here with only slight gestures of qualification he denies some of his own fundamental positions. For instance, although he insists that God can only do what befits him, he adds that he is able to do many things which he does not do; he asserts that we *do* inherit guilt from Adam and that those who crucified Christ committed 'a very grave sin' in doing so.

Until recently, scholars imagined that in his last days, at Cluny and its dependency, Abelard wrote prolifically. Both the *Dialectica* (or at least its supposed final revision) and the *Collationes* were placed in this final period. Now it appears unlikely that Abelard wrote any of his major works after the Council of Sens.[57] This would accord with what Peter the Venerable says about Abelard's last days – that he was ill and that he took up his former studies 'so far as the discomfort of his illness allowed'.[58] It has been

[55] Ed. in C. Burnett, ' "Confessio fidei ad Heloisam" – Abelard's last letter to Heloise? A discussion and critical edition of the Latin and medieval French versions', *Mittellateinisches Jahrbuch* 21 (1986), 147–55, at pp. 152–3 (*Conf. fid. Hel.; Checklist* §272).

[56] Ed. in C. Burnett, 'Peter Abelard: a critical edition of Abelard's reply to accusations of heresy', *Mediaeval Studies* 48 (1986), 111–38 (*Conf. fid. 'Universis'; Checklist* §273).

[57] See Mews, 'On dating', p. 126.

[58] Peter the Venerable, Letter 115 (I, p. 307): 'Ibi iuxta quod incommoditas permittebat, antiqua sua renouans studia, libris semper incumbebat, nec sicut de magno Gregorio legitur momentum aliquod preterire sinebat, qui semper *aut oraret, aut legeret, aut scriberet, aut dictaret*.'

argued, however, that he did undertake at this time an important revision of the *Theologia Scholarium*. The text in Oxford, Balliol, 296 contains not only a final section (543: 1400 – 549: 1632) absent from the other manuscripts, but also a number of revisions, sometimes just of a word or two, sometimes involving the substitution of whole new passages. Although none of them greatly modifies the overall argument, some seem intended to safeguard passages from the criticisms made by Abelard's accusers. These features of the revision have led to the suggestion that the Balliol manuscript contains a version of the *Theologia* modified to meet the demands Bernard made when, by Peter the Venerable's arrangement, he met Abelard and was reconciled with him.[59] The idea is a pleasant one. But in the letter where he tells of the meeting, Peter the Venerable does not say anything explicitly about Abelard's having actually corrected any of his works at Bernard's behest – a strange omission if Abelard had done so, since in his letter Peter is trying to give the best possible impression of Abelard to the Pope.[60] Moreover, the changes Abelard makes, although helpful in clarifying his argument, do not remove the aspects of the work which Bernard found heretical.[61] There is every reason to suppose, then, that the Council of Sens ended Abelard's writing as well as his teaching. Abelard retired to Cluny a sick man, to prepare himself for death.

[59] *Mews*, 285–92.

[60] Letter 98 (I, pp. 258–9).

[61] Mews (*Mews*, pp. 288–9) thinks that the changes make the first two *Capitula* of the list of heresies inapplicable. But *Capitulum* 1 (the Father is *plena potentia*, the Son *quaedam potentia*, the Holy Spirit *nulla potentia*) is based on the explanation of the simile of the seal at 463: 1676 – 466: 1750 (e.g. 463: 1682–464: 1685: 'specialiter nomine "patris" diuina potentia declaratur. . . Est autem diuina sapientia quaedam, ut ita dicam, istius dei potentia . . .') – a passage unchanged in the Balliol manuscript – and on 469: 1832–4: 'Benignitas quippe ipsa, quae hoc nomine [*sc.* Spiritui] demonstratur, non est aliqua in deo potentia siue sapientia . . .' Here the Balliol manuscript makes two changes, adding *specialiter* after *nomine* and omitting *in deo*, but these still leave the passage stating clearly that the Holy Spirit is 'no *potentia*'. *Capitulum* 2 (the Holy Spirit is not *de* – or in some versions *ex* – the substance of the Father or the Son) is based on 472: 1895–6. Here, in his first set of revisions to the full *TSch* (*TSchAP*), Abelard had added to 'Spiritus . . . minime tamen ex substantia patris est aut filii', the words 'si proprie loquimur, esse dicendus est'. In the Balliol manuscript, Abelard softens his original statement by changing it to read, 'Spiritus . . . non tamen ex substantia patris ita esse dicitur sicut filius', but then goes on (472: 1922 – 474: 1975) to explain at great length why, properly speaking (*proprie*), the Spirit cannot be said to be *ex substantia Patris*. Moreover, Abelard does nothing in the recension in the Balliol manuscript to alter his view, expounded at length in Book III, that God cannot do other than he does (the seventh in the list of heresies). This is a view he retracts explicitly in the *Confessio Fidei 'Universis'*.

HELOISE AND THE WRITINGS FOR THE PARACLETE

When, less than two years after he had entered Cluny, Abelard died, it was to Heloise that the abbot, Peter the Venerable, wrote, telling her of her husband's final months. Perhaps Peter knew that Heloise was not just Abelard's wife, nor merely his successor at the Paraclete: in the 1130s she had come to be Abelard's most important intellectual associate, and it was for her and her nuns that he wrote some of his outstanding works. During her years at Argenteuil, and even when she first took over the Paraclete, Heloise seems to have had few contacts – certainly few intellectual contacts – with Abelard. Their new association began with a series of letters.

Although Abelard was not a prolific letter-writer, a number of uncollected letters survive which he wrote to different people for various reasons: letters of dedication prefacing works, letters relating to his quarrels with Roscelin, the monks of St Denis and with Bernard, some short letter-treatises.[62] By contrast, Abelard's letter of consolation to a friend (his so-called *Historia calamitatum*) and the exchange of letters it provoked when Heloise read it circulated as a collection.[63] This collected correspondence is of enormous importance in understanding Abelard's thought and its

[62] The 'uncollected' letters are edited in Smits, *Letters* (*Ep.* 9–*Ep.* 14; *Checklist* §§278–83) except for his letter to his followers against Bernard (*Checklist* §284), ed. in Klibansky, 'Peter Abailard', pp. 6–7 (see above p. 30) and the dedicatory letters, all to Heloise, to the *Hymnarius Paraclitensis*, the commentary on the Hexaemeron and the sermons (edited along with these works). For the occasional letters, see above, p. 27, n. 84 (*Ep.* 10, to St Bernard), 18–19 (*Ep.* 11, to the abbot and monks of St Denis), 57–8 (*Ep.* 14 to the bishop of Paris). The letter-treatises are *Ep.* 9, to the nuns of the Paraclete (a set of recommendations for their studies, perhaps related to the *Rule*); *Ep.* 12 (on the superiority of monks to canons) and *Ep.* 13 (a defence of logic, which may in fact be a short note or fragment, not a letter at all). Smits comments in detail on the textual history, dating and contents of these letters.

[63] On the manuscripts of the collected letters, see Monfrin, *Historia Calamitatum*, pp. 9–31, 50–1, supplemented by *Checklist*, pp. 244–5 and C. Jeudy, 'Un nouveau manuscrit de la correspondance d'Abélard et Héloïse', *Latomus* 50 (1991), 872–81 and 'La correspondance d'Abélard et Héloïse: à propos d'un manuscrit nouveau' in *Autour de George Sand: Mélanges offertes à Georges Lubin* (Brest, n.d.). All the medieval manuscripts include Letters 1–7 except for three where copying is broken off abruptly in the middle of a piece. Although only one manuscript of the collection, Troyes, Bibliothèque municipale, 802, contains the complete text of the *Rule* for the Paraclete which Abelard attached to Letter 8, the complete *Rule* probably did belong to the original collection, since the other manuscripts (except for one) include at least the prefatory letter itself, and in two cases also an abbreviated version of the *Rule*: see C. Waddell, *The Paraclete statutes: Institutiones nostrae: introduction, edition, commentary* (Gethsemani Abbey, Trappist, Kentucky, 1987) (Cistercian liturgy series 20), pp. 45–7.

development. It is also the most controversial of all the works connected with him, since from the 1800s onwards a series of scholars has urged that the correspondence was not a real exchange of letters between Abelard and Heloise, and some recent scholars have declared the whole collection a forgery. There are, however, decisive arguments against these views and for the authenticity of the letters, which (because they are rather intricate) are set out at the end of the chapter in an excursus.

The first of the letters in the collection is written as a *consolatio*, directed to an unnamed friend who, Abelard hopes, will find his own trials easier to bear when he hears how slight they are compared to Abelard's.[64] This argument may seem to be merely an excuse and the letter-form itself a pretence, a contrivance which gives Abelard the opportunity to indulge in autobiography.[65] But the consolatory aims of the letter should be taken seriously, especially in the light of the wider philosophical concerns to which Abelard attaches them.[66] Yet, just as Boethius, in his famous *Consolation of Philosophy*, took the opportunity to explain and justify his conduct, so Abelard combined the higher aim of *HC* with a more practical purpose. At the time of writing (*c.* 1132 – a little after Pope Innocent's privilege to the Paraclete of November 1131, which it mentions), Abelard was in a most difficult position: a monk of St Denis, who had been granted leave to live away from the monastery and then to become abbot of St Gildas, but now lived in fear of being murdered by his rebellious monks, and was probably already contemplating his return to Paris as a teacher. There had earlier been rumours about his womanizing before his castration and about his unwillingness, after he had become a monk, to change his way of life; and now, after the condemnation of the *Theologia Summi Boni* at Soissons, and the attacks on him by (most probably) Bernard of Clairvaux and Norbert of Xanten, he was gaining the name of a heretic. The *Historia* seems designed to counter this public image and establish Abelard in the eyes of his readers as a man wronged both in fact and reputation. The attacks upon him were, he urges, in every case the result of envy. Although his behaviour to Fulbert had been deceitful, he suggests that he had had no

[64] Ed. Monfrin, *Historia calamitatum* (= *HC*; *Checklist* §277). In the two manuscripts which give it a title it is called 'Abaelardi ad amicum suum consolatoria'. In his *De vita solitaria*, Petrarch, following Abelard's own phrase (*HC* 63: 3–4, 107: 1561–2), referred to the work as *historia suarum calamitatum*. Duchesne (*MPL* 178, 113BC) – most probably wrongly – took this as a reference to the title of the work, rather than as a phrase describing it.

[65] See G. Misch, *Geschichte der Autobiographie* III, 2 (Frankfurt, 1959), pp. 530–1. Misch observes that the letter was an established literary form for autobiography.

[66] See below, pp. 320–1.

experience of women and was overcome by his passion. Once a monk, he shows himself as a zealous exponent of reformist rigour, disliked for this reason by his confrères and forced by their hatred out of the community. He explains that he returned to teaching partly because his abbot had pressed him, partly because the monks had made him an outcast. The trial of Soissons is portrayed as a mockery of justice and it is made clear that the condemnation there was issued only on the understanding that it would be rescinded.

Whether this letter succeeded in consoling Abelard's friend – if, indeed, he really existed – is not known. But when Heloise chanced to see a copy of it, its effect was anything but consolatory. In two letters (*Epp.* 2, 4)[67] she gives a vivid picture of her continuing grief over the loss of Abelard, describing his qualities and her love for him in superlative terms. It is she, not Abelard's friend, who, she complains, stands most in need of consolation from him. Returning to the story of their romance, told in the *Historia*, she elaborates on the arguments she had then put in her vain attempt to dissuade Abelard from marrying her. She insists that her outwardly irreproachable conduct as a nun is hypocrisy, since she took the veil not out of religious devotion, but from obedience to Abelard, and her love remains directed carnally towards him and not spiritually to God. In his replies to each (*Epp.* 3, 5) Abelard states his confidence in Heloise's wisdom and his need for her prayers and those of her nuns. He begs her to grieve no longer and exhorts her to direct her love, not to him, but to Christ.[68] Heloise begins her third and final letter (no. 6) by saying that, whilst she cannot control her state of mind, she will – out of obedience to Abelard – refrain from writing any more about her sadness. Instead, she asks him for a very different sort of remedy from the personal consolation and direction she had sought in her two previous letters: 'as the hammering in of one nail pushes out another, so a new subject of thought replaces the old' (242). Would

[67] An edition of the collected correspondence by David Luscombe is in preparation. Meanwhile, for Letters 2–5, the best edition is J. Muckle, 'The personal letters between Abelard and Heloise', *Mediaeval Studies* 15 (1953), 47–94, at pp. 68–94; for Letters 6 and 7, J. Muckle, 'The letter of Heloise on religious life and Abelard's first reply', *Mediaeval Studies* 17 (1955), 240–81; for Letter 8, T. McLaughlin, 'Abelard's rule for religious women', *Mediaeval Studies* 18 (1956), 241–92. The numbering used here (and by most scholars) counts *HC* as Letter 1. Confusingly, the editions by Muckle and McLaughlin treat Heloise's first reply as Letter 1; Muckle therefore numbers the six letters which follow 1–6, and McLaughlin describes the *Rule* as no. 7.

[68] See below, p. 321.

Abelard, she asks, provide her and her nuns – his 'handmaidens in Christ' – with two things they urgently require: a history of female monasticism and a monastic Rule which is suited to the needs and weaknesses of women? In the rest of the letter (by far her longest), Heloise not only explains, with both learning and practical awareness of the day-to-day problems of a female religious community, why a special Rule is necessary, but also gives a clear indication of the form she would prefer it to take. Abelard's responses to Heloise's two requests complete the collection.

The letters are valuable not just for their literary flair, their power to move and the insight they provide into their writers' intimate thoughts and feelings. Heloise had retained all her mental energy and she treated the problems posed by her personal predicament and her role as abbess in intellectual rather than merely practical terms. Abelard engaged with her sophisticated discussion of love and her highly original views on monasticism, and learned from them.[69] And the two tasks she set him were fruitful ones. In Letter 7, Abelard provides, not so much a narrative history of female monasticism, as an account of the religious virtues of women in antiquity, the Old Testament and the Christian era, whilst the *Rule* is one of the most important works for Abelard's practical ethics. Like St Benedict's *Rule*, it combines a set of practical instructions for ordering and running a convent with a statement of the moral and religious ideal to which the community there should aspire. But, in keeping with Abelard's general views, the themes of obedience and humility which run through and guide Benedict's *Rule* are replaced in Abelard's by an emphasis on conscience and, as Heloise had asked, moderation.[70]

The exchange of letters with Heloise probably covered the period of transition, during which Abelard finally decided to abandon St Gildas and return to the Paris schools. At the end of the *Historia* (107: 1544–55), Abelard complains that his life is in constant danger, because his monks are trying to kill him. He continues to speak of an ever-present threat to his life in both Letter 3 and Letter 5.[71] But, when Heloise talks of her own state of mind at the beginning of Letter 6, there is no indication that she is still worried about Abelard's immediate safety, as she had been before. Probably

[69] See below, pp. 300–2, 311–14.

[70] On the character of Abelard's *Rule* and its relation to earlier works, see Luscombe, 'The *Letters*', pp. 30–1 and Waddell, *The Paraclete statutes*, pp. 42–5, and cf. pp. 25–36.

[71] Letter 3, 76: 'Quod si me Dominus in manus inimicorum tradiderit, scilicet ut ipsi praevalentes me interficiant'; Letter 5, 86: 'mentione periculi in quo laboro, vel mortis quam timeo'.

Abelard had, by then, left his monastery. In his final period at Paris, besides teaching his students, Abelard also produced a set of works – of which Letter 7 and the Rule are merely two of the shorter examples – for Heloise and her nuns.[72]

Two of these works are closely connected with the teaching Abelard was doing in the schools. The commentary on the Hexaemeron which he wrote at Heloise's request does not try to escape any of the difficult or contentious problems raised by the text (often introduced, in the manner of the schools, as a hypothetical objection or by a question-formula).[73] There are long discussions of complex issues, such as the waters above the firmament, astrology and future contingents, and the different meanings of 'good'. Here, more than in any of his other later works, Abelard develops some of the ideas about goodness in general and theodicy, which he had raised in the second dialogue of the *Collationes* (which is referred to explicitly). The only significant difference in form between this commentary and that on Romans is the inclusion here of a rather perfunctory explanation of the moral and allegorical significance of part of the text. Abelard may well have lectured on the Hexaemeron as well as the Pauline letters and written up his teaching for Heloise's benefit.[74]

The *Problemata Heloissae* show even more clearly that Heloise and the nuns of the Paraclete were as eager and advanced in their studies of theology

[72] D. van den Eynde ('Chronologie des écrits d'Abélard à Héloïse', *Antonianum* 37 (1962), 337–49 at pp. 339–40) argues that, because Abelard refers to himself as an abbot even in Letter 8, the whole of the correspondence must have taken place before he left St Gildas; although he does not date this departure until 1135. But Abelard was not succeeded as abbot of St Gildas until after his death: cf. *Chronicon Ruyense* in Lobineau, *Histoire de Bretagne* II (Paris, 1707), col. 370 cited in Mews 'Abelard's *Theologia* re-examined', p. 155, n. 105. On the date of Abelard's return to Paris, see above, p. 23.

[73] Ed. in *MPL* 178, 731–84 from Avranches, Bibliothèque municipale, 135 (= *Exp. Hex.*; *Checklist* §268). This manuscript breaks off at Genesis 2: 17, whereas the other manuscripts all continue to 2: 25, still leaving the work unfinished. They also include a certain amount of extra material and changes made by Abelard. The section missing in the Avranches manuscript, the extra material, and an account of the other differences between the manuscripts are given in E. Buytaert, 'Abelard's Expositio in Hexaemeron', *Antonianum* 43 (1968), 163–94 at pp. 172–82. References to passages printed in Buytaert are prefixed by 'Buy.' The work has been edited from all the manuscripts in an unpublished PhD dissertation: M. Romig, 'A critical edition of Peter Abelard's Expositio in Hexaemeron (University of Southern California, Los Angeles, 1981).

[74] The commentary almost certainly dates from after *c.* 1133 (see Mews, 'On dating', pp. 118–19). Buytaert's suggestion ('Abelard's Expositio', p. 182; cf. p. 173) that the philosophical nature of some of the additions Abelard made in revising the piece were to fit it for a wider audience than that of Heloise and her nuns is unconvincing, since the rest of the commentary also includes difficult, philosophical material.

as the men Abelard was teaching in Paris.[75] They begin with a prefatory letter from Heloise, in which she tells Abelard how, following his advice to study scripture, she and her nuns have come across a number of points of difficulty (*quaestiones*) which they beg him to resolve for them. There follow forty-two brief questions, all except for the final one related to a particular passage or passages of the Bible, each one followed by Abelard's solution. Internal cross-references show that the questions cannot each have been despatched separately, since they are linked into groups; and it is simplest to suppose that the whole set was sent together, probably in the period between 1136 and 1139.[76]

Peter Dronke has pointed out how, behind these apparently academic enquiries, there may lie a highly personal element. Questions about true penitence (Problema 11) or about the need to keep all the commandments of the law (Problema 22) certainly fit closely the concerns of Heloise's particular situation.[77] Yet what is also striking is the continuity between Abelard's intellectual concerns, as evinced in the records of his teaching and his writings from the 1130s, and not just his solutions – as would be expected – but Heloise's questions themselves. On occasion, this is a matter of topic. For example, Problema 20 (708B) raises a fundamental difficulty about the logic of the Golden Rule ('Do to others as you would have them do to you') which frequently troubled Abelard, but not, it seems, his contemporaries.[78] Problema 24 (709D–710A) brings up another theme, discussed by Abelard both in his Rule and the commentary on Romans:

[75] Ed. in *MPL* 178, 677–730. The only surviving manuscript (Paris, Bibliothèque nationale, lat. 14511) is probably different from that used in *D'Amboise/Duchesne*, from which this edition derives; it is discussed very thoroughly in Smits, *Letters*, pp. 49–55. The *Problemata* are dated late because of their reference (710D) to the doctrine of sin as consent, which is found otherwise only in *Sc.* and the *Reportatio*; although, if the questions were not all sent together, some might date from *c.* 1133 to 1135.

[76] On grouping, see P. Dronke, 'Heloise's *Problemata* and *Letters*: some questions of form and content' in *Petrus Abaelardus*, pp. 53–73, at p. 61 (= P. Dronke, *Intellectuals and poets in medieval Europe* (Rome, 1992) (Storia e letteratura: Raccolta di studi e testi 183), pp. 247–94, at p. 309), 'Heloise's *Problemata*', p. 61 (= Dronke, *Intellectuals*, p. 309) and P. Dronke, *Women writers of the Middle Ages* (Cambridge, 1984), p. 135, n. 52. The most straightforward way of understanding the last sentence of Heloise's prefatory letter (678CD: 'In quibus profecto quaestionibus nequaquam ordinem Scripturae tenentes, prout quotidie nobis occurrunt, eas ponimus et solvendas dirigimus') is that Heloise built up a list of questions, as they arose from day to day, and then sent them all to Abelard to be answered.

[77] See Dronke, 'Heloise's *Problemata*', pp. 60–1 (= Dronke, *Intellectuals*, pp. 308–9), *Women writers*, pp. 136–8.

[78] See below, pp. 290–1.

the sinfulness of eating what one believes (even wrongly) it is unlawful to eat. More often, the similarity with Abelard is a matter of procedure. Although sometimes Heloise simply asks for elucidation of a difficult passage, more often she teases out a problem from a passage which a simpler reader would contentedly accept. When Christ says to those about to stone an adulteress, 'Let whichever of you is without sin cast the first stone', does he not thereby forbid anybody ever to punish anyone (Problema 8; 689D–690A)? Or when Christ says that we will be judged as we judge, does this not mean that if we judge unjustly we will be unjustly judged (Problema 19; 707D)?

Not all of the nuns of the Paraclete could take part in intellectual discussion of this sophistication. When Abelard sent a collection of sermons to Heloise, he explained that he had tried to make the sermons simple to understand rather than rhetorically ornate, in a way suitable for an audience of young nuns. In the finest of them (for instance, *Serm.* 1, on the Annunciation, and *Serm.* 29, on Susanna and the elders), Abelard does indeed avoid complexity of language or argument, but not of imagination, reading scriptural stories afresh and providing an account of thoughts and emotions about which the Bible is silent. The set of thirty-three sermons which survives (though not in manuscript[79]) is probably a larger collection, combining the homilies which Abelard wrote specially for the nuns with those he wrote for other audiences at other times.[80] These range from a scholarly, analytical discussion of circumcision and baptism (*Serm.* 3), to a fund-raising speech for the benefit of the Paraclete and its nuns (*Serm.* 30), to the long sermon (no. 33) which Abelard preached to the monks of St Gildas on the

[79] For the great bulk of the sermons, the only source is *D'Amboise/Duchesne*, although nos. 2, 4, 14, 25, and 30 each survive in one or more manuscripts.

[80] Ed. in *MPL* 178, 379–610 (based on *D'Amboise/Duchesne*, but using Einsiedeln, Stiftsbibliothek, 300 to improve the text of 2, 4 and 25. There is an edition of no. 30 from Colmar, Bibliothèque Municipale, 128 in A. Granta, 'La dottrina dell'elemosina nel sermone "Pro sanctimonialibus de Paraclito", *Aevum* 47 (1973), 32–59 at pp. 54–9. No. 34 (ed. *MPL* 178, 607–10 from Einsiedeln, 300) is not part of the collection printed in *D'Amboise/Duchesne* but in manner is like those addressed to the nuns of the Paraclete. Another sermon – a diatribe against the Cistercians – can probably be attributed to Abelard: it is discussed and ed. in L. Engels, 'Adtendite a falsis prophetis ... Un texte de Pierre Abélard contre les Cisterciens retrouvé?' in *Corona gratiarum. Miscellanea ... Eligio Dekkers O.S.B. ... oblata* II (Bruges/The Hague, 1975) (Instrumenta Patristica 11), pp. 195–228, at pp. 225–8. On the authenticity of the sermons, and the relationship between the surviving collection and that sent to Heloise, see D. van den Eynde, 'Le recueil des sermons de Pierre Abélard', *Antonianum* 37 (1962), pp. 2–54, as corrected by Chrysogonus Waddell, 'Peter Abelard as creator of liturgical texts' in *Petrus Abaelardus*, pp. 267–86, at pp. 277–9.

monastic ideal and its corruption using John the Baptist, Job and the ancient philosophers as exemplary figures.[81]

POETRY

Abelard mentions in his *Historia* that, during their romance, he wrote love songs to Heloise.[82] Unfortunately, there is no way of being certain which, if any, of the surviving early twelfth-century Latin love poems he wrote, although some plausible conjectures have been made.[83] Almost all Abelard's poetry in his later years – religious and moral, rather than amatory – was also connected in one way or another with Heloise.[84] He provided Heloise and her nuns with a large set of hymns, some dealing with the characteristic themes of his thought.[85] This *Hymnarius* was just a part of Abelard's often innovative work on the liturgy of the Paraclete.[86] It was probably for Heloise, too, that Abelard wrote the most complex and challenging of his poems, the set of six songs of mourning (*Planctus*) on Old Testament themes.[87]

[81] On this sermon, see Miethke, 'Abaelards Stellung', pp. 177–81 and Jolivet, 'Doctrines', pp. 110–11, 114.

[82] 73: 354–9; Heloise (*Ep.* 2, 72), too, refers to his love songs and their popularity.

[83] For instance, Peter Dronke (*Medieval Latin and the rise of European love-lyric* (2nd edn, Oxford, 1968), I, pp. 313–18 has suggested as a possibility *Carmina Burana* 169 ('Hebet sidus'). Other poems in the *Carmina Burana* (95, 117) and the Ripoll collection (22) have been attributed to Abelard by T. Latzke ('Abaelard, Hilarius und das Gedicht 22 der Ripollsammlung', *Mittellateinisches Jahrbuch*, 8 (1973), 70–89) at the end of an intricate but not entirely convincing examination. See also *Checklist* §313.

[84] One exception is a short poem on the incarnation written so as to form part of an elaborate geometrical design, ed. E. Ernst, 'Ein unbeachtetes 'Carmen figuratum' des Petrus Abaelardus', *Mittellateinisches Jahrbuch* 21 (1986), 125–46.

[85] Ed. C. Waddell, *Hymn collections from the Paraclete* (Gethsemani Abbey, Trappist, Kentucky, 1989) (Cistercian liturgy series 8–9). The more widely available edition by J. Szövérffy, *Peter Abelard's Hymnarius Paraclitensis* II (Brookline, Mass., 1975) (Medieval classics: texts and studies 3) is not entirely satisfactory: cf. H. Silvestre, 'A propos d'une édition récente de l'Hymnarius Paraclitensis d'Abélard', *Scriptorium* 32 (1978), 91–100, and C. Burnett, 'Notes on the tradition of the text of the *Hymnarius Paraclitensis* of Peter Abelard', *Scriptorium* 38 (1984), 295–302. See also C. Waddell's edition of the Paraclete breviary, Chaumont, Bib. mun., 31 (in C. Waddell (ed.), *The Old French Paraclete ordinary and the Paraclete Breviary* (Gethsemani Abbey, Trappist, Kentucky, 1983–5) (Cistercian liturgy series 3–7), which contains most of the hymns.

[86] See Waddell, 'Peter Abelard'.

[87] Ed. by W. Meyer, *Gesammelte Abhandlungen zur mittellateinischen Rythmik* I (Berlin, 1905), pp. 347–52, 366–74. There are better editions of individual *planctus*: 1, 4 and 6 – in P. Dronke, *Poetic individuality in the Middle Ages* (Oxford, 1970) at pp. 148, 119–23 and 203–9; 3 – in W. von den Steinen (in 'Die Planctus Abaelards – Jephthas Tochter', *Mittellateinisches Jahrbuch* 4 (1967), 122–44, at pp. 142–4); 6 – in L. Weinrich, ''Dolorum solatium'.

In his prefatory letter to the sermons (379–80), Abelard speaks, not just of a volume of hymns, but of 'a little book of hymns and sequences (*hymnorum vel sequentiarum*)' requested by Heloise. It is very possible, as some scholars have suggested, that by 'sequences' Abelard means to refer to this set of six *Planctus* on Old Testament themes. Other writers had put individual *planctus*, as Abelard does, into the mouths of ancient or biblical characters – Hector or Dido or the Virgin Mary. No one, however, had composed a *set* of *planctus* like Abelard's. As in some of his sermons, Abelard shows a power to rethink the scriptural material he uses, looking into thoughts, feelings and motives of the protagonists about which the Bible is silent. Sometimes Abelard uses and reshapes an extra-biblical tradition – for instance, in his presentation of Jephtha's daughter's sacrifice.[88] At other times, Abelard's portrayal of biblical characters – Samson blind and captive, Saul and Jonathan united in death – takes a turn entirely his own.[89] There is, moreover a philosophical purpose behind the *planctus* which goes beyond any individual characterization and links these poems to Abelard's abiding concerns.[90]

It was to Heloise's and his son that, sometime after about 1133, Abelard wrote his longest single poem, the *Carmen ad Astralabium*.[91] A poem of moral instruction, in the same genre as the very widely read *Disticha Catonis*, it consists of distichs, each usually containing a pithy moral maxim. To the modern reader the poem seems at first sight both loose in structure and commonplace in its ideas. A certain disjointedness is, however, characteristic of the genre, and it may have been exacerbated by the interpolation or addition of extraneous material.[92] And, on closer study, much of Abelard's

Text und Musik von Abaelards Planctus David', *Mittellateinsiches Jahrbuch* 5 (1968), 59–78 at pp. 69–72. See Dronke, *Poetic individuality*, pp. 116–18 for a balanced discussion of possible biographical references in the *planctus* which would make it likely that they were intended for Heloise.

88 See below, pp. 319–20.

89 See Dronke, *Poetic individuality*, pp. 116, 132–5.

90 See below, pp. 319–20. Chrysogonus Waddell ('*Epithalamica*: an Easter sequence by Peter Abelard', *Musical Quarterly* 72 (1986), 239–71, at pp. 241–2) has suggested that Abelard is also the author of three further sequences: *De profundis ad te clamantium* (*Analecta hymnica* 10, pp. 54–5), *Virgines castae* (*Analecta hymnica* 54, pp. 133–5) and *Epithalamica* (*Analecta hymnica* 8, pp. 45–7) (for details of eds. and MSS., see Mews, *Peter Abelard*, pp. 69–70). But the case for Abelard's authorship has certainly not yet been convincingly made.

91 Ed. J. Rubingh-Bosscher, *Peter Abelard. Carmen ad Astralabium. A critical edition* (Groningen, 1987) (=*Carmen*; *Checklist* §269).

92 Rubingh-Bosscher distinguishes three recensions and shows that the longest (I) is authentic. But this does not mean that every distich in this version is Abelard's. For instance, Peter Dronke has suggested to me, most convincingly, that the poem as Abelard wrote it may

poem turns out to be a thoughtful exposition of his central philosophical and theological views, in so far as they can provide the basis for a practical philosophy, a straightforward guide to living one's life.[93]

well have concluded with the trinitarian passage, lines. 999–1006, and that the rather inconclusive material which follows might be the relicts of rejected drafts or later additions by others.

93 See below, pp. 315–16.

Excursus 1

The letters of Abelard and Heloise

The authorship of the letters between Abelard and Heloise has been the most controversial question in Abelardian scholarship for over a century.[1] The opponents of the letters' authenticity divide into two main parties: those who believe that Abelard himself composed the whole correspondence, including the letters ostensibly by Heloise; and those who believe that, although they may use genuine material, the letters as they survive are a forgery, the work of neither of the authors who appear to have written them. The arguments against authenticity must be considered carefully, beginning with those put by advocates of the more radical position: that the correspondence (including the *Historia*) is a forgery.

The suggestion of forgery was first raised nearly two hundred years ago by Ignaz Fessler.[2] Not until the 1970s, however, was it advocated in a

[1] A detailed history of the controversy up to 1972 is given in P. von Moos, *Mittelalterforschung und Ideologiekritik* (Kritische Information 15) (Munich, 1974) and discussions from the period between 1972 and 1979 are reviewed in D. Luscombe, 'The *Letters* of Heloise and Abelard since "Cluny 1972"' in *Petrus Abaelardus*, pp. 19–39, a volume which also includes articles on the correspondence by J. Benton ('A reconsideration of the authenticity of the correspondence of Abelard and Heloise', pp. 41–52), P. Dronke ('Heloise's *Problemata*') and P. von Moos ('*Post festum* – Was kommt nach der Authentizitätsdebatte über die Briefe Abaelards und Heloises?', pp. 75–102). Contributions since 1979 include: P. Dronke, *Women writers*, pp. 107–43; H. Silvestre, 'Die Liebesgeschichte'; L. Georgianna, 'Any corner of heaven: Heloise's critique of monasticism', *MS* 49 (1987), 221–53; Waddell, *Paraclete statutes*, pp. 41–55; T. Janson, 'Schools of cursus in the twelfth century and the *Letters* of Heloise and Abelard' in C. Leonardi and E. Menestò (eds.), *Retorica e poetica tra i secoli XII e XIV* (Florence, 1988); Brooke, *Idea of marriage*, pp. 93–118; J. Benton, 'The correspondence of Abelard and Heloise' in *Fälschungen* V, pp. 95–120 (see under Silvestre); Luscombe, 'From Paris to the Paraclete'; B. Newman, 'Authority, authenticity and the repression of Heloise', *Journal of Medieval and Renaissance Studies* 32 (1992), 121–57; P. Dronke, 'Heloise, Abelard and some recent discussions' in *Intellectuals and poets*, pp. 323–42; and see also below, nn. 17 and 23.

[2] I. Fessler, *Abälard und Heloise* II (Berlin, 1806), p. 352.

coherent and detailed form, by the American historian, John Benton. Benton's was a complicated theory, which postulated at least two forgers – a 'twelfth-century epistolary "novelist"' and a 'thirteenth-century institutional scoundrel' – as well as a certain amount of authentic material; and it rested on a set of bold speculations about the practices and history of the Paraclete. Although greeted with alarmed respect by many Abelardian scholars, detailed investigation of Benton's arguments based on the liturgy and monastic institutions showed them to be without foundation It was also shown that Abelard's letters correspond with his other writings in a number of minute and characteristic ways which no forger would be likely to have imitated.

When, in 1979, Benton expounded with great candour the considerations which had made him come to doubt the arguments he had previously advanced, and retracted his theory, it might have been expected that the hypothesis of forgery had been laid to rest.[3] But this would have been to reckon without the scholarship, singlemindedness and stubbornness of the Belgian scholar, Hubert Silvestre, who set out with determination to undermine the historical credibility of a love story which is, he recognizes, 'an integral part of the cultural inheritance of France'. Long after Benton abandoned his original view, Silvestre has defended and elaborated his own version of the forgery theory which, he believes, is more firmly grounded and without the off-putting complexity of Benton's. Silvestre's thesis is, certainly, bold. The *Historia* and the correspondence are, he says, the work of a late thirteenth-century forger, working on the basis of some authentic material, who wished to uphold the right of clerics to have a concubine, and who found a powerful way of doing so by putting the arguments for clerical concubinage not into the mouth of a man, as might be expected, but of an outstanding woman. This forger was none other than the famous poet Jean de Meun, whose vast completion of Guillaume de Lorris' *Roman de la Rose*, one of the most widely read French works of the later Middle Ages, contains a passage recounting the romance of Abelard and Heloise, and who translated the *Historia* and the correspondence into French.[4]

Peter Dronke has recently provided a very powerful argument against this thesis. There are, he shows, a number of instances in the Old French translation, not explicable by variants in the Latin text or defects in the manuscript of the French, where Jean de Meun, failing to grasp the meaning

[3] 'A reconsideration, pp. 41–52. See n. 7 for details of his earlier article.

[4] Die 'Liebesgeschichte', pp. 159–64. On whether Jean was in fact responsible for the French translation, see below, n. 7.

of a phrase in the correspondence, mistranslates it.[5] How could Jean de Meun misunderstand a text which he himself had forged? Silvestre might reply that the passages in question belonged to the authentic material which Jean did not compose but incorporated into his forgery. But at least one of the passages signalled by Dronke concerns precisely the subject – Heloise's reasons for not wanting to marry – which Silvestre believes the forger himself introduced into his material.[6] And if Jean were really so accomplished a Latinist that he could imitate Abelard's style perfectly – as the hypothesis of forgery demands – how could he be capable of such errors? Silvestre might, alternatively, defend himself by suggesting that the forger of the letters was not the same person as their translator: either Jean de Meun made up the correspondence but was not responsible for the surviving Old French version, or, if Jean did make this translation, someone else forged the Latin.[7] But on either of these explanations, Silvestre's theory loses the simplicity and boldness which alone might make it plausible. In any case, the studies of *cursus* undertaken by Janson and Dronke, despite the differences in some of their conclusions, establish that the prose rhythms in the *Historia* and correspondence are characteristic of the early part of the twelfth century, not the thirteenth.[8] Janson has gone on to argue, most convincingly, that a medieval forger could not have successfully imitated the prose rhythm of an earlier age, except perhaps in a short text. Only very recently have scholars become aware of the history of medieval prose rhythm. A forger, relying solely on 'a good ear for cadences' would be most unlikely to pick up, in the authentic material he had, a rhythm which was so different to that of the prose of his own time.[9] In short, a study of prose rhythm almost certainly excludes the hypothesis that Jean de Meun or any

5 'Heloise, Abelard', pp. 326–30.

6 The translator misunderstands Letter 2, p. 114: 154–7, where Heloise is referring to the reasons she gave, and Abelard omitted from *HC*, for preferring 'love to marriage, liberty to chains'; cf. Dronke, 'Heloise, Abelard', pp. 328–9.

7 Against an early twentieth-century scholar who had suggested Jean de Meun as forger of *HC*, J. Benton had already ('Fraud, fiction and borrowing in the correspondence of Abelard and Heloise', in *Pierre Abélard*, pp. 469–511, p. 498, n. 69) raised the French translator's misunderstanding of passages in the Latin. Silvestre here ('Die Liebesgeschichte', p. 135, n. 27) mentions the possibility that Jean de Meun might not have been responsible for the translation, but later (p. 161) talks without qualification of Jean as the first translator into French of the correspondence. Dronke ('Heloise, Abelard', pp. 326–7) considers it as generally agreed that Jean de Meun was the translator of the French version, but holds back from accepting this view as completely established.

8 Dronke, 'Heloise's *Problemata*', pp. 297–302, *Women writers*, pp. 110–12, 'Heloise, Abelard', pp. 333–42; Janson, 'Schools of cursus'.

9 'Schools of cursus', pp. 183–4.

other thirteenth-century writer could have forged the letters and *Historia*.

Silvestre's thesis must be regarded, then, not simply as unproven, but rather as demonstrably false. It might seem strange, therefore, that Silvestre is able to give roughly twenty separate detailed arguments which, he says, show that the *Historia* and the letters cannot be authentic. But none of them withstands scrutiny.[10] Some are merely footling: for instance, that there is no other trace of the commentary on Ezechiel mentioned in the *Historia*; or that the papal legate, Cono, being a strong character, would not have agreed to imprison and then release Abelard. Some depend on the strange assumption that, if the *Historia* is by Abelard, it must give an entirely accurate, impartial account of events, so that (for instance) its insistence on Abelard's chastity before he met Heloise, or its failure to mention Roscelin, or its version of the quarrel over St Denis' see, must be taken as signs of inauthenticity;[11] others on the equally implausible idea that, in running the Paraclete, Heloise must have conformed completely to Abelard's instructions, so that writings attributed to Abelard must be presumed forgeries if they differ in their stipulations from the Paraclete statutes of Heloise's time, *Institutiones nostrae*. Even the few arguments which, at first sight, seem to have some force, crumble on inspection. Heloise's name does not appear in the obituary of Argenteuil – but, in fact, the obituary of Argenteuil does not survive, but merely extracts copied by Mabillon.[12] The *Historia* refers to a passage from Deuteronomy in a way which implies a division of the Bible first found *c.* 1220 – David Luscombe has shown that the numbering used here IS found in the twelfth century![13] A remark about negroes in Letter 5 seems to derive from Aristotle's *Historia animalium*, which was not translated until the thirteenth century[14] – in fact, there is *no* parallel: Aristotle's point (*Historia animalium* III, 9 (517a18–21)) is that men's teeth and bones are not always the same colour as their skin, Abelard's that an Ethiopian, being black, appears on the outside to be uglier than other men, though in some of his internal features, such as bones and teeth, he is 'more beautiful and more white'. Silvestre's persistence and scholarship have certainly helped to reach a deeper and more nuanced understanding of Abelard's

[10] Silvestre, 'Die Liebesgeschichte', pp. 136–52.

[11] See above, pp. 14–15, 8–9, 18–19 for discussion of these passages in *HC*.

[12] Printed in *Obituaires de la Province de Sens* I (Paris, 1902) (Recueil des historiens de la France. *Obituaires* I), pp. 344–51.

[13] 'From Paris to the Paraclete', pp. 253–4 and esp. n. 49.

[14] Cf. Benton, 'Fraud, fiction', p. 496 and n. 66 and Muckle, 'The personal letters', p. 84, n. 44 of his edition in *MS* 15 (1953)'.

life and work. But, just like his wider position, his detailed arguments carry no conviction.[15]

The other view which contradicts the authenticity of the correspondence is less radical and, at first sight, more plausible. It holds that the *Historia* and correspondence which follows is a literary fiction: Abelard himself is considered to have written all the letters, including those ostensibly by Heloise. Although this view goes back as far as the mid-nineteenth century, it was not until Bernhard Schmeidler's articles (published between 1913 and 1940) that the hypothesis of the correspondence as Abelard's literary fiction, was advocated in detail and with learning.[16] Schmeidler began by indicating discrepancies between the *Historia* and Letters 2–5; but he went on to argue the unity of style and thought between the letters signed by Abelard and those signed by Heloise, and between the whole correspondence and works indubitably by Abelard. Schmeidler also pointed out that Ovid's *Heroides*, well known in the twelfth-century, provided a precedent for fictional letters, and that twelfth-century letter-collections were often assembled with a particular purpose in view. More recently, Peter von Moos, in a series of learned and sophisticated studies, has revealed an even tighter and more complex web of links between the letters (both Abelard's and Heloise's) and various of Abelard's writings.[17] Tore Janson discovered a very

[15] In another contribution to the debate, Silvestre ('Héloïse et le témoignage du "Carmen ad Astralabium" ', *Revue d'histoire ecclésiastique* 83 (1988), 635–60) discusses and accepts new evidence of the authenticity of a passage from the *Carmen ad Astralabium* (lines 3790–84), where Heloise is presented, as in *Ep.* 4, as unable to repent. None the less, Silvestre maintains his view that *HC* and the correspondence is a forgery.

[16] L. Lalanne suggested this position, as one of a number of possibilities, in 'Quelques doutes sur l'authenticité de la correspondence amoureuse d'Héloïse et d'Abailard', *La correspondance littéraire* 1 (1856–7), 27–33; cf. von Moos, *Mittelalterforschung*, pp. 45–9. Schmeidler's articles are: 'Der Briefwechsel zwischen Abälard und Heloise eine Fälschung', *Archiv für Kulturgeschichte* 11 (1913), 1–30; 'Der Briefwechsel zwischen Abälard und Heloise als eine literarische Fiktion Abälards', *Zeitschrift für Kirchengeschichte* 54 (1935), 323–38, esp. pp. 331–4; 'Der Briefwechsel zwischen Abaelard und Heloise dennoch eine literarische Fiktion Abaelards', *RB* 52 (1940), 85–95; 'Abaelard und Heloise: eine geschichtlich-psychologische Studie', *Die Welt als Geschichte* 6 (1940), 93–123; cf. von Moos, *Mittelalterforschung*, pp. 60–7.

[17] See 'Palatini quaestio quasi peregrini: ein gestriger Streitpunkt aus der Abelard-Heloise-Kontroverse nochmals überprüft', *Mittellateinisches Jahrbuch* 9 (1973), 124–58; 'Le silence d'Héloïse et les idéologies modernes' in *Pierre Abélard*, pp. 425–68 (which also appeared in a revised and enlarged German version: 'Die Bekehrung Heloises', *Mittellateinisches Jahrbuch* 11 (1976), 95–125); 'Cornelia und Heloise', *Latomus*, 34 (1975), 1024–59; 'Lucan und Abelard' in G. Cambier (ed.), *Hommages à André Boutemy* (Collection Latomus 145) (Brussels, 1976), pp. 413–43; '*Post festum*' in *Petrus Abaelardus*, pp. 75–100. It is impossible

high degree of similarity in the use of *cursus* between the letters attributed to Abelard and those attributed to Heloise, so that he was led to believe it very probable 'that we have to do with one author, or at least with one editor'.[18] And John Benton (after his retraction of the view that the letters are forged) has used a computer-assisted analysis of certain recurring common phrases in the letters and in the works certainly by Abelard to argue that the correspondence is the work of a single author, and that he is Abelard.[19] Most recently, Chrysogonus Waddell – whose detailed work on the liturgy and rule of the Paraclete lends weight to his opinion – has come down in favour of the view that 'the entire correspondence . . . is from the pen of a single writer; and this writer is Peter Abelard'.[20]

Exponents of the literary-fiction theory have had widely varying views about Abelard's purpose in composing it. According to Schmeidler, at least in his earlier articles, Abelard was motivated by a desire to create a sensation and increase his own fame (and perhaps, secondarily, to exhibit his abilities as a spiritual counsellor).[21] By contrast, modern scholars such as von Moos and Waddell have attributed to him far higher motives. Abelard, they say, wished to tell the story of a double conversion – first his own, then Heloise's – from carnal love to the love of God. (A crude and extreme version of this view is put forward by D. W. Robertson, for whom it forms yet another element in his view of a Christian Middle Ages monolithically dedicated to upholding an unquestioning version of Augustine's teaching.)[22] According to von Moos, the second of these conversions is conveyed not directly, but through the rhetorical figure of aposiopesis: Heloise's silence, after the first words of Letter 6 about her own feelings. The fictional correspondence thus provides a suitable preface to the two long, final pieces:

to do justice to von Moos's complex and subtly changing views in a quick survey of the controversy: for a fuller account, see I. Pagani, 'Epistolario o dialogo spirituale? Postille ad un'interpretazione della corrispondenza di Abelardo ed Eloisa', *Studi Medievali* 27 (1986), pp. 241–318. Recently, von Moos appears to have shifted his position, but he still maintains that the correspondence is not genuine.

18 'Schools of cursus', p. 195.

19 'The correspondence of Abelard and Heloise.'

20 *The Paraclete Statutes*, pp. 41–55.

21 'Der Briefwechsel eine Fälschung', p. 30 (in 'Abaelard und Heloise', Schmeidler also anticipates the type of reason which would be given by Robertson and von Moos); Charlotte Charrier, a follower of Schmeidler's, went further and identified (*Héloise dans l'histoire et dans la légende* (Paris, 1933; reprinted Geneva, 1977), p. 24) the reason behind Abelard's composition as 'fatuité d'homme'.

22 *Abelard and Heloise*.

Letter 7, on the history of female monasticism and Letter 8, Abelard's *Rule* for the Paraclete. Von Moos and Waddell even grant that Heloise may have had some part in the composition of the correspondence – but not that she actually wrote the letters attributed to her. For this would be to allow that the letters express thoughts she really had, feelings she actually experienced, and so – they believe – to indulge in a reading anachronistically biographical and romantic.

But many do not agree. From Gilson in the 1930s to Dronke, Zerbi and Luscombe in the 1970s, 1980s and 1990s, scholars have marshalled counter-arguments to show that Heloise herself, and not Abelard, wrote the letters attributed to her.[23] They argue that the supposed discrepancies between the *Historia* and Letters 2–5 depend on misreadings and misunderstandings of the text.[24] The closeness of Heloise's letters to Abelard's in style and thought is only to be expected, they say: did Heloise not learn from her master Abelard? And did not Abelard himself perhaps learn from his pupil?[25] Moreover, recent research shows that there may be small but significant differences between the style of Heloise's letters and those of Abelard.[26] The analysis of *cursus* which has been used to suggest a single author for all the letters is not, on further examination, conclusive; and statistics which indicate that the same choice of common words is found throughout letters prove nothing about authorship: why would not a master's writing and that of his disciple resemble each other in just this way?[27] And, if the correspondence was concocted to illustrate the story of a conversion, why does its narrative end, not with Heloise's acceptance of grace, but with her silence?[28] Moreover, these scholars bring evidence to show that it is

[23] Among the most important of these contributions are: E. Gilson, *Héloïse et Abélard* (Paris, 1938); P. Dronke, *Abelard and Heloise in medieval testimonies* (Glasgow, 1976) (reprinted in *Intellectuals and poets*, pp. 247–94), 'Heloise's *Problemata*', *Women writers*, pp. 107–43; P. Bourgain, 'Héloïse' in *Abélard en son temps*, pp. 211–37; P. Zerbi, 'Abelardo ed Eloisa: il problema di un amore e di una corrispondenza' in W. van Hoecke and A. Welkenhuysen (eds.), *Love and marriage in the twelfth century* (Mediaevalia Lovaniensia Series 1, 8) (Louvain, 1981), pp. 130–61; Luscombe, 'From Paris to the Paraclete'; Dronke, 'Heloise, Abelard'.

[24] E.g. Gilson, *Héloïse*, pp. 13–24; Zerbi, 'Abelardo', pp. 154–6.

[25] Gilson, *Héloïse*, pp. 30–4; Dronke, *Women writers*, pp. 111–12.

[26] Dronke, 'Heloise's *Problemata*', p. 55, *Women writers*, pp. 110–11.

[27] Dronke, 'Heloise, Abelard', pp. 333–42 (on cursus), 325–6 (on computer-aided frequency counts).

[28] Dronke (*Women writers*, p. 129) has argued that von Moos does not satisfactorily deal with this point by his theory of aposiopesis, since aposiopesis would be plausible only if the letters were really exchanged, not a literary fiction: 'If the letter-collection were meant (even in part) as an *exemplum* of conversion, the one thing for which the figure of aposio-

neither improbable nor anachronistic to attribute to Heloise the sentiments expressed in her letters: they do not need to be explained away as exaggerations concocted so as to dramatize the story of a religious conversion.[29] In particular, Peter Dronke has shown that medieval readers such as Jean de Meun and Petrarch had no inclination to interpret the correspondence in the religious and moralizing sense favoured by twentieth-century medievalists such as Robertson.[30]

The most balanced and subtle presentation of the case for Abelard as sole author of the letters is Waddell's. He argues that the lack of any explicit reference to a conversion by Heloise is a 'non-problem' for 'the monk or nun who still lives within the monastic tradition of which Abelard and Heloise were a part', because no one is ever perfectly converted on earth: 'There is always something of a gap between sincerely expressed and sincerely held ideals and one's inward conformity to and transformation by those ideals; and, to some extent, Heloise's lament is the lament of even the most exemplary monk or nun.' In any case, 'for Abelard, the History and the Rule are meant to resolve the problem of Heloise's as yet unfinished conversion: how, indeed, could she *not* be fully converted when she has so utterly perfect a history and rule made to order?'[31] This reasoning is somewhat vitiated by the attempt to uphold contradictory hypotheses – that Heloise is never fully converted but such incomplete conversion is fully in accord with the monastic tradition, and that Heloise is fully and perfectly converted because (!) she has Abelard's *Historia* and *Rule*. Yet it may perhaps be taken as showing that the collected correspondence (Letters 1–8 including the *Rule*) can be used as a religious document, a monastic rule with a long and unusual preface. Waddell (in line with many other scholars) labours to show that the collection was indeed made with this monastic purpose in mind. Although even that position has been disputed, he is very probably right. Whoever put the correspondence together probably did think of it as prefacing the *Rule*.[32] But this still leaves open the question of whether the correspondence was deliberately produced as a collection (and therefore by a single author, or by authors collaborating, not genuinely

pesis could not be used would be the conversion itself, since this would leave the intention of the work unclear and thus make the *exemplum* lose all force and value.'

29 Dronke, *Abelard and Heloise in medieval testimonies, passim*; Bourgain, 'Héloïse', pp. 227–34; Brooke, *Idea of marriage*, esp. pp. 103–13.

30 *Abelard and Heloise in medieval testimonies*, pp. 28–9, 56–8 = *Intellectuals and poets*, pp. 275–6, 290.

31 *Paraclete Statutes*, pp. 48–50.

32 See above, chapter 3, n. 63.

corresponding), or whether there was a genuine exchange of correspondence between Abelard and Heloise, set off by Heloise's reading the *Historia*, which someone (perhaps Heloise herself) at a later date decided to collect together, for purposes of religious edification. And that is the question at issue.

What, then, are the grounds for answering it in favour of Abelard as the single author? To suggest that Abelard (perhaps aided by Heloise) composed the collection as a literary fiction is to attribute to him a method of writing, and indeed a way of thought, which neither he nor any of his contemporaries displayed elsewhere. There is nothing intrinsically impossible about the suggestion, but it requires strong evidence. This its supporters signally fail to provide. Waddell mentions examples of monastic rules which have prefaces, but he is forced to admit that there is no precedent for using an exchange of letters in this way.[33] Supposing that the letters already existed, as a genuine correspondence, it is easy to imagine a compiler arranging the material in this novel way; but much harder to envisage why, if Abelard were setting out to preface a *Rule* for the Paraclete, he should have chosen so unexampled and disconcerting a format. Schmeidler's theory gained its initial plausibility from his discovery of what he claimed were internal inconsistencies, between the *Historia* and the letters. Further research has shown these to be illusory or, at best, questionable; whilst few would now stand by the stereotyped view of medieval attitudes to love, which made Robertson so certain that Heloise could never have really felt the sentiments she expresses. Although the exponents of the literary-fiction theory often speak as if those who attribute Letters 2, 4 and 6 to Heloise are making an unwarranted leap of the imagination, whilst their own position displays a scholarly caution, in truth the positions are the reverse.

And, on further investigation, it turns out that the leap of the imagination, which makes Abelard, a Richardson before his time, into the single author of the love letters, is not merely unnecessary, but highly implausible. Were Abelard the single author of the whole correspondence, he would have been able to choose every feature of it in line with his overall purposes. Yet no such control appears to have been exercised. Letter 2 (Heloise's first reply) begins with a quick but thorough summary of the story of his life which Abelard had told in the *Historia* (68). If the letter is taken to have been written by Heloise, then this paragraph is an interesting indication that she was not writing merely privately to Abelard, but to put her case to others who might not know the *Historia*. If the letter is taken to have

[33] *Paraclete Statutes*, pp. 42–3, 54.

been composed by Abelard himself, as part of an integral fictional collection, which includes the *Historia*, the presence of the summary becomes inexplicable. Nor is it easy, on this hypothesis, to explain a great part of the content of this letter. If Abelard were trying to preface his *Rule* with letters illustrating his and Heloise's conversion (and this is the most plausible of the suggestions which the literary-fiction theorists have advanced), why should he have made the burden of Heloise's first letter the fact that he, the founder of the Paraclete, has neglected, not just her as an individual, but her as abbess, along with the nuns of the community which he himself had established? It is a theme which shows Heloise already a conscientious leader of her nuns and Abelard neither as unconverted nor converted but, from Heloise's point of view, mistaken in his choice among different spiritual priorities.

Moreover, at least two important features in the argument of Heloise's letters are hard to explain unless she, not Abelard, wrote them. Heloise pleads for an unheroic conception of the monastic life, content to win 'any corner of heaven' rather than risking disaster in striving for a sanctity which is beyond her. Nothing could be further from Abelard's view of monasticism, developed in the *Theologia Christiana* Book II and Sermo 33, in which the extremes of asceticism practised by the ancient philosophers are seen as examples to be followed by the religious of his own day.[34] True, in his own *Rule* Abelard proposes an idea of moderation in religious life which is fully in line with Heloise's request. But, whereas it is easy to imagine Abelard learning from Heloise, and changing his views because of what she has revealed of her experience in Letters 2 and 4 and of her thinking in Letter 6, it is unconvincing to posit – as the exponents of a literary fiction must – an unexplained and apparently unmotivated volte-face on Abelard's part.

Even more striking is the discrepancy between Heloise and Abelard over the relations between act and intention in determining moral guilt. For most writers about the correspondence, this has seemed an area where Heloise's letters are clearly Abelardian in their philosophical assumptions. Did not Abelard propose a morality of intention, which is assumed in many instances in Heloise's letters?[35] This supposed congruence is explained either by saying that Abelard wrote them himself or else by the fact that Heloise

[34] On these views, see below, pp. 306–7.

[35] Especially at *Ep.* 2, 72. 'Quae plurimum nocens, plurimum ut nosti sum innocens. Non enim rei effectus sed efficientis affectus in crimine est. Nec quae fiunt sed quo animo fiunt aequitas pensat'; and in her treatment of her hypocrisy in *Ep.* 4, 80–1.

was Abelard's pupil and might be expected to have absorbed his characteristic ideas. Yet in fact the view of intention in Heloise's letters accords with Abelard's only in so far as they both share the common ground of all their Christian contemporaries: that intention is central to any account of morality. But Heloise takes this in the same way as almost all the theologians of the time other than Abelard, stressing the importance of the interior state of mind and ascribing great importance to sinful thoughts, even those which are unrealized in any action. By contrast, Abelard's morality is one of intended *actions*: people are neither excused, nor inculpated, by a state of mind alone.[36] Abelard is the very last person who (except by a novelistic feat of inventing another's state of mind – a feat of which, for all his vast abilities, there is no reason to believe him to have been capable)[37] could have invented the moral perplexity expressed in Heloise's letters. From Abelard's point of view, Heloise was far from 'innocent' – having done many things which she knew, from reason and Christian teaching, to be against God's law. But neither would her unspiritual state of mind, despite her exemplary life as a nun, have seemed to Abelard a moral fault. On the contrary, though she might reject the description herself, Heloise was in Abelard's terms a heroine, no matter how she felt or thought, because of how she chose to live.[38] The apparent lack of sympathy, the failure fully to engage with Heloise's plight which many commentators have found in Abelard's replies, may owe much to this difference in philosophical outlook.

When the evidence for a position fails, there lies open another resort for its advocates: to shift the discussion to a higher plane of abstraction. Whether or not the considerations adduced are relevant, or themselves sound, such a move will confuse the opponents and lend an illusory strength to views which are indefensible. It would be unfair to accuse Peter von Moos, whose learned and subtle investigations have done so much to reveal the audacity and coherence of Abelard's thought, of having deliberately employed such a strategy. But this, though unintended, has been in practice the consequence of his adducing ideas from recent critical theories in his

[36] For Abelard's views on intention and their relation to the thought of his time, see below, pp. 253–6.

[37] Brooke (*Idea of marriage*, p. 102) comments pertinently that a great novelist such as Tolstoy or George Eliot might have created, or tried to create, a character of the complexity of Heloise.

[38] When in the *Carmen ad Astralabium* (127: 379–84), Abelard alludes to Heloise's complaint, he puts it in terms which he can recognize: those of failure to repent: 'si, nisi peniteat me comississe priora,/saluari nequeam, spes michi nulla manet:/dulcia sunt adeo commissi gaudia nostri/ut memorata iuuent, que placuere nimis' (lines 381–4).

discussions of the authenticity of the letters. He calls on scholars to look at the history of the correspondence's reception or asks them to regard the letters as literature and refrain from biographical surmises which, he believes, in the absence of further evidence can only reflect their own prejudices. Von Moos's call is reminiscent of the wish, among some literary theorists, to treat texts as if they were not the products of their authors, but independent signifiers, awaiting the reader to interpret them in one of the unlimited ways in which they can be understood. The practical value of this method is debatable. But an appeal to such an approach when an historical question is at issue must be an irrelevance. Either Heloise did or did not write certain letters. It may be difficult to determine which was the case; but there is no reason to believe that here the ordinary historical methods of gathering evidence, framing hypotheses and testing them do not apply. Nor is the question of authenticity one which a scholar should lightly ignore. Much of interest, perhaps, may be gleaned from looking at the letters merely as texts in isolation; but how much more from trying, through the texts which survive, to understand the thoughts and sentiments of Abelard (and of Heloise) as they developed within the context of their times?

Conclusion

Abelard's logic and his theology

Stormy though it was, Abelard's life gives at first sight an impression of consistency. He was a dedicated teacher who had a devoted student following but who also, as a young logician, a middle-aged monk and an elderly theologian, aroused widespread antagonism. Quarrels – with his teachers, his superiors, his colleagues and with the Church authorities – provided the backdrop to his other activities. Similarly, his work, although varied in form and subject, appears to show a high degree of continuity. There is throughout his writings the same willingness to challenge accepted views, to find and dwell on awkward questions, and to press ideas to their logical conclusions. The tools and vocabulary of logic are almost everywhere on display in his theological writings, and favourite concepts and themes recur from text to text.[1] Even the one episode which fits uneasily into a life otherwise so devoted to ideas, the romance with Heloise, is characteristic of Abelard's wholeheartedness, his disregard of consequences and his practical unwisdom.

In fact, however, the apparent consistency hides an important break. This break was the direct though paradoxical result of Abelard's romance and marriage. After his castration, Abelard became a monk. He did so, he admits, not from religious zeal but out of shame. Yet, once he had entered religious life, he quickly (if not *so* quickly as he claims) began to take the ideas of monasticism very seriously. He did not abandon intellectual work for prayer, but his main interest shifted, gradually but decisively, away from logic to theology. His life remained one of conflicts, but their character altered. As a teacher of logic, he had been embroiled in the ecclesiastical

[1] See e.g. M. Fumagalli Beonio-Brocchieri, 'La relation entre logique, physique et théologie chez Abélard' in Buytaert, *Peter Abelard*, pp. 153–62 and 'Sull'unità dell'opera abelardiana' in *Pietro Abelardo*, pp. 429–38; and J. Jolivet, *Arts du langage et théologie chez Abélard* (2nd edn, Paris, 1982) (Etudes de philosophie médiévale 57), pp. 337–63.

and clan rivalries of the time, not because of what he taught but because his teaching was seen to be outstanding. Although the political alliances and enmities he had made remained, it was the content of Abelard's theological teaching which led to the invectives and judgements against him. No longer was he an ambitious young thinker jousting for intellectual eminence and a more prestigious position: his challenge was on the level of ideas, and the challenge to him was about whether he should be allowed to write and teach them at all.

The shift from logic to theology involved more than a change of subject-matter. It brought with it also a new awareness of the past. Although the authoritative texts of logic were the works of the ancients, antiquity itself played little part in his thought before about 1120. Abelard's turn to theology coincided with a new and sophisticated understanding by him of Plato and Platonism and the construction of an idealized view of ancient life and thought. The pattern of sacred history and the doctrines of the faith had, for Abelard, to be understood in the light of this golden picture of an ostensibly pagan civilization. Abelard's awareness of the past did not, however, make him subservient to ancient models. On the contrary, where as a logician he had, despite his innovativeness, followed the structure of the accepted ancient authorities and inserted his own ideas into a borrowed framework, as a theologian Abelard set out boldly to construct his own system of doctrine.

The study of Abelard as a philosopher involves, then, not the analysis of a single pattern of thought but two distinct, though linked, areas of investigation. Part 2 will consider some of the philosophical ideas which he elaborated unsystematically in the course of his logical work. Part 3 will discuss the moral philosophy which runs through, and perhaps even holds together, Abelard's theological system.

Part II

Introduction

Abelard was a logician, a theologian and a moral thinker: how far, outside the area of ethics, was he also a philosopher? Historians have long recognized that, in his logical works, Abelard does much more than merely explore the conditions for the validity of arguments. His frequently analysed passages on universals discuss the relations between language, thought and things in the world. Elsewhere too he considers problems of signification, and also questions about the nature of possibility and necessity, facts and statements, future contingents and free will. These parts of Abelard's writing have all received close attention from modern scholars. But they have regarded them as aspects of his work as a logician. Even the one recent writer to have looked in some detail at Abelard's ontology does so merely as a prelude to examining his theory of entailment.[1]

In one sense, these scholars are right. The form of Abelard's surviving work as a logician follows the pattern of the authoritative ancient set texts,[2] and his philosophical discussions occur only when occasioned by his task as a logical exegete and instructor. None the less, in the course of expounding the logic of Porphyry and Aristotle, Abelard provides tentative explorations of some of the deepest philosophical questions: what are the ultimate constituents of the world, and how do they relate to each other and to human thought and language? Abelard did not provide systematic answers to them; some of his ideas are not fully worked, and on some questions Abelard advances different views which do not cohere with each other. He remained too closely bound to the views he took from Aristotle's *Categories* and Porphyry's *Isagoge* fully to develop his often bold insights. Yet Abelard's ontology is far more complex, wide-ranging and subtle than most historians have allowed. The extent of his achievement here emerges

[1] Martin, in 'The logic', pp. 111–13.

[2] See above, chapter 3, pp. 43–8 (and pp. 50–1 for possible exception of the lost *Grammatica*).

only by probing the limits of Abelard's discussion and by exploring its failures as well as its successes.

The aim of the following chapters is to provide such an analysis of these philosophical views, and to trace the ways in which they developed. Their place within an exposition of logic based on authoritative ancient texts creates some special difficulties for the interpreter. The philosophical point at issue is often hidden within what seems to be an exegetical dispute about a technicality of logic. Both Abelard's general procedures as an exegete and the context of each individual logical discussion need to be understood before the deeper bearing of Abelard's comments can be gauged. But first Abelard's starting point must be identified: what led Abelard the logician into wider philosophical questions?

Chapter 4

Logic, philosophy and exegesis

Abelard was led to philosophize in the course of expounding logic because the ancient and late antique logical texts on which the subject was based were not all strictly logical. Indeed, Aristotle's *Categories*, traditionally classified as a logical work, is hardly logical in content at all. Porphyry's *Isagoge* was taken as an introduction to the *Categories* and, despite Porphyry's more narrowly logical intentions, was associated with the questions raised by Aristotle's work. The *De interpretatione*, although clearly linked to syllogistic logic, contains brief but suggestive passages on language, the mind and necessity. The next section will offer a brief sketch of the ontology presented in the *Categories* and the *Isagoge*. The philosophical themes of the *De interpretatione* will be discussed separately in later chapters.[1]

THE ONTOLOGY OF THE 'CATEGORIES' AND 'ISAGOGE'

From about the first century BC, the *Categories* has been placed as the first text of Aristotle's *Organon* and regarded as a work of logic: an examination of the terms which make up statements, treated in *De interpretatione*, which, in turn, make up arguments, treated in the *Analytics*. Yet, as modern scholars have begun to recognize, Aristotle probably had no such narrowly logical intention in mind when he composed the material which became the *Categories*. The *Categories* should be seen as a treatise covering some of the same fundamental questions about what sorts of things exist as Aristotle would later raise, and answer differently, in his *Metaphysics*.[2]

[1] See below, pp. 162–3 (the mind); pp. 221–2, 226–8 (necessity).

[2] See especially, M. Frede, 'The title, unity and authenticity of the Aristotelian *Categories*' in his *Essays in ancient philosophy* (Oxford, 1987), pp. 11–28 and M. Graham, *Aristotle's two systems* (Oxford, 1987), pp. 1–19.

	NOT *de subiecto*	*de subiecto*
NOT *in* subiecto	Example: a man, a horse Boethius: particular substance	Example: man, horse, animal Boethius: universal substance
in subiecto	Example: a certain white Boethius: particular accident	Example: knowledge Boethius: universal accident

Figure 1

The ontology of the *Categories* begins from a distinction Aristotle has noticed between two types of predication (predication is here of things, not words).[3] One type is described by sentences such as 'Socrates is a man'. Such a predicate is 'said of a subject' (*dicitur de subiecto*). What is said of a subject, Aristotle explains, is not 'individual and numerically one' (1b6; *AL* 48: 5); moreover, when A is said of a subject B, then not only is the statement 'B is A' true, but it will remain true if for 'A' is substituted the definition of the item A introduces.[4] The other type of predication is described by sentences such as 'Socrates is white'. Such a predicate is 'in a subject' (*in subiecto*). Something is in a subject, according to Aristotle (1a24–5; *AL* 47: 23–4) when 'it is in something not as a part, and it is impossible that it is without that in which it is'. The second condition (inseparability) is – as will emerge – open to various interpretations.[5] Using these two technical terms Aristotle makes (1a20–1b9; *AL* 47: 19 – 48: 7) a fourfold division of 'those things which are' (*eorum quae sunt*)'. The scheme can be set out as in figure 1.

Boethius' labels (*commentary on Categories* 170BC and ff.) are a useful shorthand, but each of the four divisions requires comment. A reader might be tempted to add to the list of examples of particular[6] substances a table,

[3] For my discussion of the *Categories*, I have relied heavily on J. Ackrill, *Aristotle's 'Categories' and 'De interpretatione'* (Oxford, 1963); K. Oehler, *Aristoteles: Kategorien* (Berlin, 1984) (Aristoteles Werke in deutscher Übersetzung I, 1); Graham *Aristotle's two systems*, pp. 20–36. In my discussion I give the Latin terms used in the composite Boethian translation (*AL* I, 1–5, pp. 47–79) which was the version studied by Abelard and most of his contemporaries (see above, p. 37, n. 2); any significant divergences between this (close) translation and Aristotle's Greek are noted.

[4] 1b10–16; 3a18–20 (*AL* 48: 8–12, 51: 8–10); cf. Ackrill, *Aristotle's 'Categories'*, p. 85; Oehler, *Kategorien*, pp. 180–1.

[5] See below, pp. 120–2.

[6] The terms 'particular', 'individual' and 'singular' can cause confusion, since they are sometimes used synonymously and sometimes with different meanings. In this book, 'particular' will be used throughout as the correlate of 'universal': so we might say, for instance, that 'everything is either *particular* or universal; nominalists argue that there is nothing which is not *particular*.' In considering how one particular is separated from another, the term

for instance, or a house. But an unstated assumption behind Aristotle's discussion is that man-made things are not to be considered substances. The treatment of universal substances is clearly anti-Platonic, since Aristotle makes not them but particular ('primary') substances the basis of his ontology: 'All other things are either said of the primary (*principalia*) substances or are in them as subjects. If then [primary][7] substances did not exist, it is impossible that there should be anything else: for everything else is either said of them as subjects, or is in them as subjects' (2b3–6; *AL* 49: 21–5). Yet universal substances, though dependent, are for Aristotle in the *Categories* unquestionably among 'what there is'; although they lack numerical unity, they are none the less things.

Aristotle's account of particular and universal accidents has been the subject of much recent controversy. According to the traditional interpretation (which is the most obvious way of taking the text) the relationship between universal and particular accidents parallels that between universal and particular substances. The white in Socrates is particular, not because it differs in shade from other whites, but because it is the white which is inseparable from the particular substance, Socrates; by contrast, the universal accident white is in the universal substance snow. According to this reading, then, particular accidents are individuated by the particular substances to which they belong. The traditional interpretation was available to the Middle Ages through Boethius, though he does not keep to it consistently;[8] other, more recent interpretations are only tangentially relevant to the twelfth-century discussions.[9]

The *Categories* develops this basic ontology in two main ways. First, accidents are divided into nine groups – quantity, quality, relation, where, when, posture, having, doing and being-done-to[10] – which, along with sub-

'individuate' will be used ('Are particulars *individuated* by their accidents?'). Abelard himself used the terms *particulare*, *individuum*, *singulare* and their cognates synonymously: see J. Gracia, *Introduction to the problem of individuation in the early Middle Ages* (Munich/Vienna, 1984), p. 243, n. 8.

[7] The composite translation leaves out 'primary' here, whereas Boethius' own one more accurately includes it (*AL* I, 1–5: p. 8: 12). But the sense remains obvious.

[8] See below, p. 121.

[9] See esp. G. Owen, 'Inherence', *Phronesis* 19 (1965), 97–105 (particular accidents as ultimate specifications of a characteristic – e.g. this exact shade of white); M. Frede, 'Individuals in Aristotle' in his *Essays*, pp. 49–71 at pp. 50–63 (a translation of an article written originally as 'Individuen bei Aristoteles', *Antike und Abendland* 24 (1978), 16–39) (a more radical reinterpretation).

[10] These are literal translations of the terms found in the composite Boethian version (cf. chapter 2, n. 2): *substantia*, *quantitas*, *qualitas*, *ad aliquid*, *ubi*, *quando*, *situs*, *habitus*, *facere*, *pati* (*AL* 48: 21–2).

stance, make up the ten categories from which the treatise takes its name. Aristotle's discussion of these categories one by one occupies most of the book; his treatment of some of them (quantity, quality and relation) raises various questions which will be examined in later chapters.[11] Second, Aristotle expands his account of universal substances. Universal substances are, he explains, either 'species' or 'genera'. Any particular man is in the species Man, whilst the genus of the species Man is Animal (2a16–17; *AL* 49: 3–4). Aristotle treats each of these (particular substance: species; species: genus) as instances of the same, transitive relationship – not so much a sign that he confuses class inclusion and class membership, as that he has not consistently thought out the semantics of species and genera in class (or any other) terms.[12] (The terms 'species' and 'genus' are used relatively: so – to give an example not in the text – Animal, which is the genus of Man, is also a species of Living Thing). A few passages indicate that Aristotle has in mind a many-levelled hierarchy of genera and species: they are ones where he mentions *differentiae*.

A *differentia* is an attribute which distinguishes a given species from other species belonging to the same genus. In the scheme Aristotle implies, each species will have just one ultimate *differentia* which distinguishes it in this way. That *differentia* will also belong to every species subordinate to it, but to no species not subordinate to it; so that, for someone who knows the hierarchy of genera and species, any species can be identified just by its ultimate *differentia*.[13] Aristotle clearly has in mind a scheme whereby all particular substances belong to natural kinds, which are identified according to the scheme of genera, species and *differentiae* ('naturalism'). He also he also appears to assume that, at least in principle, we unproblematically identify the members of each kind (this might be called 'strong naturalism').

But this does not explain how *differentiae* fit into Aristotle's *ontological* scheme. The reason is that they do not really fit in at all! *Differentiae* are not substances, but Aristotle also refuses to class them as accidents, insisting that they are said of a subject and not in a subject.[14] Nor does Aristotle say

[11] See below, pp. 134–5, 135–6, 143–4.

[12] See 1b10–16 (*AL* 48: 8–12); cf. Ackrill, *Aristotle's 'Categories'*, p. 76; Graham, *Aristotle's two systems*, pp. 31–2.

[13] See 1b10–24, 3a34–b9; *AL* 48: 8–19, 51: 19–52: 3; cf. Oehler, *Kategorien*, pp. 193–5. The matter is more fully treated in *Metaphysics 'Z'*, 12 (1037b8–1038a35); by the time he wrote *De partibus animalium*, Aristotle had given up the idea of a single ultimate *differentia*: see D. Bostock, *Aristotle 'Metaphysics' Books 'Z' and 'H'* (Oxford, 1994), pp. 176–84.

[14] 3a21–8; *AL* 51: 11–17; see Oehler, *Kategorien*, pp. 216–17 and esp. Ackrill, *Aristotle's 'Categories'*, pp. 85–7.

whether there are *differentiae* of species and genera in categories other than substance, from which his few illustrations are all taken.

Twelfth-century logicians always considered the *Categories* in conjunction with a short work by the Neoplatonic philosopher and logician, Porphyry. Whether or not Porphyry intended it as such, his *Isagoge* ('Introduction') was commonly taken as an introduction, not to logic in general, but to Aristotle's *Categories* in particular.[15] Porphyry's approach to Aristotelian logic is the result of a complex series of developments.[16] Porphyry was the devoted pupil of Plotinus, the founder of Neoplatonism, but he was willing to differ from his master in his treatment of logic. Plotinus criticized Aristotle's doctrine of the categories, because it gave an inadequate account of reality. Porphyry, however, was willing to accept the *Categories*, and the other treatises of the *Organon*, but only conditionally. The truths about the intelligible world revealed by Platonic philosophy are not to be found within Aristotelian logic; nor should they be sought there, because its purpose is different. Aristotelian logic, Porphyry believed, does not offer a study of how things really are, according to the Platonic view. Rather, it is based on human language which, he thought, itself signifies concepts, common to all people, formed from the objects of sense-perception. Genus-words and species-words ('animal', 'man') would, then, have been taken by him to refer to concepts abstracted from particulars; and *differentia*-words would analyse and provide a means of ordering these concepts.

The *Isagoge*, however, was written as a text for beginners: it gives few clues to Porphyry's distinctive semantics and leaves itself open to diverse interpretations. The treatise is designed to explain the nature of genera, species, *differentiae*, *propria* and accidents. These are five different sorts of 'predicable': each can be predicated of a subject ('Socrates is an animal/man/rational/capable of laughter/white'). In his discussion of genera and

[15] Cf. Boethius *2inIs.* 143: 11–12 (and ff.): 'titulo enim proponit Porphyrius introductionem se in Aristotelis Praedicamenta conscribere'. Twelfth-century commentators invariably took the same view: e.g. P14, Abelard *sup.Por.* 2: 21–3. On Porphyry's real intentions, see C. Evangeliou, *Aristotle's Categories and Porphyry* (Leiden/New York/Copenhagen/Cologne, 1988). References to the *Isagoge* are to *Busse* and to Boethius' translation (L. Minio-Paluello (ed.) (Philosophia antiqua 48) *AL* I, 6–7, *Categoriarum supplementa* (Bruges/Paris, 1966), pp. 5–31); a useful English translation, with notes, has been made by E. Warren (Toronto, 1975) (Mediaeval sources in translation 16).

[16] The following paragraph is based especially on S. Ebbesen, 'Porphyry's legacy to logic: a reconstruction' in Sorabji, *Aristotle transformed*, pp. 141–71 (= S. Ebbesen, *Commentators and commentaries on Aristotle's Sophistici Elenchi* I (Leiden, 1981) (Corpus latinum commentariorum in Aristotelem graecorum 7, 1), pp. 133–70). See also Evangeliou, *Aristotle's Categories* and A. Lloyd, *The anatomy of neoplatonism* (Oxford, 1990), pp. 1–75.

differentia	***genus/species***		***differentia***
	substance		
corporeal	body	incorporeal substance	*incorporeal*
having a soul	living thing	non-living body	*not having a soul*
having sense-perception	animal	plant	*not having sense-perception*
rational	rational animal	irrational animal	*irrational*
mortal	man	(pagan) god	*immortal*

Porphyry follows the Aristotelian view that all living things have a soul.

Figure 2

species, Porphyry fills out the hierarchy suggested by Aristotle in the *Categories* (see figure 2).[17]

Unlike Aristotle, Porphyry recognizes that particular substances do not themselves belong to this hierarchy,[18] and his language suggests that he saw species as classes. He accepts Aristotle's strong naturalism at least as a presupposition about the world known through sense-experience. For this reason he has no difficulty in knowing when he has reached the *species specialissimae*, the most specific species which come at the bottom of his hierarchy: they are simply the various natural kinds. Whereas the classes which make up Porphyry's hierarchy (or 'tree', as it was known) are distinguished by *differentiae*, the particular members of each most specific species are distinguished by accidents.

The *Isagoge* gives brief individual discussions of *differentiae*, accidents and what he calls *propria* (*Busse* 8: 7 – 13:6; *AL* 14: 15 – 20: 15). For Porphyry, a *differentia* in the strict sense is an Aristotelian *differentia*, which distinguishes a species from the genus above it. Porphyry does not try to settle the problem left by Aristotle about placing *differentiae* in his ontology, but he talks about them rather as if they were a sort of universal accident. This view is especially strongly suggested by the fact that a *differentia* in the loose sense is described as a 'separable accident' and in the stricter sense as an 'inseparable accident'. Further overlapping occurs when Porphyry

[17] *Busse* 4.27–33, 10.3–17; *AL* 9: 24 – 10: 6, 16: 18 – 17: 10). Boethius brings these points together at *2inIs.* 208: 9 – 209: 6. Many of the early manuscripts include a diagram at this point similar to that given here (an example is reproduced in Brandt's edition, p. 209).

[18] *Busse* 5:12–15; *AL* 11: 1–4: 'specialissimum autem unam habet habitudinem, eam quae est ad superiora quorum est species, eam vero quae est ad posteriora non diversam habet'; cf. *Busse* 6:13–17; *AL* 12: 7–13.

introduces his definitions of four different types of *proprium*. *Propria* of the first three types seem to be accidents, which are marked out from other sorts of accident because they occur (1) only in one species though not to every member of it (being a doctor), or (2) in all members of a species but also in members of another species (being two-footed), or (3) only in one species, to every member but not all the time (man going white in old age). The fourth type, however, which is the 'proper' sense of *proprium*, occurs only in one species, to every member of it always: for instance, in man, the ability to laugh. Porphyry offers no explanation of why *propria* in this sense should be considered distinct from *differentiae*. There is, though, a grammatical difference in the way Boethius' translation presents *differentiae* and *propria*: *differentiae* as adjectives ('rational'), *propria* as noun clauses ('being capable of laughter').[19] This may suggest that *differentiae* are qualifications applying to classes, whereby their membership is restricted, whereas a *proprium* is an attribute belonging to members of given classes.

Porphyry's definition of 'accident' as 'that which comes and goes without its subject's being changed in substance' (*Busse* 12: 25–6; *AL* 20: 7–8: *quod adest et abest praeter subiecti corruptionem*) suggests that he is thinking primarily of particular accidents. He goes on to explain that there are two sorts of accident. Separable accidents seem, from his one example (sleeping) to be accidents of a sort which can apply to a given particular subject at some times but not at others. In the section on *differentiae* (*Busse* 8: 14–16; *AL* 14: 22–4) Porphyry had described inseparable accidents as those which are not separable in this sense: they always apply to the particular subject once it has them (such as being snub-nosed, or having a scar). He does not contradict that description here, but his examples (a crow's or an Ethiopian's being black) are instances where an accident is not merely inseparable from a substance but where, as a matter of fact, every substance of that type has an accident of this type. Even so, we can conceive of the substance, says Porphyry (*Busse* 13: 1–3; *AL* 20: 10–12), without this accident (we can conceive of a white crow, for instance).[20] Altogether, Porphyry's classification of *differentiae*, *propria* and accidents leaves many problems for its interpreters.

There is one of these interpretative problems which, to a twelfth-century reader, would have seemed the most fundamental. What are

[19] There are some instances, however, when Porphyry talks about *differentiae* using noun clauses or phrases: *Busse* 9:10, 12–13; *AL* 15: 20–21, 23–4: 'at vero aquilum esse vel simum vel rationale vel inrationale', 'nam rationale per se inest homini, et mortale et disciplinae esse perceptibile, at vero aquilum esse vel simum'. Moreover, the whole grammatical contrast is less obvious in the Greek.

[20] See below, pp. 130–1, for further discussion.

the *Isagoge* – and the *Categories*, which it was thought to introduce – about: language, thought, reality? Porphyry, as has been explained, had his own subtle theory, involving words, perceptions and concepts, which he applied to his logical work and to Aristotle's. Elements of his position were transmitted to the twelfth century in Boethius' commentary on the *Categories*, which is based on a (now lost) commentary by Porphyry.[21] Yet the twelfth-century logicians were rarely content to follow the view that the *Isagoge* and the *Categories* are primarily discussions of language and, thereby, indirectly of perceived reality which language signifies. They dutifully repeated Boethius' Porphyrean formula, that the *Categories* is a treatise about words, but words in so far as they signify things (commentary on *Categories* 160A: *de vocibus res significantibus*). For them, however, it served to point to a problem, rather than to solve it. Influenced by apparent discrepancies between remarks on the subject-matter of logic in Boethius' various commentaries, by their desire to give a word-by-word exegesis of the ancient logical texts, far more detailed than that offered by Boethius – and affected, too, by their understandable failure to grasp Porphyry's overall attitude to Aristotelian logic[22] – they began to ask themselves a more uncompromising question. Which is Aristotle or Porphyry talking about, words or things?

'IN VOCE' EXEGESIS AND THE YOUNG ABELARD

In the years immediately before 1100, some logicians who posed themselves this question began to answer it an equally uncompromising way.[23] They were not, as historians have thought, early exponents of the view that there is no thing which is not a particular – a view conventionally labelled as 'nominalism' ('nominalism' will be used in precisely this sense here and in

[21] See S. Ebbesen, 'Boethius as an Aristotelian commentator', in Sorabji, *Aristotle transformed*, pp. 373–91.

[22] They might have found a clue to this in the commentary on *Categories* 183D–184A, where Boethius explains why, since the *Categories* is concerned with words (*nomina*), primary substances are considered to be sensible rather than 'intellectible' (*intellectibiles*) substances, such as God and the soul. This remark is rarely followed up by twelfth-century commentators (although C12, Paris Bibliothèque nationale, lat. 7094A, f. 74r, does add a discussion about the relations between Platonic and Aristotelian positions).

[23] I shall provide a full discussion of the material considered briefly in this section in an article in preparation ('Exegesis, universals and ontology: Abelard and the approaches to logic at the turn of the twelfth century').

the rest of the book).[24] Rather, they were followers of a new method of interpreting the ancient textbooks. They tried to expound Porphyry's *Isagoge* and Aristotle's *Categories* as discussions entirely about words, not things – they taught logic *in voce* rather than *in re*.

A few anonymous commentaries bear witness to this approach;[25] and there are three logicians of the time who can be associated with it.[26] One is Abelard's early teacher, Roscelin (even if, later, he developed his views into a less purely exegetical theory). Another is Garlandus, who most probably wrote his *Dialectica* in the very early 1100s.[27] Roscelin's logic is known only through the remarks of his adversaries. But comment after comment in the *Dialectica* illustrates the *in voce* approach: 'we call that word "substance" along with the words placed beneath it a category'; ' "an accident is what comes and goes" [says Porphyry], that is, that word is called an accident which comes to the subject, that is to the substantive word'; 'the nature of words placed under Relation is . . .'[28] And, when he comes to define 'species', Garlandus explains that the word can be used in two ways: one applying to things, the other to words. It is with the second, verbal use of 'species' that philosophers are concerned.[29]

The third of these *in voce* interpreters is none other than the young Abelard himself. His earliest surviving commentary on the *Isagoge* (*ed.Por*) is close to Garlandus in its insistence on a purely verbal reading. Abelard probably used an existing commentary, close to one which still survives in a Munich manuscript (P7), as his basis.[30] This commentary itself uses the *in voce* method, but Abelard adds to it so as to make his *in voce* reading far more determined and explicit. For instance, whilst the earlier writer leaves it unclear whether, in defining *differentiae*, Porphyry is

[24] Even Yukio Iwakuma's fundamental new study attributes this nominalist view to them: 'Vocales, 37–111; cf. Reiners, *Nominalismus*, pp. 14–41, M. Tweedale, 'Logic (i): from the late eleventh century to the time of Abelard' in Dronke, *Twelfth-century philosophy,* pp. 192–226 at pp. 198–205.

[25] P4a (ed. Iwakuma, '*Vocales*', appendix III, 1, pp. 103–7); P4b (ed. Iwakuma in 'Vocales', appendix II, 1–2, pp. 107–10); P7 (ed. Iwakuma, 'Vocales', appendix II, pp. 74–100); notes on Porphyry at end of P7 in Munich, clm 14779, f. 36v (ed. Iwakuma, 'Vocales', Appendix II, pp. 100–2).

[26] For details of some earlier possible members of this school, such as the mysterious John, Roscelin's teacher, and Rainbert of Lille, see my forthcoming 'Exegesis, universals and ontology'.

[27] On Garlandus' *Dialectica* and its dating, see above, p. 41, n. 21.

[28] Pp. 5: 29–30, 10: 25–7, 31: 2.

[29] Pp. 7: 7–10.

[30] See above, pp. 38–9.

talking about words or things, Abelard makes it clear that Porphyry's discussion is verbal.[31] And Abelard carefully translates Porphyry's definition of an accident into verbal terms: '"An accident is", that is to say, that word is called an accident, which neither in its coming nor its going destroys its subject.'[32] Abelard was still an exponent of this method of interpretation, it seems, a few years later, when he wrote the commentary on the *Categories* (*Cat.frag.*) of which just a fragment survives. In one passage where, in his later *Categories* commentary he explicitly states that Aristotle is talking about things, not words, Abelard here insists on a tortuous verbal explanation.[33]

The *in voce* method of teaching was soon challenged. Commentators on the *Isagoge* and *Categories* recognized that there are statements in the ancient logical texts which provide authority for *in voce* interpretation, but they pointed out that there are as many which point in the other direction and suggest that Aristotle and Porphyry were talking about things.[34] Their criticisms were not based on authority alone. *In voce* interpreters were guilty, they argued, of ignoring the links between language and the world: not of having a mistaken ontology but of failing to have one at all. They insisted, by contrast, that the words which are the logician's primary object of study gain their functions and interrelations by virtue of the things they signify.[35]

This position has important consequences both for the method of exegesis and for its scope. It supports not a simple *in re* reading of the ancient texts, but a procedure which includes but goes beyond *in voce* exegesis. As a commentary (P14, probably by William of Champeaux or a pupil of his) explains, although Aristotle's primary intention in the *Categories* is to deal with words, this does not preclude him (or Porphyry) from sometimes transferring his discussion to things, since words gain their properties from things and so the nature of words is shown by a study of the nature of

[31] *Ed.Por.*, 29: 4–32: 'illa vox dicitur differentia qua abundat species ... Differentia est illa vox per quam ... ' on *Isagoge*, *Busse* 11: 1; *AL* 17: 16; cf. P9, ed. Iwakuma, 'Vocales', p. 93.

[32] 36: 13–15 glossing *Isagoge*, Busse 12: 25, *AL* 20: 7; cf. P9 (Iwakuma, 'Vocales', p. 97). Abelard also uses the *in voce* method in his commentary on Boethius' *De divisione* from the same period: see 'Exegesis, universals and ontology'.

[33] See *Cat.frag.* 58: 10–14; cf. *sup.Pred.*, 160: 29–30.

[34] For example: P3, version in Paris, BN, lat. 13368, f. 215r; P14, Paris, BN, lat. 17813, f. 2r, C8, Vatican reg. lat. 230, f. 41r. Dr Iwakuma kindly supplied a transcript of P3.

[35] For example, in the case of the ten categories (according to C8) 'Et quemadmodum sunt decem res communes quae omnium aliarum rerum principia sunt, sic etiam decem uoces sunt quae omnium aliarum uocum gratia rerum quas significant dicuntur principia esse.'

things.[36] A rationale is thus provided for reading the ancient texts as discussions of both words and things. At the same time, by accepting the links between the words which, as logicians, they consider and the things to which they refer, the opponents of *in voce* interpretation open the study of logic to the whole range of philosophical questions implicit in the *Categories* and so in the *Isagoge*. What, they must ask, is the nature of the things to which words such as *genus* and *species* refer? *In voce* interpreters (like Abelard in his early *Isagoge* commentary) could happily leave aside Porphyry's famous unanswered questions about universals, without even bothering to repeat Boethius' remarks on them. In these commentaries by their opponents, however, there are developed theories of universals – and ones which go far beyond mere repetition of Boethius: in C7 and C8 a collection theory, in P14 an indifference theory.

ABELARD'S EXEGETICAL PRINCIPLES

Both Roscelin, an *in voce* exegete, and William of Champeaux, one of his fierce opponents, were Abelard's teachers. Abelard quarrelled with each of them; and, whilst he usually referred to William's positions in logic with respect, those of Roscelin were the object of his mockery. Yet historians in this century have tended to see Abelard both as beginning from a position in logic close to Roscelin's, and as going on to refine and develop it in his mature logical works.[37] By contrast, Abelard's quarrel with William of Champeaux is generally presented, not merely as political and personal, but also as a conflict of radically opposed approaches to logic – William's realism against Abelard's nominalism.[38]

[36] Paris, BN, lat. 17813, f. 2r: 'Volunt tamen quidam Porphyrium agere de his uocibus que sunt "genus", et "species" et cetera, uel de uocibus significatis ab istis, id est de hac uoce "animal", hac "lapis" et cetera – ponentes hanc causam, quod liber iste introductio ad *Predicamenta* in quibus agitur de uocibus. Set non ualet, quia tanta afinitas est inter res et uoces quod uoces contrahunt suas proprietates ex rebus, et ideo per naturam rerum familiariter ostenditur natura uocum. Inde etiam Aristoteles considerat de uocibus transferendo se ad res. Per naturam rerum multociens aperit proprietates uocum. Item cum predicamentum aliud reale, aliud uocale sit, recte per naturam unius declaratur proprietas alterius.'

[37] After the study by Reiners, *Nominalismus*, esp. pp. 57–8. Nineteenth-century scholars had wrongly attributed to Abelard a 'conceptualist' position, envisaged as a compromise between realism and what they regarded as the 'nominalism' of Roscelin; although, for Victor Cousin, at least, Abelard's conceptualism was a moderated nominalism rather than a genuine compromise with realism.

[38] 'Realism' is used here in the traditional way as a label for those who hold that there are universal things.

Certainly, Abelard appears to have followed Roscelin's *in voce* method in his earliest logical teaching, when he was already competing with William. Yet, when Abelard emerges as a mature logician in his *Dialectica* (probably based on his teaching in the period *c.* 1113–16), he has adopted an interpretative approach very close indeed to that of William (as seen in P14) and the other opponents of *in voce* exegesis. He no longer tries to interpret every statement in Aristotle, Porphyry and Boethius as being about words. Rather, he considers that many parts of their discussion can be read in two ways: as being about things and as being about words. For example, at the beginning of his section on relatives in the *Dialectica* (83: 2–32) Abelard explains that *ad aliquid* can be taken either as a name of other words (of e.g. 'fatherhood', 'sonship') or as a word for things (principally for relations themselves, such as fatherhood and sonship). When Abelard explains the thinking behind this procedure (in the section on *differentiae* of the *Logica*), his rationale is exactly that of William and the realists:

For, even though properly the things themselves, that is to say rationality and mortality, are said to differentiate substantially and by species, because they make that to which they attach (*adveniunt*) into a substance of a given species, none the less, thanks to the things, the words (*vocabula*) too, which are imposed according to the things, are called *differentiae*. (70: 27–31)

The terms of logic have the properties they do thanks to the things which they signify. What is needed, therefore, is a dual method of exegesis. An *in voce* reading of the ancient texts is possible and useful, but it makes sense only when supported by an *in re* interpretation.

Abelard, however, adds another twist to this interpretative method. Not every passage in the *Isagoge* and the *Categories*, he believes, can be read as being about both things and words. Some apply only to things, others only to words. He continues the remark about *differentiae* quoted above by observing that

certain things are discussed about *differentiae* which properly apply only to the things <which are *differentiae*> – such as when it is said that they are qualities or forms which make a thing something else by attaching to it; but some remarks are properly applied to the words <which are *differentiae*> – such as when it is said that they are predicated of many and that they make up divisions and definitions. (70: 32–6).

Abelard exercises this option to choose whether real or verbal interpretation is suitable – or whether both are – not just in discussing *differentiae*, but wherever in logic the question seems to him to arise. For instance, in his reading of Porphyry's section on accidents, both in the *Logica* and the *Glossulae*, he takes most of what Porphyry says to apply to accidents as things, but says that his final, negative definition (*Busse* 13: 4–5; *AL* 20: 13–14) applies rather to the words for accidents.[39]

In one important way, however, Abelard differed from William of Champeaux and the realists. When he wrote the *Logica* (*c.* 1119), Abelard was a clear and thoroughgoing exponent of the view that universals are not any sort of things, but merely words.[40] That is to say, there are no real genera or species – universal substances – nor any real universal accidents or *differentiae*. Abelard appears already to have held this position a few years earlier, when he wrote the *Dialectica*, although he is not so consistent there in maintaining it.[41] The view may have links with the *in voce* method Abelard learned from Roscelin, but its basis is in argument about the nature of things, not exegetical method. As Abelard explains in the *Historia calamitatum* (65: 80–91), he met William on his own philosophical ground and showed that his analysis of universal things was self-contradictory. What Abelard's own position was at the time of this conflict (*c.* 1109) – or if he had one – is not known; but over the following years, he developed arguments against each of the various analyses of universals as things proposed by his contemporaries, and in the *Logica* he used these arguments to support the conclusion that universals are not things at all.[42]

Abelard's denial that there are universal things was a striking and unusual position and, despite some recent doubts, it is almost certain that it provided the name by which Abelard's followers came to be known: *nominales*.[43] Yet Abelard's theory of universals could be accommodated

[39] *Sup.Por.* 93: 34–5: 'Postquam definivit accidens in designatione rerum, definivit ipsum in designatione vocum'; cf. *Glossulae* 577: 27–9: 'Data diffinitione accidentalium formarum, ad ultimum ponit diffinitionem* accidentalium nominum, dicens, "ACCIDENS, id est accidentale vocabulum, EST QVOD" . . .' (*MS, Geyer *differentiam*).

[40] See below, pp. 174–5.

[41] The *Liber Partium* – the first part of the *Dialectica*, dealing with the material of the *Isagoge*, in which universals would have been discussed in detail – is lost. But there are some cross-references back to it. For example, at *Dial.* 88: 18–28, Abelard says that in the *Liber Partium* he has shown how, whereas the words (*vocabula*) 'Socrates' and 'man' are different, the essences of the things to which they refer are not. The 'substance of species is not diverse from the essence of particulars', and species can subsist only through their particulars. This, Abelard adds, applies also to forms (accidents and *differentiae*) (the *in* in 88: 26 should be deleted if the passage is to make sense). For an instance in *Dial.* where Abelard does slip into talking as if universals were real, see 90: 5–9.

[42] See below, p. 174 n. 2.

[43] The connections between the problem of universals, nominalism and Abelard's followers were challenged by M.-D. Chenu, *La théologie au douzième siècle* (Paris, 1957), pp. 95–107; C. Normore, 'The tradition of mediaeval nominalism' in J. Wippel (ed.), *Studies in medieval philosophy* (Washington, 1987) (Studies in philosophy and the history of philosophy 17), pp. 201–17; W. Courtenay, ' "Nominales" and nominalism in the twelfth century' in J. Jolivet, Z. Kaluza, A. de Libera (eds.), *Lectionum varietates. Hommage à Paul Vignaux (1904–1987)*

easily within the exegetical framework he had adopted and developed from William of Champeaux and the realists. According to this method, some passages from the *Isagoge* and *Categories* are to be read as discussing words, some as discussing things, some as discussing both. If Abelard had thought – as most nominalists have done – that properties and relations must be universal and so cannot be things at all, he would have been forced to read almost all of these two texts – everything except for the passages on particular substances – as being about words, not things. But in fact Abelard readily accepted the idea that these are particular *differentiae* and accidents though not universal ones (strange though this would probably have seemed to Aristotle), arriving at an ontology similar to that of modern exponents of 'tropes' or 'abstract particulars' – though with the very important difference that he also admits particular substances into his ontology.[44] It was, therefore, only those passages dealing with species and genera which he *had* to insist were ones about words only, although he also found that some of the passages on *differentiae* and accidents (especially *propria*) were best interpreted as being about universals, and therefore about words. By giving a further twist to his exegetical method, Abelard could also explain why certain passages in the ancient texts and Boethius' commentaries give the impression that universals are things. Sometimes, he says, logicians transfer from talking about words to talking about 'their things' – that is, in the case of genera and species, the particular things belonging to such and such a genus or species. Failure to notice such shifts of meaning, Abelard believes, has led many interpreters astray.[45]

(Paris, 1991), pp. 11–48); but see now: C. Normore, 'Abelard and the school of the *nominales*', Y. Iwakuma, 'Twelfth-century *nominales*: the posthumous school of Peter Abelard' and J. Marenbon, 'Vocalism, nominalism and the commentaries on the *Categories* from the earlier twelfth century', all in *Vivarium* 30 (1992) at pp. 80–96, 97–109, 51–61.

[44] Christopher Martin ('The logic', p. 112) has noted the connection between Abelard and such twentieth-century theories, remarking that 'he may be characterised in contemporary terms as a transferable trope anti-realist'. I am very grateful to Dr Martin for sending me a copy of a longer, unpublished version of this paper, which contains a very illuminating discussion of Abelard's ontology in these terms.

[45] *Sup.Por.* 30: 17–28: 'Notandum vero, quod licet solas voces definitio universalis vel generis vel speciei includat, saepe tamen haec nomina ad res eorum transferuntur, veluti cum dicitur species constare ex genere et differentia, hoc est res speciei ex re generis. Ubi enim vocum natura secundum significationem aperitur, modo de vocibus, modo de rebus agitur et frequenter harum nomina ad illas mutuo transferuntur. Unde maxime tractatus tam logicae quam grammaticae ex translationibus nominum ambiguus multos in errorem induxit non bene distinguentes aut proprietatem impositionis nominis aut abusionem translationis. Maxime autem Boethius in Commentariis hanc confusionem per translationes facit.'

In the logical works of his early maturity, then – the *Dialectica* and the *Logica* – Abelard regarded the whole of the *Isagoge* and the *Categories* apart from Porphyry's chapters on species and genera and Aristotle's remarks on second substances as, in principle, interpretable about things as well as (or in some cases rather than) about words. The following chapters will explore the ontology which he developed on this basis.

But there is one apparent objection to reading Abelard as putting forward such an ontology. On two occasions in the *Logica*, he makes a remark which has been interpreted by some historians to mean that he did not think that the *Categories* provides a guide to how things are, but merely an analysis of the structure of language.[46] What Abelard says is that the tenfold division of the categories is based 'rather on the meaning of words than the natures of things. Had Aristotle considered the natures of things, there is no reason why he should not have discerned more, or fewer, categories' (*sup.Pred.* 116: 35 – 117: 2 and ff.; *sup.Por.* 54: 32–4). In itself, this statement is not entirely clear, but in the light of his whole approach to the categories it is easy to see at least what Abelard is *not* saying. He is not questioning the reality of the distinction between substances and non-substances, nor the basis in reality of Porphyry's hierarchical tree: nothing in his writings would support such an interpretation. Nor is he suggesting that particular accidents (which Aristotle classifies into nine categories) – such as this whiteness, that being-six-foot-tall, this smoking-a-cigar – are not real, non-substance things. Indeed, did he not consider them real things, his comment about Aristotle's classification of them would make no sense. Rather, Abelard is arguing that, from the 'natures of things' – by which he must mean here: according to the characteristics which these accidents really have – accidents might be classed into more, or into fewer categories. It is unclear whether by this Abelard means (1) that there is a correct classification of accidents into categories, but neither he nor even Aristotle knows what it is, or (2) that there is no single way of classifying accidents which is in principle the correct one. (2) is perhaps more likely, since it is hard to see from Abelard's detailed discussion of the categories what criteria there *could* be for a correct classification

[46] E.g. M. Tweedale, *Abailard on universals* (Amsterdam/New York/Oxford, 1976), p. 94 (after quoting the comment from *sup.Pred.*): 'On Abailard's view the doctrine of categories is basically semantic rather than ontological'; J. Coleman, *Ancient and medieval memories* (Cambridge, 1992), p. 239 (before quoting the comment): 'Aristotle is not interested in how things "are" but rather how *language* signifies the properties of things, according to Abelard.'

of accidents.[47] Abelard goes on to say that the tenfold classification *does* correctly reflect the meanings of words.[48] This is not, however, a sign that he will be attending especially to language, but rather that he is aware of its limitations. A classification of accidents into more or fewer than nine categories would require the invention or redefinition of words. Since the exact classification of accidents into categories is of little importance to Abelard's ontological scheme, he is willing to go along with Aristotle's ordinary language distinctions and, in practice, pass over some categories of accident with hardly a mention, whilst attending carefully to distinctions within accidental categories such as those between discrete and continuous quantity or between the four types (*maneriae*) of quality.

[47] When he wrote the *Dialectica* (80: 9 – 81: 6) Abelard apparently believed that Aristotle had arrived at his ten categories as the result of some insight into the nature of things which was now hidden, since Aristotle's full discussion of six of the categories was unavailable. A relic of this discussion is preserved at *sup.Pred.* 258: 20–2 where, having explained how it is not always clear to things in which category certain words refer, Abelard remarks, not without sarcasm: 'Soli itaque auctoritati concedendum est de numero praedicamentorum, quorum potuit rerum naturas distinguere, quas nec cogitare valeamus.'

[48] *Sup.Por.* 54: 32 – 55: 3: 'Sed fortasse cum proprietatem inventionis decem generum diligenter attendamus, secundum eam decem generum multitudinem bene esse institutam inveniemus, in quibus, scilicet decem generibus, omnium aliorum, tam generum quam specierum, significationes incipiant quasi in supremis eorum principiis'; cf. *sup.Pred.* 117: 2–7.

Chapter 5

Substance, *differentiae* and accidents

THREE PRINCIPLES

Three principles underlie Abelard's ontology: nominalism, strong naturalism, and a very strict view of the separateness of particular things. What do they each involve and how do they relate?

Nominalism

Abelard's nominalism is to be understood as it was defined in the previous chapter: the view that there is no thing which is not a particular. It is hard to tell to what extent the view was among his deep philosophical intuitions, to what extent he reached it through force of circumstances – the early influence of *in voce* exegesis and the need to find a clear point of difference between his position and that of established teachers such as William of Champeaux. But Abelard's nominalism was certainly explicit, and he supported it with a series of detailed arguments against each of the current views which recognized universal things.[1]

Strong naturalism

Abelard took over the strong naturalism he found in the *Categories* and in his out-of-context reading of the *Isagoge*. Like Aristotle, he accepts that the world is made up of members of natural kinds, and that we unproblematically know to which kind any given particular substance belongs. He also conveniently ignores those natural kinds, like water, where the individuation of particular members is problematic. Like Aristotle, too, Abelard believes that every member of a given natural kind has the same

[1] See below, p. 174 n. 2.

underlying structure, which can be described in terms of genera, species and *differentiae*.

But how can this be, when Abelard is a nominalist and so does not accept that there are universal things? On one level this question is quite easily answered. Abelard regards *differentiae* as particular things, which attach to particular substances in somewhat the same way as particular accidents attach. He was probably led towards this position by the uncertainty over *differentiae* in the *Categories*, by Porphyry's overlapping and confusing classifications of *differentiae*, *propria* and accidents, by Boethius' suggestion that *differentiae* are non-accidental qualities,[2] and by the semantics of denomination commonly accepted at the time.[3] Porphyry's tree of genera and species is therefore seen as offering, not a hierarchy of universals, but an analysis of the structure of particular substances of different kinds from particular *differentiae*. The way Abelard develops this idea will be studied in the next section.

On a deeper level, however, the combination of naturalism with nominalism poses a very severe difficulty for Abelard, which it is not clear that he overcomes despite his reinterpretation of Porphyry's tree and various other moves. While *some* views about natural kinds would entail realism, there is no incompatibility in principle between acceptance of natural kinds and nominalism; but the question is whether Abelard developed a position which would make way for such a combination, or rather ones which tended to exclude it. This question will be considered in the discussion of Abelard's theory of universals. It cannot be answered until the main lines of his ontology, semantics and epistemology have been examined.

There are also two other ways in which Abelard modifies or develops the strong naturalism he found in his sources. First, he makes explicit what Aristotle had merely implied: that only the particulars belonging to natural kinds are substances, not objects which have been put together by human artifice. As he explains (*Dial.* 417: 23–37), human artificers do not create, they merely put together what has already been created. They do not therefore produce any new substances, but merely make accidental alterations

2 Commentary on *Categories* 191D–192D. Boethius (192B) says that a *differentia* is made (*conficitur*) from substance and quality: it is distinguished from a simple quality because its substance cannot continue to exist without it. Heat, which is an accident of water, is a *differentia* of fire because, if the heat ceases, so must the fire. Abelard, recalling this passage (*sup.Pred.* 154: 34–9), takes it to mean that *differentiae* are qualities, but they are not accidental qualities, since they make the substance the sort of substance it is.

3 See below, pp. 139–41.

to substances.[4] Second, according to Abelard, although we place substances in their kinds without difficulty, we often do not know *what* the *differentia* is which distinguishes members of one species from members of another species belonging to the same genus. For instance, we do not know the *differentia* which distinguishes stones from other sorts of corporeal, non-living substances.[5]

The separateness of particular things

Since Abelard holds that all things are particular, his view of individuation is very different from that of a philosopher for whom it would make sense to talk of a principle of individuation individuating a singular from a universal. For Abelard it must be a basic, unanalysable truth that every thing, whether a substance or a 'form' – to use the convenient term employed by Abelard and his contemporaries to cover both *differentiae* and accidents – is separate from every other thing. Accidents do not individuate substances, nor are forms individuated by the substances to which they are attached; indeed, any given form might have been attached to a different particular substance from that to which it is in fact attached. Since this is one of the more important facets of Abelard's nominalism, it is worth looking carefully at the texts where he develops the idea.

In his *Logica*, Abelard argued powerfully against the theory current in his time that substances are individuated by their accidents.[6] His own view is that substances are individuated simply by being 'personally discrete (*personaliter discretae*) in their essences'. He means by this, as he explains, that even if all the *differentiae* and accidents attaching to a particular substance were removed, that substance would be still be one particular, separate (*discreta*) from any other particular.[7] There is, then, no principle of

[4] *Sup.Pred.* 298: 33–6: 'hominum autem operatio alterare tantum materiam videtur secundum accidentia, veluti dum domum componit vel gladium, non etiam in substantiam generare'.

[5] See below, p. 236.

[6] See Gracia, *Problem of individuation*, pp. 204–10. Gracia analyses Abelard's arguments very clearly and shows that Abelard succeeded in demonstrating the incompatibility between accidental theories of individuation and the Aristotelian distinction between substance and accident.

[7] *Sup.Por.* 13: 18–25: 'Unde alii aliter de universalitate sentientes magisque ad sententiam rei accedentes dicunt res singulas non solum formis ab invicem esse diversas, verum personaliter in suis essentiis esse discretas, nec ullo modo id quod in una est esse in alia, sive illud materia sit sive forma, nec eas formis quoque remotis minus in essentialis suis discretas posse subsistere, quia earum discretio personalis – secundum quam scilicet haec non est illa – non per formas fit, sed est per ipsam essentiae diversitatem.' Gracia (*Problem of*

individuation for substances: their separateness is ultimate and unanalysable.[8] What about forms? Abelard uses their distinctness (*diversitas*) from each other as an argument against the need to individuate substances by their accidents. Forms must simply be distinct from each other in themselves, since if they were individuated by other forms this would generate an infinite regress: so why cannot substances also be individuated simply in themselves? What is remarkable here is that Abelard does not even seem to consider the possibility that forms are individuated by the substances to which they belong.

Two passages, one about *differentiae* and the other about accidents, bring out most explicitly Abelard's assumption that forms are particular in themselves and not in any way individuated by substances.[9] In the *Logica* he explains that Socrates (the stock medieval example for a particular man) might have been a man by a particular rationality other than that which, in fact, is his – either by one which did or does exist, or by one which might have existed but did not.[10] That is to say, Abelard envisages a set of men ($M_1 \ldots M_n$), a set of particular rationalities ($r_1 \ldots r_n$) and any number of hypothetical rationalities (r', r" ...). In the actual world, M_1 is informed by r_1, M_2 by r_2 and so on. But the world might have been different so that, for instance, M_1 was informed by r_2, or by *r*'. Similarly, Abelard says that the particular whiteness which makes this body white might have in fact made a different body white, although once in this body it cannot be in another (*sup.Pred.* 129: 34–6).

Abelard's view that accidents, too, enjoy this sort of separateness and qualified independence is brought out in his discussion of the inseparability condition for accidents proposed in the *Categories*. Aristotle had said that what is in a subject cannot be without that in which it is.[11] As a statement

individuation, p. 212) shows clearly that, although Abelard proposes this position tentatively, it must be his own.

8 Cf. Gracia, *Problem of individuation*, p. 211.

9 Christopher Martin has drawn attention to this aspect of Abelard's thought: see 'Logic of the *Nominales*', p. 112 and cf. above, p. 114, n. 44.

10 *Sup.Por.* 84: 14–21: 'Cum autem rationalitatem differentiam dicamus, ea autem non sit nisi haec vel illa rationalitas, oportet hanc vel illam esse differentiam. Sed profecto omnis differentia de specie universaliter dicitur praedicari et, destructa ea, necessario destrui res. At vero haec rationalitas pluribus non inest neque propter eam homo periret. Ipse quoque Socrates, sicut hic homo est per eam, ita etiam posset esse per aliam, sive quae sit, sive numquam sit'; cf. 92: 22–9: 'Sic enim rationalitas adest huic homini, ut non corrumpatur, et sic posset hic homo sine ea esse, ut ideo non corrumperetur ... Posset etiam fortassis contingere, ut sic ista careret, quod aliam rem habuisset et nunquam istam, et ideo numquam per istam corrumperetur.' For the passage omitted [...], see below, p. 129, n. 30.

11 See above, p. 102.

about universal accidents, its meaning is fairly clear: there can be no colour which is not in a body, or no knowledge which is not in a mind. Its meaning is less clear, however, in connection with particular accidents, and Boethius' commentary only complicates the issue. Some of his remarks suggest that Boethius thought particular accidents are individuated by their subjects.[12] If they were individuated in this way, then it would be logically impossible for any particular accident to exist without its subject: the accident would be this particular accident (Socrates' whiteness) just on account of belonging to this particular subject (Socrates). Yet Boethius proceeds (commentary on *Categories* 172D–173A) to interpret the inseparability condition in a much weaker sense, saying that an accident (he seems to have in mind a particular accident) 'cannot be disjoined from that in which it is'. This interpretation leaves it open to think that, in principle, a given particular accident need not be attached to what is in fact its subject, although, once attached, it cannot leave it and continue to exist. Boethius goes on (173B) to offer an even weaker interpretation of the inseparability condition. He observes that when someone's hand smells of the apple which it has just held, the smell, which is an accident of the apple (a particular accident, though Boethius does not bother to state this explicitly), has passed from one subject, the apple, to another, the hand. What Aristotle must mean then by his inseparability condition, Boethius concludes, is merely that an accident cannot exist without some subject or other, although it can change its subject. He justifies this interpretation by pointing out that 'Aristotle did not say that it was impossible for [an accident] to be without that in which it *was*, but without that in which it *is*.'

Abelard is understandably scathing about this piece of reasoning (*sup.Pred.* 130: 21 – 131: 9): if it were the case that the smell, now in the apple, would in the future pass to a different subject, then it would not now be true of this smell that it is impossible for it to be without that – the apple – in which it is. But, although Abelard rejects Boethius' weakest interpretation of the inseparability condition, his own is close to Boethius' fairly weak version, based on inseparability after conjunction. According to Abelard, Aristotle's inseparability condition means (*sup.Pred.* 129: 31–4): 'the nature of accidents cannot allow that, when accidents have once been in something, they might be able to exist (*subsistere*) afterwards without it'.

[12] E.g. commentary on *Categories* 170A: 'si vero dixero Platonis scientiam, quoniam omne accidens quod individua venit individuum fit, particularem scientiam dicit, namque Platonis scientia, sicut ipse Plato, particularis est'; 172A: 'Non autem dico quod ipsa grammatica particularis est, sed quod quaedam grammatica, id est alicujus hominis individui grammatica, quam scilicet homo particularis propria retinet cognitione.'

'Had Aristotle simply said that an accident cannot be without its subject', Abelard continues (*sup.Pred.* 129: 33–6), 'then perhaps he would have been wrong. For it seems that the whiteness of this body – which is in fact innate in this body (*quando huic corpori innata est*) – might have come to other bodies in the same way.' A few lines later (130: 6–9) he makes his position completely clear. Abelard explains that, although this particular whiteness, as it happens, belongs to this subject (say, Socrates), it might have belonged to another particular subject (say, Plato): if that had been the case, then it would have always belonged to Plato, and never have belonged to Socrates. What nature cannot allow is that an accident should change its subject – that having been Socrates' accident it should then become Plato's.[13]

Before going on to see in more detail how Abelard uses these principles in working out an ontology, it is worth pausing to ask, first, why he should have adopted them, and second, whether the view of the world they offer is a strange one. The answer to the first question is simple. The principles follow quite naturally from Abelard's nominalism combined with his intention (shared by almost all the logicians of his time) to expound the *Isagoge* and the *Categories*. The second question is more difficult. It can be posed in a non-historical or an historical way. It is not in the least strange to suggest, like (on a plausible interpretation) the Aristotle of the *Categories*, that there are real universal properties and relations which are individuated by the particular substances to which they belong; although a modern realist might prefer to do without particular properties and relations and regard properties and relations as being, by their very nature, universal. Abelard's world, where there are no real universals, but there are real properties and relations, each particular in itself irrespective of the substance to which it belongs, is harder to conceive; and even Abelard himself, it will become clear, came eventually to change his mind and think that relations and some other sorts of accident could not be given this much independence.[14] True, there are some modern philosophers who base their ontology on (just) particular properties, relations (and events); but they do not, with Abelard, also admit particular substances which are essentially differentiated.[15] As the

[13] *Sup.Pred.* 130: 6–9: 'Posset fortasse contingere ut, cum huic subiecto advenerit, alii advenisset, et ita semper in alio esset quod numquam huic contigisset. Sed non potest natura pati, cum iam alii insit, in alio iterum sit: hoc est, subiectum mutare non potest de uno transeundo ad aliud.'

[14] See below, pp. 155–61.

[15] Modern philosophers use various names for such particulars, such as 'tropes' or 'abstract particulars'. G. Stout argued along these lines early in this century; see especially 'Are the

following pages will show, Abelard would run into perhaps insurmountable difficulties trying to reconcile his view of the particularity and independence of forms with his idea of particular substances. As for Abelard's contemporaries, they all thought in terms of substances and forms. In general they accepted the existence of particular forms but, because they were not nominalists, they also accepted the existence of universal forms. Only rarely do they write in a way which makes it clear that they are referring to a particular form rather than a universal one;[16] and Gilbert of Poitiers, writing in the 1140s, the one major logician of the time who made serious use of particular forms, seems to have learned from Abelard's difficulties in developing his own, highly sophisticated theory of how substances are individuated.[17]

RETHINKING PORPHYRY'S TREE

Although Aristotle, and more emphatically Porphyry, had concentrated their attention on examining the hierarchy of genera and species, neither writer had ruled out the idea of a similar hierarchy in each of the other nine categories. For Abelard, who used Porphyry's tree as a way of analysing the constitution of particular substances, the idea that particular *differentiae* and accidents might have their own *differentiae* would have produced

characteristics of particulars universal or particular', *Proceedings of the Aristotelian Society* suppl. vol. 3 (1923) 114–22. For a recent, fully worked out version of such a theory, see K. Campbell, *Abstract particulars* (Oxford, 1990). It was, I believe, Christopher Martin (see above, p. 114, n. 44) who first noticed the parallel between Abelard's ontology and modern trope theory; the argument in this book will suggest that the parallel is less close, however, than Martin apparently holds – see below, pp. 197–201.

16 For instance, here are two examples from the late eleventh-century *Glosule* to Priscian in which undoubtedly particular forms feature (Philippus Pincius's Venice, 1500 edition of the *Institutiones*, f. 4r): 'sicut continua albedo parietis una dicitur quae in diuersis fundatur; non quia illa albedo quae huic parti adiacet sit illa indiuidualiter quae in alia parte fundatur, sed quia similis est et eadem specie iudicatur uocari eadem'; (ff. 24v–25r) 'hoc nomen "Socrates" dicunt [quidam] nomen esse substantiae et accidentium quibus formatur, scilicet albedinem, lineam, Sophronisci filiationem et cetera accidentia quae informant Socratem'.

17 On Gilbert's ontology, see J. Marenbon, 'Gilbert of Poitiers' in Dronke, *Twelfth-century philosophy*, pp. 328–52; L. de Rijk, 'Gilbert de Poitiers: ses vues sémantiques et métaphysiques' in Jolivet and de Libera, *Gilbert de Poitiers*, pp. 147–51, 'Semantics and metaphysics in Gilbert of Poitiers: a chapter of twelfth century Platonism', *Vivarium* 26 (1988), 73–112, 27 (1989), 1–35; Henry, *Medieval mereology*, pp. 180–4. Henry is under the mistaken impression that Gilbert is innovating by giving a major role to particular forms in his ontology; Marenbon 'Gilbert of Poitiers' (see esp. pp. 342–3) argues wrongly that theological considerations alone explain this role.

intractable difficulties, and he is quick to rule it out. There is no hierarchy of genera, species and *differentiae* for accidents, Abelard claims, and offers the following argument. Since *differentiae* themselves belong to the category of quality, if there were *differentiae* for the species and genera of all the categories, then for instance rationality, a *differentia* of man, would itself have a *differentia*, which would be a quality and would itself have a *differentia*, and so on *ad infinitum* (*sup.Por.* 86: 38 – 87: 38). Abelard seems to assume (wrongly) that, having shown that one of the categories of accident has no *differentiae*, it follows that only substance has them.

Consider, then, the one hierarchy admitted by Abelard: that in the category of substance as illustrated by Porphyry's tree (see figure 2 on p. 106 above). If this hierarchy is to be taken as an analysis of particular substances, the position of substance at the top of the tree is problematic. It would seem to imply that each particular substance consists of bare, particular substance plus various particular *differentiae*; so Socrates would be particular substance, plus particular corporeality, being alive, having senses, rationality and mortality. But what is bare substance? It would not be surprising if Abelard wanted to avoid an ontology which rested on so mysterious a notion, and in much – though as will emerge, not all – of his discussion, he managed to do so. His strategy relied on the bold step of making body, not substance, the starting point for his account of things. He then analysed body, not as substance plus the *differentia* bodiliness (as in Porphyry's scheme) but, rather, in physical terms.[18]

A result of this approach is that non-corporeal substances are almost entirely squeezed out of Abelard's ontology. But this consequence is tolerable for him because there are just two sorts of incorporeal substance in his view (since God is not a substance at all).[19] One sort consists of angels – but Abelard says almost nothing about them. The other sort comprises souls. Abelard was a convinced dualist. He thought that each man's (or animal's) body is one substance and his soul another, distinct substance. (He knew, through Calcidius's commentary on the *Timaeus*, of Aristotle's view that the soul is a form, not a substance, but he rejected it (*sup.Pred.* 212:

[18] In his discussion of abstraction in *sup.Por.* (25: 6–14; and cf. *sup.Per.* 329: 10–19), however, Abelard does speak of joining together bodiliness and substance. But this does not need to imply that he thinks of bodiliness as an individual *differentia*. The context here is psychological: clearly, I can regard a man merely as a substance, or as a bodily substance, or as a living thing, whether or not he has a particular form of bodiliness in the way that he does have a particular form of being-alive. For further discussion of this passage, see below, p. 189.

[19] See *TSch* 137: 609–138: 628; *TChr* 239: 1428 – 241: 1506 = *TSch* 446: 1205 – 449: 1267.

37–213: 5) as wrong – and not Aristotle's! – arguing that a form could not have qualities such as madness and anger.) He accepted, however, following the tradition of Aristotelian logic, that 'animal' and 'man' refer to bodies, which are ensouled, not to a composite substance, body and soul, which would be both corporeal and incorporeal.[20] In order to explain how we can talk about an animal having sense-perceptions or a man having knowledge, when sensing and knowing are really activities of the soul, Abelard suggested (*Dial.* 556: 21 – 558: 5) that the words for distinctively animal or human capabilities and activities are ambiguous. A word like *sensibilitas* (being-able-to-perceive-with-the-senses) refers both to a form in the category of Quality which belongs to human and animal souls, and a form in the category of Having, which belongs to human and animal bodies because they have such a soul. There are, however, some distinctively animal or human activities such as walking, eating and smelling which, unlike sense-perception or knowing, we always describe as being performed by an animal, never by its soul. But Abelard argues (*TChr* 296: 1003 – 297: 102; *Glossulae* 549: 6–11) that when we say 'An animal walks/eats/smells' this really means that the animal is being moved and stirred (in a certain way) by its soul. These ingenious linguistic analyses allow Abelard to escape saying anything very definite about the soul itself as an incorporeal substance.

Abelard's physical account of body is linked to his understanding of creation. He distinguishes between two types of creation.[21] First creation (*prima/prior creatio*) is the bringing into being of that which did not exist at all.[22] Accidents and incorporeal substances are created simply in this way (*sup.Pred.* 298: 15–19). And so was the matter from which particular bodies are made: it was nothing at all until God, in a manner beyond description

[20] Abelard makes it clear that the usual sense of 'man' is ensouled body at *Glossulae* 547: 20–37; cf. 549: 2–3. Abelard does indeed consider that there is a sense of 'man' in which it means a composite of two substances, and he tries to tackle the problems this raises in the Porphyrean scheme of things, since such a composite substance would be neither corporeal nor incorporeal: *sup.Por.* 48: 10 – 49: 11, *Glossulae* 547: 39 – 549: 3; cf. *TSum* (176: 535–8) and *TChr* (290: 853–9). The same problem also concerned Abelard's contemporaries: for instance, the earliest version of the quite widely disseminated *Isagoge* commentary (P3), in Oxford, Bodleian Library, Laud. lat. 67, dating perhaps from even before 1100, has a lengthy discussion of it (f. 11va: to SVBSTANTIA EST QVIDEM – 9: 19), which is taken up and rejected in the revised version of the commentary in Paris, BN, lat. 13368, f. 218vb.

[21] Abelard expounds his position most clearly in quite closely parallel passages of *Dial.* (418: 5 – 421: 11) and *sup.Pred.* (297: 41 – 299: 10) adding a few extra details in *Exp.Hex.* which, although written much later (probably *c.* 1133–4), keeps to the same view.

[22] *Sup.Pred.* 298: 3: 'quod cum prius omnino non esset, ad esse perducta est'.

(*ineffabiliter*), created it *ex nihilo*. Abelard looked to the beginning of Genesis in order to gain a better idea of this as-yet-unformed matter. He interpreted it in the Platonic manner which had been current since patristic times, though without making detailed reference to the *Timaeus* (perhaps because Abelard developed this theory in the context of his logic, before the period in which he became seriously interested in Plato).[23] The Bible refers to God's first creation of unformed matter when it says, 'In the beginning God created heaven and earth': by 'heaven' and 'earth' is meant all four elements, from which all bodies are made.[24] The Bible talks of the 'face of the abyss', and the poets and philosophers of 'chaos', because the elements were all mixed together into a confused mass (*Exp. Hex.* 735AB; *Dial.* 419: 6–12). The fact that the elements are confused means that Abelard does not have to admit the *differentiae* of each element (such as heat for fire) into primordial, unformed matter. Second creation (*secunda/posterior creatio*) occurs when matter, which has already been created, is made into different sorts of things through the forms (particular *differentiae*) which are added to it 'as when bodily substance becomes living through being-alive (*animatio*), or an animal through having-sense-perception (*sensualitas*) or through other forms becomes a member of one or another species – an ass or a man'.[25]

By distinguishing between two creations in this way, Abelard makes it clear that his analysis of things (which, for him, are all particular things) is not as each being particular substance plus the particular *differentiae* which make it into the kind of thing it is, but rather as body plus particular *differentiae*. Body is distinct from the *differentiae*, not merely as a matter of

[23] For a general survey of twelfth-century cosmogony and its Platonic and Calcidean background, see T. Gregory, 'The Platonic inheritance', in Dronke, *Twelfth-century philosophy*, pp. 54–80; B. Stock, *Myth and science in the twelfth century* (Princeton, 1972); J. Parent, *La doctrine de la création dans l'école de Chartres* (Paris/Ottawa, 1938). On Abelard's developing attitude to Plato, see above, pp. 56–7, 95.

[24] *Exp.Hex.* 733C; cf. *Dial.* 419: 3–6.

[25] *Sup.Pred.* 298: 6–10: 'eas vero creationes secundum quas materiam iam praeparatam per formas supervenientes in species diversas natura redigit, posteriores appellamus, veluti cum corpoream substantiam aut per animationem facit animatam aut per sensualitatem animal aut per alias formas in quascumque species variaret, ut in <asinum> vel hominem'; *Dial.* 419: 13–16: 'Secunde vero creationes sunt, cum iam creatam materiam per adiunctionem substantialis forme novum facit ingredi esse, veluti cum de limo terre hominem Deus creavit. In quod quidem nulla materie novitas, sed solius forme videtur diversitas.' By attributing this second creation to 'nature' in *sup.Pred.*, Abelard does not contradict his view that both types of creation are the work of God alone. By the work of nature, Abelard means the work of God, as he explains a few lines later (298: 32: 'non hominis opus est, sed naturae, id est Dei'); cf. *Exp. Hex.* 746 CD.

analysis, but temporally. There was a time, Abelard believes, at the creation of the world before second creation had taken place, when there was body, made up of the four elements, to which as yet no *differentiae* had been added. In the *Dialectica* (340: 30–4), he uses this idea to reject the necessity of the statement 'If every body is a body, every man is a body' – because there was a time when the antecedent was true, but not the consequent, because there were as yet no men. Abelard also believes that in the case of any bodily thing now, it is true to say that it was body before it was a man, a horse or whatever: 'this body', as he puts it in the *Logica* (*sup.Pred.* 298: 17–20) 'was first body before it was a living thing, an animal or a man'. Again, in the *Glossulae* (564: 19–21; cf. *Glossae secundum vocales* 191), Abelard remarks that, properly speaking, 'body is the matter of a man, because it precedes the man in time and precedes the forms of man as their subject'.

Abelard takes great care to make clear that, chronologically, the stages of creation are just the two he has mentioned: the creating of body, and the creating of particular substances by simultaneously adding all the *differentiae* needed to make them a substance of a given kind – a man, a horse, a stone. It would be wrong, Abelard emphasizes, to think that there ever could be, for instance, an animal which was simply an animal in general, and not an animal of a certain species. Although the ancient texts sometimes read in a way which suggests this – when they speak, for instance, of rationality 'coming to' or 'being added to' an animal and making man – Abelard insists that these remarks cannot be taken literally.[26] What 'rationality comes to an animal and makes a man' means is simply: a man exists as a subject through rationality cohering with an animal'.[27]

[26] *Sup.Por.* 68: 38 – 69: 6: 'Vel forte dicamus philosophos, cum ad doctrinam loquuntur, saepe res aliter accipere quam res sese habeant, veluti cum animalis substantiam quasi in se absque inferioribus differentiis subsistentem prius attendimus eique postea differentias animo nostro coniungimus, ordinem naturalem constituendae speciei insinuamus prius quidem animalis substantiam quasi materiam supponentes, deinde formam aptantes, tandem speciem componentes. Quae ergo simul natura composuit, quasi simul non essent, ratio distinguit.'

[27] *Sup.Por.* 68: 36–8: '... solvemus, dicentes scilicet nil aliud esse rationalitatem advenire animali et hominem facere quam hominem subsistere per rationalitatem animali cohaerentem'. Abelard also brings out the same point when he considers Porphyry's (*Busse* 11: 13–18; *AL* 18: 9–15) rather confusing analogy between the matter and form (e.g. the bronze and the shape of a statue) and the genus and *differentiae* of a substance (e.g. animal, and rationality and mortality, of a man): see *sup.Por.* (78: 24–81: 38) and *Glossulae* (564: 3 – 567: 9; closely paralleled in *Gl.sec.voc.* 190–3). For Abelard's contemporaries and predecessors, the idea of genus as matter and *differentiae* as forms was a key to solving the problems, noted by Boethius and Porphyry himself, posed by the definition of *differentia*

From these reinterpretations of Aristotle and Porphyry, there might seem to emerge the outlines of a fairly coherent ontology – of what could be called 'bundled particulars'. Particular *differentiae*, bundled together in the groupings set out in a much elaborated version of Porphyry's tree, attached to a body would produce particular corporeal substances. On this view, 'man' and 'beast' would be shorthand terms for 'a body informed by being-alive, having-sense-perception, mortality and rationality' and 'a body informed by being-alive, having-sense-perception, mortality and irrationality', whilst 'animal' would be a term which allows us to refer to a body informed in either of these ways without distinguishing them as they are in fact always distinguished.

What remains unclear in this putative ontology is how we can talk of 'a body' rather than 'body': either we must imagine that there simply are many bodies, essentially individual, or else think of particular *differentiae* individuating the original mass of body, not as a universal into particulars – there is no universal body – but as a whole into parts. This question turns out, however, to be purely hypothetical, since Abelard does *not* accept this ontology of bundled particulars, though many elements in his discussion imply it. Despite the large degree of independence he gives to particular *differentiae*, Abelard insists that particular substances are the basic building-blocks of reality. Not merely are substances essentially individuated (*not* individuated by their *differentiae*); they each have an identity apart from their *differentiae*.

Abelard's fullest presentation of this substance-based view occurs in a passage from the *Dialectica*, which follows on from his account of first and second creation.[28] Here Abelard advances three loosely formulated claims,

as 'that by which a species exceeds its genus' (*qua abundat species a genere*; *Busse* 11: 1; *AL* 17: 16; cf. Boethius (*2inIs.* 263: 2 – 265: 12)). See e.g. P3, earliest version in Oxford, Laud. lat. 67 (f. 13rb): 'Verum est quidem quod genus informatum differentiis desinit esse genus, et fit species; sed tamen cum duae res faciant speciem sua coniunctione, scilicet materia et forma, in ipsa coniunctione possunt ratione discerni quid sit ibi materia quae genus est, et quid forma quae est differentia, et etiam in ipsa coniunctione adhaeret differentia generi ut suo fundamento'; cf. f. 10ra: 'speciem nihil aliud esse quam genus formatum, et individuum nihil aliud esse quam speciem formatam' (Yukio Iwakuma discusses this comment and its background in 'The "realism" of Anselm and his contemporaries', a modified translation of his 'Abaelardus izen no fuhen ronsou (Universal controversy before Abelard)', *Zinbun* 60 (1986), 105–60); and P14, Paris, BN, lat. 17813, f. 12r–v. In the *Dialectica*, Abelard too occasionally lets himself adopt this way of regarding things: 'animal makes up man materially, but rationality and mortality make him up formally' (560: 2–3).

28 420: 30 – 421: 8: 'In quibus quidem <*sc.* primis et secundis> nature creationibus generales ac speciales constitute sunt substantie. Neque enim forme mutatio diversitatem specierum aut generum facit, sed substantie creatio. (1) Quocumque enim modo varientur forme, si

which he does not clearly distinguish (the numerals refer to the parts of the passage given in the footnote): (1) substances each have an essence which has its own identity, independent of any *differentiae*, and which is what makes them belong to one or another species or genus; (2) although it is through a *differentia* that substances of one species differ from those of another, this happens because of the diversity of the substances of the things which they [the *differentiae*] make; (3) only what the working of God has put together in the nature of a substance is part of 'specific or general nature'. In support of (1), Abelard proposes two other cases (1*) where, more obviously, diversity does not depend on diversity of *differentiae*: the distinction between the *genera generalissima* (presumably the ten categories), and that between types of accidents.

Clearly, Abelard had not entirely sorted out his thoughts when he wrote this passage (and he even includes turns of phrase which are awkward for a nominalist). What is most important to observe is that (1), (2) and (3) make claims in descending order of strength for the independence of substance; and that (1), the strongest of the claims, is borne out by other passages in later works. When Abelard is putting forward his view of the individuation of substances, he says not only that each substance is essentially individuated from every other, but that 'even if all their forms were removed from them, they could none the less subsist in what is essential to them':[29] Indeed, on one occasion he is willing to push this view even further, although he never explores its implications. He allows as a possibility that a particular substance, which is in fact a man, might never have been rational at all.[30] Since Abelard considers that there could never be a man who lacked rationality, he must be supposing here that particular substances have an identity which is prior to the kind of thing they are: so that we

identitas manserit, nichil ad essentiam generalem vel specialem agitur. (1*) Cum autem et forme nulle diverse sint, diversa tamen poterunt esse genera, ut sunt generalissima in sue discretione substantie, aut fortasse quedam species, ut de speciebus accidentium infinitatem vitantes concedimus. (1) Quamdiu itaque essentia materialis nature in se diversa atque aliud ab alia fuerit, diversa contingit esse genera vel species. Diversitas itaque substantie diversitatem generum ac specierum facit, non forme mutatio. (2) Nam etsi in speciebus substantie specierum diversitatis causa sit differentia, hoc tamen ex rerum diversitate substantie quam faciunt, contingit. Vnde etiam substantiales sunt appellate huiusmodi differentie que, in substantiam venientes, et discretionem substantie faciunt et unionem communis nature. (3) Neque enim alia in speciali aut generali natura concludimus nisi ea que in natura substantie divina univit operatio.'

29 See passage quoted above, n. 7.

30 *Sup.Por.* 92: 24–7: 'Posset enim contingere ut haec substantia hominis numquam rationalis fuisset, ideoque numquam corrumperetur propter rationalitatem, cum eam numquam habuisset.'

can meaningfully say: 'This substance, Socrates, might not have been a man at all but an elephant.'

All in all, Abelard's substance-based view is less clearly worked out than his ontology of bundled particulars and does not seem to cohere with it. Perhaps the exegetical framework in the course of which Abelard developed his ontology may have helped to prevent him from grasping and tackling this uncertainty in his thought.

DISTINGUISHING BETWEEN ACCIDENTS AND 'DIFFERENTIAE'

Many though they are, particular *differentiae* make up only a small proportion of the forms (non-substance particulars) which, along with particular substances, are the two types of thing which Abelard recognizes. The other forms he usually calls 'accidents'.[31] How does Abelard explain what distinguishes (particular) *differentiae* from (particular) accidents (including *propria* which, following Boethius, Abelard regarded simply as a special sort of accident)?[32] Before answering this question, it is important to be clear that Abelard's distinction between *differentiae* and accidents is not one between forms considered in themselves, but between forms considered in relation to the substances to which they belong: for example, heat is a *differentia* of fire, but an accident of a man – that is to say, the particular form of heat attaching to the fire blazing in my grate is a *differentia*, whereas the particular form of heat attaching to me is an accident.

Porphyry had left the difference between *differentiae* and accidents rather uncertain, but it is his definition of 'accident' which provides Abelard with the starting point for his own attempt to draw a distinction. Porphyry had defined an accident as 'that which can come to its subject and be absent from it without its subject's being changed in substance' (*Busse* 12: 25–6; *AL* 20: 7–8). Porphyry was careful to frame this definition in terms of

[31] Abelard and his contemporaries considered Porphyry's position to have been that 'accident' means 'form which is not a *differentia*'. Abelard also recognizes (in common with some of his contemporaries: e.g. P3, version in Paris, BN, lat. 13368, f. 223ra; P14, Paris, BN, lat. 17813, f. 14ra) that Boethius used 'accident' in a wider sense than Porphyry, to include every sort of non-substance, including therefore *differentiae* (*sup.Por.* 83: 24–37); and that there is a way in which Porphyry's definition of accident itself might be read which would make it fit Boethius' definition (*sup.Por.* 92: 21–33).

[32] Porphyry did not make the relationship between *propria* and accidents clear, but Boethius (*2inIs.* 276: 3–11) recognized them as accidents, and Abelard followed him (*sup.Por.* 88: 2–5; *Glossulae* 574: 1–2).

possibility, which he explained using the idea of conceivability: we can conceive of a crow or an Ethiopian changing colour but remaining the same in substance.[33] Porphyry's definition therefore implies the following criterion for distinguishing *differentiae* from accidents. If 'F' is the word for a form, and 'S' is a substance word:

(C1) F is a *differentia* of S if and only if it is impossible (= inconceivable) for S to be S without F.

With slight rephrasing, the same criterion can be put into terms acceptable to someone like Abelard, for whom all substances and forms are particulars

(C2) An F is a *differentia* of an S if and only if it is impossible (= inconceivable) for an S to be an S without an F.

Usually, Abelard is able to use something like (C2) as his implicit criterion (C2). By the time he wrote the *Glossulae* (though not earlier: see below), Abelard is able to use a criterion of this sort to distinguish even being-able-to-laugh (*risibilitas*), the stock example of a *proprium*, from a *differentia*. Although (so it was assumed) all men always have the ability to laugh, a man's *risibilitas* is an accident because 'there could indeed be a man who did not have the ability to laugh since human nature would none the less remain, even if a man's face could not make the movements of laughter' (575: 9–11; cf. *Gl.sec.voc.* 202).

There are, however, some forms which, although not *differentiae*, are not distinguished from *differentiae* by a criterion like (C2). Boethius had drawn attention to them in his *De divisione* (881BC). Besides accidents separable from the substances to which they belong 'in act and by reason', such as sitting (Porphry's 'separable accidents'), and those which can be separated from their subjects by reason, though not in act (Porphyry's 'inseparable accidents'), Boethius then mentions a third class of accidents: those which cannot even be separated from their subjects by reason, such as being-able-to-count as an accident of men. Being-able-to-count is not a *differentia* of man, yet a man would cease to be a man were this ability removed from him.

Abelard reacts to this difficulty in two different ways. The first (*sup.Por.* 90: 19–91: 3) is a desperate attempt to keep (C2) by extending the notion of conceivability beyond the limits of human reason. When Boethius talks of accidents which are inseparable by reason, he means 'by human reason', says Abelard. Ability to count is separable from human nature, although we

[33] See above, p. 107.

cannot understand how: 'There are certain things which can be discerned by reason, certain things which should be taken on authority – the reasons for which, unknown to us, were perhaps known to those who affirmed them and handed them down in their writings.'[34] Abelard's second way is bolder. He accepts that forms of the sort in question, such as ability to count, are absolutely inseparable by reason (not just by human reason) from the substances to which they belong. In the *Logica*, he is not sure whether or not such forms can be called 'accidents'. Perhaps, he says (*sup.Por.* 91: 33–42; cf. *sup.Pred.* 166: 35 – 167: 10), those accidents which are inseparable even by reason should not be called accidents in Porphyry's sense, that they can leave their subject without their subject's changing in substance; and he gives as examples not only ability to count, but also unity, being (sexually) conceived, having a body and having a soul – none of them a *proprium* but all inseparable even by reason from man. These forms, he suggests, are neither accidents nor *differentiae*.[35] In the *Glossulae*, by contrast, Abelard goes to great lengths to interpret Porphyry's definition of accident in such a way that these forms are included in it.[36]

Whether or not he calls these strictly inseparable forms 'accidents', Abelard is certain that they are not *differentiae*. But what criterion is he using to distinguish them? In the *Logica* (*sup.Por.* 91: 11–32) he explains with regard to ability to laugh (which at this stage he included along with ability to count as being inseparable even by reason from a man), that 'a man does not require (*exigit*) it, from the fact that he is a man (*ex eo quod est homo*)'. So, whilst such inseparable forms *do* satisfy (C2) – which therefore ceases to be the criterion for being a *differentia* – they fail to satisfy

(C3) An F is a *differentia* of an S if and only if, from the fact that the S is an S, it requires an F.

Abelard offers some analogies to explain what he means by the idea of requiring here. The clearest one concerns substance. No substance can exist which is not corporeal or incorporeal, but a substance is not required to be

[34] In his discussion here, Abelard includes ability to laugh as an example along with ability to count. But (as the discussion above shows), by the time he wrote the *Glossulae*, he had come to a different view about *risibilitas* and was able to explain how we could conceive a man without the ability to laugh.

[35] He brings up the same idea in *sup.Pred.* 166: 35 – 167: 10 (where the text at 167: 1–2 seems to be corrupt).

[36] Unusually, *Gl.sec.voc.* 202–4 preserves a fuller and less garbled account of Abelard's reasoning about this than the *Glossulae* (576: 24–577: 7). The relevant text from *Gl.sec.voc.*, very badly edited by Ottaviano, is given in full in the appendix to Marenbon, 'Abelard, *ens* and unity', *Topoi* 11 (1992) – Passage B, pp. 157–8; for full discussion, see pp. 154–5.

corporeal or incorporeal from the fact that it is a substance. What this seems to mean is that being corporeal or incorporeal is not part of the meaning of 'substance', although it is impossible for substances to exist without being corporeal or incorporeal. This interpretation is confirmed by Abelard's use of the term 'requires' in his discussion of entailment. Abelard glosses (*Dial.* 253: 29) his view that for p to entail q, it is not enough that it is impossible that p & $\neg q$; p must also 'require' q, as: 'from the sense (*sensus*) of the antecedent (p), the meaning (*sententia*) of the consequent (q) must be required'.[37] When Abelard talks about 'requiring', then, he is not discussing possibility and necessity, but rather talking about meaning. (C3) should be interpreted as

(C3*) An F is a *differentia* of an S if and only if 'S' means a substance which has an F as its *differentia* or among its *differentiae*.

But (C3*) – Abelard's underlying implicit criterion for distinguishing *differentiae* from accidents – begs the very question Abelard wishes to answer. He does not think that it is merely a matter of linguistic convention that certain forms are regarded as the *differentiae* of certain substances, yet it is unclear how, according to (C3*), Abelard could show that rationality and mortality, but not ability to count, unity and having a head, are *differentiae* of a man, except by appeal to the normal meaning (among logicians) of 'man'.

ACCIDENTS, BODIES AND SENSE-PERCEPTION

For the most part, Abelard restricted his examination of accidents to those which could be simply distinguished from *differentiae* by an implicit criterion like (C2). His point of departure for these investigations was Aristotle's *Categories*. At the time he wrote the *Dialectica* and the *Logica*, Abelard held that as well as words which are accidents there are accidents which are things – particular forms – belonging to each of Aristotle's nine categories other than substance. To the particular substance Socrates, there is attached a multiplicity of accidental forms (this whiteness, that sleeping, this wearing a hat, that being a father and so on).

Abelard's treatment of these accidents as things is, however, disappointingly scant. The two varieties of accident he considers most carefully in this way are quantities and sensibly perceptible qualities. His remarks on them show Abelard trying to think beyond the slight suggestions found in Aristotle and Boethius about the constitution of things, but not always achieving coher-

[37] See above, pp. 44–5.

ence or making clear how these accidents fit into either of the two ontological pictures he develops in thinking about substances and *differentiae*.

In considering accidents of quantity, Abelard began from Aristotle's discussion in the *Categories* (4b20–6a35; *AL* 54: 17 – 58: 22). When, near to the beginning of the treatise (2a1; *AL* 48: 24) Aristotle gives a set of examples of the different categories, he chooses 'two-foot-long' and 'three-foot-long' as illustrations of quantities. This accords well with Aristotle's general view of accidents: just as it is an accidental feature of Socrates that he is white, so it is an accident that he is six-foot tall and twelve stone in weight. When, in the chapter on quantity itself, Aristotle is setting out the distinctive features of quantities, he again uses examples of just this sort. But, at the beginning of the section, when he is trying to classify the different varieties of quantity, he adopts a different approach. He names as quantities, not given measurements, but rather number, speech (*oratio*), lines, surfaces and bodies, and time and place. To a modern commentator, these may seem to be, not quantities themselves, but rather the things to which different types of quantity apply (for instance, lines are measured in inches, time in minutes, speech in syllables).[38] But Abelard did not read the passage in this way. He took Aristotle at his word when he said that lines and surfaces and the rest are quantities. A quantity is 'that thing by which its subject is naturally measured and its essence bounded'.[39]

Abelard and his contemporaries elaborated Aristotle's account of lines, surfaces and bodies by developing the notion of the point.[40] Aristotle mentions the point in order to show that lines are continuous, not discrete. In order to be continuous, the parts of a quantity must be joined by a common boundary, and the point is the common boundary of any two adjacent parts of a line (5a1–3; *AL* 55: 9–11). Some of Abelard's contemporaries (cf. *Dial.* 57: 35 ff.; *sup.Pred.* 180: 33 – 181: 14) followed this idea closely, and would accept points merely as boundaries of lines and, similarly, considered that lines were simply the boundaries of surfaces, and surfaces of bodies. But Abelard – following his master, William of Champeaux – insists, despite passages in Boethius ostensibly to the contrary, that lines are actually made

[38] See, for instance, Ackrill, *Aristotle's 'Categories'*, pp. 90–1.

[39] *Sup.Pred.* 168: 7–8; very similar at *Dial.* 56: 23–4. 'Quantity' can also be used to refer to other accidents which are in a substance as a result of quantity (e.g. length, multitude) or even to the substances which are the foundations for quantities; and 'quantity' can also be used as a word for other words – the words invented to designate quantitites (*sup.Pred.* 168: 9–19).

[40] Compare, for instance, the detailed discussion of points and lines in C8 (at Vatican Reg. lat., 230, ff. 52va–53va).

up of points, and surfaces are made of lines, and bodies are made of surfaces superposed one on another. The bodies made up in this way consist ultimately, then, of indivisible points, stretching in three dimensions.[41]

These bodies are not, however, those which Abelard discusses when he is considering substances in terms of Porphyry's tree. They are 'quantitative bodies', not 'substantial bodies'. Abelard may have taken the notion of quantitative body from the pseudo-Augustinian paraphrase of the *Categories*.[42] He merely implies the distinction between substantial and quantitative bodies in the *Dialectica* (60: 7), but makes it explicitly in the *Logica*, especially in his discussion there of place (*sup.Pred.* 189: 6–24). Abelard's remarks on the relation between the two different types of bodies are, however, not entirely clear. Abelard seems to suggest that, for each bodily substance at a given moment, there is a single accident of place which bounds both the substantial and the quantitative body, whilst the quantitative body itself also bounds and measures the substantial body.[43] In a rather strange passage, Abelard also suggests that a quantitative body consists of just three surfaces: an upper, a lower and a 'middle surface', which is attached to the middle of the substantial body (*media substantia*); because the middle of the substantial body has no parts, a single surface – Abelard believes – can fill it completely and join the upper and lower surfaces.[44] It is difficult to visualize exactly what he has in mind.

Abelard thought that accidents of quality, like colours, tastes and smells, are the only things we perceive directly with our senses, without any further

[41] *Sup.Pred.* 180: 18–26; cf. *Dial.* 57: 14–34.

[42] 183: 31–4: 'Quippe inter superficies ipsa fundamenta iacent, partes scilicet substantiales corporis quae non sunt de essentia quantitivi corporis.' See the pseudo-Augustinian paraphrase (*AL* 1: 1–5, p. 149: 15–17): 'Sin autem et altitudo fuerit mensurae sociata, corpus cuncta perficiunt; quod tamen non ita accipimus quemadmodum solemus accipere naturale, ne ad usian reverti videamur.' That Abelard used this work is shown by his direct reference to it at *Dial.* 70: 19 and *sup.Pred.* 218: 25–8. Evidence that the *Categoriae decem* continued to be studied in the twelfth century is provided by C18 (a twelfth-century set of collected glosses on the work) and the twelfth-century glosses to the text in Vatican, lat. 567.

[43] 189: 8–13: 'Sicut enim totum corpus suum habet locum sese terminantem et quodammodo ambientem, ita etiam superficies vel linea vel punctum; et cum corpus quantitativum vel quaelibet pars eius substantiale corpus tantum terminent et mensurent, ipsa iterum quae mensurant substantialia corpora locis terminantur et mensurantur et in ipsis tantum proprie et loca sunt nec nisi per ea substantiis subiectis insunt.'

[44] *Sup.Pred.* 183: 34–40: 'Sicut enim pars media substantialis corporis ad extremas continuatur, ita et superficies media duabus extremis conectitur. Quippe media substantia, cui media superficies adiacet, tenuissima est nec ullas in spisso partes habet. Unde superficies quae ei inest totam eam occupat, ut ex ista parte superiorem superficiem attingat – non interposito ullo fundamento – ex illa parte inferiorem.'

act of cognition being necessary (*sup.Por.* 95: 20–2). Yet he makes up his mind only slowly and uncertainly about the nature of these sort of accidents, beginning from the idea – linked to his notion of quantitative bodies – that these accidents are also corporeal. In the *Dialectica* Abelard seems to consider that colour is attached to the outer surfaces of the quantitative body. He worries that the presence of particles of, say, whiteness on a surface will mean that the points which make up the surface cannot be contiguous and so the surface will not in fact be a continuous quantity.[45] Perhaps, Abelard suggests, 'the nature of accidents is so subtle that one accident is no impediment to the continuity of another' (*Dial.* 60: 23–4): so, although these accidents are bodily things, they are bodily things of a strange sort to which the normal laws of physics might not apply. In the *Logica*, however, Abelard's considered position seems to be that even accidents like those of colour are incorporeal.[46] Yet he talks elsewhere in the *Logica* of 'particles' of whiteness, occupying a spatial position.[47] When he returns in the *Glossulae* to the problem which had troubled him in the *Dialectica* about accidents of colour breaking up the continuity of a surface, he confidently affirms that the whiteness, for instance, of a piece of ivory is not something which is 'in a place' – implying that it is incorporeal.[48]

[45] *Dial.* 60: 18–20: 'Sed fortasse dicetur nec punctum puncto continuari propter interpositum locum vel particulam aliquam coloris vel aliquid aliud indivisibile accidens.'

[46] The only manuscript of *sup.Por.* in fact reads (and is printed by Geyer) as if Abelard were saying here that accidents are *corporeal*. But even the immediate context shows that the word *corporea* must be a slip for *incorporea*. According to the text in the manuscript, the passage (95: 24–7) reads: 'Rationabilius enim videtur, ut cum anima quae sensus habet, res incorporea sit et ipse similiter sensus res sit incorporea*, vis eorum praecipue ad accidentia, quae similis sunt naturae, id est corporeae**, dirigatur.' As it stands, something is clearly wrong. Geyer chooses to emend the second *incorporea* (marked here with a single asterisk) to *corporea*, presumably to make sense of the *similis* which relates to the word; but this leaves *similiter* (*ipse similiter sensus*) at odds with what is being said. By accepting the MS reading of *incorporea* here, and emending *corporeae* (marked with a double asterick) to *incorporeae*, sense is made of the whole passage: since the soul is incorporeal, so are the senses which belong to it; and they are directed primarily to accidents, which like it, are incorporeal. The wider context puts the emendation to *incorporeae* beyond doubt. Abelard is arguing that what the senses perceive primarily are accidents, not bodies, and that (96: 1–3) did the accident of colour not exist, bodies would not be perceived at all; and, when Abelard is *contrasting* his view with Boethius, he remarks (96: 10–11) that, according to Boethius, 'it seems to be the case that bodies are perceived, not accidents'.

[47] Cf. *Sup.Pred.* 180: 4–6: 'Sed si de essentia non sunt [*sc.* puncta], quomodo magis partes lineae continuabunt quam particulae ipsae albedinis, quae similiter insertae sunt inter se?'

[48] 549: 16–20: 'Unde colligimus, quod albedo non locale quid, quia interpositione eius nulla partium adiacentium fit distantia. Quod ita percipi potest: nam, cum in eboris medio sit albedo, non tamen facit distantiam partium eboris circa adiacentium.' The idea is repeated

The most interesting side of Abelard's treatment of accidents lies elsewhere. Particular accidents in some of the categories, especially that of relation, posed Abelard difficult questions about the relationship between language and reality. In order to answer them Abelard was, arguably, led from the mid-1120s onwards to revise his whole theory about accidents and to decide that many sorts of accident are not real things at all. This development will be studied in the next chapter.

at *TSch* 529: 946 – 530: 948, where it is also made clear that the whiteness must be considered incorporeal.

Chapter 6

Forms and language

Abelard's ideas about language, and his closely related thinking about human perception and cognition, bear on his ontology in two distinct ways. Abelard held that every thing which exists is a particular substance or a particular *differentia* or a particular accident. He also recognized, as he could hardly fail to do, that universals play a central role in language and in thinking. How is the disparity to be explained? This, for Abelard, was the nub of the problem of universals, his treatment of which will be analysed in chapter 8, after his views on perception and cognition have been presented in chapter 7. But, in the course of thinking about ontology between the time of the *Dialectica* and the mid-1120s, Abelard decided that there was another disparity between language and how things are, which he had not earlier recognized. He now decided that there are accident words of various sorts to which no particular forms correspond in the world of things: many sorts of particular accidents which had featured previously in his ontology are therefore eliminated. But, as will emerge, Abelard only goes part of the way towards explaining how statements using these accident words remain able to assert truths about the world of things.

This chapter will trace and discuss this development. It will begin by describing the idea of 'denomination', much used in twelfth-century logic to analyse the meaning of statements. Although denomination could not play exactly the same part in his theory of predication as it could in that of realist contemporaries, Abelard too initially shared what might be called the 'semantics of denomination'. His change of mind about his ontology took the form of a partial repudiation of this semantics.

THE SEMANTICS OF DENOMINATION

Denomination was not an invention of early medieval logicians, but they attached far more philosophical importance to it than the ancient grammarians and logicians from whom they had learnt the doctrine.[1] Priscian explains that denominatives are words derived from nouns.[2] His interest is in classifying the different sorts of endings which are used to transform nouns into other words (usually adjectives), and vice versa. A common sort of transformation involves an adjective and the abstract noun which designates the quality it describes: for instance, *prudens/prudentia*; *tristis/tristitia; pius/pietas*.[3] Aristotle had mentioned denominatives briefly at the beginning of the *Categories* (1a13–15; *AL* 47: 12–14), describing them as 'what take their name from something just with a difference of ending' – as the grammarian ('*grammaticus*') is named from grammar ('*grammatica*'), the brave man ('*fortis*') from bravery ('*fortitudo*'). Boethius devotes a short passage in his commentary (167D–8D) to this remark. He draws out the implications of Aristotle's view, explaining that a denominative must 'participate' both in the same thing and the same word as that from which it is denominated, but that there must be some change in verbal form. So, for instance (168AB), with regard to the denominative 'courageous' ('*fortis*'), 'there is a certain courage in which the courageous man participates', and he has participation in the word ('courage') since he is called '*courage*ous'; but 'courage' and 'courageous' are not identical words – they have different endings.

Priscian's interest is clearly that of a grammarian in the derivation of words. Boethius' language is more philosophical, but he uses the notion of participation very loosely (to apply to verbal as well as real relationships). He seems to have included the discussion of denomination only because Aristotle mentions denominatives: he does not return to the concept elsewhere in this or other works. But, for late eleventh and twelfth-century scholars, denomination became a central concept for understanding the relationship between language and the world of substances, *differentiae* and accidents they learned about from their reading of Aristotle and Porphyry.[4]

[1] Two valuable studies of medieval discussions of denominatives are: J. Jolivet, 'Vues médiévales sur les paronymes', *Revue internationale de philosophie* 113 (1975), 222–42 = J. Jolivet, *Aspects de la pensée médiévale: Abélard, doctrines du langage* (Paris, 1987), pp. 138–58, and S. Ebbesen, 'Concrete accidental terms: late thirteenth-century debates about problems relating to such terms as "*album*"' in N. Kretzmann (ed.), *Meaning and inference in medieval philosophy* (Dordrecht/Boston/London, 1988), pp. 107–74, esp. pp. 107–15.

[2] Priscian, *Institutiones Grammaticae*, ed. M. Hertz, I, 117: 3–4: 'Habet igitur [denominativum] generalem nominationem omnium formarum, quae a nomine derivantur.' Book IV (I, 117–40) is devoted to discussing denominatives. (He is also concerned in this chapter with *verbalia*, words derived from verbs.)

[3] Priscian, *Institutiones* I, pp. 118: 1, 119: 12, 128: 6.

[4] One of the earliest medieval discussions of this problem is Anselm's *De grammatico*, which has been analysed in detail by D. Henry (*The 'De grammatico' of St. Anselm* (Notre Dame, 1964) (Publications in mediaeval studies 18), which is largely superseded by his fuller *Commentary on 'De grammatico'* (Dordrecht/Boston, 1974) (Synthese historical library 8);

Consider the position of an early twelfth-century logician faced by a Latin sentence of the form *Homo est albus*, *Socrates est albus* or *Socrates est pater* – a sentence in which a proper name or a substance word is joined by the copula (*est*) to an adjective, or to a noun which is not a substance word. Each of these sentences predicates an accidental attribute of its subject: that it is white (an accident in the category of quality) or that it is a father (an accident in the category of relation). But *'albus'* ('white (man)')[5] and *'pater'* ('father') are not themselves words for accidents. To what category then, the logicians asked themselves, do these words belong? The idea of denomination helped them to find an answer. *'Albus'* and *'pater'* do not themselves belong to any category, but they are both denominated from words which fit into one of the nine accidental categories: *'albus'* from *'albedo'* ('whiteness'), a quality; *'pater'* from *'paternitas'* ('paternity'), a relation. This denomination was not regarded by early twelfth-century scholars as merely a matter of language: it reflected reality. Whiteness and paternity are real non-substance things, the attachment of which to Socrates makes true the description of him as white and a father. Garlandus, writing at about the time Abelard was beginning his career, puts the position very clearly: 'Denominative words are not in a category, because they are not subjects since they cannot exist on their own (*per se*), nor are they in a subject, because they are predicated of those things in which <accidents> have their foundation. They are, however, in a subject in a secondary way, that is through their forms which are in the subjects in a primary way.'[6] Or, as a logician writing a decade or so later, puts it: 'it is through their denominatives that forms are able to be predicated of their foundations: for example, through "white thing" whiteness is predicated of its body, that is, its foundation'.[7] Denominatives do not merely include words for *accidental* qualities. 'Rational' and 'mortal', for instance, are denominated from

The logic of St Anselm (Oxford, 1967), pp. 31–116); but Anselm avoids any direct mention of the forms from which denominatives are denominated.

5 Note that the logicians of Abelard's time called both nouns and adjectives *nomina*, because Latin adjectives, which are inflected to indicate gender, always carry with them, as well as the attribute they signify, the sense of a masculine, feminine or neuter thing. *Socrates est albus* and *Socrates est pater* are therefore more closely parallel than 'Socrates is white' and 'Socrates is a father'.

6 *Dialectica*, p. 18: 1–4. This passage provides an exception to Garlandus' usual focus on words.

7 *Categories* commentary C8 (Vatican, reg. lat. 230, f. 43ra; Paris, BN, lat. 13368 has an almost identical text): 'Iterum dicendum est quod ipse forme per sua denominatiua de suis fundamentis habent predicari, ut albedo per 'album' de corpore suo, scilicet fundamento, praedicatur.'

'rationality' and 'mortality'. Denomination thus provides the link between language and an ontology which includes accidents and *differentiae* as well as substances.

Is not this semantics simply a type of grammatical Platonism? So scholars who have discussed twelfth-century theories of denomination have tended to consider it.[8] But Platonism involves the postulation of universal forms, existing apart from and prior to particulars. Although denomination was sometimes explained in terms of such forms, it did not need to be. The case of Abelard himself proves this point. In the *Dialectica* and the *Logica*, Abelard takes over the contemporary understanding of denomination whilst denying the existence of anything which is not particular.[9]

To take just one, explicit example: when discussing (*sup.Pred.* 270: 16–31) 'whiteness' and 'white thing', which is denominated from it, Abelard explains that 'whiteness' names (*nominat*) the form in its essence of being white (*in essentia albedinis*), whereas 'white thing' names the subject as being affected with whiteness. Abelard does not, of course, restrict denomination to discussing words for accidents in the category of quality, like whiteness. Words are denominated from words for *differentiae* and from words for forms in all nine categories other than substance; in the case of the words for accidents in the categories doing and being-done-to, the denominated words can be verbs as well as nouns (cf. for example *sup.Per.* 346: 29–34).

Abelard's position here as a nominalist may seem strange. In the case of his realist contemporaries, a sentence such as 'Socrates is white' will be taken, using the idea of denomination, to mean that Socrates shares the universal form of whiteness. Their position can apparently be put easily into modern terms by saying that 'white' refers to universal whiteness. This interpretation cannot be transferred to the case of a nominalist like Abelard. If 'white' is taken, in his case, to refer to the particular whiteness by which Socrates is white, all is well so long as Socrates *is* white. But suppose that

[8] See esp. Jolivet, 'Vues médiévales'.

[9] Abelard usually talks not of denominatives but of 'derived' (*sumpta*) words. Whereas a word is a denominative only if it is related, but not identical, in verbal form to the word from which it is denominated, a derived word can be related in verbal form to that from which it is derived in any way, so long as the semantic relation is that of denomination (for instance, the relation of *grammatica* (a lady who knows grammar) to *grammatica* (grammar), of *studiosus* to *virtus*, and of *fortis* to *fortitudo* is that of derivative to that from which it is derived, but only *fortis* could be called a denominative): cf. *sup.Pred.* 122: 29 – 123: 31. The corresponding section is missing from *Dial.*, but he uses the term *sumptum* there too (see e.g. 64: 24–31). For the sake of simplicity, 'denominative' will be used in this book whether Abelard writes *denominatiuum* or *sumptum*.

he is black: 'Socrates is white' turns out to be, not false, but meaningless.[10] Yet, in fact, neither Abelard nor his contemporaries would have regarded the semantics of 'Socrates is white' in quite this way at all. One effect of the verb 'to be', they believed, is to assert the identity of what is named by the two terms it joins. (Abelard thought of this as an effect unwanted by the speaker, but inevitable none the less.)[11] In 'Socrates is white', both 'Socrates' and 'white' name the same thing, Socrates – a view which seems less strange in terms of the Latin sentence, '*Socrates est albus*', where '*albus*' can be translated as 'the white man'. (This is why, in the example above, Abelard says that '*albus*' names the 'subject' – say, Socrates – 'as affected by whiteness'; the word from which it is denominated, '*albedo*', would be needed to name the form whiteness.) The meaning which the speaker wishes to convey, however, is that Socrates is *white*. He achieves this through the signification of '*albus*', which Abelard, as much as his contemporaries, regarded as universal. How predicates can signify universally when there are no universal things is precisely what Abelard's theory of universals sets out to explain.[12]

One way, then, of explaining how Abelard shared the common semantics of denomination would be in terms of truth conditions. He and his contemporaries held in common that, where 'N-ness' is the word for a form and 'N' is denominated from it, 'Socrates is N' is true if and only if N-ness is attached to Socrates. For Abelard's realist contemporaries, N-ness will be a universal form which Socrates shares; for Abelard, it will be a particular form attached to him. The position might be put better, however, in Abelard's own language, using another term which, like 'signification', will be discussed more fully in connection with universals.[13] Abelard postulates

[10] I am very grateful to Anthony Kenny for pointing this out to me.

[11] See *sup.Per.* 360: 27 – 361: 3; *sup.Top.* 274: 16 – 275: 7; cf. Mews, 'Aspects', pp. 15–41 at pp. 23–5, nn. 37–8 and de Rijk, 'Abelard's semantics', p. 112 (both writers propose useful emendations to Geyer's text of *sup.Per.*). For the meaning of 'to be', see *sup.Per.* 347: 23 – 348: 2, 359: 23–7 – 360: 16. This area has been much discussed by recent scholars. See esp. N. Kretzmann, 'The culmination of the Old Logic in Peter Abelard' in R. Benson and G. Constable (eds.), *Renaissance and renewal in the twelfth century* (Oxford, 1982), pp. 488–551; K. Jacobi, 'Peter Abelard on the speech sign "est"' in S. Knuuttila and J. Hintikka (eds.), *The logic of being* (Dordrecht, 1985), pp. 145–80; Mews, 'Aspects', pp. 21–5; L. de Rijk, 'Abelard's semantics' at pp. 108–23.

[12] See below, pp. 184–90.

[13] See below, pp. 182–3. One reason for preferring this explanation is that, in fact, Abelard would probably not have accepted that 'Socrates is N' is true if and only if N-ness is attached to Socrates, though this has nothing to do with his views about forms but results from his strange belief that the statement 'Socrates is N' could be true through saying, not that Socrates is N but that, for instance, Plato is P; see below, p. 205, n. 8.

an initial act of linguistic 'imposition' (*impositio*) by a human 'impositor'. The imposition of each substance word involved the attachment of a group of sounds to something according to the sort of thing it is: as when '*homo*' was imposed as the word for man. The imposition of each denominative word involved the linking of a group of sounds to something on account of the form attached to it: as when '*album*' was imposed as the word for white thing. Abelard thinks, like his contemporaries, that every denominative word was imposed on account of one or many really existing forms – that the word from which it is denominated is the word for a form or forms which exist (or existed).

Given Abelard's ontological presuppositions, the semantics of denomination yields what many would regard as a strange picture of what things there are. As the last chapter suggested, there is a certain strangeness in Abelard's very notion of a particular accident, which involves a degree of independence for accidents (Socrates' whiteness might have been Plato's whiteness) not envisaged in Aristotle's *Categories*. But it is less strange to think of particular accidents of quality in this way than, say, particular accidents of having or relation. Led by the semantics of denomination, however, at the time of the *Dialectica* and the *Logica*, Abelard accepted that there are particular accidents in all nine categories of accident. His discussion of the category of relation in these works shows how he devotes great energy to interpreting Aristotle's text – contrary to its obvious meaning – to support the idea of relation as a particular accident which attaches to something which is related: fatherhood, for instance, to a father.

RELATION IN THE 'DIALECTICA' AND 'LOGICA'

Aristotle's discussion of relation is not quite parallel with that in his treatment of categories such as quality, acting, being-acted-upon or being-in-a-place. In all of these Aristotle concentrates on the accidents themselves (for instance, hotness or paleness). But in this chapter, he talks, not about relations themselves, such as paternity/sonship or mastership/being-the slave-of, but about things which are described by relational predicates such as 'father'/'son' and 'master'/'slave'.[14] One result of this decision is to make the category of relation very wide indeed, since (for instance) wing and winged thing, knowledge and what is knowable and head and headed thing

[14] Cf. Ackrill (ed.), *Aristotle's 'Categories'*, p. 98 on the extent to which Aristotle's discussion can be regarded as linguistic.

will all be relatives, although they also belong to other categories.[15] Aristotle seems to be thinking primarily in terms of language. At any rate he does not worry that the things referred to by relational predicates such as 'father' and 'son' appear to be identical with things referred to by substance predicates such as 'man'. But he is disturbed that terms for parts of the body will count as relatives ('head'/'headed-thing'), because they are not simply words which refer to things which are substances: they are words which themselves belong to the category of substance. He therefore introduces another, narrower definition (8a32–3; *AL* 62: 17–18): relatives are those for which 'to be is to be related in some way to something' (*hoc ipsum esse est ad aliquid quodam modo se habere*). But it is not clear by the end of the section exactly what Aristotle would or would not accept as relatives; indeed, Aristotle concludes (8b21–3; *AL* 63: 14–16) by describing the whole section as aporetic.[16]

In his commentary (217C), Boethius identifies the first, broad definition of relatives as Plato's, and the second, narrower one as Aristotle's correction of it. Most of his discussion is devoted to the 'Platonic' definition. Boethius takes it as being about relative things, rather than relational predicates, and he is happy to accept (220D–221A) that one and the same thing can be placed under a number of different categories: virtue and vice, he says, belong in the categories of quality, having and relation; fathers and sons, slaves and masters are all substances as well as relatives. At the end of the section, he comments on Aristotle's narrower definition, without trying to reconcile it with what he has said before.

In both the *Dialectica* and *Logica*, Abelard's main interest is – as with other types of accidents – in the particular accidents which belong to the category of relation: this particular fatherhood, that being-a-son. In the *Dialectica* he accepts, as with the other categories, that *ad aliquid* can also be used to refer to words (83: 3–5) and to the things which are informed by relations (83: 20–1); and he recognizes that, according to the first, Platonic definition, all things which can be related to each other through their proper names are relatives. But the proper and substantive definition which, according to Abelard, Aristotle put forward in place of Plato's treats relatives as the relations themselves: paternity, sonship, mastership and being-the-slave-of (83: 24–32). And Abelard is quite sure, not merely that Aristotle rejected the Platonic definition, but that his entire account of this position

[15] See *Categories* 6b36ff., 7b24 ff, 7a15ff.; *AL* 59: 23ff., 61: 9ff., 60: 4ff.

[16] For further discussion and references, see C. Kirwan (ed.), Aristotle: Metaphysics Γ, Δ and E (2nd edn, Oxford, 1993), pp. 208–14.

is designed to reveal its weakness.[17] Whereas Boethius happily accepted the idea that the same thing might belong to more than one category, to Abelard this leads to an absurdity which Aristotle reveals in order to 'mock and discredit' the Platonic position.[18] Indeed, Abelard is so convinced of the unacceptability of the Platonic position that, towards the end of the section (91: 18–31), he speculates that Aristotle might have been led by envy to distort his master's position. He adds as an afterthought (91: 32 – 92: 20) the idea that Plato and Aristotle are not, after all, at odds over relatives, because Plato's definition concerns 'a verbal construction', whereas the Aristotelian definition is about 'the natural relation of things'. It is this idea which Abelard develops in the *Logica*. We are not to think that there was a controversy between two such great philosophers. Aristotle's definition concerns the nature of things. Plato's defines a class of words; but Plato's definition does not even define the words for the things which, according to Aristotle, are relations, but rather takes 'relation' in a different and broader sense (*sup.Pred.* 217: 8–17; cf. 201: 7–12).

Abelard, therefore, goes out of his way to twist Aristotle's text to conform to his idea of relations as, primarily, particular accidents. In the *Dialectica* (87: 21–9) he considers a possible objection to this position. Take this particular fatherhood: by the narrower (in Abelard's view authentically Aristotelian) definition, its being (*esse*) is its being related – that is, being related to this particular being-the-son-of. Therefore this particular being-the-son-of is 'substantial' (that is, 'essential' in modern terminology) to this paternity and therefore to paternity in general, since whatever is essential to the particular is essential to the species. If then this particular being-the-son-of is destroyed, paternity in general will disappear. If my son dies, there will be no more fatherhood. Abelard answers this (88: 17–34) by pointing out that there is no substance of a species apart from the essences of its particulars, and stressing that what are related are particulars – particular accidents – not species. It is perhaps a sign of the greater firmness with which Abelard had established his doctrine of universals as words not things that in the *Logica* he does not even raise this hypothetical objection. In both works he also accepts the idea that there will be as many particular accidents of, for instance, paternity, as there are such relations: a father will be

[17] Abelard was not alone among his contemporaries in reading Aristotle as entirely rejecting the first, 'Platonic' view: see C7, Paris, BN, lat. 17813, f. 35r.

[18] 84: 21–4: 'ipse platonicam de relativis diffinitionem manifeste deridet et improbat, cum species eius generis qualitates ostendit esse quod in Ad aliquid Plato recipiebat: est enim impossibile genus alteri predicamento quam species supponi'.

informed by a different paternity for each of his children.[19] This indicates how definitely, at this stage, he regarded accidents of relation, like other accidents, as particular things; although, by the way he puts it, Abelard also shows that he has grasped the special, reciprocal character of accidents of relation: for each being-a-son-of, he says, there will be a paternity.[20]

Even the similarity between one thing and another is regarded by Abelard in terms of particular accidents attaching to the things.[21] Abelard's difference here from some of his contemporaries was that he placed similarity and dissimilarity in the category of relation, not that of quality. Aristotle had noted in his *Categories* (11a15–19; *AL* 68: 9–13) that it is by virtue of qualities alone that things are said to be similar or dissimilar. Abelard pointed out (*Dial.* 105: 15–19) that, if this is taken to mean that similarity and dissimilarity are themselves qualities, it will be difficult to avoid an infinite regress (since this similarity and that will be similar by another similarity and so on).

HINTS OF CHANGE

There are, however, isolated points in the *Logica* when the results of trying to talk in terms of particular accidents seem so untoward that Abelard momentarily abandons the semantics of denomination.

One of these cases is in his treatment of time. The 'common view' in Abelard's day (*sup.Pred.* 184: 38 – 185: 6) was that each particular substance has in it its own times (particular accidents in the category of quantity) by which it is measured. And so I have in me my own instants, days and months by which I am measured, and another person has his own. In the course of one day 'there persist the essences of many days (*multae dierum essentiae permaneant*), although they are all counted as a single day according

[19] *Dial.* 89: 20–31 (answering an objection at 87: 29–31); *sup.Pred.* 218: 32 – 219: 20. The argument in the last lines of this passage (219: 8–20) is not very clearly stated and might be confusing. Abelard's point is this: just as there is a separate paternity by which Socrates is related to each of his children, so there is a different wholeness by which a whole is related to each of its parts. It is indeed true that, in a whole made of two parts, if one part is destroyed, then the whole ceases to be a whole. But this is not because the whole was related to both parts by virtue of only one wholeness, but rather because there cannot be a whole which consists of just one part. Other logicians of Abelard's time also adopted the view that a father has a separate paternity for each of his sons (cf. C7, Paris, BN, lat. 17813, f. 35rb), for otherwise it could not be explained what happened if one son died.

[20] *Dial.* 89: 21–2: 'quot sunt in diversis filiationes, tot erunt in ipso paternitates'; repeated almost verbatim in *sup.Pred.* 218: 38–9.

[21] *Dial.* 105: 9 – 106: 12; *sup.Pred.* 249: 1–36 (clearer and better organized).

to the revolution of the sun from the east to the west'. This view was accepted without question by Abelard in the *Dialectica*.[22] For Abelard's realist contemporaries, the particular hours and days measuring particular substances could be regarded as participants in a universal, individuated by their particular subjects; but for Abelard himself particular times would have to enjoy the same independence he attributed to all particular accidents. Perhaps this is why, in the *Logica* (*sup.Pred.* 185: 6 – 186: 14), Abelard abandons the common view and suggests rather that there is just one day which is in all temporal substances and by which they are measured.[23] In the passage which follows (185: 18 – 186: 4), he goes on to question the applicability of denomination when analysing the meaning of some temporal adjectives. If we say, as he is suggesting, that each thing does not have its own times – that is, particular accidents in the category of quantity – how do we explain what is meant when something is described as 'annual' or 'daily', which seem to be denominated from accidents of quantity? He answers that words such as these, although they signify (*significant*) times, are not denominated from them: either they are denominated from properties other than quantities 'or, perhaps, it is more rational to think that they are not denominated, but invented from a common cause (*ex communi causa inventa*), because they *do* signify quantity: although they are not denominated from quantities, they reply to the question "How much?"' (185: 41 – 186: 3).

The other case where Abelard departs from the semantics of denomination is during his discussion of the passage in the *Categories* specifically about denomination (*sup.Pred.* 124: 13 – 125: 3). There Abelard gives a list of words – 'unity', 'being-an-accident' (*'accidentalitas'*), 'potency' (*'potentia'*), 'change', 'signification' and 'being-a-species' (*'specialitas'*) – which, he says, are 'numbered among denominative nouns, but do not have an attached thing (*res adiacens*) because, if they did, there would be an infinite regress'.[24] By this terse comment Abelard means to say that the words in this list are indeed words from which others are denominated ('one', 'accident', 'able

[22] 62: 27–31: 'Cum autem res singule sua habeant tempora in se ipsis fundata, sua scilicet momenta, suas horas, suos dies vel menses vel annos, omnium tamen dies simul existentes vel menses vel anni pro uno accipiuntur, secundum volutionem solis ab oriente in occidente<m> vel totius circuli sui cursum.' Very similar words are used in *sup.Pred.* to describe the *communis sententia* which Abelard there rejects.

[23] 185: 8–10: 'Potest enim una dies toti simul mundo, id est omnibus temporalibus substantiis, inesse, secundum quam vel totus mundus mensuretur vel quaelibet singularum rerum.'

[24] 124: 15–17: 'Quae omnia cum denominativis nominibus participent, rem tamen adiacentem non habent propter infinitatis inconveniens.'

to' (*'potens'*), 'changing', 'is signified' and 'species'), but if we suppose that there therefore exist particular accidents of unity, being-an-accident and so on – in the way that there are particular accidents of whiteness or being-six-foot-tall – there will be an infinite regress. The reason for the regress is that a particular accident of unity is itself one, a particular accident of being-an-accident is itself an accident, a particular accident of *potentia* is itself *potens*, and so on. Therefore (to take the example of 'unity'), if something is one because a particular accident of unity attaches to it, then, since that particular accident of unity is itself one, it will have to be one because another particular accident of unity attaches to it, and so on to infinity.

In fact, Abelard is willing to allow that there are particular accidents of unity.[25] He cuts off the regress by suggesting that, when the word 'one' is applied to (a particular accident of) unity it is not denominated from anything, but means merely 'discrete (*tantum valere quantum discretum*)'. He goes on to explain that 'discreteness' should not be understood as the word for a type of form (by which he means here 'particular accident'). Rather, when we use 'one' to mean 'discrete', 'we are denying (*removemus*) the essences of other things with regard to that which we call "one", as if we were to say, "It is such that it is not any other thing".' In this use, 'one' is a word given 'from a common cause' – just like the word 'non-man'.[26] Similarly, Abelard provides analyses of 'the potency is able to be in something', 'the change changes' and 'the signification is signified' in which the only particular accidents which need to be postulated are those referred to by the subject terms. With regard to 'accident', Abelard goes further and appears to suggest that there do not exist any particular accidents of being-an-accident. The difficulty with 'species' (125: 3 – 126: 7) arises only, says Abelard, for those who, unlike him, think that there are real genera and species. He counsels that they might do best to deny that there is any such form as being-a-species or being-a-genus. In the rather hypothetical discussion which follows, Abelard suggests – at odds with his main discussion of relation – that there could be instances where things can be related without this involving the existence of any particular accidents of relation. 'Genus' and 'species' should be considered (on the realist

[25] *Pace* Marenbon, 'Abelard, *ens* and unity', p. 153.

[26] 124: 21–9: 'Dicimus itaque "unum", quando de unitate praedicatur, non esse denominativum nec sumptum ab aliquo, sed tantundem valere quantum "discretum" . . . non ut discretionem formam aliquam intelligamus, sed potius ceterarum rerum essentias ab eo quod "unum" dicimus removemus, ac si diceremus: est tale quid quod non est aliqua aliarum rerum. Et est quidem vocabulum commune ex communi causa datum sicut "non-homo" vel "non-equus", licet non sit subiectum vel substantiale.'

hypothesis) to be related, not because they signify relations, 'but with regard to the way in which they are imposed (*modum impositionis*) – that is, that this thing is called by this name in respect of that' (to call something a 'genus' means that it contains species, and to call something a 'species' means that it is contained by a genus).

One aspect of these departures from the semantics of denomination is clear enough. Certain sorts of particular accident (those of the measures of time belonging to each substance, those of being-an-accident), which would exist according to the semantics of denomination, are declared not to exist. Abelard trims the luxuriance of his ontology – a little. But Abelard still considers that the apparent denominatives, which he has unmasked as not really being denominatives, are words which can be used meaningfully in describing how things are in the world. How? Abelard's explanation in each case is that the word is 'invented' or 'given' from 'a common cause'. Abelard speaks (*Dial.* 565: 1–36) in the same way about the words '*ens*' ('an existing thing') and '*res*' ('a thing'), and also what were called 'unbounded names' (*nomina infinita*), like 'not-man': they each have 'one cause of imposition'. (Abelard also brings the idea of a 'common cause of imposition' into his discussion of universals, in a distinct but related sense.)[27] When Abelard talks in these cases of a single or common 'cause', he has it in mind that the usual reason for inventing or imposing a word – that it picks out a certain sort of substance or a certain sort of form – does not apply. The pseudo-denominatives (like '*accidens*') are in this respect exactly like '*ens*' and '*res*' – words which can be used for *any* sort of substance or form, and like boundless words. By talking of a 'cause', Abelard wishes to insist that there is none the less a consistent reason behind the use of each of these words. He goes on to show, with varying success, what these reasons are. In the case of the time words, he merely makes a gesture: they answer the question 'How much?' In the case of sentences in which 'one' is predicated of an accident of unity, he goes further and suggests that they must be analysed as making a statement quite different from what their surface form would suggest. The success of this analysis depends on whether it is considered self-explanatory to say of something that 'It is such that it is not any other thing', or whether this explanation merely begs another.

In the *Logica*, then, Abelard makes some very rare departures from the semantics of denomination, but provides only hints of the semantics he might put in its place.

[27] See below, pp. 191–5.

ABELARD'S NEW SEMANTIC THINKING: DIFFERENCE IN PROPERTY

From the mid-1120s, Abelard became bolder in rejecting the universal applicability of the semantics of denomination, although he still did not go very far in providing an alternative semantic or ontological account. The *Theologia Christiana* is the surviving work in which this change of mind is clearest. The key to Abelard's new thinking there is analysis of the meanings of the words 'same' (*idem*) and 'different' (*diuersum*). It is first introduced, in connection with the Trinity, in the *Theologia Summi Boni*; and it then appears, with some changes and developments, in the *Glossae secundum vocales*, the *Glossulae*, the *Theologia Christiana* (the most elaborate account) and the *Theologia Scholarium*.[28]

A little background is needed to make clear what these distinctions involve. As explained in the preceding chapter, Abelard considered all forms as particular things, each essentially discrete and each of which might not have attached to the substance to which it in fact attaches. But he also recognized the strongest ties between forms and the substances to which they are in fact attached (and apart from which they cannot now continue to exist). In the case of *differentiae*, these two points of view give rise to Abelard's two different, and not entirely compatible approaches: that based on 'bundled particulars' and that based on substances. More generally with all forms, Abelard can look on each particular form as numerically one,

[28] Besides the special development in *TChr* which will be discussed, there are some other divergences between the accounts. At *TSum* 142: 745 – 150: 959, Abelard distinguishes six meanings of 'same' – same in essence, same in number, same by definition, same by likeness, unchanging, same by effect – and six exactly corresponding meanings of 'different'. At *Gl.sec.voc.* (*Phil. Schr.*, p. 58), the same meanings are more briefly explained. *Glossulae* (558: 11 – 560: 15) gives, at rather greater length and differently arranged, the same six meanings, but with one important change: identity in essence is explicitly said *not* to be the same as identity of predication – whereas Abelard himself had claimed that they *are* the same in *TSum* (143: 757–8) and *Gl.sec.voc.* (ed. Geyer, p. 588: 10–11). This change is the result of his noticing a new sort of difference – that by property, first discussed in *TChr* (see below, pp. 151–5). At *TChr* (247: 1677 – 255: 1936) Abelard lists five main meanings of 'same' – in essence ('that is, in number'), in property, by definition, by likeness and unchanging – to which correspond five main meanings of different, although he adds that parts of wholes do not differ in number but do in essence. Abelard also mentions (254: 1937 – 255: 1975) other meanings. In *TSch* (454: 1411–87) Abelard simplifies his list to three meanings of 'same' – by likeness, in essence or number, and by definition or property – and three meanings of 'different' – in essence, in number and by property or definition.

but also as part of a whole – substance plus particular *differentiae* plus particular accidents – which is itself one in number.

Abelard's treatment of sameness and difference takes this idea as a point of departure. Consider a substance – Socrates, for instance – to which a number of different predicates can be applied, such as 'man', 'white thing', 'solid thing', 'substance', 'bodily substance', 'body'. According to his analysis of sameness and difference, Abelard would say that, in this case, Socrates, the man, the white thing, the solid thing, the substance, the bodily substance and the body are all the same thing, not merely in number (as Socrates and his hand – or any whole and its parts – are the same in number), but also in essence. With regard to the body and the bodily substance Abelard would go further: they are the same, not just in essence and number, but also in definition: from the fact that it is a body, it is a bodily substance, and from the fact that it is a bodily substance, it is a body. By contrast, Socrates, the man, the white thing, the solid thing, the substance and the body/bodily substance are all different by definition. Although the thing is one and the same in essence – the man we know as Socrates – its being white does not require its being solid, its being a substance does not require its being a body, nor does its being a body require its being a man.[29]

In the *Theologia Christiana* (247: 1699 – 248: 1739), Abelard introduces a new type of difference – by property.[30] Difference in property is a particular sort of difference by definition, which Abelard finds especially interesting for theological and other purposes. In the example given above, the white thing and the hard thing, different by definition, are the same in property, since the white thing participates in the hardness, the property of the hard thing, and the hard thing participates in the whiteness, the property of the white thing. The statements, 'The white thing is hard' and 'The hard thing

[29] *TSum* 147: 892 – 148: 897: 'Diuersa autem diffinitione sunt que eadem diffinitione sententie terminari non possunt, hoc est que talia sunt ut sese mutuo non exigant, licet eadem res sit utrumque, sicut est substantia et corpus, uel album et durum. Non enim ex eo quod substantia est corpus est, uel eo ex quod album est durum est, cum hoc sine illo queat esse neque ex se illud exigat'; and the continuation: *TSum* 148: 897 – 149: 931; cf. *TChr* 252: 1875 – 254: 1923 (very close); *TSch* 457: 1490–1504; *Glossulae* 559: 18–29.

[30] In *TSum* (175: 501 – 176: 538) Abelard had already begun to explore the apparent paradoxes in statements about things the same in what he would call, in *TChr*, property. It is very possible that Abelard was first stimulated to think about this area by Aristotle's discussion of predication *secundum accidens* in *De interpretatione* (21a). Abelard comments on this in *ed.Per.* 129: 8ff., *Dialectica* 116: 6 – 117: 9, *sup.Per.* 476: 15ff.; and in both *TSum* (176: 539–41) and *TChr* (290: 859–62), he gives – with an explicit reference to *Dial.* – an example of this sort of predication immediately after mentioning the type involving a difference by property.

is white' are true. Things essentially the same differ by property as well as by definition when their properties remain 'entirely unmixed together'. This occurs, for instance, in cases where the things considered are the material and what is made out of that material. Abelard's example, here and elsewhere, is that of an image in wax (as in a wax seal). That which is made from the material (*materiatum*), the wax image, and the material, the wax from which it is made, are the same in essence and number, but they differ, not only by definition but property. As Abelard puts it (248: 1724–6): 'The property of the material is that very priority, according to which something comes to be materially from it. The property of that which is made from the material is that very posteriority which is the converse <of the priority>.'

What is involved in difference by property can be made clearer by another example (not, of course, Abelard's). Historians talk of Stalin as a private man and as a public man, without this implying that there was more than one being who was Stalin. But the statement, 'The private man was the public man', is false. The reason for its falsehood is that 'private man' means 'the person considered with the attributes characteristic of him as a private person and without the attributes characteristic of him as a public figure', whilst 'the public man' means 'the person considered with the attributes characteristic of him as a public figure and without the attributes characteristic of him as a private person'. The case is the same in Abelard's example: the wax, the material, and that which is made from it, the wax image. When we say 'the material', we mean 'the thing considered with the attributes it has always had and without the attributes it came to have when it was imprinted', and when we say 'that which is made from the material' we mean 'the thing considered without the attributes it has always had and with the attributes it came to have when it was imprinted'. (Abelard puts this more neatly, but perhaps less clearly, in terms of priority and posteriority.) Abelard's example is, however, more potentially confusing than that of Stalin as private and public man, because whereas 'private man' and 'public man' are clearly descriptions of Stalin, in Abelard's example it is easier to overlook, or forget, the fact that there is a thing of which 'the matter' and 'that which is made from the matter' are both correct descriptions.[31]

Abelard's way of speaking about difference by definition and by property might seem to be based on an error. On a hasty reading, his discussion might appear to move from the fact that we can use different descriptions of the same thing to the idea that exactly the same thing (for instance, a

[31] See below, pp. 178–9.

hard, white stone), described in different ways, is somehow a number of different things (a hard thing, a white thing). This impression is certainly misleading. Abelard stresses that Socrates, the white thing, the hard thing, or the material and that which is made from the material, are one in essence (and therefore in number).[32] Indeed, there is no reason *in principle* why Abelard's new distinctions should not have been merely a novel way of explaining how descriptive terms are used to talk about particular substances and particular forms, and any apparent oddness merely a reflection of the genuine oddness of an ontology in which a white, hard stone is one thing in number but consists of a substance and a whole variety of particular forms. To say, 'The white thing differs by definition, but not in essence or number, from the hard thing' is a shorthand (and perhaps somewhat confusing) way of saying: 'Here is a substance to which are attached a particular accident of whiteness and a particular accident of hardness and so which may correctly be described by these two phrases which each have a different meaning – "white thing", "hard thing".' And, in principle, this analysis could be extended to difference by property, since the wax in Abelard's example could be held to become a wax image by receiving certain particular accidents.

In fact, however, Abelard uses distinction by definition and, especially, distinction by property as far more than another way of speaking about the ontology and semantics he had followed in the *Logica*. Why he does so becomes evident in the light of the theological aims for which these distinctions were introduced. Abelard's intention is to explain, at least to some extent, how it is that the Father, Son and Holy Spirit are one in essence but three persons with three distinct properties: the Father has the property of begetting the Son, the Son of being begotten by the Father and the Holy Spirit of proceeding from the Father and the Son. Difference by property provides Abelard with the analysis he needs. The persons of the Trinity are one in essence, but differ by property: although we can say that the Father, Son and Holy Spirit are all one God, we cannot predicate of one the personal property of another, nor say, for instance, that the Father is the Son, or the Holy Spirit is the Father.

Does this mean, then, that 'Father' (for instance) describes God as having the form of begetting attached to him, but not that of being begotten or of

[32] Note how in *TSch* Abelard formulates the position very carefully so as to avoid any misunderstanding: (457: 1490–94) 'facile in singulis rebus assignari potest, et unam numero atque essentialiter rem permanere, et ipsi plures inesse proprietates secundum quas aliqua diuersa sint diffinitione, non numero, et eadem res diuersa in sensu uocabula sortiatur'.

proceeding? By no means. Abelard rejects the idea that there are any forms in God (256: 2005 – 259: 2122) and fiercely attacks those theologians who think otherwise (*TChr* 301: 1106–27; *TSch* 440: 1015–20, 1028–34). Indeed, before introducing his analysis of difference, Abelard explains that he needs to go beyond Porphyry's account because it is limited to considering differences which are based on forms, whereas there are no forms in God.[33] When we talk about the 'properties' of the persons of the Trinity, Abelard adds a little later, we must not think that this word implies the existence of any forms in God. He points out that Aristotle, too, had talked on occasion of what was 'proper' to something without this being a matter of forms – as when he says that all substances have it in common that they are not in a subject, cannot be described as 'more' or 'less' and are not contrary to anything.[34]

So does this imply that, since God is just one thing, undifferentiated by any variety of forms, the difference between Father, Son and Holy Spirit is a matter merely of words? Abelard also rejects this alternative. 'It is asked . . . whether the Trinity of persons which are in God should be understood verbally or in reality (*in uocabulis an in re potius sit accipienda*). For our part, we state that it should be understood as a matter of reality itself (*in re ipsa*), in this way: that from eternity that unique, entirely simple and individual thing, which is God, has been three persons . . . It was not because a distinction of names was made in this way, that there is this Trinity, but because there has been this Trinity from eternity that at some point in time the distinction of names was made.'[35] To say that the persons of the Trinity differ by property is to say that they are really different, but this difference cannot be explained in terms of things (contrast the case of the white thing and the hard thing, which are one in essence but different by definition because 'white thing' is truly predicated of it on account of a particular accident of whiteness, which is a different thing from the particular accident of hardness on account of which 'hard thing' is also truly predicated of it).

Such ways of speaking may seem – at least without further explanation (and none is forthcoming) – mysterious. But then the Holy Trinity is, to believers, a mystery. Abelard had explained at length, from the time of the

33 *TSum* 141: 729 – 142: 732 (= *TChr* 246: 1661–5): 'Ibi quippe solummodo differentias tractat [*sc.* Porphirius] que in formis consistunt, quando uidelicet res discrete diuersis ab inuicem formis distant, uel eadem res per formas sibi inuicem succedentes permutatur. In deo autem nulle forme sunt.'

34 *TSum* 151: 984–91 = *TChr* 256: 2005–12.

35 1st quotation: *TSum* 157: 2–6 = *TChr* 266: 2–6; 2nd quotation: *TChr* 268: 75–7.

Theologia Summi Boni, that human language is not adequate for talking about God, and that words change their ordinary senses when their application is transferred from creatures to God.[36] Abelard might, then, have confined the use of his new distinctions to theological discourse, where ordinary rules of explanation do not apply; or at least he might have insisted that in its earthly analogues difference by property could be fully explained in terms of things, although this did not remain true when it was transferred to talking about God. But, in fact, Abelard thought the analogy was far closer. Although he developed his notions of property and difference by property or definition in order to discuss the Trinity, he believed that they applied also to the ontology of created things (as is shown by his treatment of relation, *sermones* and even universals)[37] and, as a result, he abandoned in part the semantics of denomination.

ACCIDENTS, WORDS AND THINGS: THE LATER THEORY

Abelard's willingness to rethink his view of created things in the light of his views about properties in God is most strikingly evident in the *Theologia Christiana*. There (259: 2109–22) in the course of stressing that, when God is called Father or Son, 'these properties of being related (*proprietates relationum*) are not any things other than God himself', Abelard chooses to reinforce his point by a reference to relations in human beings: 'many things in ourselves are regarded relatively, when no one of sense would accept that these relations are anything other than ourselves'.[38] The example which Abelard chooses is the relation of similarity (and its contrary, dissimilitude or oppositeness) – which in the *Dialectica* and *Logica* Abelard had treated, like other relations, in terms of particular accidents.[39] Whereas, in these earlier works, Abelard had held that an infinite regress could be avoided so long as similarity and dissimilarity were taken as accidents in the category of relation, not that of quality, he now points out that, if the relation of similarity or dissimilarity is regarded as a thing, different from the substance which it informs, then there will be an infinite regress, since this particular similarity will be similar to that by another particular similarity, and so on.

[36] See *TSum* 137: 623 – 141: 721; *TChr* 241: 1497 – 246: 1642; *TSch* 448: 1259 – 453: 1399; see also pp. 54–6 above.

[37] See below, pp. 155–8 (relations); 178–9 (*sermones*); 199–200 (universals).

[38] 259: 2108–10: 'Nam et in nobis ipsis multa relatiue accipiuntur, cum nemo discretus relationes ipsas aliud a nobis esse concedat.'

[39] See above, p. 146.

He ends by adding another argument: 'What . . . could be more ridiculous than that when someone is born now to whom I am similar, something new should come to existence in me which, when he perishes, will of necessity disappear?' Abelard is still talking about similarity, but the same point could be made about many other relations, such as fatherhood and being-the-son-of. Indeed, just a little earlier (258: 2057–60), Abelard asks himself: 'Because we call those properties relations, should we understand them to be different things (*res diuersae*) from the substance itself which, from them, is said to have a relation to something?' And he replies, 'Most certainly not!' More generally, Abelard remarks (285: 676–8) that no one who rightly understands unity or 'many other forms' so separates them from the substances which are their subjects that 'he considers them different from these substances in number or essence'.

Abelard, then, has had a complete change of mind about the ontology of some, if not all accidents (including at least all those in the category of relation): no longer does he regard them as particular things. He brings out his position most clearly, and offers some explanation for it, in a passage from later in the *Theologia Christiana* (342: 2434 – 344: 2532).[40] The initial question is a theological one, which is couched in strictly linguistic terms. Can the words for the properties of the divine persons ('fatherhood', 'sonship', 'procession') be predicated of God, in the same way as the words for other properties (such as 'omnipotence', 'charity' and 'wisdom')? Would we be right in saying, 'God is fatherhood'? This linguistic question is followed immediately by an argument about the relationship between God and things. There is nothing in God save God himself. Either, then, the personal properties are not things at all, or we must admit they are God. That they are God is supported by the fact that everything which exists is a creature or the Creator; but these properties are eternal and so cannot have been created. Abelard seems poised to accept statements such as 'God is fatherhood', but then observes that such ways of speaking are never used by the Church Fathers. To find a way out of the problem, Abelard turns from the special question of relations in God, to relations in other things (342:

[40] The whole of this passage is discussed very differently by Tweedale (*Abailard on universals*, pp. 188–204). Tweedale takes it as presenting Abelard's constant view about, it seems, all accidents, not – as suggested here – a change of mind about some categories of accident, such as relations. He also considers that Abelard is far more successful in his attempt to ' "eliminate" certain abstract entities' (p. 196) than will be argued here. In his brief comments in 'Logic (i): to the time of Abelard' (p. 221), Tweedale seems to have changed his view and accuses Abelard (not without justice) of wanting to have his 'ontological cake whilst throwing it out at the same time'. See also Mews, 'Aspects', pp. 31–3.

2458–9). There, he says, we neither hold relations to be different things (*res diuersae*) from their subjects, nor do we predicate their names of their subjects – we do not say 'Socrates is fatherhood'. The fatherhood which Socrates has is, however, not another thing from Socrates, 'nor perhaps is it the same thing, since rightly speaking it cannot be called a thing at all: it has no true essence in it which would make it something one in number essentially discrete from whatever is not itself'.[41] Like relations in other things, the properties of the divine persons, says Abelard (343: 2472–80), are neither God nor things in God: they are not things at all, not essences (*essentiae*), not the existences of any things (*rerum aliquae existentiae*), but merely properties within something (*in una re consistentes proprietates*).

Abelard, it seems, has given up his earlier position (linked to the semantics of denomination), according to which 'I am a father' is true because there attaches to me a particular fatherhood, which is a thing, a particular accident in the category of relation. Now Abelard is sure that this fatherhood is *not* a thing (just as God's Fatherhood is not a thing). Yet, even in denying that it is an essence, Abelard continues to speak about it as a quasi-thing. So Abelard goes on to argue (343: 2481 – 344: 2504) that, when we say, 'Paternity exists', we mean that something is a father; from which it would seem to follow that to say that *x* has the property of paternity means simply that the statement 'he is a father' is true of *x*. Yet Abelard puts this point in the same manner as he has discussed paternity in the preceding passage: he speaks of paternity (not the word 'paternity') and then denies that it has an essence, rather as if it were both a thing and not a thing.[42]

The next and final section of the discussion (344: 2505–32) continues in the same way. Abelard explains why, although fatherhood is not a different thing (*diuersa res*) from a father, neither 'Fatherhood is a father', nor 'A father is fatherhood' is true. From the first of these statements, he says, it would follow that fatherhood is a substance – one, indeed, capable of fathering a child – whereas it is rather a 'property or relation of substance'. With

[41] 343: 2466–70: 'cum tamen ipsa paternitas non sit res alia ab ipsis, nec fortassis eadem, cum res omnino recte dici non possit, quae in se ueram non habet essentiam, ut sit in se una res numero a ceteris omnibus quae ipsa non sunt rebus essentialiter discreta'.

[42] The text printed by Buytaert reads (343: 2486–91): 'Cum enim dicimus hominem esse, tale est ac si ponamus hominem in sua manere substantia, hoc est aliquem in se ipsum esse siue aliquid esse hominem. Si uero dicamus paternitatem esse, tale est ac si ponamus aliquid esse patrem, non ipsam paternitatem esse suam essentiam.' As it stands, the meaning of the final clause is unclear ('not that fatherhood itself is its own essence'). But the reading in Tours, 85 of *essentia* supports an emendation of the last two words to *sua essentia*, so that the clause would mean: 'not that fatherhood itself exists by its own essence'.

regard to the second, Abelard points out that 'to be someone who is a father is not the same as his having paternity in him, that is, as his being a father'. Both explanations take it as their starting point that, although fatherhood is not a particular thing, it can be talked about as if it were. If Abelard had ceased to regard fatherhood as a thing entirely, he would have declared that 'A father is fatherhood' and 'Fatherhood is a father' are both meaningless, unless they are taken to read 'A father is "fatherhood"' and '"Fatherhood" is a father', which are obviously false.[43] By sticking to the idea that fatherhood is a property – but a property is not a thing – Abelard stops himself from thinking further and providing an alternative ontological explanation to that which, in his earlier works, was given by positing particular accidents of relation.

Although Abelard's new attitude to (some categories of) accidents was occasioned, it seems, by theological considerations, the *Theologia Christiana* talks about the theory as one already established in logic about relations in created things. Abelard refers his readers explicitly to his *Grammatica*, where the new theory of categories which he uses is worked out fully. The tantalizingly brief and professedly incomplete exposition of some of this theory here makes the loss of this treatise – more, it seems, a work of logic than what we would regard as grammar – all the sadder.[44]

There is, however, at least one remaining query about Abelard's new position to which other evidence may provide an answer. In the *Theologia Christiana*, Abelard is usually talking about accidents in the category of relation (because these are of particular importance in connection with the Trinity). Yet he certainly does not exclude the idea that his analysis could apply to other sorts of accidental forms, and in one passage (285: 676–8: discussed above) he denies that unity – an accident in the category of quantity – and 'many other forms' are essentially different from their subjects. Does Abelard now believe that *no* sort of accident is a thing, or does his new theory apply only to some of the categories of accident?

In the part of Avranches, 232 which also contains the *De intellectibus*,

[43] Abelard initially presents his position as being that (544: 2510–11) we cannot join *sibi inuicem per praedicationem* 'father' and 'fatherhood'. This might mislead a modern reader into thinking that he *is* saying that 'Fatherhood is a father' and 'A father is fatherhood' are meaningless. But Abelard uses 'to predicate' in the sense of 'to predicate truly' (see *sup.Por.* 16: 39 – 17: 28; cf. 58: 28 – 59: 4); and, in the discussion which follows 'Fatherhood is a father' and 'A father is fatherhood' are clearly taken to be meaningful sentences which – so Abelard wants to show – express statements which can be shown to be false: 344: 2526–8: 'Non est itaque pater paternitas ... neque e conuerso paternitas est pater.'

[44] On the *Grammatica*, see above, pp. 50–1.

there are some notes on matters of logic and ontology. One of them gives a series of different current views about forms, including that which it attributes to 'Abelard and his followers', who are described in terms that are not only flattering but suggest that Abelard must have been still alive and teaching when the note was written.[45] According to this report, Abelard and his followers hold that some forms are essences (*essentie*), some by no means. Only certain forms[46] are essences, and only those which do *not* fall into one of the following classes: those which the subject itself is sufficient to make exist (for instance, quantities); those which depend on the disposition of the parts of their subject among themselves (for instance, curvature of the nose) or in relation to something else (for instance, sitting); those which are present due to something outside the subject (for instance, being the owner of a horse); and those which are such that a substance must be added when they leave (for instance, not-being-ensouled).

Although the distinction proposed here applies both to *differentiae* and accidental forms, it in fact allows almost all *differentiae* to continue to be regarded as essences. Even a negative *differentia* such as immortality would not be disqualified under the criteria proposed, since when it leaves its subject what must be added is not a substance, but another *differentia*, namely mortality. By contrast, most varieties of accident must be judged, by one or other of these criteria, not to be essences. Quantities, place and perhaps time are eliminated by the first criterion: they exist simply by virtue

[45] (f. 69r) 'Alii autem qui quasdam formas essentias esse, quasdam minime perhibent, sicut Abaelardus et sui, qui artem dialecticam non obfuscando sed diligentissime perscrutando dilucidant. Nullas formas essentias esse approbant nisi quasdam qualitates que sic insunt in subiecto quod subiectum ad esse earum non sufficit, sicut ad esse quantitatum ipsum subiectum sufficit; uel partium dispositio ad inuicem uel cum alio non est necessaria, sicut ad curuaturam digiti necessaria est dispositio partium ad inuicem et ad esse sessionis necessaria est dispositio partium subiecti et aliud ubi subiectum sedeat; uel que non insunt gratia alicuius extrinseci ita quod sine illo esse non possent, sicut proprietas aliqua inest in aliquo quia equum uel bouem possidet quanquam nullo modo remaneret destructo illo extrinseco; uel ad cuius recessum non est necessarium addi substantia subiecto, sicut ad recessum inanimationis necessarium est addi substantia subiecto, scilicet animam. Nullam enim formam essentiam esse asserunt cui aliquid istorum poterint assignari: uel subiectum adesse illius sufficere, uel dispositionem partium ad inuicem siue cum alio, uel que inerit gratia extrinseci ita quod sine illo esse non posset, uel ad cuius recessum necesse est addi substantiam.' The passage was edited (with some errors and mispunctuations) by V. Cousin in his *Fragments philosophiques* II (2nd edn, Paris, 1840), at pp. 494–6.

[46] The writer uses the word *qualitas* here, but in the sense of 'form' not of 'accidental form in the category of quality': his remark would make no sense if the word had the latter meaning, since he goes on to refer to accidents in categories such as quantity and relation, and certain *differentiae*, as varieties of *qualitas*. On the various meanings of *qualitas*, see *Dial.* 93: 3–7, *sup.Pred.* 223: 29 – 224: 3.

of the existence of the subject. The second criterion rules out some accidents of quality and of doing, whilst the fourth rules out those in the classes of relation, posture, having and being-done-to. This leaves just some accidents in the classes of quality and of doing/acting to be regarded in the way in which, formerly, Abelard had considered all particular accidents – as things.

The note in the Avranches manuscript is at second-hand, but there are two considerations which suggest that it *does* accurately represent Abelard's later thought about the ontology of accidents. First, there is a brief remark in the commentary on the Hexaemeron (768BC) which asks whether everything besides God is a creature: are merely substances creatures, or do they include substances and their accidents, such as 'any sort of thing (*res aliqua*)' like 'sitting (*sessio*)'? Abelard begins to answer his question by saying that 'we do not say when it happens that someone sits that some thing now exists which did not formerly exist, nor that some thing has perished which formerly existed in the person when he was standing'. Even though he does not pursue the subject any further, Abelard has made it fairly clear from this comment that, although he calls an accident of sitting *res aliqua*, he does not in fact wish to regard it as a thing at all, in the sense of 'existing thing' or 'creature'. A remark elsewhere in the same commentary suggests, however, that – just as the Avranches passage indicates – he is willing to allow existence to some accidents of quality.[47] Second, Abelard's discussion of evil in the *Collationes* (probably written a few years after the *Theologia Christiana*) requires accidents such as sadness and pain to be things[48] – but these are precisely the sort of accidents which the criteria in the Avranches passage would still allow to be considered as real existents.

There is nothing, however, in Abelard's later writing to suggest that he sorted out the confusion which he produced in the *Theologia Christiana* by talking about accidents which are not things as if they were things to be talked about: indeed, the report in the Avranches manuscript itself follows just this way of speaking, when it explains that some forms are essences, and some forms are not. Equally, there is no sign that Abelard posed himself

[47] Abelard has been saying (Buytaert, 'Abelard's Expositio', pp. 172–3 (Text 1)) how, by contrast with bodily substances, incorporeal accidents such as whiteness cannot change from what they are without ceasing to be altogether. He very clearly uses the vocabulary of existence here in connection with these accidents ('nec umquam id quod est albedo prius aliquo modo aliquid exstitit quam albedo esset, et cum ipsum albedo esse desinet, nullis essentiae statum retinebit'). He finishes by saying: 'Unde nonulla accidentia quanto minus quam substantiae variabilia vel mobilia sunt, tanto eis verius esse assignaverunt.' (Note the following correction to Buytaert's text: *in corporeis rebus* (173: 5, should read *incorporeis rebus*.)

[48] See below, pp. 241–2.

the difficult ontological questions which his manner of speaking about these accidents tended to conceal. By changing his ontology and semantics from that of the *Dialectica* and the *Logica*, Abelard succeeded in removing some of the strangeness of the scheme he had set out there, but not without raising more questions than he resolves.

Chapter 7

Perception and knowledge

It might now seem time to turn to look at Abelard's treatment of universals. But there is an important preliminary. In his various discussions of universals, Abelard makes extensive use of his developing ideas about perception and knowledge. His theory of cognition therefore provides a background against which his theory of universals, and the changes he makes to it, become easier to understand. Here, as in his ontology, Abelard starts from a body of philosophical material transmitted in ancient logical works, but often reinterprets it in accord with his own views, becoming bolder the more he writes and thinks about the area.

COGNITION: ABELARD'S SOURCES

Abelard developed his account of human cognition on the basis of Aristotle – as transmitted by Boethius in his logical commentaries. Aristotle's analysis of cognition (found in the *De anima*, to which Abelard had no direct access) rests on his metaphysics of matter, form, potency and act. The interpretation of Aristotle's theory has been controversial since antiquity and remains so. The sketch which follows is intended only to set out roughly some points which will be important for understanding Abelard.

Aristotle presents the senses and, for the most part, the intellect as receptive rather than active. Just as, in sensual perception, the senses take on the accidental forms which they perceive (my touch becomes hot from the form of hotness), so in intellectual perception the intellect is informed by the substantial form which makes the thing perceived the sort of thing it is. The form man informs matter to make a particular man, but it also informs the potentiality of my intellect when I think of a man. There must, Aristotle adds, be an active aspect of the intellect which discerns the universal form within the perceptions acquired by the senses. Intellectual cognition is therefore of universals alone, although Aristotle remarks that it must always be accompanied by 'images (*phantasmata*)', which are connected with the senses. The central feature, then, of Aristotle's theory is that, when we think, we understand the world by grasping universals, which really exist in the world, although only in individual concrete wholes of matter and form.

Abelard, who held that there were no universal things, and who thought of the soul as active rather than merely receptive, could hardly build on a theory of this sort without at the same time transforming it. But he was also affected by the way in which his only direct sources, Boethius' commentaries on the *Isagoge* and *De interpretatione*, presented Aristotle's theory.[1]

The long commentary on *De interpretatione* was especially important. At the beginning of this work (16a2–8; *AL* 5: 4–9) Aristotle remarks that words (*voces*) are marks of affections (*passiones*) in the mind, these affections are likenesses (*similitudines*) of real things. Boethius' explanation of what this description implies (25: 15 – 52: 27) draws on Aristotle's *De anima* as well as later exegesis. Boethius establishes (27: 18–22) that the affections of the mind cannot be sense impressions, since sense impressions are affections of the body. He goes on to show that the affections of the mind also cannot be identified with what he calls *imaginationes* ('images'), his equivalent of Aristotle's *phantasmata*. These images, he states, following Aristotle, are distinct from thoughts, although thoughts must always be accompanied by them. Sense impressions and images, he continues (29: 1–10), are the initial figures on the foundation of which the intelligence works. In the same way as a painter first draws an outline as a basis for his portrait and then adds the colours so as to portray someone's face, so sense impressions and images underlie the perceptions of the mind. When we sense something or begin to consider it, first there must be an image of it. Only then does our intellect supervene and disentangle the different parts which were there, undifferentiatedly, in the image.[2]

The likenesses which Aristotle calls 'affections of the mind' are described by Boethius, not as *imaginationes* but as *imagines*. First, he says (34: 2–19), a thing is grasped by the imagination, and then the intellect perceives it, and this involves a being-done-to, an affection (*passio*). With his closest allusion here to Aristotle's ideas about matter and form, Boethius likens

[1] For this area of Boethius' work in general, see J. Magee, *Boethius on signification and mind* (Leiden/New York/Copenhagen/Cologne, 1989) (Philosophia antiqua 52).

[2] 29: 6–10: 'Nam cum res aliqua sub sensum vel sub cogitationem cadit, prius eius quaedam necesse est imaginatio nascatur, post vero superveniat intellectus cunctas explicans partes quae confuse fuerant imaginatione praesumptae.'

this affection to the impression of a figure and adds that the way a *figura* is within a thing is different from the way when this form is transferred to the mind. Boethius is not quite clear in his account of these *imagines* or likenesses, but they seem to have the role of unit-thoughts or concepts. He refers to the likeness of a sphere or square (35: 1–6), but also to the likeness of 'the good' (41: 26–7). So far as natural goodness – as opposed to the laws and customs of particular states – is concerned, everyone who regards something as good has the same affection of the mind, the same likeness of good.

In his second commentary on the *Isagoge* (164: 3 – 167: 20), Boethius elaborates this account of cognition in describing the process of abstraction by which we grasp universals.[3] The rational soul takes from the senses things which are undifferentiated and mixed together and distinguishes them by its own power and thought, separating what is incorporeal by nature from the body to which it must be attached. It can, for instance, regard a line separately from a body or, by collecting a single likeness (*similitudo*) of humanity from many men, all of them different, it can know the species, man – since, for Boethius, this likeness, which is sensibly perceptible in each individual, *is* the universal when it is grasped in thought. Earlier, in the preface to this commentary, Boethius had brought out another element to the theory of cognition, by distinguishing the imagination – shared by man with at least some other animals – as a separate power of the soul, distinct from the senses and the reason.

Abelard's reaction to this source material was a penetrating and developing one. He worked, with increasing clarity, towards a theory which, like Aristotle's, makes all human knowledge begin with sense perception, but one which also emphasizes the intellect's active power to penetrate the structure of particular things and to think about them in different ways. He sketched an inchoate form of his theory of cognition in his *Logica* when discussing the passage on universals from the *Isagoge* and developed a first full form of it at the beginning of the commentary there on *De interpretatione*. In the *De intellectibus* he changed and developed his theory in some very important ways.[4]

[3] Boethius does not use the word 'abstraction' (which Abelard would borrow) frequently, but he does do so at the beginning of this discussion: 'quod si hoc per diuisionem et per abstractionem fiat, non quidem ita res sese habet, ut intellectus est, intellectus tamen ille minime falsus est' (164: 12–14).

[4] There are very useful observations on the development of Abelard's theory of cognition (especially about the the shift in emphasis from mental images to abstraction) in T. Shimizu,

THE EARLIER THEORY OF COGNITION

Abelard's first attempt to think about human cognition in the *Logica*, in the commentary on Porphyry, is closely bound up with the problem of universals, which he is in the course of discussing. Abelard wishes, at this stage, to argue that there are 'common conceptions' in our minds which universals 'signify',[5] and here he identifies these common conceptions with a certain sort of common likeness formed by the mind. Sense perception and intellectual perception, he begins by remarking (20: 20 – 21: 27), are distinct but parallel. The senses have for their objects bodies and their sensory accidents. But the intellect, 'just as it needs no bodily instrument, so it has no need of a bodily object towards which to direct itself'. Rather, its act of understanding (*suae intelligentiae actio*) is directed towards a likeness (*similitudo*) of the thing, which the mind makes for itself. Sense-perceptions are not the same as their objects, nor are thoughts the same as their objects – the likenesses of things made by the mind. A thought is 'a certain action of the mind' – a phrase which implies that it is a particular thing, an accident in the category of doing; by contrast, the form to which it directs itself is imaginary and feigned – neither a substance nor an accident – like the imaginary town of which we dream or the idea a craftsman forms in his mind of what he is going to make. Some people, says Abelard, consider that these likenesses are the same as thoughts. But Abelard insists that what are properly called likenesses are not the thoughts, but what is thought. Consider, for instance, the likeness of a tower: it has a certain height and shape, but these accidents of quantity and quality cannot be real accidents They must be feigned ones. But a real thing, such as a thought, cannot be informed by a feigned accident. These accidents must therefore inform feigned substances – that is to say, the likenesses which are, in Abelard's view, not things. Abelard's feigned likenesses are not the same as Boethius' likenesses, the *similitudines* or *imagines* which Boethius equates with Aristotle's affections of the mind and so with thoughts. Nor are they exactly equivalent to Boethius' confused *imaginationes*, which precede and accompany thoughts. Boethius describes *imaginationes* as if they arose from sense-impressions, whereas Abelard's likenesses seem to be the mind's own creation, as he indicates by the analogies which he chooses – the imaginary

'From vocalism to nominalism: progression in Abaelard's theory of signification', *Didascalia* 1 (1995), 15–46, at pp. 36–42.

[5] See below, pp. 184–6.

towns of which we dream and the craftsman's conception of what he is about to make.

Abelard's line of argument here can be explained on the presumption that he does not have any clear notion of the difference between a thought and the content of a thought, although he is acutely aware of the questions such a distinction would help to answer. He does not, therefore, see how descriptions of what is thought can be applied to the thought itself. Yet he is not content just to say that there are things in the world which have certain attributes (for instance, a square tower), and that we have thoughts about them which do not have these attributes, but those of an accident in the category of doing. (Had he taken this straightforward path, he would have been unable to solve the aspect of the problem of universals he was then considering in the way he wished to do at this stage.[6]) He therefore postulates the likenesses in the mind, which he regards purely as contents, which are qualified by feigned attributes, such as being square or being ten metres tall, and are really not any thing at all. He places these in relation to thoughts as their immediate objects – but only, it seems, when the real thing is not present. When the object of thought is actually being perceived, says Abelard (21: 18–23), the mind has no need for a likeness of it. This comment suggests a rather different view of likenesses from that which he has been taking, as if they were memory-pictures which substitute where necessary for real things.

Abelard ends this account of cognition by discussing the idea of abstraction (25: 1 – 26: 3). In doing so, he implicitly assumes the idea of a content for the act of thinking – distinct both from the act as an act, and from the direct object of thought. Already, in the very process of elaborating his theory, he seems to be leaving behind his earlier construction, which needed to use likenesses as the objects of thoughts. Abstraction is not for Abelard, as it was for Boethius, a matter of discerning a real universal by collecting sense-impressions of many particulars of the same kind. Rather, according to Abelard, when it abstracts the intellect attends to a form or forms without considering the matter to which they are attached, or to the matter, without considering its forms. For instance, I might attend to a man just as substance, ignoring all the other forms which characterize him, or I might attend just to his bodiliness, or I might join together his substance and his bodiliness in my mind, whilst still leaving out of account his being-alive, rationality and the rest. Abelard has to explain why thoughts gained through abstraction are not erroneous (*cassi*), even though they conceive things other

[6] See below, pp. 185–6.

than they are (a man is not just substance, or just bodily substance). When I regard a man only as substance or only as a body, he explains, I am not conceiving anything in his nature which is not there, but I am not attending to all which he has. My thought would be erroneous if I regarded his nature as being only substance or only body. There is nothing erroneous, however, about regarding him only as substance or body: the 'only' must apply to the regarding, not to the way in which the man exists.[7]

In the commentary on *De interpretatione* in the *Logica* (*sup.Per* 312: 12 – 334: 17) Abelard develops the ideas he had broached in the discussion of universals, and presented there in a not entirely coherent form, into a more systematic theory of cognition. His strategy now is, following the suggestion of Boethius in the preface to his second commentary on the *Isagoge*, to distinguish three sorts of cognition: by the senses, through imagination and by the intellect.

Abelard sets out his scheme in some detail. Sensory perception, by which we gain a loose grasp of the thing in question (*rem leviter attingimus*), is described as a merely mechanical process. We can be sensing something even if we are not paying any mental attention to it: I am, he would say, hearing the birdsong now, although I am so preoccupied by the sentence I am writing that I am not aware of it.[8] Once we go beyond the stage of unconscious, mechanical perception, Abelard considers that we are using imagination. Although Abelard continues to hold, as he does in commenting on Porphyry, that there is no need for an imaginary likeness when the object of which we are thinking is present (315: 14–18), he also cites and supports Aristotle's view (316: 20 – 317: 7) that thoughts cannot be had without *imaginationes*. The apparent contradiction is explained by saying (317: 9–11) that 'when the mind first applies itself, that application and beginning of thought, before it distinguishes the nature or any property of a thing, is called *imaginatio*'. When the object about which we are thinking is not actually present, the initial stage of mechanical sense perception is omitted. Imagination in this case consists of attending to a mental image, rather than fixing the attention of the mind on the thing itself. Abelard says a good deal about these likenesses or images. As in the *Isagoge* commentary, they are distinguished from thoughts (Boethius' 'likenesses') and, even

[7] 25: 23–8: 'Cum enim hunc hominem tantum attendo in natura substantiae vel corporis . . . profecto nihil nisi quod in ea est intelligo, sed non omnia quae habet attendo. Et cum dico me attendere tantum eam in eo quod hoc habet, illud "tantum" ad attentionem refertur, non ad modum subsistendi, alioquin cassus esset intellectus.'

[8] *Sup.Per.* 317: 25–30; cf. *sup.Por.* 21: 22–6.

more emphatically, Abelard insists that they are not things of any sort.[9] Abelard sometimes talks of these likenesses as if they were memory pictures (314: 1–3, 8–12). But he also, as before, compares them (315: 18–20) to dream-images of non-existent things – imaginary castles and cities; and he considers that we use images in order to think about incorporeal things, such as rationality.

Abelard can afford to take this rather broad and vague view of mental images, because he now has a very firm view about the imagination, of which they are a function, as a mere preparation for thought. Imagination, Abelard suggests (318: 11–22), is an imperfect type of cognition, but one needed in order that perfect cognition through thought may be gained – just as there can never be a house without there being half a house. Abelard is therefore insistent that the images are 'undifferentiated'.[10] No longer are the images or likenesses what is signified by any sort of words, unless someone is speaking explicitly about mental images. Rather, they are used by the mind as mere intermediaries, in order to think about things – rather as we might use a statue of someone as a way of seeing the person it represents.[11] It is because they function in this way that Abelard finds their use in thinking about incorporeal things unproblematic. In these cases, each of us may well form entirely different images, and yet we are thinking about the same thing: since the images are merely being used as pointers in our minds, the difference between my images and yours does not affect our thoughts.[12]

Thoughts are sharply distinct from images of any kind. We *think* about a thing when, using our reason, we consider its nature or one of its properties (317: 32–5).[13] Thought, then, necessarily involves abstraction. Now that images have been very clearly shown not to be the objects of thoughts, Abelard concentrates on developing the discussion of the contents of think-

[9] *Sup.Per.* 314: 25–7: 'Si quis autem quaerat utrum ipsae imaginariae formae, secundum quas imaginatio sive intellectus habentur, aliquid sint, negamus. Non enim vel substantiae sunt vel formae a substantiis sustentatae'; cf. 315: 5–6.

[10] See e.g. *sup.Per.* 316: 19, 317: 2.

[11] See below, pp. 186–7.

[12] 329: 3–9: 'Cum enim vim et naturam rerum insensibilium attendimus, sicut spirituum vel qualitatum quas non sentimus, alius aliam fingit imaginem et alius aliam, cum tamen utraque vim naturae recte attendat. Cum enim de rationalitate ego et alius cogitamus eamque in eo attendimus, quod animam potentem discernere faciat, vera est utriusque attentio et eadem, licet diversas imagines pro eo constituamus.'

[13] 317: 32–6; cf. 317: 12–15: 'Ubi vero attendit naturam aliquam rei in eo quod res est vel ens vel substantia vel corpus vel alba vel Socrates, intellectus dicitur, cum quidem de confusione quae imaginationis erat ad intellectum per rationem ducitur.'

ing, which he had already begun developing when treating abstraction in the *Isagoge* commentary. Just as the intellect can attend to the same thing in different ways – as a substance, a piece of wood, a bodily thing – so it can attend to the same image in different ways and so with different thoughts (329: 10–19). When we think, we grasp a certain property or properties of a thing and leave others out of account. We might think of something completely unitary, such as (this particular) rationality. But we might also think of man, as we do when we hear the word 'man', and this will involve our thinking of a rational, mortal animal. Yet, Abelard insists (325: 19–25), this will still be a simple, non-composite thought. There is a single action of the mind, by which the substance and the *differentiae* which inform it are considered. If, by contrast, I hear the phrase 'mortal, rational animal', my thought will be composite, involving three separate actions. In the case of the thought stimulated by the word 'man', animal, mortality and rationality are already joined together, whereas the phrase 'rational, mortal animal' requires the mind to do the joining, which it does, Abelard suggests, by running from one image to another (326: 21). The very process of thinking thus involves assembling (or taking apart) images. But this process has its limitations, and it is not identical with thought, as Abelard goes on to explain (328: 1 – 329: 28). Suppose that Socrates is sitting down and I hear the (true) statement, 'Socrates stood' or 'Socrates will stand': I form a conception (*conceptio*) which joins together the image of standing and that of Socrates (328: 7–17). But there is nothing in this conception, which I have at the moment before my mind, to connect it to the past or the future, rather than the present. The truth of our thoughts must be judged, therefore, not according to 'a conception or the disposition of images' (*conceptio vel dispositio imaginum*), but rather according 'to the attention of the mind'. Although I put together at this moment the images of Socrates and standing, I do not do so in order to attend to them as if they were together at present.[14] A little later (330: 23–6), Abelard will make it clear that the attention of the mind can vary, not merely to regard things as past or future, but also as hypothetical. Images, indeed, belong to the imagination, which man shares with other animals, whereas the power of discernment is the characteristic of reason. And so the correctness of a thought depends entirely on the 'attention of the mind': it does not matter, ultimately, how the images – which are mere signs, used by the mind – are disposed, nor what these signs are. Once he has seized upon this point,

[14] 328: 22–4: 'Non enim ad hoc imagines in animo colligo praesentialiter ut praesentialiter sic esse attendam, sed sic antea contigisse vel contingendum esse.'

Abelard tends to forget about the joining of images and to talk in terms of mental acts of attention. For instance, when we understand a phrase such as *homo rudibilis* ('a man who can bray': the example plays on its similarity in sound to *homo risibilis*, the standard illustration of a *proprium*) there are three attentions or actions of the mind: one regarding each of the things – a man, and something which can bray – and a third which joins the two together (and shows us that this is an empty thought) (330: 11–18).[15]

THE LATER THEORY OF COGNITION

The theory of cognition Abelard advances in the *De intellectibus* can seem deceptively close to that of the *Logica*: the terminology is the same, and some passages are almost the same in wording. Yet Abelard has taken the chance to revise his earlier views substantially and to remove some of the uncertainties and inconsistencies which arose from the disparity between his own theory of universals and the Aristotelian basis on which he was working.

It is with regard to the imagination, the notion which produced most of the difficulties in the *Logica*, that Abelard concentrates his revisions in *De intellectibus*. Abelard emphasizes the point he had already made in the *De interpretatione* commentary, that imagination, like sense-perception, is common to men and beasts.[16] No longer is imagination, in one of its forms, seen as a fixing of the mind on a thing being perceived by the senses. When a thing is being perceived by the senses, then not merely (as in the earlier theory) is there no need for an image or likeness: imagination itself has no part at all.[17] Whether or not a sense-perception is attended to depends

[15] Abelard also holds that thought itself, although it represents reality, does not make some of the distinctions made by language, between for instance asserting something (as a statement does) and saying the same thing without asserting it: there is no distinction in the thought produced by 'white man' and that produced by 'the man is white' (except perhaps the time signified by the present-tense verb), nor between 'the running man' and 'the man is running'; nor is there a distinction between the thought produced by 'Would that the King would come!' and that by 'I wish the King would come' (*sup.Per.* 327: 7–41).

[16] *De int.* 106: 26–34: 'Et notandum quod ubicumque sensus esse potest, et imaginatio. Nam et bruta animalia, rebus quas senserant abscedentibus, imaginationem earum, teste Boetio, retinent, ipsis adhuc rebus quas senserant per quamdam recordationem adhaerentia ex imaginatione, sicut antea facerant ex sensu; et prout valent, quaedam longius, quaedam brevius hanc imaginationem deferunt quam sensus in eis reliquit impressam'; cf. *sup.Per.* 317: 30–2.

[17] 106: 18–19: 'Ubi enim sensus agit, imaginatio simul in ipsum agere non potest'; cf. 105: 30–2.

on the intellect, not the imagination. Imagination does, however, have an important role in retaining sense-impressions of things no longer there. It does for absent things exactly what the senses do for those which are present.[18] The perceptions of imagination are, like those of the senses, 'undifferentiated' – that is, they have not yet been sorted out by the discerning and deliberating intellect (105: 30–3).

Abelard's argument so far would seem to suggest that the images in our imagination can only be of things we have perceived with our senses. But he must explain Aristotle's view, relayed by Boethius, that we cannot have thoughts which are not accompanied by images (106: 38–40). Since many of our thoughts are about incorporeal things, and many features even of corporeal things are not sensibly-perceptible, imagination will also include perceptions which are not derived from the senses at all.[19] In his earlier theory, Abelard had presented such images of non-corporeal things as figments which our minds produce to act as signs and help us in our process of thinking. Now his approach is quite different. Our thoughts – even those of incorporeal things – are, indeed, accompanied by images, but this is not an aid to thinking but a distraction. As a result of human weakness, all our cognition must begin from sense-perception, and there is thus instilled in us the habit of conjuring up images of sensible things, even when they are not required.[20] For example, suppose that I want to think just about the human nature in a particular man – to regard him as a rational, mortal animal, leaving aside all his many other features. None the less, the imagination forces all sorts of other things into mind against my will: his colour, his height and various other of his accidental features which I know from having seen him. And, when I try to think of something incorporeal, I am compelled by the habit of my senses, to imagine it corporeally: when I think of an uncoloured object, for example, I must imagine it as coloured (107: 12–26). Even when I think about an object which I am also perceiving at the same time with my senses, I will not be free from images of the imagination. Suppose I am looking at a stick and thinking about it: my

[18] 106: 19–22: 'abscedente sensu, locum eius supplet (*sc.* imaginatio), non quidem sentiendo, sed rem absentem absque ulla discernens diiudicatione, sicut et sensus facit percipiendo'.

[19] 106: 40 – 107: 5: 'Unde, cum plerosque de incorporeis rebus habeamus intellectus – sunt de his quoque corporeis quae nullo unquam sensu attractavimus – oportet iuxta Aristotelem imaginationem dici quam nos supra descripsimus: omnem videlicet confusam animae perceptionem sine sensu, sive illa quidem perceptio ex sensu surrexerit, sive minime.'

[20] 107: 7–12: 'dum in aliqua re per intellectum aliquam eius naturam aut proprietatem deliberare nitimur, eamque sola attendere curamus, ipsa sensus consuetudo a quo omnis human notitia surgit, quaedam per imaginationem ingerit animo quae nullo modo attendimus'; cf. 103: 19–26.

imagination will form an image of, for instance, its hardness, which I am not actually sensibly-perceiving at the time. Can we ever think about things without this undesired accompaniment of sensory images? Abelard suggests that this form of pure thought is what Boethius had in mind when he wrote about 'intelligence' (*intelligentia*) (107: 31 – 108: 13). Boethius apparently believed that a few men might enjoy this type of cognition on earth, but Abelard concludes that, in Aristotle's view, intelligence was open to God and to men in this life only through special, ecstatic revelation.

Now that images play only the role of impediments in the process of thought, Abelard gives far more attention to the act of thinking itself. For example, in the *Logica*, thinking about things involved joining together images (for instance, images of Socrates and of standing), although as Abelard developed his account he tended to ignore this feature. In *De intellectibus* there is no more mention of putting together images in order to put together thoughts. Instead (110–14) Abelard speaks in terms of a succession of acts of thinking. The word *concipio* takes on a new meaning. Rather than being linked to the formation of mental images, it is used as a way of talking about the contents of an act of thought. For instance, Abelard glosses Aristotle's comment that 'sound thoughts' (*sanos intellectus*) are 'likenesses of things' as meaning that they are ones 'conceiving a thing in the way in which the thing is'.[21] In the Porphyry commentary, Abelard had used the term 'conception' (*conceptio*) to stand for a mental image or likeness; in the *De interpretatione* commentary Abelard used the same term to refer to conjoined images;[22] but in the *De intellectibus*, when Abelard talks in terms of 'things being conceived', there is no suggestion that he means anything but the way something is thought about. For example, Abelard explains that there are many different concepts in which one can think of human nature, not just the concept of 'man', the name of a species, but also the concept of a sitting man or a horned man, or even of a particular man (124: 31–8).[23]

Some modern readers might feel that Abelard's revised view of thought

[21] 115: 1–5: 'Sanos autem intellectus Aristoteles in eodem rerum similitudines appellat, hoc est ita concipientes ut rei status sese habet, veluti cum hominem intelligo vel etiam hominem esse risibilem vel non esse risibilem.' The point of adding 'non esse risibilem' is to stress that even if I think of the false statement 'Man is not capable of laughter', my thought of man is not empty – there really are men. This passage is also cited by Shimizu ('From vocalism', p. 40), who rightly says that it shows Abelard thinking in terms of the relationship 'between contents of *intellectus* and actual states of things'.

[22] See e.g. *sup.Por.*, 23: 32, 24: 1; *sup.Per.*, 328: 13, 19.

[23] See below, p. 190 for this quotation and further discussion.

and imagination is less persuasive than his earlier one, and that it represents a retreat from an authentically Aristotelian acceptance of sense-perception to a more typically twelfth-century and Platonic emphasis on the intelligible. This would not be fair. For Aristotle, intellectual knowledge, though desirable, is incomplete because, by its nature, it is knowledge of universals, not particulars. For Abelard, who does not accept the existence of real universals, all knowledge must, ultimately, be knowledge of particulars, although the intellect can, if it wishes, disregard their particularity. Aristotle needs to posit images as an accompaniment to intellectual cognition in order to help link it back to the world of particular things (and thirteenth-century thinkers such as Aquinas would show on this basis that, in an indirect sense, the intellect could know particulars). From Abelard's point of view, however, as he came to see clearly in *De intellectibus*, these images can only be an obstacle to thought, even if they are useful as records of past sense-impressions.

All these changes show Abelard carefully moulding his own views, although he keeps to the vocabulary he has inherited and is anxious to seem to follow the authority of Aristotle and Boethius. The next chapter will explain how some of these developments are also important for the way they affected Abelard's treatment of universals.

Chapter 8

Universals

For Abelard, there is not really *a* problem of universals, but three different, related ones. The first is the problem posed by the question: are there any universal things? It has been explained here already that Abelard is sure that the answer is negative. He may have been predisposed to this view because of the special way (*in voce* exegesis) he had learned, as a young logician, to interpret the *Categories* and *Isagoge*.[1] But he is able to support it by a series of arguments in the *Logica* (*sup.Por.* 10: 17–16: 18) and the *Glossulae* (513: 15 – 522: 9) to show that each of the various ways in which his contemporaries held that there are universal things leads to contradiction. These arguments have been carefully analysed by modern scholars and need no further commentary.[2] Abelard considers that, if there are no universal things, universals must be words. This leaves him with two further problems. The first, on which he concentrates most of his attention, is a problem about semantics. Abelard holds that every thing is particular, but he also recognizes that our language and thinking depend heavily on universals. In statements such as 'Socrates is a man' and 'Plato is white', the predicates 'man' and 'white' signify universals. But how can they do so if there are no universals? Using his theory of cognition as a basis, Abelard develops a sophisticated answer to this question in the *Logica*, which he revises in the *Glossulae* and *De intellectibus* in line with his new analysis of imagining and thinking. The second question is ontological. Among Abelard's underlying principles is not only nominalism, but also what has been called here 'strong naturalism'. Abelard considers that every substance belongs (and is unproblematically known to belong) to a natural kind. This assumption runs through his entire ontology, and it is also an element in Abelard's semantics of universal words. Abelard needs to show *how* it is

[1] See above, pp. 108–10.

[2] See esp. Tweedale, *Abailard on universals*, pp. 89–132.

compatible with his nominalism: to explain in what way things can really belong to the same kind, if every thing – substance and form – is particular. For many thinkers, the semantic and the ontological questions about universals are very closely related. Many realists, for instance, say that things belong to the same kind because each shares in the same universal properties, and that predicates for properties refer to these real universals. For Abelard, however, the two questions are sharply distinct. He tackles the ontological question far less openly and clearly than the semantic one, and his solution, in so far as he has one, is surprising.

There are, however, three preliminaries which need to be treated before the central thread of Abelard's thought on universals can be clearly presented. First, what Abelard means when he says that universals are words must be explained. This is a matter of ground-clearing – of showing that an issue which might seem to be central is merely peripheral. Second, it is necessary to comment on what might seem to be a radical difference between how Abelard conceived of the problem of universals and how a modern philosopher would present it. Third, the technical terms which Abelard uses to analyse the semantics of universals need to be glossed.[3]

[3] There is a considerable literature on Abelard's theory of universals. Long before *sup.Por.* and the *Glossulae* were made available, it was discussed on the basis of his brief comments in the *Historia*, second-hand reports and inauthentic texts. The first discussion to take account of the most important textual evidence was by Abelard's editor, B. Geyer, 'Die Stellung Abaelards in der Universalienfrage nach neuen handschriftlichen Texten' in BGPMA Supplementenband 1, 1913, pp. 101–27. On Geyer's interpretation and the other analyses published up until about 1970, see Tweedale, *Abailard on universals*, pp. 3–7. Important modern discussions include P. Vignaux, 'Note sur le nominalisme d'Abélard' in *Pierre Abélard*, pp. 523–7; W. Gombocz, 'Abaelards Bedeutungslehre als Schlüssel zum Universalienproblem' in *Petrus Abaelardus*, pp. 153–64; G. Küng, 'Abélard et les vues actuelles sur la question des universaux' in *Abélard. Le 'Dialogus', la philosophie de la logique* (Geneva/Lausanne/Neuchâtel, 1981) (Cahiers de la revue de théologie et de philosophie 6), pp. 99–113; C. Wenin, 'La signification des universaux chez Abélard', *Revue philosophique de Louvain* 80 (1982), 414–47; Shimizu, 'From vocalism'. Three recent scholars, in especial, have written extensively on the subject: Jean Jolivet, L. de Rijk and Martin Tweedale: Jolivet, 'Comparaison des théories du langage chez Abélard et chez les nominalistes du XIVe siècle' in *Peter Abelard*, pp. 163–78; 'Non-réalisme et platonisme chez Abélard. Essai d'interprétation' in *Abélard en son temps*, pp. 175–95; 'Trois variations médiévales sur l'universel et l'individu: Roscelin, Abélard, Gilbert de la Porrée', *Revue de métaphysique et de morale* 1 (1992), 111–55 at pp. 128–41. Tweedale: *Abailard on universals*; De Rijk: 'The semantical impact of Abailard's solution of the problem of universals' in *Petrus Abaelardus*, pp. 139–50; (more briefly) 'Abelard's semantic views and later developments' in H. Braakhuis, C. Kneepkens and L. de Rijk (eds.), *English logic and semantics* (Nijmegen, 1981) (Artistarium supplementa 1), pp. 1–58 at pp. 1–5, 50–1. For de Rijk on Tweedale see his 'Martin M. Tweedale on Abailard. Some criticisms of a fascinating venture', *Vivarium* 23 (1985), 81–97, answered by Tweedale in 'Reply to Prof. de Rijk', *Vivarium* 25 (1987), 3–

THREE PRELIMINARIES

Voces and *sermones*

Abelard himself does not just propose his nominalism by denying that there are any universal things. He also asserts what universals are – they are words. Or, more precisely, in the *Logica* he asserts that universals are *voces* (the usual term in Latin for a spoken or written word); but in the *Glossulae* Abelard argues that universals are *not voces*, but rather *sermones*. *Sermo* means 'a speech': it is a term not used before by logicians writing about universals, to which Abelard wishes to give a new, technical meaning. It is natural to imagine that, when he sharply repudiated his earlier view that universals are *voces*, Abelard was signalling an important change in his thinking about universals. Most historians have, indeed, placed great emphasis on this shift.[4] Yet, on examination, Abelard's new terminology turns out to do no more than clarify the way in which he had earlier stated his position on universals. It does not contribute to his really important task: that of *justifying* this position.

When, in the *Logica*, Abelard argued that universals are *voces*, he very clearly wished to insist that they are not things of any sort. But, someone might object, words (*voces*) themselves *are* things. To a modern reader, this might seem a merely pedantic quibble. For a philosopher who shared the twelfth-century understanding of *voces*, it had to be taken seriously.

'Word' is not a completely accurate translation of *'vox'*. Literally, *vox* means "a voice". Following Priscian, twelfth-century grammarians and philosophers also used *'vox'* by synecdoche to refer to the sounds produced by the vocal chords of men and other animals. These sounds might be without meaning (as with nonsense words such as *'blityri'*, or a baby's babble), or meaningful. Meaningful *voces* (*voces significativae*) might have their significance naturally (as with the bark which indicates that a dog is angry) or by human imposition and convention: such *voces* (*voces significativae ad placitum*) are what is ordinarily meant by the term 'words'. Usually, when Abelard talks of a *vox*, what he has in mind is a *vox significativa ad placitum* (which is why 'word' is usually a good translation for *vox* in Abelard's writing). When he says that universals are *voces*, he means that

22; de Rijk's own 'Postscript' to the exchange is on p. 23. Peter King has written a Princeton PhD thesis (1982), 'Peter Abailard and the problem of universals'. He has informed me, however, that the work no longer represents his views on the subject, and so I have not made use of it.

4 See e.g. de Rijk, 'The semantical impact', pp. 139–44.

they are *voces significativae ad placitum*. This does not, however, answer the objection that *voces* are things. Whether it has meaning or not, a *vox* is what is produced by the action of the vocal chords: it is, in the definition given by Priscian, 'very fine air which has been struck'.[5] It is, then, a thing: what *sort* of thing was the subject of great controversy among logicians and grammarians at the beginning of the twelfth century.[6] Some argued that the *voces* are air (as Priscian's words seem to imply) and so are substances.[7] Others, relying on the authority of Boethius and Aristotle, and finding some means to explain away Priscian's definition, held that *voces* are the measurements of the air which has been struck by the vocal chords – and therefore accidents in the category of quantity.[8] Abelard – at least by the time he wrote the *Logica* – treated the controversy itself as a merely verbal one; but he insisted (against the view of his Master – presumably William of Champeaux) that what carried meaning was a quantity (a measurement of the air) rather than the air itself.[9]

In any case, whether *voces* are regarded as substances or quantities, they will be (in Abelard's view) things. Having decided that universals are *voces* because it can be shown that no thing can be predicable of many, in the manner of a universal, the 'vocalist' – the exponent of the view that universals are *voces* – is now forced to concede that *voces* are themselves things. After ridiculing the idea that there is such a thing as a universal man, wholly present in every particular man, the vocalist has been forced into asserting, far more ridiculously, that it is a puff of air, or the quantity measuring it, which is both one and many. He may protest that this is not what he wishes to do. He is talking, not about words as things but as

5 Hertz, *Prisciani . . . Institutionum* II, p. 5: 1: 'Philosophi definiunt vocem esse aerem tenuissimum ictum.'

6 A full account of the different views is found in the Priscian *Glosule* (1500 edn, ff. iii^v–iiii^v; the whole section on *vox* has now been edited in I. Rosier, 'Le commentaire des Glosulae et des Glosae de Guillaume de Conches sur le chapitre De Voce des Institutiones Grammaticae de Priscien', *CIMAGL* 63 (1993), 115–44 at pp. 119–30). Abelard refers to the controversy in his discussion of quantity at *Dial.* 65: 23–71: 14 and *sup.Pred.* 173: 6 – 177: 3. Treatment of *voces* as both substances and quantities plays a part in discussion of other logical questions – for instance, the meaning of *substantia*: cf. the *Categories* commentary, C8, Vatican, Reg. lat. 230, ff. 44v–45r.

7 The Priscian *Glosule* expound their views (1500 edn, ff. iii^v–iiii^r; ed. Rosier, pp. 119–25).

8 Cf. the Priscian *Glosule* (1500 ed., ff. iiii^{r-v}; ed. Rosier, pp. 125–7).

9 *Sup.Pred.*: 174: 11–13, 31–3; cf. *Dial.* 67: 5–15 where Abelard's Master is identified as holding that only the air properly 'is heard, sounds and signifies'. Abelard's reason for considering the controversy verbal is that much of the discussion hinged on the exact relation in meaning between *oratio* – which Aristotle considers to be a quantity – and *vox*, which Priscian seems to identify with air, which is a substance.

carriers of meaning. Yet, Abelard would suggest in *Glossulae* (523: 40–2) the term *vox* does not allow him to make this distinction: 'when we say, "This *vox* is a genus", it is as if we were to say, "This essence of a *vox* is predicable of many".' And this, as Abelard immediately remarks, is false.

In the *Logica*, Abelard's approach to this problem is simply to ignore it. When he talks of universals as *voces*, he obviously wishes to consider them just as bearers of meaning, but he does not say this explicitly. In the *Glossulae* (522: 10 – 524: 20) Abelard tries to make the position clearer. He thinks that he can do so by giving a new, technical meaning to the word *sermo*, which he contrasts with the meaning of *vox*.[10] In any given case, the *vox* and the *sermo* are 'identical in essence', but they differ in origin. The *vox* owes its origin to nature, Abelard claims – his idea is that a *vox* is either a puff of air or the quantity measuring it. The *sermo*, Abelard says, owes its origin to human convention (*institutio*) – his idea is that a *sermo* is a word as bearer of meaning, and that words convey meaning because a certain group of sounds is accepted, by convention (following an original act of imposition) as the name for things of a given sort.[11]

Abelard provides an analogy – that of an image in stone and the stone from which it is made. Although they are one and the same thing, their origin is different: the condition of being a stone (*status lapidis*) is due to God, the condition of being an image (*status imaginis*) to human craft. This example is close to that of wax and a waxen image, used in the *Theologia Christiana* to illustrate difference in property and, although Abelard does not mention this type of difference here, he seems to be thinking along the same lines.[12] A difference in property occurs when something, *x*, can at the same time be described truly as both '*p*' and '*q*', but 'the *p* is the *q*' is false; this occurs because to say '*p*' implies a property P which is incompatible with the property Q which is implied by saying '*q*'. So, for instance, we can say 'The material (the stone) is not that which is made from the material

[10] At *sup.Por.* 16: 24, Abelard does talk of universal *sermones*, but, *pace* Tweedale (*Abailard on universals*, pp. 141–2), he does not appear to give any special meaning to the term to distinguish it from *uoces* and *uocabula*.

[11] 522: 17–23: 'Quid enim aliud est nativitas sermonum sive nominum, quam hominum institutio? Hoc enim quod est nomen sive sermo, ex hominum institutione contrahit. Vocis vero sive rei nativitas quid aliud est quam naturae creatio, cum proprium esse rei sive vocis sola operatione naturae consistat? Itaque nativitas vocis et sermonis diversitas, etsi penitus in essentia identitas.'

[12] Tweedale (*Abailard on universals*, pp. 142–62) provides a very different analysis of this discussion; he does not think (p. 153) that there is any close parallel between this passage and the treatment of sameness and difference in the *TChr*; cf. also de Rijk, 'The semantical impact', pp. 139–44.

(the image in stone)' because to call something 'the material' is to imply the property of being made by God, not man, and to call something 'that which is made from the material (the image in stone)' is to imply the property of being made by man, not God. The case is parallel if '*vox*' is substituted for 'the material', and '*sermo*' for 'that which is made from the material'. In his discussion of *vox* and *sermo* Abelard goes a stage further, however, and considers a case where what has P is able also to have a further property S which is incompatible with Q. When we describe something as 'a *sermo*', we imply the property of being established by human convention, which is compatible with predicability of many; when we describe something as 'a *vox*', we imply the property of not being established by human convention but being made by God, which is incompatible with predicability of many.

The distinction between *vox* and *sermo* brings out a serious point: that words are universals only because of the human conventions which make them words at all, rather than just sounds. Yet, in one respect, Abelard's position is deceptive. He defends with great ingenuity the position that (523: 37–42) whilst both (a) 'This *vox* is this *sermo*', and (b) 'This *sermo* is a genus' are true, (c) 'This *vox* is a genus' is false. His arguments are convincing, so long as it is understood that '*vox*' means 'a word regarded just as a physical entity, and not with regard to human conventions'. What Abelard does not bring out (and what his way of talking about differences between things which are numerically the same tends to obscure) is that there is something of which it is true *both* that is a physical entity and that it has been established with a meaning according to human conventions and so can be a universal.

There is an unexpected postscript to this topic. Whilst Abelard's view of universals was itself highly influential, at least for a few decades, his attempt to introduce *sermo* as a technical term had little success. In revising the *Theologia Summi Boni* to make the *Theologia Christiana*, Abelard had dutifully substituted *sermones* for *voces* in a passage where he was explicitly contrasting the utterance of words with their function of signifying.[13] But even in the *Glossulae* themselves, Abelard tends not to use the word *sermo* after his initial discussion of it. He prefers to use terms more common among logicians, such as *vocabulum* and *nomen*, to mean 'words as instituted to bear meaning' (by contrast with *voces*). Indeed, very shortly after Abelard introduces the term *sermo*, he glosses it with the more familiar *nomen* (522: 17, 18–19) and a little later (524: 3–5) he explicitly says that statements such

[13] *TSum* 150: 950–3 modified at *TChr* 255: 1955–9. The change is noted and discussed in Mews, 'Aspects', at pp. 16–19.

as *hoc nomen est genus* and *hoc vocabulum 'animal' est genus* are to be accepted. It is hardly surprising, then, that those who adopted Abelard's views about universals, and on many other issues, became known in the second half of the twelfth century, not as 'sermonalists' but as 'nominalists' (*nominales*).[14]

Universal substances and universal forms

When modern philosophers discuss universals, they are usually concerned with properties and relations – in Abelard's terms, 'forms'. They wish to ask, for instance, whether in the sentence 'Socrates is white', 'white' is the word for a real universal property of being white, or whether there are no such universal properties. By contrast, Abelard and his contemporaries discussed universals mainly when commenting on a remark near the beginning of the *Isagoge* about genera and species.[15] Genera and species are universals indeed, but they are universals in the category of substance: that is, they are substance words and, for the realist, substances. When Abelard considers universals, what he has in mind therefore are usually universal substances (as discussed in the theories he attacks) and universal substance words; the sentences he scrutinizes are ones such as 'Socrates is a man', 'Plato is an animal'.

In one sense, this difference between Abelard's approach and that of a modern philosopher is less important than it may seem. Although Abelard concentrates, for the reason explained, on universal substance words, he makes it clear that his theory applies to universals generally. At the beginning of his discussion in the *Logica* (9: 13–17) he comments that, in his treatment of genera and species, Porphyry 'touches on the nature of all universals generally' and he proposes to do the same. In the extended treatment of the passage from Porphyry both here and in the *Glossulae*, Abelard usually talks of 'universals', and only occasionally (under the influence of the text of the *Isagoge*) of 'genera' and 'species'. He defines a universal, following Aristotle, as 'a word which has been so devised that it is appropriate for it to be predicated of many things singly' and, in the *Logica* (*sup.Por.* 16: 39 – 17: 6; cf. 18: 1–2) he brings out very clearly that this definition does not just include substance words. Any word, he claims, which is joined to another by the force of the copula to form a true statement

[14] See Marenbon, 'Vocalism, nominalism' pp. 51–4.; cf. above, p. 113, n. 43.

[15] On this definition and its exact relation to Aristotle's, see Shimizu, 'From vocalism', pp. 16–19.

is said to be 'predicated'; and even verbs are predicated of many things (and therefore are universals), since they contain the 'force' of the copula – 'the man runs' is equivalent to 'the man is running'.[16] From all this, it is clear that Abelard intended his analysis of sentences like 'Socrates is a man (*Socrates est homo*)' also to apply to those like 'Socrates is white (*Socrates est albus*)'. Even the apparent grammatical dissimilarity between these two sentences disappears in Latin: *albus* is, like *homo*, a 'name (*nomen*)' and can stand on its own to mean 'white man'.

In another sense, however, Abelard's concentration on substances in his discussion of universals has very important consequences, since (as will become clear) it makes it far easier for him to focus on the semantics of universals and leave the ontological question he also needs to answer aside, to be considered in a briefer and less explicit analysis.

Signification, imposition and naming

Abelard discusses the semantics of universal words using three main technical terms, current among the logicians of his time: 'signification (*significatio*)', *impositio* (imposition) and *nominatio* (naming). Since none of them corresponds simply to any term used by philosophers nowadays, it will be clearest to look closely at what Abelard says about each of them, and then to ask how they can best be understood to fit together.[17]

The most potentially troublesome of them is 'signification'.[18] At the beginning of the twelfth century, logicians tended to use the word both in a

[16] Cf. *sup.Per.* 348: 15–30. A great deal has been made by some scholars of Abelard's observation that a predication might be analysed into three parts (Subject – copula – predicate: *homo est currens*) or into two (Subject – predicate: *homo currit*) (cf. the references given in p. 142, n. 11), and Tweedale (*Abailard on universals*, pp. 283–304) and Küng ('Abélard', pp. 99–103) make the idea of two-part predication a centrepiece of their reconstruction of his theory of universals. These views are hard to reconcile with an early dating of the *Dialectica*, and lay excessive weight on an element of his thought which Abelard himself never emphasizes; cf. above, p. 41.

[17] There are too many divergences to draw useful analogies between *impositio*, *nominatio* and *significatio* and the Fregean terminology of reference and sense which is so influential in modern semantics: for two attempts which (after giving warning about the many dissimilarities) discover more general parallels between Abelard and Frege, see Tweedale, *Abailard on universals*, pp. 305–27 and K. Jacobi, 'Abelard and Frege: the semantics of words and propositions', *Atti del congresso internazionale di storia della logica (San Gimignano, 1982)* (Bologna, 1983), pp. 81–96.

[18] On signification in the late eleventh and early twelfth century, see especially de Rijk, *Logica modernorum* II, 1 and K. Fredborg, 'Speculative grammar' in Dronke, *Twelfth-century philosophy*, pp. 177–95.

broad sense, according to which any sort of way in which language stands for a thought or a thing is a type of signification; and in a stricter sense, as a term for the particular type of signification-in-the-broad-sense they thought most important. (In modern usage 'meaning' can be similarly equivocal.) A good example of Abelard's use of 'signification' in the broad sense is when, in the *Dialectica* (111: 27 – 112: 13), he distinguishes four main types of signification: by imposition, determination, generation and exclusion (*remotio*).[19] In the section of the *Dialectica* which immediately follows the fourfold division of signification, Abelard shows how he also, even at this early stage, had in mind a stricter or proper, as well as a broad, sense of the term. According to the 'correct and proper definition' of 'signification', he says, a word signifies only those things which are conceived by the mind through it – a definition which corresponds roughly to what he has just called signification by 'generation'.[20] Abelard became even surer of this view as his thought developed, and he tended to use 'signify' in this stricter way.[21] In its proper sense, then – and from now on, the term will be used here in this sense, unless otherwise noted – 'to signify *x* (to someone)' means for Abelard (and more generally in medieval discussions from his time onwards) 'to cause a mental act of understanding *x* in someone' or, to put it more briefly, 'to a cause a thought of *x* in someone'.[22]

'Imposition' has been mentioned in an earlier chapter. The idea of impo-

[19] For signification by imposition and generation, see below; signification by representation (a term frequently used in Abelard's time) is the relationship between a word and an accident of the substance it names which is contained in the sense of the word: so in 'Socrates is a man' and 'Socrates is a rational thing', 'man' and 'rational thing' signify rationality by representation. 'Signification by exclusion' is Abelard's name for the relationship between an unbounded word (*nomen infinitum*) like 'not-man' and what it excludes (man).

[20] 114: 6–15: 'Si tamen "significare" proprie ac secundum rectam et propriam eius diffinitionem <as>signamus, non alias res significare dicemus nisi que per vocem concipiuntur ... Laxe tamen nimium sepe auctoritas ad omnem impositionem "significationis" nomen extendit.'

[21] See e.g. *sup.Per.* 309: 17–21, 335: 29–30; *Glossulae* 530: 24–8 (quoted in note 22); cf. M. Fumagalli Beonio-Brocchieri *La logica di Abelardo* (2nd edition, Milan, 1969); trsl. S. Pleasance, *The Logic of Abelard* (Dordrecht, 1969), pp. 29–36 (of translation); de Rijk, *Logica Modernorum* II, 1, pp. 193–5, 'Abelard's semantics', pp. 85–6.

[22] I copy this excellent definition from P. Spade's review of Tweedale, *Abailard on universals* in *Nous* 14 (1980), 479–83; cf. P. Spade, 'Some epistemological implications of the Burley-Ockham dispute', *Franciscan Studies* n.s. 35 (1975), 213–22, at 213–14 and Gracia, *Individuation*, p. 222. See e.g. *sup.Por.* 18: 37–19: 2 (quoted by Spade); *Glossulae* 530: 24–8: 'Solet enim quaeri de significatione et intellectu istorum universalium nominum, quas res scilicet significare habeant. Nam cum audio hoc nomen "homo" ... quam rem in ipso intelligam, quaero.'

sition is used to answer the question: how did this or that group of sounds or written signs ('man', 'horse') come to mean what they mean? Abelard (*Dial.* 576: 35–7; *sup.Pred.* 112: 9–14) postulates an original imposition, in which the impositor attached a certain group of sounds to a certain sort of thing: 'man' to men, 'horse' to horses and so on. Abelard sees this imposition as having had a double effect. On the one hand, that group of sounds is thenceforth the word for any thing of that sort: 'man', for instance, is said to be imposed *on* all men. But imposition does not just fix the extension of words, it also determines what would now be called their 'intension'. We must, says Abelard, distinguish between those things *on which* a word is imposed and that *according to which* it is imposed. He brings this out clearly by contrasting a definition and the word for the thing defined. 'Mortal, rational animal' is an adequate definition of man (since all men and only men are mortal, rational animals) but, says Abelard, it does not include all the *differentiae* of man (he may have in mind, for instance, 'two-footed'). Whilst, then, 'mortal, rational animal' and 'man' are imposed on all the same things, the definition is imposed just according to *some* of what man is essentially – a mortal, rational animal – whereas 'man' is also imposed according to the other *differentiae* of man.[23] The intension of a word thus depends on what the original impositor had in mind. Suppose (by contrast with the example just given) that the impositor of 'man' did not have all the *differentiae* of man in mind when he imposed the word, then the meaning (*sententia*) of 'man' should be taken as restricted to just those he envisaged. But there is an important qualification to this idea. The word 'man' should be considered to have been imposed according to all the *differentiae* of man, so long as this is what the impositor intended, even if he did not in fact grasp all of them distinctly.[24] Putting together these different suggestions, it seems that Abelard thought of an original impositor pointing to a member of a natural kind (say a man) and establishing that (i) 'man' will be the word for every thing of that sort and that (ii) 'man' means a substance with the structure of *differentiae* which the substance being

[23] *Dial.* 335: 30–8: 'maximeque illa attendenda est vocum significatio que prima est, idest que in voce ipsa denotatur et secundum quam ipsa vox imponitur, non ea cui imponitur. Nam et cum diffinitio et diffinitum ad ea<m>dem prorsus substantiam habeant impositionem atque enuntiationem, sepe tamen non idem prorsus de ipsa notant. Nam "animal rationale mortale" secundum id tantum hominis substantie datum est, quod est animal informatum rationalitate et mortalitate; "homo" vero secundum ceterarum quoque formarum differentiarum informationem.' Cf. *sup. Pred.* 112: 40–1; 115: 39–40.

[24] *Dial.* 595: 26–8: 'Licet autem impositor non distincte omnes intellexerit hominis differentias, secundum omnes tamen quaecumque esse<n>t, tamquam ipsas confuse conciperet, vocabulum accipi voluit.'

pointed to has, whatever exactly that structure may be. Abelard also (*Dial.* 595: 32–9) thought of denominative words being imposed in the same type of way, although he does not explain exactly how this could take place.

In Abelard's usage, a word 'names (*nominat*)' a thing if and only if the thing falls within the extension of the word. So, for example, 'white thing (*album*)' names this white page and that white house.[25] Both 'man' and 'Socrates' name Socrates, although 'man', Abelard explains (*Dial.* 563: 1–5), does not 'properly demonstrate him': Socrates is not in what can be understood from the word (*intelligentia vocis*). 'Naming' therefore includes both the semantic relationship which would now be called 'naming' ('Socrates' to Socrates) and also generally that of reference ('man' to Socrates, Plato, this man, that man . . .).

THE SEMANTICS OF UNIVERSALS: THE COMMON CONCEPTION THEORY OF SIGNIFICATION

As soon as Abelard has proposed in the *Logica* his view that universals are not things, but words, he realizes that he faces a considerable task to justify it: *maxime de eorum significatione dubitatur* (18: 7) – there is the greatest question about what they signify. 'Signify' here is meant in the broad sense – a complete semantic account of universal words is needed. In the following passage, Abelard identifies two different ways of approaching the problem.[26] One approach asks about the imposition of universal words. If there are no universal things, what is the cause according to which universal words are imposed? The other approach asks about what universal words signify. It will be clearest to begin (in this section and the next) by examining what Abelard says about what universal words signify.

Abelard explains (18: 23–37) that, if we say, for instance, 'Socrates is in the house', there is a thing, Socrates, of which the word 'Socrates' produces a thought. But if we use a universal word and say 'A man (*homo*) is in the house', then – even if Socrates is the only person in the house – there is no thing of which the universal word *homo* produces a thought, since there are no universal things and the universal word 'man' is not such as to produce a thought of Socrates or any other man or collection of men.

[25] Cf. *Dial.* 563: 4–5; 111: 32, 113: 6. Abelard's use of *nominare/nominatio* was standard: see e.g. the passages from the Priscian *Glosule* quoted by Mews, 'Nominalism and theology', p. 18, n. 37 and by de Rijk, *Logica modernorum* II, 1, p. 228; cf. Tweedale, 'Logic (i): to the time of Abelard', p. 211.

[26] The two different aspects of Abelard's discussion are well distinguished by Shimizu, 'From vocalism', pp. 21–4.

'Therefore', says Abelard (18: 37 – 19: 2), 'neither "man" nor any other universal word seems to signify, since there is no thing of which it produces a thought.' To put it in terms of the definition of 'signify' given above: if 'to signify *x*' means 'to cause a thought of *x* in someone', what can be the *x* in the case of universal words, if there are no universal things?

Abelard's strategy, here in the *Isagoge* commentary of the *Logica*, is to identify an *x* which is not a thing. There is, he argues, an object of which the thoughts caused by universal words are thoughts, but that object is not a thing. What, then, is it? The theory of cognition he held at this time gives the answer – indeed, it may well have been devised especially to provide it. According to this theory, the object of a thought is a thing when that thing is actually present, but otherwise it is a mental likeness.[27] The likeness (or 'form' or 'image') may be of a particular, but it may be 'common' – 'containing in it a resemblance to many things although considered in itself as one thing'.[28] When I hear the word 'Socrates', a likeness of the particular person Socrates appears in my mind. When I hear the word 'man', a representation springs up in my mind which is common to all men and particular to no one of them.[29] These common conceptions are the object for the thoughts conveyed by universal words, and so, therefore, are what universal words signify (22: 25–7; 24: 28–31). And, as Abelard stresses, mental images are not things: they are figments – nothing rather than something.[30]

Abelard's common conception theory provides a direct answer to the question about the (proper) signification of universal words. When he claims that mental likenesses or conceptions are not things, Abelard is making a perfectly sensible point, if a little unclearly. As explained, he regards these likenesses purely in terms of their content and it is not unreasonable to say that mental contents are not things. Had Abelard developed his implicit theory of mind more fully and set out his common conception theory more clearly, he would have distinguished between the mental act of thinking

[27] See above, p. 166.

[28] 22: 12–17: 'Rem etiam subiectam intellectui possumus vocare sive veram rei substantiam, veluti quando simul est cum sensu, sive rei cuiuscumque formam conceptam, re scilicet absente, sive ea forma communis sit, <ut> diximus, sive propria; communis, inquam, quantum ad similitudinem multorum quam retinet, licet tamen in se ut res una consideretur.'

[29] 21: 32–6: 'Unde cum audio "homo", quoddam instar in animo surgit quod ad singulos homines sic se habet, ut omnium sit commune et nullius proprium. Cum audio "Socrates", forma quaedam in animo surgit quae certae personae similitudinem exprimit.' The same idea is repeated at the end of Abelard's discussion of abstraction (27: 29–34).

[30] See above, p. 166.

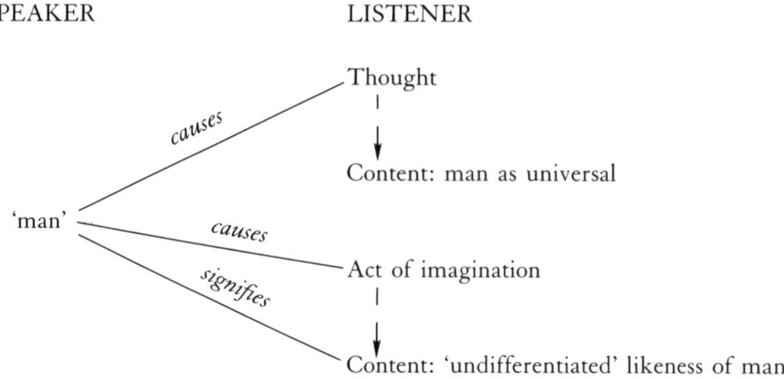

Figure 3. The common conception theory of universals

(which is a thing) and its content (which is not a thing), and the mental act of producing a likeness (which is a thing) and its content (which is not a thing). Figure 3 presents this idealized version of the common conception theory.

There are, of course, many problems, not explicitly considered by Abelard, about the idea of an 'undifferentiated' likeness of, say, man. Abelard seems to be thinking of the likenesses as mental pictures; but how can such a mental picture be without the features which would link it with one sort of man or another (female men or male men, black men or white men, for instance)? Abelard might also be accused of simply begging the large epistemological questions his theory raises: why do we group things together as we do, so that we all form a common likeness of man, but not a common likeness of man and dog? As a strong naturalist, Abelard just assumed that things do belong to natural kinds which we recognize unproblematically.

THE SEMANTICS OF UNIVERSALS: THE LATER THEORY

By the time he looked at the problem of universals again, in the *Glossulae* and the *De intellectibus*, Abelard had abandoned his common conception theory. In fact, he seems to have abandoned it, by implication, even when (perhaps only a few months later) he drew up his discussion of cognition in the *Logica* commentary on the *De interpretatione*.[31] Mental likenesses are

[31] *Sup.Per.* 312: 12 – 332: 7: see above, pp. 167–8.

no longer taken to be the objects of thought, but mere intermediaries used by the mind in the process of thinking. As such, Abelard no longer wishes them to be what is signified by universal words or any words at all. It is quite wrong, Abelard approvingly reports Aristotle as saying, to believe that words were invented to talk about these likenesses in the mind. They were invented, rather, in order to communicate knowledge about the nature of things. Words do indeed produce in the mind of the listener a feigned likeness, but this is merely a means by which they achieve their speaker's object, which is to communicate a thought (*intellectus*).[32]

By the time he wrote the *Glossulae* and *De intellectibus*, Abelard had gone even further and he now envisaged these likenesses as obstacles rather than aids to acquiring a grasp of the nature of things.[33] He could no longer, therefore, explain the signification of universal words as he had done previously, making mental images (which are not things) into the objects of the thoughts caused by universal words. Yet Abelard initially puts the problem to himself in much the same terms as he had used in the *Logica*.[34] 'What things might there be for universal words to signify, or what thing is thought in them?' Suppose I hear the universal word 'man', what thing do I think of in it (*quam rem in ipso intelligam*)? Abelard then gives what he explicitly says is the right answer: what I think of is man (*homo*). This means, as Abelard glosses it a few sentences later:

(A) I conceive through my thought human nature, I attend to that sort of animal (and not, he implies, any particular man).

Abelard devotes the rest of his discussion to answering a critic who argues that (A) is incompatible with Abelard's nominalism – the claim that (N) every thing is particular. The critic argues that if

(1) Man is thought of (*intelligitur*) [by someone]

[32] 315: 28–37: 'Non enim propter similitudines rerum vel propter intellectus similitudinem voces repertae sunt, sed magis propter res et earum intellectus, ut videlicet de rerum naturis doctrinam facerent, non de huiusmodi figmentis, et intellectus de rebus constituerent, non de figmentis, sed tantum per figmenta, quando pro rebus absentibus ipsa constituimus quasi quaedam intersigna rerum. Unde potius voces per ea quibus quasi intersignis utimur, intellectus de rebus non de ipsis constituunt, cum videlicet voces animum audientis ad similitudinem rei applicant, ut in ea non ipsam, sed rem pro qua ponitur, attendat.'

[33] See above, pp. 171–2.

[34] The whole passage, posing the problem and giving the solution, is at *Glossulae* 530: 24 – 531: 29; *De int.* 123: 22 – 124: 38; cf. Tweedale, *Abailard*, pp. 180–185 (an analysis, including translation of extracts) and de Rijk, 'Semantical impact', p. 147; 'Abelard's semantic views', pp. 50–1 (but neither Tweedale nor de Rijk uses *De intellectibus*).

and

(2) Every man is this man or that man (from N)

then

(3) He thinks of (*concipit*) this or that man.

If this syllogism were true, it would imply that (A) could never be the case. Since (A) clearly can be the case, the critic's implication is that Abelard should give up (N). Abelard answers by claiming that (3) does not follow from (2), but rather from

(2') Every thought which is a thought of man (*omnis intellectus intelligens hominem*) is a thought of this man or that man.

But (2'), he says, is not true.

In fact, however, both Abelard and his imaginary opponent are right, depending on how 'think of *x*' is understood. The expression is ambiguous. '*x*' can stand for the object of the thought: this is how in his earlier discussions Abelard took the expression, and how his opponent now takes it. But '*x*' can also stand for the content of the thought. Abelard's objection to his opponent's inference is correct only if '*x*' is taken to stand for the content of the thought, not its object. Abelard's insistence that (3) follows, not from (2), but from the false (2') should, then, be read as claiming (evidently justly) that what is true of the objects of thoughts (for example, that they are particular) need not be true of thought contents.

Abelard has, therefore, modified his earlier view of what is required for a word to signify. He has given up the attempt to find objects for the thoughts caused by universal words. He feels it is enough to point to the contents of these thoughts to show that universal words signify. He brings this out very clearly at the end of his discussion in the *Glossulae*, where he uses statements of wanting as an analogy. 'What do you want?' has two senses: 'What is the thing about which you have a want?' and 'What want do you have?' In the second sense, the question can be answered without there being any thing in the world which is what I want (for example, when what I want is a golden castle). The same applies to thinking. When I hear the word 'man', there is something for me to understand – and so the word is significative – even though there is no thing which is a man and not a particular man: it is enough that the thought of man which the word produces has a content.[35]

[35] 532: 30 – 533: 9; cf. 531: 39 – 532: 3. This passage is well discussed by de Rijk, 'The semantical impact', pp. 147–9 (and see following note).

Does this mean that the signification of universal words simply depends on what happens in people's minds, and is not related to how things are in the world?[36] Clearly this was not Abelard's view. In his earlier theory, the signification of universals was linked to the world by the common conceptions, undifferentiated likenesses of things. In his later theory, as the *De intellectibus* shows, Abelard wished to use the mind's power of abstraction to make the connection between things and the contents of the thoughts caused by universal words.

Abelard had already introduced the idea of abstraction into his discussion of universals in the *Logica*. There (*sup.Por.* 25: 1 – 26: 3) he had explained that the mind 'abstracts' when it attends just to one aspect (*natura vel proprietas*) of something, although in reality the thing has many aspects. An abstracted thought is not a misleading one, however: the abstracted aspect is regarded separately from the other aspects, but not as being separate.[37] Abelard goes on to say (27: 18–34) that abstraction is always involved in thinking of universals, but he then tries, confusingly, to connect this with what he has said earlier in the discussion about undifferentiated conceptions.[38]

In *De intellectibus*, the idea of abstraction is the same, but its connection with universals is more fully developed. Abelard explains (118: 1–5) that thoughts are said to be 'by abstraction' when they regard a form in itself, without its subject (for example, the colour of something is considered apart from the coloured thing), or when 'they dwell on a certain nature indifferently – that is, apart from its division into particulars (*naturam quamlibet indifferenter – absque suorum individuorum discretione meditantur*)'. When I abstract in this way, I do not attend to the distinction which separates one thing from another (*personalis discretio*) and so I consider, for instance, man just in so far as he is a rational, mortal animal, not in that

36 De Rijk has been accused by Tweedale ('Reply', p. 21) of interpreting Abelard in this way, when he says ('The semantical impact', p. 149; cf. n. 33 on p. 151) that a universal 'does not exist in the outside world. Its existence, rather its being given, is just due to some productive way of thinking, and, accordingly, never exceeds the *realm of thinking*' (although 'it *does* exceed the area of *my* (and *your* etc.) thinking'). Tweedale may well be unjust, since de Rijk seems to be saying just that, for Abelard, there are no real universal things, not that there is no basis for them in reality at all.

37 25: 26–8, 32–3: 'Et cum dico me attendere tantum eam in eo quod hoc habet, illud 'tantum' ad attentionem refertur, non ad modum subsistendi, alioquin cassus esset intellectus . . . Separatim namque haec res ab alia, non separate intelligitur'; an explanation along similar lines (distinguishing two senses of *intelligo rem aliter quam sit*: (a) (abstraction) where *aliter* qualifies *intelligo*; (b) (misleading, empty thought) where *aliter* qualifies *quam sit rem*) is found in *De int.*, 120: 21 – 121: 22.

38 Nothing is added in *sup.Per.*: see 331: 6–11.

he is this or that man.[39] Abelard does not think that abstraction is the *only* way through which I can consider human nature. If someone says 'Socrates', the thought produced by that word is one by which I conceive human nature. Here the thought does have a particular thing in the world as its object, Socrates. But Abelard wishes to insist that there are many thoughts by which I also conceive human nature – those, for instance, caused by the words 'white man', 'sitting man', 'man' and even 'horned man' – where I do not have this or that man as the object of my thought.[40]

Even more clearly than in the case of his earlier view, Abelard's new theory about the signification of universal words cannot stand on its own. It rests, just as his earlier theory did, on the ontological presumption that substances have natures, and the epistemological presumption that we can know these natures. His account of abstraction now perhaps suggests a reason for his epistemological presumption. We conceive of man even when we think of any particular man; conceiving just the nature of man is, then, simply a matter of disregarding the distinction which separates one thing from another.

THE SEMANTICS OF UNIVERSALS: IMPOSITION

In the *Logica*, Abelard does not only put forward his theory about the signification by universal words of common conceptions. He also examines the imposition of universal words. One effect of imposition, according to Abelard, is to determine a word's extension – in his terminology, what it 'names'. Since a universal word's extension consists of particular things, Abelard can say straightforwardly that universal words 'in some way signify by naming many different things'. 'Signify' here is used in its broad sense: Abelard says explicitly that what universal words signify in the proper

[39] *De int.* 118: 13–19: 'Sed cum naturam humanam quae singulis inest hominibus ita indifferenter considero ut nullius hominis personalem discretionem attendam, hoc est simpliciter hominem excogito, in eo scilicet tantum quod homo est, id est animal rationale mortale, non etiam in eo quod est hic homo vel ille, universale a subiectis abstraho individuis.'

[40] *De int.* 124: 27–38: 'Non est itaque necesse ut, si hominem intelligam vel aliquem conceptum habeam in quo naturam humanam concipiam, ideo hunc hominem vel illum attendam, cum multi alii et innumerabiles conceptus sint in quibus humana excogitatur natura, sicut et ipsa simplex conceptio huius specialis nominis quod est homo, vel hominis albi simpliciter,** vel hominis [*so MS; Ulivi mistakenly prints* homini] sedentis, vel etiam hominis cornuti – etsi numquam ille sit; et in quibuscumque conceptionibus natura humanitatis attenditur – sive cum discretione certae personae, ut Socratis vel alicuius alterius, sive indifferenter, absque ulla scilicet personae certitudine.' Cf. *Glossulae* 531: 14–19 which is nearly identical up to**.

sense – that of which they produce a thought – are not the many particular single things, but the 'common likeness', although the thought 'is linked (*pertinens*)' to the particulars (as his theory of common likenesses or conceptions explains).[41] But, as well as considering *on* what a word is imposed, Abelard must discover *according to* what it is imposed. In order to do this, he asks what is the 'common cause (*communis causa*)' according to which a universal noun or adjective (*nomen*) is imposed.

The use of the expression 'common cause' may seem surprising. Abelard usually talks of a common cause of imposition in just those cases where no thing or things exist to explain the imposition – where, for instance, there is a denominative word but no particular form from the word for which it is denominated.[42] 'Man' and most other universal words do not seem at first sight to fit this category at all, because in the case of every man there are the particular *differentiae* of rationality, mortality and so on, by virtue of which he is a man. What Abelard must have in mind, however, is that he requires an explanation for why 'man' and other universals can be imposed universally on things of a given kind. The particular rationalities and mortalities of Socrates or Plato do not explain this universality. And were Abelard to posit a thing of any sort as an explanation, he would immediately be conceding the argument to his opponents who say that there are universal things. Here then, as elsewhere when he invokes common causes, Abelard is offering an explanation for how words are used which avoids a direct link with things.

What, then, is the common cause of the imposition of a universal word? Abelard explains that, for instance, 'man' is imposed on many different men from the common cause 'that they are men'. Men, he says (19: 18–20), 'come together in this, that they are men'. 'I do not say', he is careful to add, 'in man – since no thing is a man which is not discrete – but in being a man (*esse hominem*).' Another phrase Abelard uses for 'being a man' and 'that they are men' is 'the *status* of man'.[43] Elsewhere Abelard tends to use

[41] 19: 7–9: 'Nam et res diversas per nominationem quodammodo significant, non constituendo tamen intellectum de eis surgentem, sed ad singulas pertinentem. Ut haec vox "homo" et singulos nominat ex communi causa, quod scilicet homines sunt, propter quam universale dicitur, et intellectum quendam constituit communem, non proprium, ad singulos scilicet pertinentem, quorum communem concipit similitudinem'; cf. 20: 15–16.

[42] See above, pp. 147–9.

[43] Abelard introduces the term *status* part of the way through the discussion (20: 3–4: 'hunc et illum in statu hominis, id est in eo quod sunt homines, convenire dicimus'; 20: 7–8: 'Statum autem hominis ipsum esse hominem, quae non est res, vocamus'). De Rijk ('Martin M. Tweedale', pp. 93–4) argues that *in eo quod sunt homines* should be translated as 'in their being-men' and that *ipsum esse hominem* should be translated as 'just the being-a-man'.

status qualified by the adjectives *specialis* or *generalis* to mean 'the condition of being something which belongs to such and such a species or genus': when something undergoes substantial change, it is said to lose its *status specialis*.[44] To say the *status hominis* means, then, 'the condition of being this sort of thing – a man'. *Status*, Abelard insists, are not things (20: 1, 6; cf. 19: 25–9). There is nothing untoward, Abelard goes on to show (20: 9–12), in saying that a cause – here a cause of the imposition of a word – is not a thing. Often causes are not things. For instance, we say 'He was whipped because he did not wish to go to the forum.' His being whipped is, for Abelard, a thing, an accident in the category of being-done-to; but *not* wishing to do something is nothing at all.[45]

Although in the *Glossulae* (and *De intellectibus)* Abelard concentrates on discussing the signification of universals in terms of thought contents, there is one passage where he explains (531: 30 – 532: 8) that every thing is one in number, like Socrates and Plato, and yet also that 'they are the same, coming together from something, that is to say, from their being men (*convenientes ex aliquo, ex eo scilicet quod sunt homines*)'. He goes on to amplify this comment a little, commenting that this coming-together is not from any thing (*ex aliqua re*) in which they participate, but it is from something (*ex aliquo*) – 'from this, that they are men'. These brief comments indicate that Abelard retained his theory of *status* when he wrote the *Glossulae*, without having developed or changed it.

What is the relationship between *status* and the common conceptions or

The problem with these versions is that (a) they obscure the grammatical structure of the Latin, and (b) they simply are not English.

44 See e.g. *sup.Por.* 84: 9–10: 'res aliqua speciei statum amittit'; cf. 92: 13; *sup.Pred.*, 166: 21–3: ' Unitas vero in substantiam speciei nihil promovet, quia per se nullius speciei statum complet, sicut rationalitas, mortalitas ad complendam substantiam rationalem sufficit, etiamsi omnes aliae formae deessent'; 297: 4–5: 'res quaelibet substantialiter permutatur, specialem statum vel relinquens vel assumens'. Cf. also *sup.Por.* 84: 26, where *status rerum* means 'how *things* are', 'the condition of *things*'; *TChr* 281: 518–30, where *status navigabilis/risibilis* means 'the condition of being able to sail/able to laugh'.

45 The sentence immediately following this justification of why *status* are not things has caused controversy. In Geyer's edition it reads (20: 12–14): 'Statum quoque hominis res ipsas *in* natura hominis statutas possumus appellare, quarum communem similitudinem ille concepit, qui vocabulum imposuit.' The manuscript reads not *in* but *non*. Tweedale (*Abailard on universals*, p. 207) argues that the manuscript reading should be restored and, on this basis, produces a translation which is severely criticized by de Rijk ('Martin M. Tweedale', pp. 94–5), who himself proposes an emendation to *nunc*. Yet Geyer's emendation produces the best sense: 'We can also call *status* those things set up [*statutas*] in the nature of man [that is, the particular mortalities, rationalities and so on], the common likeness of which was grasped by the person who imposed the word <'man'>'; cf. below, p. 195.

thought contents in terms of which Abelard explains the signification of universal words? According to the *Logica* (24: 33–7), it is due to both that universal words have their commonness, although especially to the common cause (the *status*), which is based on the nature of things (*secundum rerum accipitur naturam*). It is tempting to conclude – and some interpreters have done so – that *status* are themselves signified by universal words: that is to say, the common conceptions (in the earlier theory) and the thought contents (in the later theory) are not, in fact, the ultimate objects of the thoughts caused by universal words, but merely their proximate objects, since they themselves have *status* as their objects.[46] An argument for such a reading might be made on the following lines, starting from the idea (recalled at the beginning of this section) that words are not just imposed by their original impositor *on* certain things, but also *according to* something:[47]

(1) That according to which a word is imposed is that word's signification.
(2) The common cause of the imposition of a word is that according to which it is imposed.
(3) Abelard says explicitly that the common causes of the imposition of universal words are *status*.

Therefore

(4) According to Abelard, universal words signify *status*.

The conclusion of this argument, (4), follows uncontentiously from its premisses. Yet there are grounds for thinking that Abelard in fact rejected (4), and that he was able to do so because he did not accept (1).

For Abelard appears deliberately to refrain from stating that universal words signify *status*, and there is an important passage in the Porphyry commentary of the *Logica* (22: 28 – 23: 30) which suggests that he holds a much subtler view. Abelard refers to Priscian's view that universals signify the common conceptions of things in God's mind. According to Abelard, God's common conceptions are indeed of the *status* of things (23: 11–12), but he sharply distinguishes divine common conceptions from human ones (23: 1–2: 'Now this common conception is well attributed to God, not to

46 Tweedale, for example, takes this view, linking it to his theory of two-part predication: see e.g. *Abailard on universals*, p. 304: 'The conclusion of all this is that universal expressions signify types [Tweedale's translation of *status*], but types are not themselves denotable and thus are not at all things.'

47 On imposition, see above, pp. 182–4. Note that even in the *Dialectica* Abelard does not commit himself to the view that signification derives directly from imposition, although some of his phrasing might suggest this (e.g. 595: 18).

man'), contrasting God's knowledge of what he makes with human ignorance.[48] It would seem to follow that human common conceptions (which, according to Abelard, universals do signify) are *not* of the *status* of things. Yet Abelard then remarks that 'the whatever names of whichever existing things' *do* convey knowledge, because (as he had already explained in the *Dialectica*), although the original impositor of a word may not have been able to analyse well the nature or property of the thing (*nec ipse bene excogitare sciret rei naturam aut proprietatem*), he intended to impose the word according to 'some natures or properties of things'. Abelard then goes on to say that universal words signify human common conceptions, for which they are like proper names.

Abelard's argument here makes sense if it is allowed that, plausible though it may be, he does not identify a word's signification with that according to which the word is originally imposed (that is, he rejects (1) above). Rather, Abelard is saying that universal words are intentionally related to *status*, because their original impositors, even if ignorant of the *status* of things, intended them to be imposed according to a thing's nature and properties. He is also distinguishing this open intentional element in universal words from their signification, which is of human common conceptions. There is a good reason to make such a distinction. If a word's signification is that of which it causes a thought, it needs to be more definite than a mere place holder like 'the thing's *status*, whatever it is'.[49]

In the course of this passage, Abelard also remarks (23: 18–20) that we have merely opinion, not knowledge, about 'inner forms which do not come to the senses, such as rationality and mortality, fatherhood, being-in-a-sitting-position'. Abelard can hardly mean by this that words such as 'rational' and 'father' cannot be used to convey knowledge about the world. He remarks explicitly in his commentary to the *De interpretatione*, for instance, that you and I can both think about rationality as that which makes the soul able to discern.[50] Probably what Abelard wants to say, then, is that we

[48] Abelard also mentions this view, which he now associated with both Priscian and Plato, in *sup.Per.* 314: 13–24; 315: 20–1, 26–7. Here he does not bother to make the careful distinction between God's ideas and human common conceptions, perhaps because (see below) universal words are no longer held to signify common conceptions.

[49] If this interpretation is correct, then Jolivet's view that '[l]e fondement des noms universels . . . serait donc, en dernière instance, le système des Idées divines' ('Non-réalisme et platonisme chez Abélard. Essai d'interprétation' in *Abélard et son temps*, pp. 175–95 (= *Aspects*, pp. 257–78), at p. 194, would need to be rejected; cf. also Wenin, 'La signification', pp. 442–3, where Jolivet's line is followed. I discuss Abelard's references to divine ideas in more detail in 'The Platonisms of Peter Abelard' in L. Benakis (ed.), *Neoplatonism in medieval philosophy* (forthcoming).

[50] See above, p. 168, n. 12.

share a conception of these forms through their effects but have no knowledge of what they are in themselves.

Abelard's concentration throughout his discussion of universals on substance words makes it difficult to attribute to him with confidence a complete theory about the semantics of universals. None the less, the discussion in the paragraphs above suggests the following tentative reconstruction. All universal words signify common conceptions (according to the earlier theory) or signify by virtue of producing thoughts with contents derived through abstraction (according to the later theory). The signification of different sorts of universal words is differently related, however, to the real natures of things. In the case of denominatives denominated from sensibly-perceptible forms, which Abelard believes we cognize fully and unproblematically, there is no gap between common conception or thought content and the real nature of the forms. We all know what an accident of, say, whiteness is, and on this knowledge there is based the common conception of whiteness which is signified by 'white' in 'Socrates is white'. In the case of denominatives denominated from non-sensibly-perceptible forms, we know the forms in question only by their effects, and it is on them that our common conceptions or thought contents are based. We can, therefore, use words such as 'rational' and 'father' meaningfully, but without having any grasp of what the forms rationality or fatherhood are in themselves. In the case of substance words, the human common conceptions or thought contents which they signify (unlike divine common conceptions) need not in principle be based on the distinct knowledge of a *status*. But substance words are always linked to a *status* by an open intentional connection: if 'horse', for instance, is imposed on horses, then the word carries with it, from its imposition, the intention that it should be imposed according to the properties of a horse, whatever they are. Moreover, Abelard certainly does not exclude the possibility that, in the case of *some* substance words ('man', for instance),[51] we *do* know the *status* and it is reflected in our common conception, which becomes in such instances like a divine common conception.

THE ONTOLOGY OF UNIVERSALS

Abelard's semantics of universal words, it has been argued, depends on his strong naturalism. If his theory is to be satisfactory, Abelard therefore needs to explain how this position is compatible with his nominalism. On the face of it, such an explanation is provided by his theory that the common causes

[51] See the text discussed in n. 45 above.

of the imposition of universal words are not things, but rather *status*. It is also easy to accept the idea that *status* are not things. Indeed, the appearance of paradox – that there is a something which is not a thing – is mainly due to Abelard's decision to use a noun, *status*, in this special technical way, in place of a noun clause. To urge that, if 'S' is the word for things of a certain sort, then being an S is not a thing, seems very reasonable.

The theory of *status* does not, however, go very far in explaining what is the common cause on account of which universal words are imposed. Rather, it indicates how to go about providing such an explanation. We are directed to look to what the members of a natural kind have in common in a way which does not involve considering this as a thing which they share. Did Abelard let his discussion of universals rest at this point? To judge from his two set-piece discussions of universals in the *Logica* and the *Glossulae/De intellectibus* – and from most of his modern commentators – he did. But a wider look at his logical writings suggests that he carried on his ontological query another stage.

Consider first a line of thought which Abelard hints at, but does not pursue. Certain passages suggest that Abelard may have thought about natural kinds in terms of law. He quite often writes about the 'nature' of a given sort of thing 'permitting' certain attributes and 'disallowing' others; what is possible for a thing is that which 'is not repugnant to its nature' – anything which has, will or may happen to any member of the species to which it belongs.[52] If Abelard interpreted having a given *status* – for instance, that of man – as following certain laws (coming ultimately from God), he would secure a solid basis for his naturalism without compromising his nominalism, since he would have admitted no universal things into his ontology.[53] Yet Abelard did not develop any explicit argument along these lines. Why? Most probably because he thought primarily of things which shared a *status* as all having the same structure of particular *differentiae*.[54] A man is for him primarily not something which obeys the laws of human nature (though he sometimes talks in this way) but a rational,

[52] See e.g. *Dial.* 385: 4–5: 'id tantum quisque possit suscipere quod eius natura permittit, idque non possit quod natura expellit'; cf. *sup.Por.* 88: 21–2. On repugnance to nature and possibility, see below, pp. 222–3 (and references in p. 223, n. 22, on Abelard's view of nature).

[53] I am very grateful to Simo Knuuttila for suggesting to me this possible way of looking at Abelard's theory.

[54] *Sup.Por.* 90: 36 – 91: 3 makes very clear how Abelard indeed tends to construe the laws pertaining to the nature of a thing in terms of what forms it must have (*differentiae*) and those it can lack (accidents, including even *propria*): cf. above, pp. 130–3.

mortal animal: that is, a particular substance with particular *differentiae* of rationality, mortality and so on. This then leaves the problem: by what is one particular *differentia* of a certain sort (Socrates' rationality, for instance) like others of the same sort, so that they can all be called by the same name ('rationalities')?

Abelard's ontology, it was mentioned above, has much in common with that of modern 'trope' theorists. To hold, as the trope theorists do, that there are real properties and relations, but they are particular, does not in itself resolve the problem of universals. As David Armstrong has argued: suppose, as these theorists say, this ball is round by its particular roundness, that ball by its particular roundness, no universal need yet be involved. But we must then ask by what principle this, that and all other roundnesses are grouped together. The possible replies include all the various types of nominalism, and also types of realism.[55] If, however, the trope theorist chooses to explain the grouping by similarity, he has at least gained one advantage. A straightforward resemblance nominalist encounters difficulties because he has to point out a given property or relation by which one thing resembles another: the balls resemble each other by their roundness. A resemblance trope theorist can say simply that this roundness and that roundness are similar, and he can try to claim that such similarity is not further analysable.[56] It would have been quite easy for Abelard to have devised an argument along such lines. He might have said that rationalities come together in the *status* of rationality (or even that whitenesses come together in the *status* of whiteness). He does not. Two passages from his treatment of *differentiae* – one in the *Logica*, one in the *Glossulae* – show what direction his thought *does* take.

The problem of how particular *differentiae* can be *differentiae* of the same sort (of rationality, for instance) arises because Abelard wishes to hold both that (a) there attaches (for instance) to every man a particular *differentia* of rationality, but that (b) there is no necessary connection between the particular man and the particular *differentia* of rationality by which he happens to be rational: Socrates might have been rational by the rationality by which, in fact, Plato is rational.[57] For Abelard, (a) does not mean, as it might seem, that one of the particular rationalities which have existed, exist or will exist, must attach to any given man. As he points out in the *Logica*, it is possible

[55] See D. Armstrong, *Nominalism and realism: universals and scientific realism* I (Cambridge, 1978), pp. 77–8 for a longer account and bibliography.
[56] See Campbell, *Abstract particulars*, pp. 27–40.
[57] See above, pp. 119–20.

that a man might have been rational by a rationality which in fact never does exist. Every universal word – denominatives such as 'rational' and substance words such as 'man' – has an unlimited (*infinita*) cause of imposition. Just as the word 'man' can apply to any man – not just those who exist, have existed or will exist, but also to any hypothetical man who might exist or have existed – so too the extension of 'rational' exceeds all actually existent, past or future rationalities. But what is this unlimited cause of imposition of 'rational'?[58] In the *Logica*, Abelard gives no answer to this question. He sticks, rather, to talking about the species. He says (*sup.Por.* 84: 21–6) that when we say that the *differentia* is predicated universally of its species (for instance, every man is rational), this is a statement about the universal word which is called a *differentia* (about 'rational'); and when we say that a thing belonging to the species cannot be without its *differentia*, this is a statement about the common cause of imposition of the word for the species – that is, of 'man', for instance. The cause of imposition of 'rational' is not considered.

In the *Glossulae*, however, the same problem leads Abelard to confront more directly the need to explain by virtue of what different rationalities (for example) are all rationalities. As before, Abelard is trying to explain that no man can lack rationality – rationality is, as he now puts it, 'essential (*substantialis*)' to man – but he could certainly lack any given particular *differentia* of rationality – the particular *differentia* is not essential, but 'accidental'. He presents his view in the following terms: 'when we agreed that rationality is essential [to man] we did not agree that this or that rationality is essential; rather, they are accidental'.[59] This is a very surprising way for Abelard to speak. There is no doubt that he is talking here about things, not words (he deals separately, later (573: 15–19), with the same question posed about *differentiae* as *vocabula*), yet he seems to be allowing that as well as particular *differentiae*, this or that rationality, there are non-particular *differentiae* which, alone, are essential. In fact, Abelard quickly tries to correct this impression. Yet it remains true that Abelard's approach to universals *is* different here from elsewhere. Abelard wishes both to insist

[58] *Sup.Por.* 84: 26–85: 16. There are a several mistakes in the text of the manuscript in this passage, some of which Geyer fails to correct: 84: 38 should read 'potest esse homo ita quod <non>'; 85: 4 should read 'possit esse illud ita, quod <non> sit'; 85: 10 should read 'numerum rerum <in>definitum habebat'. For a discussion of this passage from a rather different perspective, see Jolivet, 'Trois variations', pp. 135–6.

[59] 570: 5–7: 'Unde cum rationalitatem substantialem esse concedimus, neque hanc neque illam substantialem esse concedimus, sed accidentalem.'

that there are no rationalities which are not particular rationalities (and therefore accidental);[60] but that these rationalities can also be considered as essential. He is willing to stand by the apparently self-contradictory statement that 'rationality is that which is in no way essential [to a man] and that which is in some way essential [to a man]'.[61]

Near the beginning of his discussion (570: 41 – 571: 8), Abelard tries to explain his position by bringing in the human mind. The statement

(4) Rationality is in a man, in such a way that he cannot exist without it

can be understood, he says, in two ways. Either the relationship between the pronoun 'it' and the noun it stands for ('rationality') is 'according to thought (*secundum intellectum*)'. This means, Abelard explains, that 'it' produces exactly the same thought as the word it stands for ('rationality') earlier in the sentence (*ut sicilicet penitus eundem intellectum habeat cum nomine praemisso*). Or the relationship between 'it' and 'rationality' is one of identity of number, so that (4) means

(4') Rationality is in a man, in such a way that he cannot exist without that particular rationality.

(4') is false; whereas (4) is true if 'it' is taken 'according to thought'. What this amounts to saying is that, in thought, we grasp the notion of rationality in general, and that each particular man must have a particular *differentia* which would fit this general mental notion. Yet Abelard does not believe that what makes certain forms rationalities (and not, for instance, irrationalities, mortalities or whitenesses) is just that this is how we regard them (any more than he believes that certain substances are men just because that is how we regard them): we regard them as rationalities (or men) because that is what they are. This explanation, therefore, which merely echoes Abelard's account of the semantics of universals, is insufficient.

Perhaps that is why, near the end of the discussion, Abelard puts forward a bolder alternative explanation. He now contrasts identity of number not with identity 'according to thought' but with identity 'by definition': when we say

[60] In addition to the analysis which follows, cf. Abelard's replies (571: 34 – 572: 3, 572: 12–20) to the objections he raises to his thesis at 571: 30–3, 572: 4–11.

[61] 572: 21–2: 'Item concedimus, quod rationalitas est quod nullo modo est substantiale et id quod aliquo modo est substantiale.'

there is one form which is essential, another which is accidental, 'one' and 'another' are not here being used to indicate numerical diversity, but rather diversity of definitions or properties, since no form could be found which is essential.[62]

There are, then, according to Abelard's view here, forms which are essential to their substances, but they are identical in number, and different only by definition, from the accidental forms. Abelard does not speak here explicitly of universal and particular forms; but he has made clear that accidental forms are particular ('this or that'), and it is hard to see what the essential forms could be if not universals. In any case, Abelard goes on explicitly to say (572: 31–2) that, in general, it is difference by definition which is involved when one thing is called singular, another universal: *cum dicitur res alia universalis, alia singularis*.

So Abelard, in thinking about *differentiae*, has come to a theory of universals not only distinct from any of the forms of the view he advances in his main treatment of universals, but sharply at odds with it, because it admits universal things. Or, at least, it admits universal things in a certain sense. We can talk, he allows, of universal things or of *differentiae* essential to their substances, but they are not things different in number from the particulars. The difference which does apply, difference 'by definition', is that considered by Abelard at greater length in the *Theologia Summi Boni* and its subsequent versions; he even mentions here two of the same examples as he uses there.[63] Abelard's view of difference by definition, as has been explained earlier, is not completely clear. Although in many cases it might be explained in terms of alternative descriptions of the same composite thing (substance plus *differentiae* plus accidents), in which one or another feature is highlighted (as the hard thing differs by definition from the white thing), Abelard's use of the distinction in discussing the Trinity leads him to suggest that in some sense it distinguishes things which are different and yet the same. If Abelard wishes to say here merely that a 'non-essential *differentia*' and an 'essential *differentia*', or 'a particular' and 'a universal' are different descriptions of the same things, it is hard to see

[62] 572: 26–30: 'Sic igitur dicemus rationalitatem nec tamen hanc vel illam cum ita dicemus, "forma alia substantialis, alia accidentalis". Ibi "alia" et "alia" non ad diversitatem numeri ponitur, sed magis ad diversitatem diffinitionum vel proprietatum, cum nulla possit reperiri quae sit substantialis.'

[63] 572: 32–4: Infinity according to number and time, and constitutive and divisive *differentiae*; see *TSum* 148: 922 – 149: 931; *TChr* 253: 1908–17; *TSch* 456: 1474–87 gives only the second of these examples. On difference by definition in the *TSum*, *TChr* and *TSch*, see above, pp. 151–5; the notion is also used earlier in the *Glossulae*, in the treatment of *sermones* – see above, pp. 178–9.

how he succeeds in explaining anything. If, as the parallel with his trinitarian discussions suggest, he is suggesting that in some sense there are universal things, then he will, in effect – when faced squarely with the problem of what ultimately makes one thing like another – have abandoned the nominalist position he always explicitly holds on universals. The parallel with Duns Scotus is hard to resist. Like Abelard, he invokes a special sort of distinction to explain how the persons of the Trinity are different, though one in essence. Like Abelard (arguably, in this passage), he uses this very distinction to differentiate the particular from the universal. But, whereas Abelard has his place in history as one of the earliest nominalists, Scotus is regarded as a sophisticated realist.

Too much weight should not be put on a passage which is isolated and difficult to interpret. So long as Abelard concentrates on the signification and imposition of universal substance words (with it vaguely in mind that his account would apply to other universal words too) he adheres rigorously to his nominalism, and there is nothing as such incompatible between it and his strong naturalism. But his understanding of natural kinds in terms of a common structure of *differentiae* demands that he give an explanation of why one particular *differentia* is of the same sort as another. At this point, Abelard could – like a modern trope theorist – have produced an explicitly nominalist account, even if just by asserting that such *differentiae* are unanalysably similar. He certainly makes no such move and, where he tackles the problem most unflinchingly, ends (to put it at the mildest) by using language tinged by the realism which elsewhere he has so conscientiously avoided. Does this betray an unsureness about the basis of his ontology? Abelard's treatment of the *dicta* of statements, which will be examined in the next and final section of Part II, suggests that it well might.

Conclusion

Dicta, non-things and the limits of Abelard's ontology

For Abelard, the problems about words, thoughts and things raised by the *Isagoge*, the *Categories* and the opening of the *De interpretatione* were no more than a prelude to his main task, as a logician, of studying statements linked together into arguments. His treatment of statements, syllogisms and topical argument is one of the richest and most innovative parts of his entire work, but most of it falls outside the bounds of this investigation into the specifically philosophical questions Abelard tackled in the course of his logical work. There is, however, an important exception. Abelard's notion of non-things has already been mentioned in connection with his theory of universals. In the *Logica* he is careful to point out that neither common conceptions nor *status* are things at all – they are nothing rather than something. In his treatment of statements and arguments Abelard introduces another sort of non-thing: what statements say – *dicta propositionum*, as he called them from the *Logica* onwards. The concept of the *dictum* is central to Abelard's logical thinking, since it is in terms of their *dicta* that he analyses the truth of entailment statements. Yet, as the following paragraphs will show, Abelard's discussion of *dicta* begs rather than answers the ontological question it raises. By indicating very clearly the limits of Abelard's thought about what there is, it also marks the point where the investigation of this aspect of his philosophy must conclude.

The main lines of Abelard's theory of *dicta* have been well studied and can be described quite briefly.[1] Abelard is brought to talk about *dicta* principally by his need to explain the basis for the truth of conditionals. When

[1] See especially G. Nuchelmans, *Theories of the proposition* (Amsterdam/London, 1973), pp. 139–63; cf. also Jolivet, *Arts du langage*, pp. 77–85; L. de Rijk, 'La signification de la proposition (dictum propositionis) chez Abélard' in *Pierre Abélard*, pp. 547–55; A. de Libera, 'Abélard et le dictisme' in *Abélard. Le 'Dialogus'*, pp. 59–92; N. Lewis, 'Determinate truth in Abelard', *Vivarium* 25 (1987), 81–109, at pp. 84–8; Martin, 'Logic of the *Nominales*', pp. 113–21. My account is indebted to all of these, although my conclusions are rather different.

we say, 'If *p*, then *q*', what do '*p*' and '*q*' stand for? Statements (*propositiones*), or thoughts (*intellectus*) or something else? Behind this question lies Abelard's view about what is necessary for the truth of a conditional: that the antecedent must of itself require (*exigit*) the consequent. If antecedents and consequents are to be linked together in this way, what must they be? The first possibility, that they are simply statements, is easily dismissed, since, for Abelard (in common with the whole medieval tradition), statements are not abstract entities but a particular sort of string of words.[2] Could they not be, then, the thoughts caused by statements?[3] Abelard has a variety of arguments to show that it cannot be thoughts, either, which are entailed in conditionals. In the *Dialectica* (154: 30 – 155: 11) he argues that, if they are based on thoughts, only conditionals which repeat the same proposition ('If he is a man, then he is a man') will be true. Others will lack 'the necessity of entailment', because the thought generated by the antecedent could well be without that generated by the consequent. 'If he is a man, then he is an animal' is a valid entailment; but my thought joining together (for instance) Socrates and man need not involve my joining together Socrates and an animal. And it would be absurd to imagine that every time we grasp the thought signified by 'every man is an animal', we also have in mind the numberless statements it entails – not merely, 'every man is a body' and 'some man is an animal', but also 'some man is not a stone/a piece of wood/ a colour ...' In the *Logica* (*sup.Per.* 366: 2–6) Abelard remarks that the thought signified by a statement lacks the necessity to found a conditional, because it is transitory.

A similar sort of argument is one of the strongest which Abelard mounts against another possibility. Since neither statements themselves nor the thoughts they produce will serve, some say that it must be the things themselves about which statements are made that provide the basis for true

[2] *Dial.* 156: 1–21. At *sup.Pred.* 291: 26–8, Abelard rejects as false, 'If there is a man, then the statement "There is a man" is true', because 'it often happens that something is the case although no statement has been made about it'. On the medieval meaning of *propositio*, see N. Kretzmann, 'Medieval logicians on the meaning of the *propositio*', *Journal of Philosophy* 67 (1970), 767–87. For Abelard a statement (*propositio)* is not even a sentence-type but a sentence-token, so that if I say 'Socrates is sitting' now and repeat it five minutes later, I will have made two different statements (*Dial.* 54: 9–10; *sup.Pred.* 161: 21–4). Abelard, indeed, goes so far as to say (*Dial.* 54: 5–7; *sup.Pred.* 161: 24–6; *sup.Top.* 225: 31–6) that 'true' and 'false' are not contraries when used of statements, because the same statement can be true and false – e.g. if I say now 'John is writing about Abelard' this is true of John Marenbon but not of John Major.

[3] On how statements cause thoughts, and their relation to the thoughts caused by single words, see above, pp. 169–70.

conditionals – for instance, roses and flowers in the conditional 'If it is a rose, it is a flower'. But this explanation, Abelard points out (*sup.Per.* 366: 6–12), fails to show how 'If it is rose, it is a flower', would remain true, as he insists it does, even if there were no roses and no flowers.[4] What, then, are conditionals about? Not statements themselves, not the thoughts they produce, not the things their parts signify, but, rather, what the statements say – their *dicta*, to use the term Abelard coined in this technical sense in the *Logica* and used regularly in this sense from this time onwards.[5] Abelard can also fit this idea of *dicta* neatly into the scheme of Aristotelian logic: when, in the *Categories*, Aristotle talks about negation and affirmation as opposites, he is talking about the *dicta* of statements, Abelard insists (*sup.Pred.* 275: 3–13): for instance, the *dictum* of 'Socrates sits' – that Socrates is sitting – is opposite to the *dictum* of 'Socrates does not sit' – that Socrates is not sitting.

Dicta, then, play an important role in Abelard's scheme of things, but what precisely are they? Abelard follows two different approaches in describing what is said by statements. The first approach links them closely to the world of things, though they are not things but how things are. So, in the *Dialectica* (154: 11), he describes what statements speak of as the existence or non-existence of a thing (*existentia rei vel non existentia*), or (155: 26) as 'the essence (*essentia*) of things'. A conditional, understood (as, according to Abelard, it should be) in terms of what statements say, should be interpreted as, for instance, 'if it is thus in reality (*ita est in re*) that every man is an animal, so it is in reality that every man is a body' (155: 27–8). And, at the end of the section, Abelard explains that statements do not simply designate things as names do. Rather, they propose how things stand with regard to each other. What statements express is 'as it were the way things stand'.[6] The same approach is also found in the *Logica*. For statements to be true or false according to their *dicta* is glossed as 'stating that

[4] The same argument is put forward in *Dial.* (160: 17–21): 'Omnibus enim rebus destructis incommutabilem consecutionem tenet huismodi consequentia: "si est homo, est animal"; et quecumque vere sunt consequentie, vere sunt ab eterno ac necessarie" cf. 282: 25–7. Abelard gives further arguments against the position at *sup.Per.* 368: 1–39.

[5] See e.g. *sup.Pred.* 275: 5–6, 291: 41; *sup.Per.* 327: 20, 366: 27, 37; *sup.Top.* 226: 27. For use in *Coll.*, see below, p. 247. In *Dial.* Abelard once uses *dictus* (4th decl.) (372: 10: 'nec Aristoteles de dictu propositionis mentionem facit') in much the same sense as he would give to *dictum* a few years later.

[6] 160: 29–36: 'Non itaque propositiones res aliquas designant simpliciter, quemadmodum nomina, immo qualiter sese ad invicem habent, utrum scilicet sibi conveniant annon, proponunt . . . Et est profecto in re, sicut dicit vera propositio, sed non est res aliqua quod dicit. Unde quasi quidam rerum modus habendi se per propositiones exprimitur, non res alique designantur.'

which is or is not in reality (*quod in re est vel non est in re*)' (*sup.Per.* 327: 20–1). *Dicta*, although not things, are the 'quasi-things' (*quasi-res*) of statements (*sup.Per.* 367: 12–13) – what Aristotle calls the 'thing' of a statement when he says that, that Socrates is a man (*quod Socrates est homo*) and that he is not a stone are the causes of the truth of the statements which state that it is thus (*sup.Per.* 367: 24–6). Very much in line with this approach, too, is Abelard's tendency sometimes to use 'event' (*eventus/eventus rerum*) apparently as a synonym for *dictum*, especially in his discussion of future contingents.[7] And when, a little later, Abelard uses the notion of *dicta* in the *Collationes* ('it is good that there is evil') he is again very obviously talking about how things are (160: 3146–9).

Abelard's other approach links what is said by statements far more closely to the world of statements than the world of things. The first of the two most important manifestations of this approach is Abelard's claim, made in the *Dialectica* (154: 11–17) and repeated in the *Logica* (*sup.Top.* 225: 25–9, 225: 39 – 226: 8), that 'true' and 'false' apply to what is said by statements. There are, then, true *dicta* and false *dicta* and, indeed, Abelard considers that when a statement is called true or false this is primarily because it states a true or a false *dictum*.[8] (Taking truth and falsity to apply primarily

[7] *Dial.* 210–22 (see e.g. 221: 3–5: 'Aristoteles . . . demonstrat ipsas affirmationes et negationes in proprietate veri ac falsi sequi illos eventus rerum quos enuntiant, gratia quorum tantum vere esse vel false dicuntur'; *sup.Per.* 417–31; for Abelard's treatment of future contingents, see below, pp. 226–32. Neil Lewis ('Determinate truth', pp. 87–92) argues against identifying *eventus* and *dicta*. He claims that at *sup.Per.* 422: 41 – 423: 27 Abelard identifies two possible views about events (*eventus*) – that they are things, and that they are *dicta*, but does not give his own view. But Abelard's aim in this passage is simply to show that, whichever view is taken about events, not all statements about the present and past will have determinate events. In *Sent.Par.* (22: 2–12) it is stated explicitly that events are not things (and here they are very closely assimilated to *dicta* since it is said that they are the causes of the truth of statements). Lewis also identifies with the event the *res* which is contrasted with what a statement says at *Dial.* 213: 21–8: in fact, here the contrast is obviously between the thing itself, a battle, which does not yet exist, and what is said by the statement. Moreover, Lewis's suggestion, on the basis of this passage, that *dicta* are tensed is unconvincing: Abelard seems rather to be saying that the same *dictum* is expressed by differently tensed statements uttered at different times (an idea which he would use in connection with prophecy and faith: see immediately below). It is, none the less, true that 'event' and '*dictum*' did not mean the same thing for Abelard: '*dictum*' is a wider term since false statements have *dicta* but there are no events which correspond to them.

[8] This is brought out very strikingly by Abelard's view (*sup.Pred.* 291: 29–42) that, if we say that the statement (for instance) 'There is a man' is true, this means just that 'what it says is as it is in reality', so it will not follow that it is true that there is a man, because 'There is a man' might be true through a different *dictum* (e.g. 'There is an ass') which is also true. Abelard does allow that 'true' or 'false' used of a statement can be derived from the truth or falsity of the thought it produces, but he has to insist (*sup.Per.* 327: 18–21) that in the case of the definition of a statement, it is only the truth or falsehood of *dicta* which

to *dicta* enabled Abelard to explain the abiding truth of belief in, for instance, the Virgin Birth, which has now to be stated in the past tense – 'A virgin has conceived' – but once had to be stated in the future – 'A virgin will conceive').[9] The second manifestation (closely linked to this) is Abelard's confidence throughout his discussion that he can talk about *dicta* or what statements say in the case of false as well as true statements, and impossible statements as well as contingently false ones. Indeed, many of the conditionals Abelard considers, and interprets as being about *dicta*, involve false statements ('If Socrates is a pearl, then Socrates is a stone').

There are, then, two main ways (which do not seem to belong to different chronological stages) in which Abelard thought about what statements say or (as he came to call them) *dicta*. According to the first, *dicta* are states of affairs: they are not things, but how things are, and they are what make statements true or false. According to the second, *dicta* are what some twentieth-century philosophers have called 'propositions': they are what sentences, understood in their context, express, and they may be true or false contingently or necessarily. Most commentators have described Abelard's view of *dicta* mainly according to the first approach: *dicta* are 'positive and negative states of affairs', 'propositional contents' (Martin); *Sachverhalten* (Jolivet); the objectivized content of a thought (de Rijk). Nuchelmans rightly points out the difficulty raised by the *dicta* of false statements, if we identify the *dicta* of true statements with 'states of affairs which are actually the case in reality'.[10] Lewis recognizes a 'two-sided character' to Abelard's *dicta*, propositions on the one hand, states of affairs on the other. 'Many philosophers wedded to a correspondence theory of truth', he admits, 'would have trouble here'; but he alludes to other philosophers whose views 'collapse facts and true propositions and ... suggest a more general identification of propositions and states of affairs'.[11] Lewis is right to point out that a philosopher might on good grounds propose a view of things which leaves no room for the distinction between propositions and states of affairs. But Abelard gives no indication of having considered the problems in this area and arrived at such a solution. His wider terminology and discussions invite the distinction between propositions and states of affairs to be made – but he overlooks it.

The most celebrated feature of Abelard's *dicta* is their ontological status,

are meant, since he believes that the thought produced by 'Socrates running' – which is not a statement – is the same as that produced by 'Socrates runs'.

9 Cf. Marenbon, 'Vocalism, nominalism', pp. 58–61.

10 *Theories of the proposition*, pp. 160–1.

11 'Determinate truth', p. 87.

or rather lack of it. In the *Dialectica*, Abelard is already insistent that what statements say are not things of any sort. He asks (157: 14–16) 'whether those existences (*existentie*) of things which statements say are any existing things (*alique de rebus existentibus*) – whether one thing or many?' This question is answered very clearly in the negative. In part, what Abelard is arguing here is that what statements say are not the things they talk about (Socrates in the case of 'Socrates is Socrates'; Socrates and a stone in the case of 'Socrates is not a stone'). But Abelard also wishes to indicate that what a statement says is not a thing at all: hence his contrast, already mentioned, between 'any sort of thing' and 'how things stand'. By the time of the *Logica*, Abelard has become firmer in excluding the language of being when talking about what he now, accordingly, calls not 'existences' but '*dicta*'. He insists that *dicta* are 'not essences (*essentiae*) of any sort' (*sup.Pred.* 275: 6; cf. *sup.Top.* 226: 12), 'they are not at all essences, neither one nor many' (*sup.Per.* 366: 37–8), 'they can be called entirely nothing (*nil omnino*)' (*sup.Per.* 368: 39) – or, going even further than this (*sup.Per.* 369: 37–9): 'Nothing can be said affirmatively of the *dictum* of a statement – as, for instance, I might say that it is nothing – but rather negatively, that it is not anything.' In reply to someone who asks how can *dicta* be the cause of statements being true if they are nothing and can be nothing, Abelard explains that not eating can be the cause of someone's dying and he points to the case of commands, where the action commanded – which is the cause of the command – is nothing at the time the command is given, and may never be anything if it is not in fact performed (*sup.Per.* 368: 40 – 369: 18). This explanation is not, however, very illuminating since, on analysis, these instances too turn out themselves to involve *dicta* as causes ('That he did not eat caused him to die'; 'That the room will be warm caused me to tell you to light the fire').[12]

For a philosopher to describe a certain sort of item (call it 'I') as a 'non-thing' need be neither paradoxical nor question begging. It can be a way of saying that, although we talk as if Is were things, and perhaps it is convenient to do so, the proper analysis of statements containing 'I' does not involve postulating the existence of any Is. The case of *status* – one of Abelard's non-thing items – illustrates this point. When we talk of the *status* (of, for instance, man), we should not think that there exists some thing which is this *status*; rather, we use the word 'status' in order to talk about

[12] In *sup.Pred.* (293: 21–36), Abelard considers the same question. Here he says that since what a statement says is not an essence, it cannot properly be called a cause, but it can be called one *magnificative*, in the same way as victory can be called the cause of a war.

particular things (such as men) in a certain sort of way. Scholars have often noted the closeness in Abelard's thought between the notion of a *status* and that of a *dictum*; and, indeed, Abelard uses some of the same terms and examples in talking about both (for instance, when explaining that a cause need not be a thing).[13] Yet there is a very important difference. Abelard is committed to holding that there is a *status* of S (where 'S' is a substance word) only if Ss exist. Indeed, since he talks of the *status* of S in order to explain the imposition of 'S' as a universal word, and he states explicitly (*sup.Por.* 30: 1–5) that 'S' would not be a universal if no Ss were in existence (although it would still signify, through its power to produce a thought), it seems likely that he would have held that, if there were no Ss, there could be no *status* of S. By contrast, one of the important characteristics of *dicta* is that they do not depend on the existence of any things. For instance, the *dicta* of the statements 'it is a rose' and 'it is a flower' can be used to form a true conditional even if there exist no flowers, and there is no reason why the existence of any other things besides flowers should be required by these *dicta*. The language of *dicta* cannot, therefore, just be a certain way of talking about things, and this leaves Abelard's insistence that *dicta* are non-things as a rather desperate expedient, an implicit promise of further explanation which cannot possibly be fulfilled.[14]

Despite the contrast which has just been made, there *is* a close parallel between Abelard's problem about *dicta* and the difficulties of his *status* theory. For, as the last chapter makes clear, Abelard does *not*, as he might have done, give an explanation of *status* which would bear out his nominalism. On the contrary, when he most squarely faces the problem they pose, he apparently gives up his nominalism and allows himself to speak of real universals. Why? Perhaps because Abelard is unwilling to think of natural kinds except as providing a necessary structure for how things *must* be. His naturalism was strong, not just in the epistemological sense, but also in the sense that it encompassed not just how things are, but how they *must* be. Perhaps, given a certain view of God as legislator, Abelard might still have succeeded in reconciling such naturalism with his nominalism. But Abelard does not explore this avenue.

Had Abelard set out, in his later work, to establish a system on the basis of the ontology he set out in the *Dialectica* and the *Logica*, he would have

[13] Tweedale's interpretation of Abelard depends on this closeness; see *Abailard on universals*, esp. pp. 282–3, where he lists the parallels in the ways *dicta* and *status* are discussed.

[14] Jolivet ('Non-réalisme et platonisme', pp. 193–4) suggests that Abelard founds the eternal truth of necessary entailments on the Ideas in God's mind. This would, indeed, have been a sensible course for him to take, but there is no passage in which he does so.

been building on insecure foundations. His achievements in recasting much of what he took from the *Isagoge* and *Categories* to fit a world in which everything is a particular are remarkable. His grasp of the philosophical issues raised by the ancient logical texts is firmer than has been recognized; his semantics of universal words more sophisticated. Yet he never fully overcame the initial problem of trying to combine a conception of a world made up only of particulars with a conception of a world founded on substances, belonging to natural kinds.

But Abelard did not use his ontology as a foundation for his later thought. Rather, he chose to construct a theological system which does not have an ontological basis but an ethical one: God as an agent who can do only what he does because he always does what is best. Elements of Abelard's thought about what there is, including the notion of *dicta*, are used occasionally in working out this system, but it does not rely on them.[15] Abelard never renounced the ontological theories he devised mainly in connection with his logic, and he continued to work on aspects of them in the mid-1120s. But, especially in the 1130s, when he was working out his ethics, they no longer appeared to have held much interest for him. Perhaps Abelard showed not just audacity in developing his ontology, but prudence in judging its limitations.

[15] In one of the most sustained recent studies of Abelard's thought, *Non-ontological constructs. The effects of Abaelard's logical and ethical theories on his theology: a study in meaning and verification* (Berne/Frankfurt/New York/Paris, 1988) (Basler und Berner studien zur historischen und systematischen Theologie 56), Daniel Blackwell gives an account of Abelard's logic which gives pride of place to his theory of non-things and relates his approach to theology to it. Interesting though many of his observations are, the investigations of the preceding chapters would suggest that he has distorted the balance of Abelard's thought; and his reconstruction of Abelard's intellectual progress relies on a dating of the works which few scholars would now find acceptable.

Part III

Introduction

The system which Abelard elaborated as the second phase of his work was (in a broad sense) a theological one: an explanation of Christian doctrine. Yet, even more clearly than the first phase, it also contains a philosophy. Working as a logician, Abelard had been led by the ancient logical texts themselves into problems of ontology, epistemology and semantics. As a theologian, Abelard had from the start tended to see his subject in predominantly ethical terms. Philosophical ethics is not, then, a by-product of theological reflection, or a simple accompaniment to it. Rather, it guides Abelard's whole approach to Christian doctrine. For, although the form of Abelard's thought in its second phase is theological, the ethical theory Abelard develops both provides its underlying structure and allows it to fulfil its aims. His view of God and his works is, at base, an ethical one; and the purpose of his theology (no less than that of his great opponent, St Bernard) moral reformation.

Abelard explicitly recognized both the importance and the breadth of ethics: it is 'the end and fulfilment of all other disciplines' (*Coll.* 88: 1263–4), which has as its task to discover what is the highest good and how it may be attained (*Coll.* 98: 1508–9; cf. 88: 1265 – 89: 1269). Ethics, then, embraces discussion of God, as the highest good, and his ordering of the universe, analysis of the most general evaluative terms and of the acts they are used to qualify, theoretical examination of laws and conduct, and practical consideration of social arrangements and individual behaviour. Abelard's systematic, though developing, treatment of these areas is found, then, not only in the two works clearly devoted to ethics, the *Collationes* and *Scito teipsum*, but through the whole range of his broadly theological writing from about 1125 onwards, including his poetry and his letters to Heloise.

The philosophy which Abelard developed in connection with his logic is, as the previous chapters have shown, unsystematic, needing to be recovered by the historian from the exegetical contexts where it is often hidden.

In this it reflects the unsystematic nature of Abelard's logic itself, rooted to the order of the ancient texts. By contrast, Abelard's ethical thought needs no searching out. Although it is complex and in some respects changing, it is presented clearly within the body of theological writings to which it gives direction and internal coherence. Abelard works out this ethical theory on three interrelated levels. At the highest, most abstract level, it is concerned with the most general questions about good, evil and their relation to God. What does it mean to say that God is omnipotent? How is his omniscience compatible with human free will? How can there be evil in a world which he orders in the best possible way? What are the various senses of the terms 'good' and 'evil'? This most abstract level of Abelard's ethics will be discussed in the chapters 9 and 10. At a second, less abstract level, Abelard's moral theory analyses the ethical act – the subject of chapters 11, 12 and 13. Finally, Abelard considers the detailed working of his ethics in particular circumstances, practical ethics in groups and society and, through examples, ethics in practice – the subject of chapter 14.

By understanding Abelard's ethics in this way, on a number of levels, it is possible to avoid the narrow focus of a whole succession of commentators.[1] From the eighteenth century to the twentieth, many historians have all but identified Abelard's ethics with one of its levels: the analysis of the ethical act.[2] Even here they have been selective, concentrating on the links Abelard makes between God's will, guilt, intention, consent and contempt of God, and saying little about his views on virtue, merit and love. They have been

[1] Important exceptions to this rule, who have taken a broader view of the subject, are F. De Siano, 'Of God and man: consequences of Abelard's ethic', *The Thomist* 35 (1971) 631–60; M. de Gandillac, 'Intention et loi dans l'éthique d'Abélard' in *Pierre Abélard*, pp. 585–608; D. Luscombe in his introduction to *Peter Abelard's 'Ethics'* (Oxford, 1971), pp. xviii–xxiv; G. Verbeke, 'Ethique et connaissance de soi chez Abélard' in J. Beckmann, L. Honnefelder, G. Schrimpf, G. Wieland (eds.). *Philosophie im Mittelalter* (Hamburg, 1987), pp. 81–101; and P. Delhaye, 'Quelques points de la morale d'Abélard' in *Sapientiae doctrina: Mélanges de théologie et de littérature médiévales offerts à Dom Hildebrand Bascour O.S.B.* (= *RTAM*, num. spec. 1, 1980), pp. 38–60.

[2] For example, see: *Histoire littéraire de la France* XII (Paris, 1763), 'ABÉLARD ', pp. 86–152 (this article is reprinted in *MPL* 178, cols. 9–54: see 47–8); J. Cramer, *J. B. Bossuet: Einleitung in die Geschichte der Welt und der Religion fortgesetzt* VI (Leipzig, 1785), p. 439; J. Frerichs, *Commentatio theologico-critica de Petri Abaelardi doctrina dogmatica et morali* (Jena, 1827), pp. 28 ff.; C. Stäudlin, *Geschichte der christlichen Moral* (Göttingen, 1808), p. 76; J. Buhle, *Geschichte der neueren Philosophie* I (Göttingen, 1800), pp. 842–3; W. Tennemann, *Geschichte der Philosophie* VIII (Leipzig, 1810), pp. 196–7; L. Saltet, *Thèse sur l'Ethique d'Abélard* (Montauban, 1852), pp. 28–30; S. Deutsch, *Peter Abälard. Ein kritischer Theologe des zwölften Jahrhunderts* (Leipzig, 1883), pp. 349–51; J. Sikes, *Peter Abailard* (Cambridge, 1932), pp. 179–200; J. Rohmer, *La finalité morale chez les théologiens* (Paris, 1939) (Etudes de philosophie médiévale XXVII), pp. 31–40.

led in this direction by the fact that *Scito teipsum* is usually made the centre of any study of Abelard's moral theory and, in its unfinished state, it is almost entirely devoted to discussing sin. And the problem has been compounded by the fact that the most detailed modern study of any part of Abelard's ethics forms is in a monograph explicitly on the doctrine of sin.[3]

The result has been that even some of the most recent writers on Abelard's ethics have tended to concentrate on Abelard's analysis of intention in terms of consent and, as a result, left the impression that Abelard's concern was with rather narrow logical distinctions rather than broader and deeper moral issues – a view which fits well with the received picture of Abelard in general as brilliant but not profound, a critical rather than a constructive thinker, whose great achievement (or, from another point of view, great error) was to apply his logic to theology.[4] A broader study of his ethics will show, by contrast, that his ethics shares the boldness of the theological system in which it is developed. Abelard does indeed engage, sometimes brilliantly, in logical and linguistic analysis; but he does far more than just this. In both his philosophical ethics, and the theology which it shapes, Abelard presents a new and radical understanding of fundamental issues.

[3] R. Blomme, *La doctrine du péché dans les écoles théologiques de la premiére moitié du XIIe siècle* (Louvain/Gembloux, 1958) (Universitas catholica Lovaniensis. Dissertationes ad gradum magistri . . . consequendum conscriptae, series III, 6), Part 2, pp. 103–294.

[4] See, for instance, the discussion by one of the foremost authorities on Abelard, L. de Rijk ('Abelard and moral philosophy', *Medioevo* 12 (1986) 1–27), which arrives at the following conclusion (p. 27): 'Logic did not make Abelard unpopular, rather it was *his* logic. His way of handling logic made him hated, that is, logic not as a procedure, but as a life-style.'

Chapter 9

Ethics, God's power and his wisdom

The starting point for Abelard's ethics is that of his theological system itself: the bold principle, announced in the *Theologia Summi Boni*, and frequently reiterated in later writings, that when Christians speak of the Father, Son and Holy Spirit, what they are talking about are the power, wisdom and goodness of God.[1] From this assertion, it follows that one of the theologian's central tasks in trying to understand God, in so far as he can be understood, will be to investigate these divine properties. Abelard sees them as each posing one particular main question, and in each case the answer he gives is ethical in content or bearing.[2] In connection with God's power, he asks whether God can do more things or better things than he in fact does. By considering the relation between God and ethical values, Abelard's treatment of this question provides a basis for his whole discussion of morality; whilst by answering in the way he does Abelard gives to his theological system its underlying ethical structure. God's wisdom raises another question central to ethics: if God foreknows all things, how is human free will possible? Abelard's treatment of these two questions will be the subject of this chapter. God's goodness poses for Abelard the problem of theodicy: why, in a world ordained by a good and omnipotent God, is there evil? Abelard's answer – discussed in the next chapter – brings in his general study of the meanings of 'good' and 'evil'. It provides the link between his

[1] See above, pp. 54–5.

[2] The main questions raised in connection with God's power and his goodness are, of course, closely related. In the *Sententie* and *Sent.Par.* they are all considered under the heading of God's power, and only a brief discussion remains in connection with God's goodness. But in *Sent.Flor.* and, so far as can be judged from what remains of the section, *TSch*, the problem of theodicy is treated in connection with God's goodness and the discussion about God's power restricted to the central problem of whether he can do more or better than he does.

thought about ethics in connection with God and his thought about human morality.

GOD'S POWER: ETHICAL VALUES AND OMNIPOTENCE

Abelard answers his central question about God's power in an uncompromising way. God cannot do otherwise than he does. It is necessary that he does what he does and does not do what he does not do. Abelard gave a great deal of attention to proposing this view and resolving the related problems. A first, lengthy discussion appears in the *Theologia Christiana* (358: 417 – 372: 819), but Abelard rewrote it almost entirely for the *Theologia Scholarium* (511: 375 – 524: 771), tightening and developing his argument.[3]

The starting point for Abelard's argument is the same as that of almost every Christian thinker: God does nothing which is not good.[4] How did Abelard derive from this a position which, as he recognized, few would accept and which was, indeed, quickly condemned as heretical?[5] Abelard takes over from Augustine a rather broad definition of omnipotence. For God to be omnipotent means, not that he can do everything, but that he is able to bring about whatever he wishes (*potest efficere quicquid uult*).[6] Unlike most other definitions of omnipotence, this is compatible with Abelard's view of the necessity of divine actions, but Abelard's view is not entailed by it. Rather, Abelard's position derives from his particular way of understanding the relationship between God and what is good. A look at how Aquinas avoids a position like Abelard's on divine necessity makes this clear. Aquinas agrees that God orders all things to his goodness as their end, but he adds that the divine goodness 'is an end which exceeds beyond all proportion (*improportionabiliter*) created

[3] Parts of the revision are found in the extra material of *TChrCT*: see 360–3, marginal notes 33–5. Brief expositions of Abelard's view (closer to *TSch* than *TChr*) are found in the various *Sentences* based on his teaching: *Sententiae* §§146–50; *Sent.Flor.* 11; *Sent.Par.* 20: 13 – 21: 7.

[4] As Kenny (*The God of the philosophers* (Oxford, 1979), p. 110) suggests. Kenny's whole discussion of Abelard's theory (pp. 110–13) is very illuminating; see also, Deutsch, *Abälard*, pp. 215–27; Sikes, *Abailard*, pp. 122–3. Considerable light is also thrown on Abelard's position by Ivan Boh's analysis of some of the arguments brought against it in the 1150s and later: 'Divine omnipotence in the early *Sentences*' in T. Rudavsky (ed.), *Divine omniscience and omnipotence in medieval philosophy* (Dordrecht, 1985), pp. 185–211.

[5] See *TSch* 519: 618–21: 'id solum posse facere arbitror quod quandoque facit, licet haec nostra opinio paucos aut nullos habeat assentores, et plurimum dictis sanctorum et aliquantulum a ratione dissentire uideatur'.

[6] *TChr* 356: 352–60 = *TSch* 509: 326–34. Following Aquinas, Kenny (*God of the philosophers*, p. 113; cf. pp. 91–2) suggests that such a definition is inadequate, because according to it a wise man who restricts his wants to what is within his power would be omnipotent.

things'. The order of things imposed by a wise maker on what he makes and does derives from their end. When that end is proportioned to the things, his wisdom is indeed limited to choosing one determinate order. But when the end is beyond all proportion to the things ordered to it, there is no such limitation.[7] It is as a result, therefore, of the unbridgeable gulf between God's infinite goodness and his finite creation that, for Aquinas, God is able to choose between many possible orders of things, and so can do other than he does. For Abelard, by contrast, God is indeed the highest good and, as such, a far greater good than any created thing. But – in spite of what he says on some occasions about words changing their meaning when applied to the divinity, and in spite of his describing divine goodness as 'ineffable' – his underlying assumption is of there being a common measure between God's goodness and that of other things.

This assumption is evident in the way in which Abelard makes the argument about divine necessity in the *Theologia Christiana* and, even more strikingly, in the *Theologia Scholarium*. In the earlier work, Abelard argues that since God is perfectly good, he does everything as well as he is able and does not omit to do anything which should be done. Nor can he cease from doing what he does and not do what should be done. God's goodness, Abelard adds, is not, like ours, accidental but 'substantial' – essential – to him. He cannot, therefore, not have the good will which he has and, since his will is always efficacious, whatever he does, he does necessarily.[8]

In the *Theologia Scholarium* Abelard brings out his underlying assumption more clearly. It is not merely that he emphasizes the independence of the criterion of goodness from God's will. God does not act like those tyrants who do what they wish – 'This is my will, this is my order; no need for reasons – I wish it so' – rather than consider what is good: rather, God wills what is good.[9] In itself, this position would be accepted by

[7] *Summa Theologiae* I, q. 25, a. 5: 'Manifestum est enim quod tota ratio ordinis, quam sapiens rebus a se factis imponit, a fine sumitur. Quando igitur finis est proportionatus rebus propter finem factis, sapientia facientis limitatur ad aliquem determinatum ordinem. Sed divina bonitas est finis improportionabiliter excedens res creatas. Unde divina sapientia non determinatur ad aliquem certum ordinem rerum, ut non possit alius cursum rerum ab ipsa effluere.'

[8] *TChr* 358: 424 – 359: 456; 366: 588–611.

[9] 514: 459–67: 'Tale est ergo quod ait Ieronimus: "Non enim quod uult hoc facit, sed quod bonum est hoc uult deus", ac si diceret: non ita ut estimat Nabuchodonosor operatur deus, more uidelicet eorum qui in his quae faciunt, non tam quod bonum est attendunt quam ut suae satisfaciant uoluntati, qualiscumque ipsa sit. De qualibus scriptum est: "Hoc uolo, sic iubeo. Sit pro ratione uoluntas" [Iuvenal *Satire* 6, l. 223]. Sed magis uelle dicendus est singula ut fiant, quia bonum esse ut fierent uidit.' See also *Sententie* §152.

Aquinas and many other theologians who uphold the primacy of God's intellect over his will. More important, Abelard tends to refer to a notion of what is good which is apparently independent of God, although always followed by him.[10] God can do only what it is good for him to do (*quae bonum est ipsum facere*) (e.g. 511: 382–3). Abelard takes it as obvious that what is good to be done, what is fitting (*conuenit*) to be done, what it is good for God to do and what it befits (*conuenit*) God to do are all the same; and that this is identical with that 'which has a rational cause (*rationabilis causa*)'.[11] Behind the idea of 'rational cause' lies a quotation from the *Timaeus*, already used in the *Theologia Christiana* but which Abelard does not link to his argument about God's omnipotence until the *Theologia Scholarium*: 'Everything which comes forth comes forth from some necessary cause. For there is nothing the origin of which is not preceded by a legitimate cause and reason.'[12] Abelard also supports his position with another argument cited from the *Timaeus* – one which he had mentioned only with reservations in the *Theologia Christiana*. God, being free from all envy, wished to make the world as much like himself as possible: therefore, he could in no way have made the world better than he made it.[13] In this Platonic argument, it will be seen, there is no indication that God's goodness is out of all proportion to that of his creation; whereas it is precisely the lack of proportionality between divine goodness and that of his creation which enables Aquinas to preserve God's freedom of indifference.

[10] Abelard does not entirely omit mention of God's goodness which is essential to him (see 524: 758–60), but it is no longer central to the argument as it was in *TChr*.

[11] See e.g. 511: 385 – 512: 390: 'Idem autem facere et dimittere non conuenit eum, nec bonum est. Nichil quippe simul et fieri conuenit et dimitti . . . Nec rationabilis causa subesse potest qua idem fieri et dimitti debeat'; 515: 490–1: 'quid fieri bonum est, et rationabilem habet causam qua faciendum sit'.

[12] *Timaeus* 28a (ed. Waszink, p. 20: 20–2), *TSch* 513: 437–9; this is quoted (outside the discussion of omnipotence) at *TChr* 73: 33–5 and (the second sentence only) at *TChr* 349: 97–8 = *TSch* 502: 91–2. See also below, pp. 233–4.

[13] The passage from the *Timaeus* is at 29d–30a (ed. Waszink, p. 22: 17–23). After quoting it in *TChr* (361: 499–362: 507) Abelard says that Plato's words imply that everything was made by God as good as it could be'; he rejects the view–'Quod tam a ueritate quam a nostra remotum est opinione' (362: 509 – 363: 511) – and promises (vainly) to return to the point later. In *TSch* (512: 404–15) Abelard gives the same quote and draws the same implication, but so far from rejecting it he describes it (512: 402) as 'Platonis uerissima ratio'. Why was there such a sharp change? Probably what Abelard found objectionable in Plato's words was the implication that, for instance, God could not have made man better than he is, and so man is so good that he could not be better. In the *Sententie* (§149) and *Sent.Par.* (20: 29 – 21: 7) Abelard shows how a statement like Plato's can be understood without this implication. This is probably why Abelard's attitude to it changes. For a fuller discussion, see my forthcoming 'The Platonisms of Peter Abelard'.

None the less, on its own, Abelard's notion of a criterion of goodness common to God and his creation – fundamental though it is to his ethics and his theological system – would not imply that God can do only what he does. For, granted that God always does what is best for him to do, might there not on some occasions be a number of equally good courses of action? In the *Theologia Scholarium* (515: 480–501) Abelard anticipated and answered this objection, and in his final revision of the work he added an extra passage to his initial exposition in order to make it clearer why he would not accept such a counter-argument.[14] In the extra passage Abelard explains that there could not be a 'rational cause (*rationabilis causa*)' why something should both be done and not be done. If it is good for something to be done it cannot be good for it not to be done: the contrary of good can only be evil. But suppose an opponent objects that there might be two alternative courses of action, *x* and *y*, which are both equally good; and, to Abelard's argument that, if *x* is good, it cannot be good not to do *x* and do *y* instead, the opponent answers that when he says *x* is good, he means *x* is good only if *y* is not done. To this Abelard responds that, if *x* and *y* are equally good, then it must also be the case that *y* is good only if *x* is not done, and so it (like *x*) is not good without qualification and so, if God does *x* or *y* he will be bringing about something which is not good.[15]

What concept of good lies behind these apparently strange arguments? Anthony Kenny has remarked that, according to Abelard, God acts according to a 'morality of rightness', like that of modern utilitarians for whom 'there is at each juncture a single action which is right and morally obligatory'.[16] But Abelard's position is rather more extreme. Utilitarians are able to achieve such certainty in principle about how we should act because they have a single common measure (usually, the amount of pleasure produced). Yet they would admit that, at least in theory, there might be instances where alternative courses of action would produce exactly the same total

[14] 511: 382 ('nec nisi . . .') 512: 397 ('eum facere dimittit') in Oxford, Balliol, 296 only.

[15] 515: 493–8: 'Sin autem dicas de altero quod factum non est, quia non erat bonum ut fieret, nisi ita ut alterum cessaret, profecto eadem ratione de altero, quod factum est, non erit simpliciter concedendum ut bonum esset illud fieri, cum aeque concessum sit tam hoc quam illud fieri bonum esse. Fecit itaque deus quod non erat bonum fieri? Absit!' Although some of Abelard's vocabulary (e.g. *cessaret*) might suggest that Abelard is thinking, not of alternative synchronic possibilities, but of abandoning one course of action for another, other comments (e.g. *quod factum non est*) make it clear that Abelard *is* trying to think of *x* and *y* as synchronic alternatives, although his language for doing this is not well developed. See also below, pp. 222–3.

[16] *God of the philosophers*, pp. 115–6.

amount of pleasure, and so each of them would be right. By contrast, Abelard considers that if one course of action is good, no alternative course can also be. Parallels to this way of thinking can be found, but outside the moral sphere: in a properly constructed chess problem, for instance, there is just one set of moves which is good (the one which solves it). If we objected that moral choice cannot rightly be regarded in this manner, Abelard might reply that, true though this is for human beings, it is not the case where the actions, based on rational causes, of an omnipotent and omniscient God are concerned.

A discussion about whether God can do other than he does is, by its very nature, concerned with modality. But, from the arguments he gives for it, Abelard's view about the necessity of God's acts cannot itself be traced back to his understanding of possibility and necessity. Indeed, it is striking that Leibniz, the later thinker who came nearest to Abelard's views on divine necessity, analysed possibility and necessity in a way sharply different from Abelard. When it comes to defending his view about the necessity of divine action against objections, however, Abelard gives a solution which relies implicitly on what might be called an unanalysed notion of 'possibility *for*'.[17] The meaning of this notion, and its usefulness for him, becomes clear in the light of Abelard's analysis of modal statements.

Abelard is well known as being one of the earliest medieval logicians to recognize the difference between what he called the compound or *de sensu* interpretation (*de dicto* in the language of later medieval and modern logicians) and the divided or *de re* interpretation of modal statements. The statement *possibile est stantem sedere* can be interpreted either as a true *de re* statement

(1) He who is standing can be sitting at some time (*is qui stat possit sedere quandoque*)

or as a false *de sensu* one

[17] This exposition of possibility *for* draws on, but modifies in a number of important ways, my article 'Abelard's concept of possibility' in B. Mojsisch and O. Pluta (eds.), *Historia philosophiae medii aevi* (Amsterdam/Philadelphia, 1991), pp. 595–609, esp. pp. 597–602. On Abelard's theory of modality, see also S. Knuuttila, 'Time and modality in scholasticism' in S. Knuuttila (ed.), *Reforging the great chain of being* (Dordrecht/Boston/London, 1981), pp. 163–257 at pp. 178–87 and *Modalities in medieval philosophy* (London, 1993), pp. 82–96; H. Weidemann, 'Zur Semantik der Modalbegriffe bei Peter Abelard', *Medioevo* 7 (1981), 1–40; K. Jacobi, 'Statements about events: modal and tense analysis in medieval logic', *Vivarium* 21 (1983), 85–107, at p. 104 and n. 62.

(2) It is possible that the standing man should sit while he remains standing (*possibile est stantem sedere manentem stantem*).[18]

The distinction between (1) and (2) can be analysed as that between

(3) $\exists x\,(Fx \,\&\, \Diamond \neg\, Fx)$ (Someone is standing and it is possible that he is sitting)

and

(4) $\Diamond\, \exists x\,(Fx \,\&\, \neg\, Fx)$ (It is possible that someone is standing and sitting).

Abelard seems to have accepted the analysis of (2) as (4), but the analysis of (1) as (3) raised disturbing questions which he wished to avoid. (3) can itself be interpreted in two ways. One way allows for synchronic possibilities. According to this interpretation, (3) entails that it is possible that someone who is standing now is sitting now. The other way admits only diachronic possibilities: it holds that (3) entails merely that it is possible that someone who is standing now is sitting at some time other than now. Abelard's ancient sources would have encouraged him to follow this second, diachronic interpretation. But, although some turns of phrase (for instance, *quandoque* in (1) above) suggest that he does so, he appears to have been reluctant to adopt this view explicitly, but also reluctant to admit the idea of synchronic possibilities.[19] Instead, he sought a way out of the problem. He found it by relying on an unanalysed notion of possibility *for*.

Rather than treat *de re* possibility in terms of what it is possible may be the case about the thing in question, thereby raising the interpretative question he wishes to avoid, Abelard prefers to restrict the discussion to what is possible *for* the thing: that is, simply to listing which properties a thing may have or lack.[20] To make these lists, Abelard thinks in terms of the species to which a particular thing belongs (and he keeps his enquiry to particular substances). A particular man, for instance, may have any property which is not repugnant to the nature of man.[21] For a property P not to be repugnant to the nature of man, it is a sufficient but not a necessary condition that some man has had, does or will have P. Abelard believes that we use our knowledge of men (or whatever the species in question is)

[18] *Sup.Per.* (M) 13: 15–14: 4. Abelard makes the same distinction, but does not regularly use the same terms for it, in *Dial.*: see Marenbon, 'Abelard's concept', p. 597, n. 9.

[19] This argument is made in more detail in Marenbon, 'Abelard's concept'.

[20] This approach to possibility is closely related to one of the dominant ancient approaches, which views possibility in terms of potentiality. See Knuuttila, *Modalities*, pp. 23–30, 37–8, 46–8.

[21] See e.g. *Dial.* 193: 34–7, 200: 25–31; *sup.Per. (M)* 21: 3, 27: 23–6, 43: 4–6.

to determine what *is* repugnant to their nature, and so there is left an indefinitely large number of properties any man may have – of what is possible *for* him.[22] On this view, it will be possible *for* a man whose legs have been amputated to walk (*sup.Pred.* 229:34–6; 273:39 –274:18), and indeed for him to run a mile in 200 seconds, even if (as a matter of fact) no one will ever succeed in running so fast. If Abelard had gone on to express this possibility *for* in terms of possibility *that* – of what it is possible may be the case about the man – he would have been forced to admit that (3) must be interpreted in terms of synchronic possibilities. But this is precisely what he wants to avoid doing and therefore, so far as he can, he presses his analysis no further and thinks just in terms of possibility *for*.

Abelard's notion of possibility *for* is *not*, then, to be taken as a way of considering *de re* possibility which a modern thinker might usefully adopt. On the contrary, modern possible worlds semantics offers a very clear way of analysing *de re* possibility. A statement about *de re* possibility can be seen as picking out a thing referred to and tracing it across possible worlds. 'It is possible that Socrates is standing and sitting' is false *de dicto,* since there is no possible world at which Socrates stands and sits at the same time, but it is true *de re*, because there are many possible worlds at which, at the moment when in the actual world Socrates is standing, Socrates is sitting. And Abelard's comments about lack of repugnance to a thing's nature can be fitted into this framework. They set limits to what properties a thing can have in *any* possible world. Socrates, who in the actual world is a blind, one-legged peasant, is a normally sighted, two-legged bishop in some possible world, but there is no possible world in which he is three-legged or can fly. But the point at issue is not how Abelard's intuitions about modality can be put into a more satisfactory analytical framework than he established, but how he himself analysed, or failed to analyse them. Abelard's idea of possibility *for* represents his escape from a problem rather than a solution to it, but this makes it no less important in understanding his thought.

Abelard uses the idea of possibility *for* to counter an obvious objection to his view of divine necessity. Abelard's view, it can be objected, seems to imply that it is not possible for a man whom God is going to damn to be saved, and so not possible for him to perform the good actions by which

[22] On Abelard's concept of nature, see J. Jolivet, 'Eléments du concept de nature chez Abélard' and D. Luscombe, 'Nature in the thought of Peter Abelard', both in *La filosofia della natura nel medioevo* (Atti del terzo congresso internazionale di filosofia medioevale) (Milan, 1964), at pp. 297–304 and pp. 314–19, and T. Gregory, 'Considérations sur "ratio" et "natura" chez Abélard', *Pierre Abélard*, pp. 569–85.

he would be saved. If he could be saved by God, then God could save him, and so God could do something other than what he does. But this is exactly what Abelard denies. Human beings would therefore be bound by necessity and would be unjustly condemned by God for actions they could not have avoided.[23]

Abelard answers this objection by observing that, although it is the same 'for someone to be saved by God (*aliquem saluari a deo*)' and 'for God to save him' (*deum saluare eum*), it does not follow that

(5) If (a) it is possible for someone to be saved by God, then (b) it is possible for God to save him.

Abelard first formulated this approach to the problem in the *Theologia christiana*, developing it in his oral teaching and elaborating it considerably in the *Theologia scholarium*.[24] His central point throughout is that possibility *for* God must be distinguished from possibility *for* his creation, even when the same event (and so the same possibility *that*) is being considered. What is possible *for* someone is whatever is not repugnant to his nature as a man; what is possible *for* God is just whatever it is fitting that he should do. Abelard has two favourite analogies to make the point clearer. A sound is audible (can be heard by someone), a field can be ploughed, even if there is in fact no one to hear the sound or plough the field. It is enough that, by their natures, the sound is suitable to be heard and the field to be ploughed.[25] Similarly, when we say of someone who will be damned:

> that he can be saved by God we consider possibility with regard to the potentiality (*facultas*) of human nature, as if we were to say that this is not repugnant to human nature, that he will be saved who is in himself mutable so that he might consent as much to his salvation as to his damnation and offer himself to God to be treated just as much in this as in that way. But when we say that God can save a man who is not at all worthy to be saved, we consider possibility with regard to the very nature of God, as if we said that it is not repugnant to the nature of God that he should save him. And this is entirely false. For indeed it is entirely repugnant to God's nature to do what lessens his dignity and what it does not at all befit him to do. (*TSch* 521: 669–79)

Whenever, in speaking of God, we mention the possibility of something

[23] *TSch* 516: 527 – 517: 554. The same objection is put in different words at *TChr* 360: 459 – 361: 487.

[24] *TChr* 371: 781 – 372: 819; *Sent.Flor.* 11: 15–17; *Sententie* §151; *Sent.Par.* 23: 2–23; *TSch* 520: 657 – 523: 743. develop at some length solutions along the same lines as *TSch*.

[25] *TSch* 521: 680–522: 692; cf. *TChr* 372: 810–19; *Sententie* §151; *Sent.Flor.* 11: 18–20; *Sent.Par.* 23: 10–17.

happening otherwise than it does, we must be referring, not to God, but to things or people and their possibility *for*. A parallel is provided by a statement like 'A chimaera is thinkable (*chimera est opinabilis*)', which does not refer to the chimaera, which is non-existent, but says that someone can think about a chimaera. When, therefore, Augustine says that God could have redeemed us in a different way from that he chose, we must understand this statement, Abelard says, as referring to the 'subject thing' and meaning that things were such (*ratio in rebus fuit*) that another way of redeeming us would have been possible.[26]

Abelard's solution to his problem of determinism may seem to be a piece of verbal subterfuge. True, he can say, given his understanding of possibility *for*, that it is possible for Judas who will be damned to be saved, but all this seems to mean is that Judas is a man and some men, though not Judas, might in principle be saved. Such a position provides no escape from the problem of determinism – that, whatever may be the case for other men, Judas' damnation is necessary and so he cannot be said to be free to choose good or evil. This argument, however, does not take account of the fact that, in the example, the man who will be damned is *ex hypothesi* worthy of damnation (*damnandus*), because of the state in which he dies (which, for Abelard, comes about as a result of the way in which he freely chooses to ignore the grace which God offers to everyone).[27] Since it is fitting that someone who deserves to be damned is damned, and God cannot fail to do what is fitting, he must damn whoever merits damnation.[28] The only way in which it remains possible for the *damnandus* not to be damned is precisely the generic possibility captured by Abelard's concept of possibility *for*. But the inevitability of the person's damnation derives not from any divine determinism but simply from the hypothesis being considered. No one is in fact *damnandus* until, through his own freely chosen actions and intentions, he has died out of a state of grace.

[26] *Sent.Par.* 23: 24–242: 'Augustinus dicit, "Fuit et alius modus possibilis Deo." Sed iste modus potentie refertur ad rem subiectam, sicut cum dico: "chimera est opinabilis", opinionem refero ad rem subiectam, non ad chimeram, quia, cum dico, "chimera est opinabilis", non dico quod chimera possit opinari, sed dico quod aliquis potest opinari chimeram. Similiter cum dico, "Fuit et alius modus possibilis Deo", id est, ratio in rebus fuit, quod modus redemptionis aliter fieret'; more briefly in *Sententie* §151.

[27] On Abelard's view of grace, see below, pp. 325–7.

[28] This is brought out particularly clearly by a couple of analogies which Abelard gives to (5) in *TSch* (521: 660–6) but not elsewhere, both of which involve a modal statement which is true when interpreted *de re*, but false *de sensu*. (5b) yields a false *de sensu* modal statement only when, given that God cannot but do what is fitting, it is fitting that the man in question be damned.

GOD'S WISDOM: DIVINE FOREKNOWLEDGE AND HUMAN FREE WILL

Abelard's idiosyncratic view of divine necessity does not, therefore, imply determinism for God's creatures. But, if he was to propose an ethics based on human free will, Abelard also had to show how human freedom was compatible with an aspect of God's nature which almost every Christian thinker has accepted – his omniscience. If God infallibly foreknows that I shall choose this course of action and not that, is not my choice determined before I make it and so not free? This is the problem which Abelard discusses in connection with God's wisdom in the *Theologia Christiana* and the *Theologia Scholarium*. Unlike many of the questions connected with divine omnipotence, it was a well-rehearsed topic: Abelard had already considered it in his *Dialectica* and *Logica*, and for his starting point he turned not merely to Boethius but also to the teacher with whom he had fought so vehemently, William of Champeaux.

Abelard's underlying position is one proposed succinctly by Boethius: God foreknows what will happen, but in the case of contingent events he knows that they will happen contingently, in such a way that they might have happened differently.[29] Similarly, William of Champeaux had remarked that God knows not only human acts, but their modes – so God has foreseen not just that I am now sitting, but that I am sitting in such a way that I am able not to sit.[30] In the *Logica* (*sup.Per.* 428: 41 – 429: 18). Abelard develops the same idea at length. God foresees future things in the way in which they will be future – contingent things, therefore, as being able not to happen. Suppose I am walking now, then God has foreseen both that I am walking and that I am able not to be walking: both are equally in God's providence.[31] The problem for Abelard was to see how he could maintain this view when faced with apparently tight logical arguments which seemed to make determinism the consequence of God's prescience.

[29] *2inDeIn*. 226: 9–13: 'Novit enim futura deus non ut ex necessitate evenientia, sed ut contingenter, ita ut etiam aliud posse fieri non ignoret, quid tamen fiat ex ipsorum hominum et actuum ratione persciscat.'

[30] *Lottin* §238, p. 197: 18–21: 'Nota etiam quia Deus non solum prouidet actus hominum, sed etiam omnes modos. Cum enim modo sedeam, hoc prouidet Deus et modum etiam, scilicet posse non sedere; sedere enim et posse non sedere non sunt contraria.'

[31] 429: 13–18: ' Si ergo integre providentiam eius consideremus, quae omnia simul praescivit, quae ad meum actum sive possibilitatem pertinebant et ita me ambulare modo et simul posse non ambulare providit, secundum eius providentiam et me ambulare contingit et posse non ambulare, quia utrumque in eius providentia aequaliter praeexistit.'

Abelard considered in detail two main examples of these arguments. One of them states that

(5) If (a) it is possible for something to happen otherwise than it does, then (b) it is possible for God to be mistaken.

William of Champeaux had already discussed the problem in a similar form.[32] From (5a) William allows that it can be inferred that something is able to happen otherwise than as God has foreseen, and that therefore the contrary of divine providence can come about, but

(6) If (a) the contrary of divine providence can happen, then (b) the providence of God can be false

is invalid, because (6a) is true but (6b) false. William is right, but he offers no explanation of why (6b) does not follow from (6a), as it may seem to do.[33] By contrast, Abelard was able, even at the time he wrote the *Dialectica* (218: 24–9), to identify the problem neatly and dispose of it.[34] (6a), he notices, is ambiguous in much the same way as *possibile est stantem sedere*.[35] It can be expounded either as

(6a') The following is possible: that something should happen otherwise than as God has foreseen (*de sensu;* cf. (2))

or as

(6a'') For a thing it is possible to happen otherwise than as God has foreseen (*de re*; cf. (1)).

Only if (6a) is expounded as (6a') does it entail (6b) (since the possibility of the consequent follows only from the possibility of the *whole* of the

[32] *Lottin* §237, 195: 1–16.

[33] William also (196: 58–70) notices that the non-modal entailment statement 'If things happen otherwise, then God is or was mistaken' is correct, but not the modal version, 'If it possible for things to happen otherwise, then it is possible for God to be mistaken.' But he cannot explain *why* without falling back on what he knows from authority – that it is impossible for God to be mistaken.

[34] For Abelard's analysis here, see my 'Abelard's concept', pp. 607–8, material from which is used in this and the next paragraph. Recently, H. Weidemann ('Modalität und Konsequenz. Zur logischen Struktur eines theologischen Arguments in Peter Abaelards Dialectica', in K. Jacobi (ed.), *Argumentationstheorie. Scholastische Forschungen zu den logischen und semantischen Regeln korrekten Folgerns* (Leiden/Cologne, 1993) (Studien und Texte zur Geistesgeschichte des Mittelalters 38), pp. 695–705) has provided a different, but not incompatible, analysis of this passage.

[35] In the parallel discussion in the *Logica*, Abelard himself used the sentence *possibile est stantem sedere* as an example (*sup.Per.* 430: 6–9).

antecedent); but (6a'), Abelard considered, is clearly false.[36] (6a'') is, by contrast, true; but it does not imply (6b).

Abelard was satisfied with this analysis and repeated it, with some clarifications, in the *Logica* (*sup.Per.* 429: 26 – 431: 12) and the *Theologia scholarium* (546: 1489–1513).[37] One of its consequences was to make Abelard think, fleetingly, in terms of alternative providential possibilities, since behind the logical distinction Abelard makes, there lies the idea that, as he puts it in the *Dialectica*, 'if things were to happen otherwise, God would have had a different providence which the event would have followed, nor would he ever have had the providence which he now has' (218: 19–21): this event might indeed be other than it in fact will be, without God being mistaken, because, if it were other, God would have foreseen it as other. But, whereas some of Abelard's contemporaries used the idea of alternative providential possibilities to work towards a view of modality which anticipates Duns Scotus and Leibniz, Abelard was distinctly unhappy with this way of thinking.[38] In the *Logica* (430: 23–6), after repeating the idea that God would have foreseen differently if things were to have been different, he goes on to show that, after all, this supposition is not needed (*sup.Per.* 430: 39 – 431: 12). In (6a''), he says 'otherwise' should be understood 'not relatively but negatively'. Events, he suggests, are merely *dicta propositionum*, not things which can be altered in some respect or another; and there can only be one event at a time. The correct interpretation of (6a'') is, then, that it is possible that the event may not happen at all. And – Abelard concluded – understood in this way (6a'') does not imply that, if God is infallible, it must be possible for him to have a different providence from the one he does. We do not doubt that it is possible for events not to turn out in accord with the way a stone foresees – because a stone does not foresee at all. Yet we do not say that the stone must therefore either be mistaken or else have had a different providential disposition. Why should the case be different for God?

The second form of the argument from divine prescience to determinism

[36] *Dial.* 218: 26–9: 'Dicimus autem ea<m> [*sc.* regulam] quodammodo intellectam veram esse, cum scilicet antecedens quoque ipsius falsum* est, alio vero modo falsam, cum videlicet ipsum antecedens verum** accipitur'; cf. *sup.Per.* 430: 12–21. The text given is that of the unique manuscript, but Cousin (*Ouvrages inédits*, p. 290) and de Rijk emend the *falsum* marked * to *verum* and the *verum*, marked ** to *falsum*. See J. Marenbon, *Early medieval philosophy* (1st edn, London, 1983) p. 141 and 'Abelard's concept', p. 607; Weidemann ('Modalität', pp. 701–2) has come independently to the same conclusion about the text here.

[37] In the various *Sententie*, however, Abelard does not consider this form of the problem, but only the second, discussed below. In *TChr* there is no discussion of divine prescience and necessity, because there is no section dealing with God's wisdom.

[38] See Knuuttila, *Modalities*, pp. 75–82, 95.

considered by Abelard puts the problem the other way round. It argues from God's infallible foreknowledge of all that happens to the conclusion that everything takes place by necessity. The temporal aspect of this problem has engaged many of the philosophers who have tackled it – that God knows *today* what I shall do *tomorrow*. Abelard, however, gives almost no attention to this side of the problem. His view about what statements signify may cast light on this surprising gap. For Abelard, the *dictum* of the different past, present and future-tense statements referring to my writing now is the same – and it is this *dictum* which is the object of God's knowledge.[39] Whilst, then, for some thinkers, what God foreknew at t is a future-tensed statement ('John will be writing at t + 1'), for Abelard it is a tenseless *dictum* (that John writes [tenseless] at t + 1 (= D)); and it is exactly this *dictum* D which is said by the statement 'John is writing' uttered by Maximus at t + 1 when he sees me writing. Superficially, then, for Abelard the position with God's foreknowledge is much the same as with our knowledge in general; and this may explain why he had little to say about God and time. Still, even if God's knowledge is of tenseless *dicta*, God knows at t the truth of the *dictum* D; whereas we cannot know the truth of D until, at the earliest, t + 1. Of course, if Abelard accepted Boethius' well-known view, put forward by Boethius in Book V of *De consolatione Philosophiae*, that God exists in an eternal present and perceives all things (which for us are past, present and future) simultaneously, he would avoid this problem.[40] A remark in the *Sententie* might suggest that Abelard had adopted this view;[41] but, although Abelard refers during his discussion in the *Theologia Scholarium* (544: 1433 – 545: 1453) to this book of *De consolatione*, he says nothing there about Boethius' idea of an eternal present; and, indeed, he regularly speaks of God as *having* foreseen an event. Abelard is open, then, to the charge of having simply overlooked the problems which arise from the temporal aspect of divine prescience.[42]

[39] See above, pp. 202–6: in the present context, *dictum* has roughly the sense of 'propositional content', although (as explained there) in some other discussions its meaning is closer to that of 'state of affairs' or 'event'.

[40] For a detailed discussion and an attempt at justification of Boethius' notion of God's eternal present, see E. Stump and N. Kretzmann, 'Eternity', *The Journal of Philosophy* 78 (1981), 429–58 (reprinted in T. Morris (ed.), *The concept of God* (Oxford, 1987), pp. 219–52).

[41] *Sent.* §163; Bu. 98: 35–6: 'nichil est inter eius [*sc.* Dei] eternitatem et ultimum temporis momentum'.

[42] In particular, Abelard remains open to the following argument from divine prescience to determinism, which is far stronger than any which he in fact considers. If God has foreseen *x*, *x* will happen. But 'God has foreseen *x*' is a statement about the past and so, if true, is necessarily true, because the past cannot be changed; and, since what is entailed by a

The central difficulty, as Abelard sees it, is the following. It is a necessary truth that, if I know *p*, then *p* is true. We readily accept that we know things which are happening now and yet they are not necessary: but how is this so? Boethius had introduced the distinction between simple necessity (for instance, that the sun will rise tomorrow) and conditional necessity (that, if someone knows I am walking, then I am walking) by way of explanation, and Abelard quotes him enthusiastically.[43] It might be expected that Abelard would have gone on to use Boethius' distinction to show why an inference from 'God knows *p*' to '*p* is necessarily true' is invalid, by distinguishing between what Aquinas and later medieval writers would call the necessity of the consequence and the necessity of the consequent – showing that, whilst 'Necessarily, if God knows *p*, then *p*' is true (necessity of the consequence), it does not imply that *p* is necessarily true (necessity of the consequent). In fact, both in the *Logica* (*sup.Per.* 429: 18–25), where he considers it briefly, and in the *Theologia Scholarium* (541: 1335 – 546: 1488), where he discusses it at length, Abelard presents the problem rather differently. Rather than consider what can or cannot be inferred from the simple statement 'God knows *p*', Abelard considers complex statements of the form

(7) It is necessary that what God has foreseen will so come about, when he has foreseen it.[44]

In a statement such as (7), the clause introduced by 'when' (*cum*) is called 'a determinator' (*determinatio*). Abelard's main concern is to insist that from such a statement with a determinator it is never possible to infer the statement without the determinator (*TSch* 542: 1350–1: *simplex necessarii predicatio nequaquam consequatur determinata*); so (7) does not entail

(8) It is necessary that what God has foreseen will so come about.

necessary statement is itself necessary, *x* will necessarily happen. This argument was discussed by Aquinas and later scholastic thinkers. Kenny (from whom this formulation of it is taken) looks at it in some detail in 'Divine foreknowledge and human freedom' in A. Kenny (ed.), *Aquinas: a collection of critical essays* (Notre Dame/London, 1969), pp. 255–70 at pp. 260–70 and in *God of the philosophers*, pp. 55–8; see also A. Plantinga, 'On Ockham's way out', *Faith and philosophy* 3 (1986), 235–69 (= Morris, *Concept of God*, pp. 171–200). The argument cannot, of course, be made if the Boethian view of God's eternity as eternal presentness is accepted.

43 *TSch* 544: 1435 – 545: 1453 quoting from *De consolatione* Book V, pr. 3 and Book IV, pr. 1.

44 *TSch* 543: 1402–3. The example in *sup.Per.* (429: 19–20) has the same underlying structure: 'It is impossible for the thing not to happen thus, when God has foreseen that it will happen.'

The case is analogous, Abelard believes, to

(9) It is impossible for this man to have two feet, after he has lost them,

from which it does not follow that

(10) It is impossible for this man to have two feet (*sup.Per.* 429: 21–5).

Abelard explains Aristotle's 'that which is, necessarily is, when it is' along the same lines,[45] and he understands Boethius' distinction between types of necessity in the same way, substituting (*TSch* 545: 1454) 'absolute' for Boethius' 'simple' and 'determinate' (i.e. 'with a determinator') for his 'conditional'.

Why does Abelard concern himself with the inference from (7) to (8) rather than the simpler inference analysed in this context by the later scholastics? Perhaps it is because this choice enables him to see the problem of divine prescience from the same point of view as he approaches it in his analysis of (6). Abelard does not merely wish to observe that (7) does not entail (8); he also holds that (8) is false. (7), not (8), he is claiming, gives the correct account of divine prescience. What exactly does this claim involve? Consider an event *e* which is foreseen by God (for instance, that as soon as I open the printed copy of this book, I shall find a misprint). Abelard, it seems, by denying (8) wants to say (much as he does in (6a")) that it is possible for *e* to be other than the event as which God has, in fact, truly foreseen it: *e* has the potentiality for not being the event it will in fact be. But not only does such a way of thinking raise problems about the nature of events, of which Abelard himself shows awareness in his discussion of (6). It is also uncertain how far it really succeeds in preserving the contingency of future events. As his comments elsewhere show, in the analogy of a man's having two feet, Abelard would always consider that (10) is false; where the man has lost his legs, the truth of his situation is given by (9), from which (10) does not follow (just as (7), which does not entail (8), gives the true account of divine prescience). It is always possible for a man to walk, since to walk is not repugnant to his nature as a man.[46] But this species-based possibility *for* offers little comfort to the man who is now in fact legless. And if the same model really can – as Abelard seems to think – be applied

[45] *TSch* 541: 1326–34; cf. Knuuttila, *Modalities*, p. 91.

[46] See *Dial.* 385: 11–14; *sup.Pred.* 229: 34–6, 274: 10–12; cf. Knuuttila, *Modalities*, p. 90; Abelard uses either someone who has lost his legs having them or being able to walk, or someone who has been blinded being able to see, as his examples.

to a future event, it will fall similarly short of showing that the event, though foreseen, is contingent in any usual sense.[47]

Abelard himself, at least, believed he had succeeded in showing how future events can be foreseen and yet contingent, thereby providing good rational grounds for dismissing a determinism which would have been incompatible with his, and perhaps any Christian, moral scheme. Yet these discussions (unlike his treatment of God's omnipotence) contain little which contributes to Abelard's individual theological system and to the ethics bound up with it. By contrast, when he comes to discuss God's goodness – the third person of the Trinity – Abelard develops some of the fundamental features of his moral theory.

[47] Compare Abelard's position, examined in the previous section, on divine predestination. *There* Abelard's views on grace offered an escape from the unintended deterministic implications of his position.

Chapter 10

God's goodness: theodicy and the meaning of 'good'

Just as God's omnipotence and his wisdom are each linked to a particular main problem, so God's goodness (*bonitas/benignitas*) raises its special difficulty for Abelard – one which he shares with almost every Christian thinker: how is the goodness of an omnipotent God compatible with the existence of evil?

THE PROBLEM OF EVIL

Abelard first discussed the problem of God's goodness and the existence of evil in the *Theologia Christiana*. Although the work ends before the section which would have covered the subject, at the very beginning of the treatise Abelard anticipates his treatment of the area. Where in the *Theologia Summi Boni* he had confined himself to a very brief explanation of the Holy Spirit, equated by him with God's benignity, in terms of mercifulness, he now describes it (72: 14–17) as 'that highest goodness by which he orders each of those things which the highest wisdom has made to the best end, always using even evil things well and miraculously arranging whatever deeds are performed wickedly in the best way'. Abelard adds a series of quotations from Augustine, each to the effect that, whatever evil God allows, he uses well: God creates good natures and arranges evil wills; when the devil uses good natures badly, God uses evil wills well.[1] To these Abelard attaches the two quotations from Plato's *Timaeus* mentioned in the last chapter, which are central to his argument that God's creation and providence are

[1] Extract a: 72: 19–22 = *Enchiridion* III, 11 ((Turnhout, 1969) (CC 46), p. 53: 29–34 with omission); Extract b: 73: 24–7 = *De ciuitate Dei* XI, 17 (ed. B. Dombart and A. Kalb (Leipzig, 1928) I, p. 484: 28–485: 1); Extract c: 73: 27–9 = *De ciuitate Dei* XI, 17 (I, p. 485: 5–7); Extract d: 73: 30–2 = *De ciuitate Dei* XI, 18 (I, p. 485: 15–18). Dombart and Kalb's edn of *De ciuitate Dei* is reprinted with minor changes in CC 47–8 (Turnhout, 1955).

the best possible and could not be different.[2] And, he adds, not only does God make all things as good as they can be, but also 'he disposes evil things well, through his highest and incomprehensible devising'.

This assemblage of quotations already indicates clearly Abelard's distinctive approach to theodicy. Since Augustine bases his theodicy on the Neoplatonic tradition, it might seem that, by combining texts from Plato with those from Augustine, Abelard would do no more than show his adherence to a certain, single tradition. Yet, in fact, there were important differences between Plato's approach and that of Augustine. Augustine took directly from Neoplatonism the view that evil is a privation, a lack of being. It still, however, remained for him to ask what place there is for evil, even if regarded merely as a privation, in a universe created and ruled by a benevolent, omnipotent God. Plato and his pagan followers had not had to answer quite this question, although they too needed to find what is the cause of evil. For Plato himself, there was not a single omnipotent deity, but (as twelfth-century scholars recognized) three principles: the demiurge, the Ideas and matter. A Neoplatonist might bring together the first two of these principles and describe the world of Ideas as an emanation from the One, the highest of all beings, but matter remained as an independent principle to which the presence of evil – not an existence but an absence of being – could be attributed. By contrast, Augustine and the whole tradition of Christian thought recognized in God alone the creator of all things, including matter. A cause other than matter had to be found for evil, and Augustine found it in the one element in the universe not directly under God's control – the free will of rational creatures, men and angels. It was part of God's beneficence that he should have created rational beings: beings who, by definition, have free will, which they might use or abuse. First the rebel angels, then Adam and Eve, chose to misuse their will, and so evil – not a thing but a privation – entered God's creation. But God is omnipotent, and sacred history is the plan by which he saves the goodness of his creation from the evil which was not of his making. Although there are passages in Augustine's work – even in late works such as the *De ciuitate Dei* – where he advances an aesthetic image to explain the presence of evil in the universe, his emphasis, especially in his mature writing, is on the economy of salvation: man's responsibility for his sin, the redemptive sacrifice of Calvary and the unearned, inexplicable grace by which God saves his chosen people.[3]

[2] 73: 33–44. The two passages from the *Timaeus* are from 28a (Extract e: trsl. Calcidius, p. 20: 20–2) and 29c–30b (trsl. Calcidius, 22: 18 . . . 23: 4); cf. p. 219.

[3] R. Jolivet, *Le problème du mal d'après Saint Augustin* (2nd edn, Paris, 1936) remains the clearest exposition of Augustine's position. See also the fine analysis in C. Kirwan, *Augustine* (London/New York, 1989), pp. 60–81.

By his choice and juxtaposition of texts from Plato and Augustine, Abelard succeeds in seeing Plato through Augustine's eyes and Augustine through Plato's. He makes Plato's pronouncements answer Augustine's questions and, by his selection of material from Augustine, makes the Church Father's answers seem far more Platonic than he ever intended. When, in the *Timaeus*, Plato writes about the perfect ordering of the world, he has in mind the world of immaterial ideas, and the motions of the stars: he is not claiming, as Abelard makes him do, that every event in our human world is ordered according to a best possible providential plan. Augustine *does* think of God as providentially planning human history. But, in his work as a whole, he envisages this providence as executed on the one hand in the sweep of sacred history and, on the other hand, towards each individual through God's free gift of grace (or the withholding of it). Abelard does not, of course, reject the pattern of sacred history, but he does not bring it to bear in answering the problem of evil; and his markedly un-Augustinian theory of grace makes efficacy a matter of the individual's choice, not God's.[4] In handling the question of theodicy, he picks just those passages from Augustine which seem to reflect on the problem in a timeless and generalized manner: those which offer the picture of a God who has so organized every event that, even where the free will of rational creatures intends evil, all that happens is part of the best possible providence.

The main lines of this approach would remain unaltered throughout Abelard's work. In the *Collationes*, written soon after the *Theologia Christiana*, Abelard integrates his views on theodicy into an analysis of the different meanings of the words 'good' and 'evil'. This allows him to present his insight with technical precision, and to make clear the relation between his views on God's goodness and his theory of the ethical act. And in later works he extends the discussion of theodicy so as to examine a further question raised by his position: if the world is perfectly ordered by divine providence, what place is there for sorrow and grieving?

GOOD THINGS[5]

'Our authors', complains the Philosopher in the *Collationes* (159: 3132 – 160: 3135), 'say that some things are good, some evil, some indifferent; but they do not distinguish these by any definitions and rest content with giving

[4] See below, pp. 325–7.

[5] An earlier treatment of some of the ideas put forward in this section will be found in my 'Abelard's ethical theory: two definitions from the *Collationes*' in H. Westra (ed.), *From Athens to Chartres* (Leiden/New York/Cologne, 1992), pp. 301–14 at pp. 309–14.

examples to illustrate them.' The Christian's attempt to supply a definition allows Abelard to develop a general analysis of good and evil. He approaches the problem, as the Philosopher's question indicates, in terms of language. But this does not mean that he is simply enquiring what people usually mean by 'good' and 'evil' and trying to draw some analytical distinctions on this basis. As the Christian explains (161: 3169 – 162: 3188), being able to use a word correctly is not at all the same as being able to define what it means. From the practice of speaking we learn how to use a certain word, but do not know the word's true meaning.[6] For instance, we are able to use the word 'stone' correctly to refer to the things which are stones. But we do not know what the *differentia* is which distinguishes stones from other inanimate bodies – we do not even have a word for it.[7] It seems, then, that Abelard's Christian envisages himself as being (or, at least, as expected to be) not an investigator of language but an enquirer into a truth which, at present, is hidden and unexpressed. Yet there remains a linguistic side to his search. First, it seems from the parallel case of 'stone' that ordinary usage will be a guide to where to look, if not for what. Just as, for Abelard, the natural scientist begins from particulars of the kind we call 'stones' and asks what it is that makes them similar; so the starting point for the moral philosopher is the fact that various sorts of things, intentions and *dicta* are called 'good' or 'evil' in ordinary speech. Second, Abelard finds not just the use of a word illuminating, but also (as so often) the grammatical constructions in which it is employed. This is evident from the way Abelard structures his analysis and from how he begins it.

The overall division Abelard's Christian makes is between 'good', 'evil' and 'indifferent' used of things, and 'good' and 'evil' used of *dicta*. The sense of 'good' as used of intentions is examined in connection with indifferent things.[8] The Christian's starting point is a linguistic distinction which the Philosopher had made earlier in their conversation (129: 2335–50). It was a well-known observation of Aristotle's that some adjectives can change their meanings according to the noun they qualify: a man may be good and a cobbler, but not thereby a good cobbler (*Categories* 20b36; *AL* 53: 20). It is probably this distinction on which the Philosopher draws when he

[6] 161: 3172–4: 'Pleraque nominum quibus rebus conveniant ex locutionis usu didicimus; que vero sit sententia eorum vel intelligentia minime assignare sufficimus.'

[7] 161: 3179–83; cf. above, p. 119.

[8] Unfortunately, these clear lines are rather obscured in the course of the dialogue, since in reply to a query from the Philosopher about his definition of 'good thing', the Christian enters a long discussion (162: 3196 – 169: 3385) which dwells both on intentions and *dicta*: see below, p. 248, n. 28.

wishes to explain why it does not follow from the fact that a punishment is good, in the sense that it is just, that it is 'a good thing'.[9] The Philosopher illustrates this difference between the two senses of 'good' by making an analogy with a more straightforwardly definable adjective: 'composite'. He takes the example of an atomic and a composite (or 'hypothetical') statement. When we talk about 'a composite statement' we mean a statement which is composite *as a statement* – that is to say, one which is made up of more than one atomic statement. But we can also say of a statement, not that it is composite as a statement, but that it is 'a composite thing'. Every statement is a composite thing, since it is made up of individual terms.[10]

The Christian in the dialogue uses the distinction implied by the Philosopher and tries to set it out more explicitly. To call something 'a good thing' is, he says, to call it good 'without qualification (*simpliciter*)'. This is to be distinguished, he says, from using 'good' in a different way – what will be described here as using it in a 'specified sense'. The Christian considers that 'good' has a specified sense whenever it directly qualifies a noun. He notes (160: 3136–46) that 'good' changes its meaning according to the word it qualifies. When people speak of 'a good man', 'a good craftsman', 'a good horse', 'good' has a different meaning in each case. A man, the Christian explains, is called 'good' because of his behaviour (*ex moribus*), a craftsman from his knowledge, a horse from its strength and swiftness 'or those things which pertain to its use'. To spell out Abelard's point: if 'E' stands for any word which denotes a substance – either a substance word, such as 'man', or a denominative word, such as 'cobbler' – then when 'good' is used in a specified sense, 'E is good' means 'E is good as an E'. Abelard

[9] The Philosopher talks about a change in sense according to a change in gender (129: 2336–7: *generum permutatio in adiectivis nominibus sensum variat*) because, in Latin, by putting the adjective standing for F into the neuter, the sense of 'F-thing' is obtained: e.g. *omnis propositio est composita* means 'every statement is a composite proposition' whereas *omnis propositio est compositum* means the same as *omnis propositio est res composita*, 'every statement is a composite thing'.

[10] The Philosopher also (129: 2338–41) uses the example of a bronze statue, which is an everlasting thing (because its matter will never cease to exist) but not an everlasting statue. But this illustration is a little confusing. In the case of the composite statement or the punishment (and in the case of the uses of 'good' the Christian will raise), the distinction is between the meaning of the adjectives in each case (e.g. 'composite' = made up of parts; 'composite' = made up of parts which are statements). In this example, however, 'everlasting' retains the same meaning, but what it qualifies differs by, as Abelard would say, property: in 'the statue is an everlasting statue', 'statue' refers to the *materiatum*, that which is made of the matter, whereas in 'the statue is an everlasting thing', 'statue' refers to the *materia*, the material from which the statue is made. On this distinction, see above, pp. 150–5.

seems to think it fairly obvious in each case what is meant by 'good as an E', whichever noun is substituted for E – a view which involves some highly questionable hidden assumptions, at least when E stands for a substance word. (The Philosopher's analogy proves to be rather misleading, since it *is* immediately clear what it is for a statement to be composite as a statement.) Such casualness would make the discussion very shallow were this path the one to be pursued. Abelard, however, is almost exclusively interested in 'good' in its unqualified sense ('a good thing').

It is this which the Christian proceeds to define. Something is good without qualification, he says, 'which is fitted to some use and which does not of necessity hinder the dignity or commodity of anything'. By contrast, something is called 'an evil thing . . . when of necessity one or other of these is brought about by it'.[11] What, exactly, does Abelard mean by this definition of a 'good thing' and an 'evil thing'? The definition of 'good thing' contains two elements: the thing must

(a) be fitted to some use;

and

(b) not of necessity hinder the dignity or commodity of anything.

The definition of 'evil thing' contains just one element, which is the negation of Requirement (b) for 'good': the thing must

(b') of necessity hinder the dignity or commodity of something.

Requirement (a) is very lax. In his reply to the Philosopher's objection (examined below), the Christian makes it clear that a thing has a use if it can be fitted into the plans of men or of God. But in God's plan everything, even what is bad, has its use. It might seem, then, that there is *no* thing then which would fail to meet (a) and so it is a redundant requirement. In fact, Abelard does think that there is a certain class of what he regards as things which do fail to meet (a): this will become clear when his definition of 'indifferent' is discussed. But the weight of his definition of 'good' certainly falls on (b).

Requirement (b) is built around two terms which Abelard feels no need to explain: *dignitas* and *commodum*. *Dignitas* was used, both in classical Latin and by Christian authors, to mean the worth or value of something or

[11] ' "bonum" simpliciter, id est "bonam rem" dici arbitror, que, cum alicui usui sit apta, nullius commodum vel dignitatem per eam impediri necesse est. E contrario "malam rem" vocari, credo, per quam alterum horum conferri necesse est' (160: 3154–7).

somebody.[12] In Augustine's usage, the term could take on the sense of the true worth of something, as opposed to its mere usefulness for us. So, in the section of *De ciuitate Dei* (XI, 15–16) on which Abelard drew repeatedly for his discussion of theodicy, Augustine remarks on how, estimating things according to their use, we often value a horse or a jewel more than a slave, although by nature every living thing is higher in dignity (*dignitas*) than inanimate objects, and rational beings are higher than irrational ones, just as angels precede all things except God in the dignity of their nature (*dignitas naturae*). In classical Latin *commodum* means 'comfort', 'advantage', 'pleasantness'. Already Seneca had used the word to contrast *commoda* with true goods. Sometimes Augustine gave this usage a pejorative implication, in which *commoda* (often qualified by the adjective *temporalia*, 'worldly') are the transitory, earthly things we desire, often in place of what is genuinely good.[13] In *De ciuitate Dei*, however, Augustine discusses how the Stoics call *commoda* what everyone else, except the Stoics, would recognize as goods and, following this line, Anselm of Canterbury used *incommoda* simply to mean what modern philosophers would call 'natural' as opposed to 'moral' evils – for instance, sadness and pain.[14] In his *Dialectica*, Abelard uses *commodum* as a synonym for *utile* (97: 18–22); and, a few years after writing the *Collationes*, Abelard would adapt a theory of love which used Augustine's contrast so as to distinguish a mercenary love – love for the *commoda* someone can provide – from disinterested love. In this theory, however, these *commoda* include any sort of gain, not just what is worldly and transitory; even, indeed, eternal beatitude itself.[15]

[12] In using the term, Abelard probably has particularly in mind Cicero's *De inventione*, which he had used (see below, pp. 284–7) in framing definitions of the virtues. Cicero (II, 52, 157) defines one of the three sorts of desirable things as that which 'sua vi nos allicit ad sese, non emolumento captans aliquo, sed trahens sua dignitate.'; justice, he says a little later (II, 53, 160) is the virtue 'suam cuique tribuens dignitatem'.

[13] Seneca, Epistola 74 (ed. O. Hense (Leipzig, 1914), p. 265: 6–11): 'bona illa sunt vera, quae ratio dat, solida ac sempiterna, quae cadere non possunt, ne decrescere quidem aut minui: cetera opinione bona sunt et nomen quidem habent commune cum veris, proprietas in illis boni non est. itaque commoda vocentur et, ut nostra lingua loquar, producta'. Augustine, *De sermone domini in Monte* II, 25, 82 (ed. A. Mutzenbecher (Turnhout, 1967) (CC 35)), p. 182: 1890–2: 'Temptatio autem duplex est: aut in spe adipiscendi aliquod commodum temporale aut in terrore amittendi'; cf. *De diversis quaestiones lxxxiii*, no. LIX, 3 (ed. A. Mutzenbecher (Turnhout, 1975) (CC44A)), p. 115: 111–12.

[14] Augustine: *De ciuitate Dei* IX, 4 (I, p. 37: 24–5). Anselm: *De concordia* I, 7 (Schmitt, *Anselmi opera* II, p. 258: 22–7); cf. *De conceptu virginali* (Schmitt, *Anselmi opera* II, pp. 146: 30 – 147: 1), *De casu diaboli* (Schmitt, *Anselmi opera* I, p. 274: 13–15). I am grateful to Simo Knuuttila for his advice about this point.

[15] See below, pp. 298–303.

From this various evidence, it seems reasonable to suggest that, when Abelard's Christian speaks of *dignitas*, he means a thing's intrinsic worth. When he refers to its *commodum*, he is talking not about intrinsic value, but value in terms of the meeting of desired ends. This view is confirmed by what Abelard says on the other occasion when he uses *dignitas* and *commodum* as a pair. There he explains that a power, as opposed to a weakness, must serve someone's *dignitas* or *commodum* – that is, it must add to his intrinsic worth or help him achieve the ends he desires.[16] There is, then, a certain asymmetry between the two terms. Socrates' *dignitas* is his, Socrates', intrinsic worth; his *commoda* are those things which have value for him because they meet his desires. The asymmetry is, however, diminished by the fact that, for Abelard, the characteristics which give Socrates his intrinsic worth are particular forms (his rationality, for instance, and his various virtues); and the things which he values because they meet his desires, although they may include independent substances such as the water he drinks, also include particular forms such as health and joy.

In using the pair *dignitas/commodum* the Christian is, therefore, trying to be as inclusive as possible of different types of value: intrinsic value (*dignitas*) and value as what fulfils somebody's desire (*commodum*). The fact that the Christian bases his definition of 'good' and 'evil' on two such all-inclusive evaluative terms, which he does not attempt to define in their turn, shows what sort of analysis Abelard is attempting. He is *not* trying to find a basis for making evaluations which is not itself evaluative – like, for instance, the type of utilitarian who says that every statement of value is, properly speaking, a quantification of pleasure produced or pain avoided. Abelard uses as his starting point the idea that things can have value instrumentally (*commodum*) – they are what is desired – and also (what some philosophers would find harder to accept) that they can have value intrinsically (*dignitas*). He is not concerned with the problem of determining which things have intrinsic value and which lack it: indeed, he seems to think that such valuations can be made uncontroversially and unproblematically. He is working from inside a world of values. What he wishes to do is to use his two most basic evaluative terms – those for intrinsic and for instrumental worth – in order to reach a definition of 'good (thing)' which has a wider extension than that of both *commodum* and *dignitas* together and, correspondingly, a definition of 'evil (thing)' which is narrower than one which

[16] *TChr* 354: 286–94 = *TSch* 507: 268–76. A similar argument about *potentie* and *impotentie* is put forward at *Dial.* 97: 17–37 and *sup.Pred.* 230: 11–22, using the pair *utilitas/dignitas* rather than the pair *commodum/dignitas*.

would include anything lacking in both intrinsic and instrumental worth.

Abelard achieves this aim by making requirement (b) both modal and negative. Any thing which does not *necessarily* impede (or, as he adds (*Coll.* 169: 3389, 3390) diminish) the intrinsic or instrumental worth of something is good. But, wide though (b) is in extension, it is not all-embracing. When the Christian returns to discussing it near the end of the dialogue (169: 3386 – 170: 3394), he makes it clear that there are some things of which (b) is not true and which are, therefore, by his definition, evil.

He explains this by using Aristotle's idea of contraries. Contraries are opposites *par excellence*: as Abelard had stated in his *Dialectica* (374: 33 – 375: 2), two contraries (sickness and health; black and white) cannot be in the same thing at the same time. In the discussion of contraries in his logical works, Abelard had followed Aristotle and Boethius in thinking only in terms of accidental forms in the category of quality. But here he includes both accidental qualitative forms and *differentiae*; in each case, of course, particular forms, since for Abelard all forms, like all substances, are particular. Forms are things, but things which cannot exist apart from the particular substance to which they are attached, given that they have been attached to it.[17] It follows, then, that if one of a pair of contrary forms is attached to a substance, it will perish if its opposite supervenes. If I become sick, I cease to be healthy: the particular accident of health by which I was healthy ceases to exist when I am informed by a particular accident of sickness. Health is one of many accidents – Abelard also lists life, immortality, joy, knowledge and chastity – which have some *dignitas* or *commodum*. When their contraries supervene, they cannot remain. The *dignitas* or *commodum* of something is necessarily impeded or diminished. And so the implication is, therefore, that these contrary qualities – particular forms of death, mortality, grief, sickness, ignorance and unchastity – are themselves evil things.

All this is sketched out very quickly by the Christian, in such a way that it is easy to lose sight of whose or what's values are lost or diminished. From the evidence of what is written here, and earlier when the definition was first given, it seems that Abelard's Christian envisages a substance – say, Socrates. Socrates has a certain intrinsic worth by virtue of the forms attached to him (for instance, knowledge and chastity), and other forms (health, joy) are valuable to him because they meet his desires. Should the forms of ignorance, unchastity, sickness and grief supervene, these forms (knowledge, chastity, health and joy) will perish, and so Socrates will lose the intrinsic worth of the first two and the value of the second two in

[17] See above, pp. 121–2.

meeting his desires. The *dignitas* and *commodum* of Socrates will thus be impeded or diminished. Abelard has, it is true, been guilty of a looseness in stating this argument. The *dignitas* of Socrates' knowledge is part of Socrates' *dignitas*, but the *commodum* of his joy is not one of his *commoda*. Rather, the joy itself is a *commodum* of Socrates, something which he values because it meets his desires. When the Christian talks of the *commodum* of forms such as joy and health, he must mean 'the fact of their being a *commodum*' (perhaps this is what he wishes to indicate by the phrasing *aliquid habeant dignitatis vel commodi*). The line of reasoning is, in any case, firm. When Socrates becomes sick, he will cease to be healthy: the arrival of the form of sickness will mean the loss of something he values – his health.

Although there are then, by the Christian's definition, things which are evil, it also follows, as he immediately goes on to state, that every *substance* is a good thing. There is no substance which, simply by virtue of the sort of thing it is, must *of necessity* hinder the dignity or commodity of something. For even in the case of a wicked man, who leads a life which is corrupt or corrupts others, he might not have been wicked; and so, with regard to his substance (man), he is a 'good thing'.[18] In his commentary on the Hexaemeron (766D) Abelard makes the same point with regard to the angels who rebelled: they were created as good spiritual creatures and, even after their sin, the nature of the spiritual substance remains good. But here Abelard goes on to blur the lines of his argument slightly by introducing (without clearly distinguishing) yet another sense of 'good' – this time an explicitly theological one. He explains that, whilst a newborn baby or foal is not yet a good man or a good horse, it is nevertheless a good creature:

[18] 170: 3394–9: 'Sic et quaslibet substantias constat bonas res esse dicendas, quia, cum aliquid conferre ualeant utilitatis, nichil per eas dignitatis uel commodi necesse est prepediri. Nam et peruersus homo, qui corrupte uel etiam corrumpentis uite est, sic esse posset ut peruersus non esset, ideoque per eum *nichil* deteriorari necesse esset.' Thomas prints *nonnichil* for *nichil* here, following the text in Vienna, 2486. But the other (usually better) manuscript, Oxford, Balliol, 296 reads *nichili*, giving excellent external grounds for suggesting *nichil* as the correct reading. It must so read if the passage is to make sense. The Christian begins (170: 3394–6) by stating that 'all substances whatsoever' (*quaslibet substantias*) are to be described as 'good things', 'because, whilst they are able to bring something of use, it is not necessary that through them anything of dignity or *commodum* should be obstructed'. He goes on to cite the example of the wicked man in order to make his point: 'For even the wicked man, whose way of life is corrupt or corrupts others, might not have been wicked; and, in that case, it would not have been necessary that anything should have been made worse by him.' I am very grateful to Giovanni Orlandi (with whom I am collaborating on an edition and translation of the *Collationes*) for checking the manuscript readings here.

it has from God's creation whatever is fitting to it.[19] Abelard also argues (767B–768B) that apparently useless or harmful things can be described as good creatures, because, when God created them, poisonous plants and fierce animals were not harmful to man; they became so only after the Fall – and even now they are put to good use not only by reminding us of how much we have lost by disobeying God, but also by carrying out just punishment on guilty people and freeing just men from the difficulties of this life and even by serving various uses which men have found for them (undergrowth which destroys vines if it is not cut down can be used, for instance, as firewood).[20] As well as the specified sense of 'good', by which many substances are not good, and the unqualified sense of 'good', according to which every substance, but not every thing, is good, there is then a third sense, 'good' meaning good as a creature, which is rather vaguely defined in relation to God's creative activity. Every substance (every thing? Abelard gives no clue as to whether he would call any or every form 'good' as a creature), it seems, is good in this sense too.

What, though – it might well be asked – is the point of all these complicated definitions? Abelard deserts the idea of 'good' in its specified sense (which seems promising for ethics) in order to define 'good' in its unqualified sense very widely, and in a way which itself relies on presupposed value judgements. His purpose becomes clear, however, once it is seen that Abelard is not here trying to put forward a general ethical theory but to consider the particular problem of the place of evil in a universe ruled by an omnipotent God. In especial, through his definitions of good and evil Abelard wishes to present a sharply different way of treating this problem from that common among his contemporaries. Usually they answered the question of how there can be evil in a universe created by a good and

[19] *Exp.Hex.* 767A (Avranches Bib.Mun. 135, f. 86r): 'Etsi enim infans cum nascitur, quamuis nondum bonus homo dicatur, quod ad mores pertinet, bona tamen est creatura. Sic et pullus cum nascitur, quamuis nondum sit bonus equus et ad usitandum idoneus, bona tamen est creatura et quantum ei conuenit in ipsa creatione a Deo accepit, qui nichil sine ratione uel facit uel fieri permittit'; cf. *Coll.* 130: 2358–64.

[20] Compare Augustine's discussion of the same problem in *De ciuitate Dei* XI, 22 (I, 490: 16 – 491: 10). Abelard adds to the unclarity here when he tries to draw a distinction between creatures being good and being 'exceedingly good' (*ualde bona*) or best. On the one hand, he suggests (767A) that God, by giving to each creature just what befitted it, made it, not just good, but 'exceedingly good'. On the other hand, he argues (766C), with a reference to Augustine, that individual things are good in themselves, but 'exceedingly good' when considered all together 'because what, considered in themselves, seem to be worth little or nothing are most necessary when all things are taken together as a whole (*in tota omnium summa*)'.

benevolent God in straightforwardly Augustinian terms: evil is nothing, a privation of being, rather than an existing thing – it does not belong to the creation of God, who is the source of all being.[21] And, although Anselm of Canterbury had hesitated on the matter, most of them insisted on the non-being not only of sin but also of what would now be called natural evils, such as pain, blindness and sorrow.[22] By contrast, Abelard did hold that there are really existing evils. He admits that no evil is a substance (although not every substance is a good instance of the sort of thing it is). He also allows that sin 'subsists in not-being rather than being', because it consists in not doing or not giving up what we know we should do or give up for God.[23] But he insists that there are evils (both natural evils, like pain, and evils which are the direct results of sin, such as unchastity) which are real things, although accidents not substances. The link between God, being and goodness is thus broken. Abelard is able to break it, as will become clear, because he thinks of God's best providence not in terms of things, but in terms of how things are.

INDIFFERENCE, ACTIONS AND INTENTIONS

The Christian does not confine himself to giving definitions of 'good thing' and 'evil thing'. He also defines what it is to be an 'indifferent' (*indifferens*) thing. The notion that many things are neither good nor evil but indifferent is a feature of Stoic ethics. Stoic moralists described many of the things which people usually value – fine food and clothing, wealth, honour and fame – as indifferent.[24] Abelard certainly knew of this doctrine from Boethius' commentary on the *Categories* where, discussing opposites (268B), Boethius says that Aristotle believed that not everything is good or bad, but

[21] For Augustine on evil as a privation, see e.g. *Confessiones* III, vii, 12; 'quia non noueram malum non esse nisi priuationem boni usque ad omnino non est'; cf. Jolivet, *Le problème du mal*, pp. 35–8 and, for a succinct critique of the idea, Kirwan, *Augustine*, pp. 61–3. On the doctrine in early twelfth-century theologians, see Blomme, *Doctrine du péché*, pp. 9–14.

[22] In *De casu diaboli* 26 (I, pp. 274: 8–13), Anselm says that whilst moral evil (*malum quod est iniustitia*) is nothing, some sorts of natural evil (*malum quod est incommoditas*), such as sorrow and pain, are something. But he seems to step back from this position in *De conceptu virginali* 5 (II, pp. 146: 30 – 147: 1), where he describes sorrow and pain as evils which *seem* to be something. For the type of view common in Abelard's time, see e.g. *Principium et causa omnium*, p. 69, where it is argued that every sort of evil is simply the absence of a thing's natural goodness.

[23] *Sc.* 6: 2–10; on the definition of sin, see below, pp. 265–7.

[24] See M. Lapidge, 'The stoic inheritance' in Dronke, *Twelfth-century philosophy*, pp. 81–112, at p. 89 (for indifferents), pp. 91–9 (for transmission of Stoic ethics to the twelfth century).

that he had no word to describe such things. He adds that, later, the word 'indifferent things' (*indifferentia*) was introduced, and that the Stoics thought that riches and beauty were among these indifferents. Abelard explicitly recalls and repeats these remarks in his own commentary (*sup.Pred.* 267: 13–18). He employs a similar idea of indifferent things in his *Rule* (probably written about five years after the *Collationes*) when he remarks that 'the consumption of meat and wine, just like marriage, is counted among the things intermediate between good and evil, that is, among indifferent things'.[25] The view he puts forward in the *Collationes* is, however, not quite the same. Indifferent things are, indeed, those which are neither good nor evil, as his three-fold definition implies. But Abelard's Christian does not here envisage putting meat or wine or beauty or riches into this category. Indeed, it is hard to see how, by the definition he has given of 'good' and 'evil', all these things are not to be classed among good things: all of them are of some use, and of none is it true that it must *necessarily* impede or diminish the *dignitas* or *commodum* of anything. The Christian of the *Collationes* defines an indifferent thing ('neither good nor evil') as one 'through the existence of which it is not necessary that any good things should be brought about or impeded'. He goes on immediately to give as an example 'the chance motion of a finger or other such actions'; and then he continues:

> For actions are judged as good or evil only according to the root of intention. In themselves, they are all indifferent and, if we look at the matter carefully, they (which are not at all from themselves good or evil) confer no merit, since the very same actions are equally appropriate to the damned and to the elect. (160: 3158 – 161: 3165)

This definition and the illustration of it which follows raise a number of problems. First, it seems strange that Abelard should give, as his example of a type of thing, a sort of action. Second, it might seem that the definitions of 'good thing' and 'evil thing' which have already been given are such as together to comprehend everything. Third, the transition from talking about unconsidered actions ('the chance movement of a finger') to every action whatsoever is abrupt and unexplained.

In the Christian's rather brief remarks on his definitions, no explicit solution to these problems is offered. Using ideas Abelard advances elsewhere, however, the difficulties might be resolved along the following

[25] 267: 'Usus autem carnium ac vini, sicut et nuptiae, intermedia boni et mali, hoc est indifferentia, computantur.' Note that *computantur* is a word which carries a certain reserve; and Abelard goes on to say that marriage is not entirely without sin and wine is the most dangerous of foods. For a discussion of this theme, see below, p. 312.

lines. For Abelard, actions are things – they are accidents in the category of *agere*; and Abelard went on thinking of these types of accident as things, even once he had stopped regarding many other types of accident in this way.[26] It is not, then, surprising that a sort of action should be used as an example of a type of thing. The definitions of 'good' and 'evil' do not include everything. Consider once again the Christian's definitions. There are two requirements for a thing to be good: (a) it must be fitted to some use; (b) it does not of necessity hinder the dignity or commodity of anything. There is just one requirement for a thing to be evil: that it fulfils (b'), the negation of (b). It is this asymmetry between the definitions of 'good' and 'evil' which leaves room for the possibility of indifferent things. If something fulfils (b), but not (a), it will be neither evil nor good – and so indifferent. But is there anything which does not fulfil (a), since (as remarked above) Abelard considers that whatever can be fitted into God's plan has a use, and that God's plan has a place, it seems, for everything, even what is evil? The Christian's comment on indifferent things suggests that, for Abelard, there is a sort of thing which fails to fulfil (a): actions. Although Abelard never explains the rationale behind this suggestion, it would have been reasonable for him to hold that, whereas every substance and most sorts of forms are fitted to some use, this is not true of actions. It is rather through actions that the uses for which other things are fitted are accomplished, than actions which themselves are fitted to any use. It would also be reasonable to suppose that no action fulfils (b'); that no action is, therefore, in itself evil. Although some actions are likely to hinder the dignity or commodity of something, it would be wrong to say that of any action that it must *necessarily* do this. It is always possible that something will intervene. As things, then, all actions are indifferent – they are not fitted to any use and so not good; nor can they fulfil the requirement for being evil.

This way of looking at an action, simply as a thing – leaving out of consideration the intention informing it – is, of course, a very unusual way of regarding actions, since usually even the roughest description of an action takes account of a presumed intention. Abelard's abrupt transition from talking about the chance movement of a finger to every sort of action might be interpreted as his way of recognizing just this point. Every action, considered just as a thing apart from the agent's intention, is like the chance movement of a finger. Abelard will go on to insist that actions gain their value, not as things, but through the intentions behind them. Any inten-

[26] See above, p. 160.

tional action is to be valued, according to the intention in which it is rooted – an idea which is central to Abelard's discussion of the ethical act, which will be discussed in the next chapter. But a good or evil intention is not a good *thing* or an evil *thing*.

Abelard, then, uses the category of 'indifferent things' as a way of linking the moral evaluation of action with his more general scheme of good and evil things. Actions in themselves are things which are neither good nor evil. Intentions, however, are good or evil, but they are not things, and very different criteria must be used for judging them. A man – who is a good thing, whatever he does – becomes a good man or an evil man through his behaviour, which must be judged according, not to actions themselves, but to the intentions which inform them.

THE GOODNESS OF HOW THINGS ARE: ABELARD'S OPTIMISM

Things and intentions are not alone in being described as 'good'. When he first gives his definition, the Christian makes sure to add (160: 3146–9) that

> we sometimes apply the word 'good' not just to things themselves, but also to what is said about things, that is to the *dicta* of statements; and in such a way that we can even say that it is good for there to be evil, although we would not at all allow that evil is good.

Although any *dictum* might be described as good, Abelard's Christian immediately turns to the extreme case of the *dictum* of the statement, 'evil exists'. This helps to show where Abelard's concerns lie. At the end of the dialogue (170: 3403–6), the Christian paraphrases 'for this to be/not to be is good' as 'this is necessary for some excellent plan (*optima dispositio*) of God's to be fulfilled, even if this plan is entirely hidden from us'. The idea of 'good' as a description for *dicta* gives Abelard a technically precise way of stating his answer to the problem of God and evil. Divine providence functions, not on the level of things, but of how things are – the *dicta* of statements. There are good and evil things in the world, as Abelard's definition makes clear. There are also good and evil intentions: things are done well or badly. But 'good' and 'evil' used of intentions and used of things need to be distinguished from their usage in connection with *dicta*. Even the statement 'it is good that someone acts well' (that is, with a good intention) may not always be true: the person's intended act – though not what he succeeds in doing – may not fit with God's ordination of things.[27] 'Who does not know', asks the Christian (162: 3211 – 163: 3215), 'that the highest goodness of God, which allows nothing to take place without a cause, preordains even evil things well and uses them too in the best way, so that it is even true that it is good for there to be evil, although evil is by no means good?'[28] The position is supported with a set of quotations from Augustine and the *Timaeus*, similar to those which Abelard had used at the beginning of the *Theologia Christiana* and which he would use in the *Theologia Scholarium* in connection with the necessity of God's actions.[29]

Not only are things, even evil things, so ordained by God that they are for the best. God, argues Abelard, has also made this excellent disposition evident to men. It is on the evident excellence of the way the universe is ordered that he bases his arguments in the *Theologia Christiana* (348: 62 – 352: 193) and the *Theologia Scholarium* (500: 58 – 504: 179) both for God's existence and his unity. And, in his commentary on the Hexaemeron, Abelard insists that when the Bible says, 'And God saw that it was good', it means not just that God's creation is good, but that its goodness is evident to us.[30] Abelard is therefore even willing to argue that to lament the death

[27] 170: 3406–9: 'Non enim aliquem etiam bene facere bonum est, si hoc eum facere alicui divine ordinationi non competit, sed potius obsistit, quia nec bene fieri potest, quod rationabilem cur fiat causam non habet. Tunc autem rationabilem non habet causam cur fiat, si quid a Deo dispositum prepediri necesse esset, si illud contingeret.' Note the final clauses, which make it clear that the intended action will not actually take place if it goes against God's providence.

[28] This discussion of providence occurs, not as part of the treatment of 'good' applied to *dicta*, where it really belongs, but in the Christian's answer to an objection by the Philosopher to his definition of 'good thing'. Why, the Philosopher asks (162: 3194–5) does not Requirement (a) suffice: that a good thing be 'fitted for some use'? The Christian argues against this by pointing out that good things can be used badly and bad things well. His prime example is the way in which God uses all things for the best, although he also points to the devil, who uses good things badly and the good ruler, who uses well the very sword which a bad ruler uses badly. At this point (163: 3226–30), however, the Christian's reasoning becomes tangled. From the fact that anything can be used well or badly, he infers that any man, whether good or bad, is the cause of both good and bad things: the good man differs from the bad, not because he does what is good, but because he acts well. This, in the form stated, is a *non sequitur*. It is true, however, that in view of God's supreme ability to use all things for the best, judgement of men's behaviour can never rightly be based on its effects, which are all part of the best divine providence, but must look to intended actions.

[29] 166: 3309–11 = Extract e; 168: 3349–51 = Extract b; 168: 3353–4 = Extract c; 168: 3356–8 = Extract d; 168: 3360–1 = unknown!; 168: 3363 – 169: 3368 = Extract a (slightly longer); 169: 3370–80 = *Enchiridion* XI; p. 236: cf. above p. 233, n. 1.

[30] This is why (747D–748A) the Bible does not say that God 'saw that it was good' after the description of the second day – God has still not shown us what good or use there was in

of martyrs, who will go to heavenly glory, is irrational (though excusable as resulting from ignorance or from an excess of love) – as is the behaviour of the man who grieves intensely at seeing his aged and beloved father about to die.[31]

Abelard's distinctively optimistic approach to theodicy is brought out especially clearly in a passage near the end of his commentary on the Hexaemeron.[32] The verse under consideration is Genesis 2: 17, where God prohibits Adam from eating the fruit of the Tree of Knowledge. Abelard's main source here was almost certainly Ambrose's *De Paradiso*. There Ambrose raises the question of why God, who is omniscient, gave a precept which he could foresee would be disobeyed.[33] After making it clear that the fault lay with Adam who broke the precept, not God who gave it, Ambrose adds that, had there been no sin, then 'perhaps' there would have been no virtue either: virtue 'might not have been able to subsist or shine out were there not some seeds of wickedness'. And then, rather inconsistently, Ambrose goes on to argue that, even if God had not given a commandment, there still would have been the possibility of sin. We know naturally what is evil: we read the laws of God not 'inscribed in tablets of stone' but 'impressed in our hearts by the spirit of the living God'.

The direction of Abelard's discussion is exactly the same. He asks why God made a prohibition which he knew would be broken and, after showing the good which in fact resulted, he goes on to argue that, even without God's prohibition, men would have been able to sin, since we know by natural reason what offends God: 'It is by no means to be conceded that they would have remained free from sin had they been given no commandment to obey, since without a commandment they could have acted wickedly against their conscience.' Abelard's presentation of the beneficial effects

the waters above the firmament (Ambrose (Hexaemeron *MPL* 14, 143A) and Bede (*In Genesim* (*Opera omnia* II, 1, ed. C. Jones (Turnhout, 1967) (CC s.l. 118a) 9: 195–8)) provide partial precedents for this view); and why the Bible uses a roundabout expression – 'God saw all things that he had made, and they were very good' – at the end of describing the fifth day: (766AB; Avranches 135, f. 85v): 'Non enim – iuxta hoc quod exposuimus de singulis "uidit Deus quod esset bonum", hoc est, "uidere hoc nos et intelligere fecit ex manifesta eorum utilitate" – potuit de omnibus dici quod uiderit cuncta bona, propter operationem saltem secundae diei de suspensione aquarum, quarum diximus utilitatem nondum probare ualemus.'

31 *Sent.* (§§187–9; Bu. 114: 19–37), *Sent.Par.* (25: 4 – 26: 4) and *TSch* (547: 1557 – 548: 1579).

32 The Avranches manuscript, which was used for the edition in *MPL*, finishes in the middle of the first sentence of this comment; but the complete text of this (and the rest of the remaining section) is edited from the other manuscripts in Buytaert, 'Abelard's Expositio', see pp. 174–6 for this passage.

33 *MPL* 14, 291D–293A.

of the Fall is, however, far more direct and extreme than Ambrose's. By sinning, he claims, man was able to become better than he had been before he sinned, because Christ redeemed us through his own death and we love God all the more because we thereby have a greater reason to love. By loving God more after the Fall than we did before, we are made better than we were, so that 'through God's mercy that evil of ours was turned into the greatest good for us'. Now 'one woman is worth more to God and through her merit is more pleasing to him than many thousands of people he would have made if they had persevered always without sin'. Where would there be a crown of victory, were there no struggle against enemies? Abelard emphasizes his point by quoting the liturgy for Easter Vigil: 'O truly necessary sin of Adam which was cancelled out by Christ's death! O happy fault which merited such and so great a redeemer!'[34]

This treatment of Adam's *felix culpa* does not merely illustrate Abelard's optimism, related to his view that God can do only what is best. It also shows how he tries to reconcile such optimism with human free will. Adam's sin is, for Abelard as much as for Augustine, an act of free will. But Abelard's God acts in such a way as to make this freely chosen, sinful act a necessary part of a scheme of things which could not have been so good had Adam not sinned. In his oral teaching Abelard was fond of using aesthetic metaphors which depict God using evil in order to make the way things are better than it would be otherwise, like a master painter using a colour which is less beautiful than others in itself, but makes the whole picture more beautiful.[35] Given Abelard's theory of grace,[36] Adam's progeny acts with no less freedom than he did. But God incorporates whatever things and intentions are evil into his inscrutable best providential plan of how human actions interrelate with one another and with natural events. Sometimes evil (and indeed, sometimes, good) intentions are not realized in action at all; sometimes they are realized, but their apparently evil consequences are part of a greater good. So goes Abelard's theory – but it would be a shallow one were it not merely one part of a complex view of ethics. Abelard realizes that there is a gulf between the excellence of divine providence and individual ethical agents, striving to avoid sin as they act within a web of circumstances encompassed by God's, but not their, knowledge. This level of Abelard's discussion – the ethical act, its context and evaluation – will form the subject of the next three chapters.

[34] Buytaert, 'Abelard's Expositio', p. 175.

[35] *Sententie* §154, *Sent.Par.* 24: 7–16 and cf. *Coll.* 168: 3360–1. The comparison is quoted from Augustine, of whose theodicy this aesthetic analogy forms a strand, but not the central one.

[36] See below, pp. 325–7.

Chapter 11

Act, intention and consent

Abelard inherited two different sorts of vocabulary for analysing the morality of human behaviour. His predecessors and contemporaries talked in terms of vices and virtues, and also in terms of sin and merit. Vices and virtues, as Abelard's reading of Aristotle had taught him, are settled states; sin and merit, by contrast, however they are analysed, must be seen in terms of individual moral choices. Abelard's understanding of ethical acts is structured around this distinction, which at once unites his analyses of good and evil behaviour and separates them. Just as he draws a sharp contrast between vice and sin, so Abelard distinguishes virtue from merit. But whereas, in examining wrongdoing, he concentrates his attention on sin, and discusses the vices only in order to explain why sin must not be confused with them, Abelard approaches good behaviour mainly by examining the virtues and their relation to the supreme virtue of charity and treats merit rather as an afterthought. It is for this reason that it is clearest to examine his views on acting badly separately from those on acting well (Abelard himself makes such a separation when he presents his ethics systematically in the *Sententie*). And it is for the same reason too that it is for the most part in connection with sinning that Abelard investigates the relation between action and moral judgement. This chapter will consider Abelard's distinctive view of this problem, which provides the starting point for his wider treatment of human morality.

INTENTION

Abelard considered that true moral judgement (such as that which God makes) is according to what he calls the agent's 'intention' (*intentio*). This position is one he repeats frequently, from the mid-1120s onwards, very often putting it in terms of a contrast between *opera* ('actions', with the implication: actions as they would strike an observer unacquainted with the circumstances) and intention. So – to give just a few examples – in the *Theologia Christiana* (369: 696–8), Abelard remarks that 'the whole quality of deeds should be taken according to the root of intention (*radix intentionis*)'.[1] In the Commentary on Romans, he writes of the 'judgement of true justice, where all things which are done are weighed up according to intention rather than to the sort of actions they are'; and the *Sententie* (§275; Bu. 154: 40–3) argue that God 'does not care for actions, which are indifferent in themselves, but demands purity of intention'. Here Abelard adds to his emphasis on intention the corresponding negative point, about the indifference of actions: as he had put it even more directly in the *Collationes* (160: 3161–3): 'Actions are not judged good or bad except according to the root of intention: in themselves, they are all indifferent.'

Is there anything distinctive to Abelard about this view of intention and act? An emphasis on intention is characteristic of patristic moral thought and was adopted by most of Abelard's contemporaries. By claiming that sin is to be judged according to intention, they usually meant something more than what a modern thinker would understand by this claim: not merely that acts (as they appear to an observer) are not sufficient basis for judgement, but also that sin requires or can be partly identified with a given mental act or series of acts, hidden from other people, but patent to both the agent in question and God. Much modern discussion of intention has been devoted to rejecting such 'mentalist' accounts in favour of theories which account for the intentionality of acts without postulating mental acts of intending preceding each external act. Although Abelard's analysis of sinning discusses both dispositions and mental attitudes, and although the link Abelard makes between intentions and external acts is (as will emerge) very close, there is every reason to think that he too identified sins with mental acts (wholly rather than partly, as other thinkers did, since he claimed that actions in themselves are 'indifferent').[2]

In a very general sense, then, Abelard's views on intention may be seen as the continuation and development of a long tradition, which was shared by all the thinkers of the early twelfth century. But, here as elsewhere, Abelard developed his ideas in a characteristically subtle and distinctive way.

[1] On the implications of saying '*root* of intention', see below, pp. 255–6.

[2] See above, pp. 244–7 and below, p. 256.

ACTS AND INTENTIONS: ABELARD'S PREDECESSORS AND CONTEMPORARIES

Although Abelard certainly read patristic discussions of sinning, especially Augustine's, and found problems and examples there which stimulated his thought, the immediate background against which he worked was provided by the two main theories about the nature of sin current among Abelard's immediate predecessors and contemporaries.[3] Both of them, in line with the general patristic approach, envisaged sin in terms of intention. The first, which might be called a 'defect of justice' theory, was that propounded by Anselm of Canterbury. A rational being sins, Anselm thought, when he fails to act in accord with justice. Neither the will (*uoluntas*), which is created by God, nor even the desires which have occasioned the sinful act, are themselves sinful. Sin is found, rather, in the failure of the will, in its lack of justice.[4] The main motivation behind this theory was not ethical but theological and metaphysical. It was designed to show that evil is not an existing thing and so not a creation of God's.[5] William of Champeaux, Abelard's teacher and enemy, proposes a rather cruder version of this theory in one of his *Sententiae*. The will itself, so far as its nature goes, is good; but it has been given freedom of choice by God and is able, therefore, to choose what goes against his commands: in that case, the will – the particular act of willing – is bad.[6]

The other theory, which might be called a 'stages' theory, was Anselm of Laon's, but it was closely related to Augustine's thought. It analyses sin by looking, chronologically, at the stages of thought and action in a case of

[3] The opening chapters of *De libero arbitrio* were particularly fertile for Abelard as a source of problems and examples: for instance, the man who kills his lord to save himself from injury or the man who kills someone with a stray dart I, iv, 9 (ed. J. Martin (Turnhout, 1972) (CC 32), pp. 215: 10–18, 216: 29–30); cf. also below, p. 290, n. 17. On the underlying differences between Abelard's approach and Augustine's, see R. Saarinen, *Weakness of the will in medieval thought. From Augustine to Buridan* (Leiden/New York/Cologne, 1994) (Studien und Texte zur Geistesgeschichte des Mittelalters 44), pp. 20–43.

[4] This is a very crude summary of a complex theory, which is expounded and developed in a number of Anselm's works, but put with especial clarity in *De conceptu virginali* III (II, pp. 142–4). On Anselm's ethics, see R. Pouchet, *La 'rectitudo' chez saint Anselme* (Paris, 1964).

[5] See e.g. *De conceptu virginali* (II, p. 146: 5): 'Iniustitia autem omnino nihil est, sicut caecitas.' The whole argument of *De casu diaboli* centres around this idea.

[6] *Lottin* §277, p. 221: 1–7. William of Champeaux uses *uoluntas* to refer both to the will, as a capacity, and to a particular act of willing.

sinning.[7] First, there is suggestion (*suggestio*). Suppose, for instance, I see a married woman and I feel a sexual attraction to her. Anselm would not consider that, at this stage, I am guilty of any sin: he would say that my body (as a result of human weakness) is putting into my mind a certain evil idea.[8] But, as soon as I begin to turn over in my mind whether or not I will try to sleep with her, then I begin to sin.[9] The next stage is when I consider the sinful action with pleasure (*delectatio*). In some cases, Anselm would say that I could, if I wished, avoid this. Instead, however, I might give consent (*consensus*) to these thoughts and so increase my delectation.[10] Finally, I give my consent to the sinful action and actually carry it out, sleeping with the married woman and committing the sin of adultery.[11]

The stages theory was very popular among writers in the early twelfth century, especially those of the 1130s to 1150s.[12] What view of intention and act does it involve? According to it, intentions take place in the mind and can be analysed into different stages; acts are performed in the world. Both intentions and acts are subject to evaluation. Intention alone can be sinful. A man may sin merely by indulging, for instance, his sexual attraction to a married woman, even if he would never actually go so far as to commit adultery with her. But the exponents of this theory also seem to have accepted the traditional view that certain categories of action are sinful in themselves, whatever the intention behind them. True, Anselm of Laon stresses the importance of intention when he insists that it can be evil to perform what is, as a matter of fact, a good deed, if it is done from an intention to cause harm. But the very way he put this point shows his

[7] An exposition of this view by Anselm himself is found in *Lottin* §85, pp. 73–4; cf. Blomme, *Doctrine du péché*, pp. 21–6. It is to a variant of this view that William of Champeaux refers at *Lottin* §278, p. 222: 9–14. The basis of the scheme (*suggestio*, *delectatio*, *consensus*, *actus*) had a long tradition: cf. Blomme, *Doctrine du péché*, p. 24, n. 1.

[8] *Lottin* §85, p. 73: 12–17: 'Suggestio . . . ipsis suggerentibus semper est peccatum, non autem semper ei cui suggeritur . . . Talis enim suggestio nihil aliud est quam quidam motus carnis reducens in mentem aliquod malum sine delectatione.'

[9] *Lottin*, §85, p. 74: 25–7: 'dicitur peccare per suggestionem quando apud se dubitat de illo malo, utrum ipse faciat an non et deliberat apud se, nondum delectatus uel consentiens'.

[10] *Lottin*, §85, p. 74: 32–3, 54–6: 'Peccatum delectationis duobus modis consideratur. Alia namque est euitabilis, alia ineuitabilis . . . Nam consensus ille [*sc.* qui comitatur delectationem] est quando aliquis fauet illi euitabili delectationi et producit eam ut magis delectetur.'

[11] At *Lottin*, p. 74: 22, Anselm defends the four stages, *suggestio*, *delectatio*, *consensus*, *opus*; at p. 74: 50–4 he distinguishes the act itself from the *consensus* which accompanies it.

[12] See Blomme, *Doctrine du péché*, pp. 27–53. Some of these alter the stages theory in a way which brings it closer to Abelard's ideas: it is quite possible that this was due to the influence of Abelard's teaching and writing.

underlying view: 'everything done with intention of harming one's neighbour is an evil, whether it is good or bad'.[13]

ACTS AND INTENTIONS: ABELARD'S THEORY[14]

Abelard adopted neither the defect-of-justice nor the stages theory, although he was influenced by both of them. He shared the concern for the problem of theodicy which was one of the motivations for the defect-of-justice theory, but he tackled this question, as has been shown, in a different way, through his distinction between 'good' used of substances, accidents and *dicta*. In much of his writing, however, he did, like the exponents of this theory, talk of sin as a *uoluntas*, although finally he rejected this description. He was also attracted by the emphasis in the stages theory on the intentions preceding the sinful act itself but, finally, he used this theory's vocabulary of consent to work out a theory of sin quite different from that of its exponents. Although this highly individual theory is fully developed only in *Scito teipsum* (and clearly present in just two other texts from the same period, the *Problemata* and the London *Reportatio*) it offers, not a dramatic change in perspective, but rather the clear and explicit expression of what was always implied by Abelard's underlying views on intention.

In his various comments on intention, Abelard does not, as might appear at first sight, draw a direct antithesis between intentions and actions but, rather, says that actions *in themselves* are indifferent, and that judgement must be made according *to the root of* intention. It is a point which Abelard already makes at the time of his earliest prolonged reflections on ethics.[15] In his last ethical treatise, *Scito teipsum* (46: 4–12), the argument is developed in detail. Abelard makes the point with regard to a good intention, but it would apply equally to a bad one. When we talk of someone's good

[13] *Lottin* §70, p. 61: 4–8.

[14] In *Doctrine du péché*, pp. 113–219, Blomme provides a very thorough, detailed and finely nuanced analysis of the notions of sin, guilt, intention, will, consent, desire and vice in Abelard's work. Many of my conclusions in the following paragraphs, on these subjects, accord with Blomme's, although Blomme tends to emphasize Abelard's 'interiorization', whereas here attention is drawn particularly to the central place of intended acts in Abelard's ethics. Blomme was sometimes hindered from making the best sense of the differences and similarities he noticed in his material by having accepted a dating for *Coll.* after *Sc.*, and by considering the *Sententie* (and *Sent.Par.*) as independent works by followers of Abelard.

[15] See above, p. 252 (quote from *Theologia Christiana*); cf. also *SN*, 609–10 (this passage, found in just one manuscript, is labelled 'ABAIELARDVS', clearly indicating that, unlike the other material in *SN*, it is Abelard's own).

intention and his good deed, Abelard says, we distinguish two things, the intention and the deed, but there is just one goodness – of the intention. It is just as if, says Abelard, we were talking about a good man and the son of the good man: there would be two men, but only one goodness. Similarly, an intention is called 'good' from itself, a deed not from itself but because it proceeds from a good intention.

Although, then, Abelard holds that actions in themselves are indifferent – a view which was condemned at the Council of Sens and might seem to make his view of sin even more starkly intentional than those of his contemporaries – he does not strip actions of ethical value, but he insists that it is a derivative value. Actions are rightly described as good or bad, but only by virtue of the intentions from which they spring. But intentions, although they belong to the life of the mind, are sinful only in relation to a definitely intended (although perhaps prevented) action. This view is, therefore, in one way the direct opposite of that which underlies the stages theory. Instead of holding that intentions and acts should each be evaluated, Abelard believes that acts cannot be judged except through the intentions which inform them and that intentions cannot be judged except in relation to the acts which result from them, or would have resulted had they not been thwarted.[16]

This outlook had two contrasting consequences on how Abelard determined when a person was sinning or not, one of which made his standard of judgement in a certain way laxer than would have been usual, the other of which made it more severe. Unlike many of his contemporaries, Abelard held that neither dispositions to act sinfully, nor any physical or mental process or attitude other than the final mental act of choosing to perform the sinful act, were blameworthy. But he also argued that, by the same token, an agent's attitude of disapproval towards a sinful action does not at all excuse him, if he none the less performs the action. The sin – the mental act of choosing this course of action under the circumstances – is not affected by mental attitudes such as this.

The rest of the chapter will trace in more detail the two central distinctions just raised. First, Abelard's contrast between sin and vicious dispositions will be considered, and then his attempts to distinguish between a sin and the feelings, thoughts or mental attitudes surrounding and related

[16] *Coll.* (III: 1868–75) may seem to offer an exception to Abelard's usual view, since the Christian allows the possibility that sin might consist in deed or in will; but this is only so as to put in the most sweeping form his rejection of the position that all sins are equal (see below, p. 308).

to the sin. To some extent, Abelard's discussion of these distinctions can be regarded as an investigation into what would now be called the philosophy of action. But, for Abelard, the moral and theological aim of his enquiry always remains primary: to show what sin is and is not. As a result, questions and concepts which a twentieth-century philosopher would keep distinct are often merged in a way which the modern interpreter could only separate at the cost of leaving behind Abelard's argument altogether.

SIN AND VICE

The main sort of vicious dispositions which Abelard contrasts with sin are those which he considers innate. In the *Collationes*, the Philosopher explains, with the tacit agreement of his interlocutor, the Christian, how at their birth men contract from the balance of elements in them many vices – for instance, that they are of an irascible or sexually excitable nature (130: 2368–71). He does not make an ethical point about these vices here, but in the *Sententie*, Abelard develops the moral implications of the position.[17] No one can be blamed for what he is born with, and so innate vices, although they incline people to sin, must be sharply distinguished from sins: they are not themselves blameworthy – they are, indeed, the occasions for merit. 'Vice is a defect in nature such that it makes a man lacking in power (*impotens*) to resist an unlawful inclination or unwilling to give each man his due – for instance, quickness to anger, sexual indulgence, greed and so on. But sin is to will to become angry, indulge in sexual appetite and so on' (§267; Bu. 150: 27–31).

Abelard's point is that a person is not bound to act in the way to which an innate weakness inclines him.[18] Although he does not state it explicitly, he is clearly thinking of what Aristotle, in the *Categories*, calls a 'natural weakness'.[19] When he discusses quality in the *Dialectica* (96: 18 – 99: 24) and the *Logica* (*sup.Pred.* 229: 15 – 231: 32), Abelard explains that Aristotle means by these terms, not any sort of natural potency or weakness, but just those which result from the particular make-up of certain members of a

[17] The Philosopher does, however, make an analogous ethical point with regard to a natural disposition which is not regarded as a vice (116: 1990–2000). If a man is born who lacks sexual appetites, this natural chastity or frigidity is not, says Abelard's Philosopher, a virtue. Nor is there any merit when this man remains chaste, since he has not had to overcome any desire.

[18] §267; Bu. 150: 38–9: 'Multi siquidem sunt qui, cum proni sunt ad hoc, uoluntatem tamen cohibent.'

[19] 9a14–27; *AL* 64: 14–24.

species and so are not shared by all its members. Natural potencies of this sort are, for instance, being able to fight easily or run easily, but not simply being able to fight or being able to run. Everyone can naturally fight or run; but some people, through the way their limbs are naturally formed, can do these things easily.

In *Scito teipsum* (*Sc.* 2: 20 – 4: 25), Abelard's main discussion of what he now calls 'vices of the mind' follows exactly the lines set in the *Sententie*. At the very beginning of the work, however (2: 6–8), Abelard describes 'vices of the mind' quite differently. They are, he says, the opposites of the virtues: injustice, for instance, or intemperance.[20] The virtues of justice and temperance, as will be explained, were held by Abelard not to be natural but acquired. In talking about the vices opposite to them, Abelard must therefore be drawing into his account a sort of disposition distinct from natural weaknesses.[21] This equivocal use of 'vice' is confusing, but it underlines Abelard's insistence that a sin – which is a particular intention to act – cannot be identified with any sort of disposition.

WILL AND CONSENT

When he wrote his commentary on Romans, Abelard already was concerned to distinguish between a sin – which he envisages as a definite mental act (preceding the external act or, in the case where the external act is thwarted, standing on its own)[22] – and the various thoughts, feelings and mental attitudes surrounding the sin. But he has a serious problem of vocabulary. Both the defect-of-justice theory and the stages theory describe sin and sinning using the noun *uoluntas* and its cognate verb *uelle*. This vocabulary would have been especially attractive to Abelard, because it helps to draw a clear distinction between sin and external acts. Abelard therefore adopts this common terminology and declares that sin is a *uoluntas*.[23] But

[20] Blomme (*Doctrine du péché*, pp. 166–7) seems not to notice this, remarking that 'in the opening pages' of *Sc.* Abelard 'appears to be thinking of natural predispositions'.

[21] He had already used 'vice' with this sense, completely different from his usual one for the word, in the *Collationes* (115: 1986–7) and the *Sententie* (§265; Bu. 149: 1–14; cf. *Coll.* 126: 2270 – 127: 2283). Vices are also presented as the opposites of the virtues in *Serm.* 5 (423A). *Vitium* is sometimes used by Abelard with a less precise sense in exegetical contexts – see *Comm.Rom.* 185: 16–17 and *Serm.* 6, 427CD, 428B.

[22] Note, for instance, Abelard's willingness (65: 640–2) to talk of the 'mind' (*animus*) in which something is done, and the phrasing in the passage quoted in n. 24 below (*ex uoluntate quacumque praeeunte*); cf. below, p. 260.

[23] See e.g. *Comm.Rom.* 164: 354–7: 'Pluribus autem modis peccati nomen Scriptura sacra accipit: uno quidem modo et proprie pro ipsa animi culpa et contemptu Dei, id est praua

uoluntas and *uelle* are words with a very wide range of meaning in Latin, and Abelard also uses them when he is talking about precisely what he wants to distinguish from sin. He thus argues (206: 635 – 207: 682) that there are cases where someone might be said *not* to will (*uelle*) an action and yet to sin by it. Suppose that I am forced to kill a man in order to avoid being killed by him myself, or suppose that I sleep with someone else's wife, ardently wishing that she were unmarried and that I was not committing adultery. I cannot, in the first case, be said to will (*uelle*) to kill the man. What I will to do is to save my life – and that is not a sin. Nor can I be said, in the second case, to will (*uelle*) to commit adultery. What I will to do is to sleep with the woman – and that, too, is not a sin. Yet Abelard insists that in each case I do commit a sin which is 'willed' (*uoluntarium*). He tries to sort out this ambiguity by saying that the sin is willed in the sense that there was a volition which preceded the action of sinning, but not in the sense according to which 'will' can be identified with '*concupiscentia*'.[24] Abelard seems to be searching for a word with which to talk about this feeling or attitude of desire or approval which he cannot identify clearly but he is sure is distinct from the mental act which constitutes sin. '*Concupiscentia*' may not be a very good choice, however, because its meaning is definitely pejorative and it has strong sexual and physical connotations. To make matters worse, on at least two occasions in his Commentary on Romans (158: 147–8, 196: 314–16 and ff.), influenced by the text of St Paul, and by his wish to stress that sin does not consist in bare actions (and perhaps also by the popular stages theory), Abelard identifies *concupiscentia* with sin.[25]

In his latest writings, Abelard introduced a new term in order to escape the confusion caused by the different meanings of *uoluntas/uelle*.[26] Sin, says

uoluntate nostra qua rei apud Deum statuimur'; *Sententie* §269; Bu. 151: 52–6; *Coll.* 164: 3254 – 165: 3270; cf. Blomme, *Doctrine du péché*, pp. 174–81, 184–8.

[24] 206: 635–9: 'Cum itaque dicitur "omne peccatum uoluntarium" et cum dicitur "nemo peccare inuitus", de actu hoc peccati, non de concupiscentia est intelligendum. Omnis quippe actus peccati inde uoluntarius potius quam necessarius dicitur quod ex uoluntate quacumque praeeunte ipse descendit.'

[25] Cf. Blomme, pp. 188–9.

[26] Examples of the new usage in the four works in which it occurs (*Sc.*, *Problemata*, the London *Reportatio* and the *Sententie Magistri Petri*) are given in the notes following. Abelard does use the word *consensus* occasionally outside these four, but it does not have the special role in his definition of sin which he would give it there. At *Comm.Rom.* 119: 102, for instance, *consentire* is used – 'agree to/bring to pass' in a positive sense – in his death Christ 'consented' to our salvation. (At *Comm.Rom.* 80: 132–4 and 291: 86, *assentio* is used where later Abelard would use *consentio*, showing very clearly that at this stage he had not introduced his technical usage – although *assentio* is used for *consentio*, very rarely in *Sc.*:

Abelard in *Scito teipsum*, is properly speaking *consent* (*consensus*) to what is not fitting.[27] 'We consent to that which is not allowed', Abelard explains, 'when we do not at all draw back from carrying it out and are entirely ready to do it, if the chance is given.'[28] Consent, then, is not just a matter of thinking about something in a certain way: it is being ready to do it. None the less, like the volition (*uoluntas*) with which he previously identified sin, consent is a mental act. As in the Commentary on Romans, Abelard is willing to talk of 'the mind' (*animus*) with which something is done;[29] he describes God as the 'inspector' of our 'intentions and consents' (*Sc.* 42: 4); and he calls a sin which does not affect others and remains entirely unknown to them 'a hidden fault of the mind' (*Sc.* 42: 20–1).

A number of scholars have observed that Abelard was far from original in using the term 'consent'.[30] It was employed, they explain, both by the Fathers and by Anselm of Laon, as well as in some writings roughly contemporary with Abelard. So indeed it was: but not consent *to perform an action*. When these writers use the term, they speak either of consent to desire, consent to temptation, consent to appetites, or sometimes, vaguely, just of consent.[31] In some cases, they do indeed make the moment of consent the

cf. 24: 20.) *Consensus* is used frequently in *Serm.* 1 (381D–382A), but in the special sense of consent to carnal relations within marriage (not a sin, though something which both Mary and Joseph wished to avoid): see below, pp. 317–18. In the *Rule* (276) Abelard uses *consensus* in the same sense as he would in *Sc.*, but immediately parallels it with *uoluntas*, which he would later distinguish from it ('Nec timendum est quidquid agatur in corpore si animus ad consensum non trahitur. Nec confidendum de munditia carnis si mens voluntate corrumpitur').

27 4: 27–30: 'Vitium itaque est quo ad peccandum proni efficimur, hoc est, inclinamur ad consentiendum ei quod non conuenit, ut illud scilicet faciamus aut dimittamus. Hunc uero consensum proprie peccatum nominamus.' Sin is also defined formally as *consensus* in the London *Reportatio* (f. 108v): 'Ad quod magister P. dicit quia peccatum non est nisi consensus eius operis cui non est consentiendum', and in the *Problemata* (no. 13; 696A): 'consensum, qui proprie peccatum dicitur', cf. also no. 24 (710D). The *Sententie Magistri Petri* use the language of *consensus* – fragment 24 (p. 183): 'Concupiscere alienam uxorem sive concumbere cum alterius uxore non est peccatum, sed solus in hoc consensus et contemptus Dei peccatum est' and cf. fragment 17 (p. 182).

28 14: 17–19: 'Tunc uero consentimus ei quod non licet, cum nos ab eius perpetratione nequaquam retrahimus parati penitus, si daretur facultas, illud perficere.'

29 *Sc.* 28: 10 and 40: 9–10; and cf. Luscombe's note (p. 28, n. 3).

30 Blomme, *Doctrine du péché*, esp. pp. 46–9; R. Peppermüller, *Abaelards Auslegung des Römerbriefes*, BGPMA 10 (Münster, 1972), pp. 143–4; Luscombe, *Peter Abelard's 'Ethics'*, p. 14, n. 1.

31 See e.g. (from the passages cited in the references given in the preceding note): Augustine, *Expositio quarundam propositionum ex ep. ad Romanos* (*MPL* 35, 2066): 'Non enim in ipso desiderio pravo, sed in nostra consensione peccamus' (consent to desire); *De continentia* ii, 3 (ed. J. Zycha (Prague/Vienna/Leipzig, 1900) (CSEL 41), p. 142: 27–143: 1: 'Si autem consensit, iam corde dixit, etiamsi ore non sonuit . . . (consent involving an internal

moment when a person first starts to commit sin. But they still see it as the moment when the sinner surrenders to his desires. It seems that, when Abelard was developing his ethical theory, he deliberately avoided using the term 'consent', perhaps because it was not, in general usage, associated with the idea of intended action which was at the centre of his thought. But then he decided that he could helpfully employ the term for his own purposes by shifting its use and talking of consent to an action. Perhaps his initial caution was justified. The term 'consent' does allow him to clarify his theory, but on at least one occasion in *Scito teipsum* it leads him into talking for a moment rather like a stages-theorist, even though he quickly rights himself.[32]

Now that Abelard has chosen a special, technical term to carry one of the meanings of *voluntas*, that in which it is what constitutes a sin, he vigorously objects to describing sin as *voluntas*. This, as Blomme has explained, is not therefore a radical shift in outlook but a development in terminology.[33] (There is a parallel here to the way in which, once he had decided to use for 'a word *qua* bearer of meaning' the new technical term *sermo*, Abelard argued strongly that universals are not *voces* but *sermones*.)[34]

Abelard is now able to re-state more clearly and fully the examples of reluctant action he had given in the Commentary on Romans. Those of us who would prefer (*uellemus*) that the woman with whom we sleep were not in fact married to another are contrasted with those adulterers who glory in the very fact of cheating another man. In the first case, Abelard says that the adulterers do not will (*uelle*) to commit adultery (16: 16–22). In the case of the man who murders in self-defence, Abelard (*Sc.* 6: 24 – 10: 27) denies that there was any bad *voluntas* on his part. Abelard has sharpened the example, by making the murdered man, not the murderer's

dialogue); *Contra Secundinum Manichaeum* (ed. J. Zycha (Prague/Vienna/Leipzig, 1892) (CSEL 25), pp. 926–7): 'anima ergo cum consentit mali, ipsa substantia est. consens uero eius non est substantia' (consent used vaguely: the context is ontological, not ethical); Gregory the Great, *Moralia in Iob* XXI, iii, 7 (CC 143A) p. 1068: 20–2: '... aliud esse quod animus de temptatione carnis patitur, aliud uero cum per consensum delectationibus obligatur' (consent to the temptation of the flesh, binding it to the pleasurable consideration of what is sinful); Anselm, *De conceptu uirginali* (II, p. 144): 'Quare non eos [*sc.* appetitus] sentire, sed eis consentire peccatum est' (consent to appetites); (probably Anselm of Laon) *Glossa marginalis* to II Corinthians (Lyons, 1590, vol. VI, col. 449 – quoted Blomme, *Doctrine du péché*, p. 47, n. 2): 'Tentatio autem cui non consentitur non est peccatum, sed materia exercende virtutis' (consent to temptation).

[32] 32: 23 – 34: 3; cf. *Reportatio*, f. 108v.

[33] *Doctrine du péché*, esp. pp. 190–7.

[34] See above, pp. 176–80.

enemy, but his lord. By killing his lord, the vassal would knowingly be putting himself in danger of death as punishment or revenge: how then, asks Abelard, can he have committed the murder 'voluntarily' (*uoluntarie*)? As before, Abelard accepts that the vassal had the will (*uoluntas*) to avoid death, but explains that this was not a bad will. Yet, he can now state clearly, the vassal sinned because he 'consented' to commit the murder. Abelard goes on to raise and answer a fresh objection. It might be said that the vassal did 'will to kill his lord, in order to escape death' (*Sc.* 8: 21–2: *uoluit interficere dominum suum propter hoc ut mortem euaderet*). Abelard answers that this does not make the bare statement 'he willed to kill his lord' true. He gives this parallel. If I say to someone, 'I will that you have my hat if you pay me five *solidi* for it', I am not thereby forced to accept that it is true that I will it to be yours. Abelard also raises other examples of reluctant actions, such as undergoing surgery or letting one's son be put in prison as a hostage for oneself, as well as the case of people who are overcome by 'the weakness of the flesh' and 'compelled to will that which they do not will to will' (*Sc.* 16: 23–4: *uelle coguntur, quod nequaquam uelle uellent*). In all these cases of reluctant action, Abelard insists that there is consent, and that they are therefore sins, but they are not 'voluntary' in the ordinary sense of the word.

Is it possible to reach a better understanding of exactly what Abelard understood by the distinction between *consensus* and *uoluntas* (which he had earlier tried to work out in terms of different meanings of *uoluntas*)? The meaning Abelard gave to *consensus* – that of a mental act preceding and prompting the performance of the outward sinful act – is in a sense clear, although one might well regard the notion of such mental acts, and their relation to the physical world, deeply puzzling. But what Abelard means by *uoluntas*, when he contrasts it with *consensus*, is more immediately puzzling.

For some of the time, he seems to have been thinking of *uoluntas* in terms of irrational drives, such as sexual drive. This is evident from his tendency to gloss this sense of *uoluntas* by *concupiscentia*, and by the way in which he describes a man struggling against sexual temptation, in which his mind 'is touched by the pleasure of the flesh' (*Sc.* 10: 31 – 12: 13). Yet this cannot be the sense he has in mind when he insists that the man who kills his lord or who commits adultery but would prefer the woman not to be married does not will (*uelle*) to commit murder or adultery. The information about what the two men do not will concerns the way they regard the action they perform. 'Not willing' here seems rather to be a mental attitude related to the mental act of consent, but distinct from it.

This suggests the following reconstruction of Abelard's understanding of *uoluntas/uelle*.[35] As a preliminary, it should be observed that although Abelard claimed to be giving a theory which covered both sins of commission and omission, he concentrated his attention on those sins which he could identify with a particular mental act of consenting to perform an action – especially those which involve the breaking of a prohibition. Abelard was fully aware that there are many different correct descriptions which can be given for any action, and that we consent to perform an action under only some of them. This was his point in insisting that acts can only be judged according to 'the root of intention'. When we sin, one of the descriptions under which we consent to the action is, Abelard believes, that it is a sin (of a particular sort).[36] But there are other descriptions, too, under which we consent to the sinful action: for instance, 'sleeping with a woman', 'killing a man'. The cases of sinning which interest Abelard are usually ones where the action is carried out reluctantly, because the agent would choose it under one of its descriptions, but not under another. Abelard uses the terms *uelle/uoluntas* to clarify this idea, by describing what choices to act an agent would make under just one given description. According to Abelard, someone wills to perform an act of ϕ-ing, if it is an act he would choose to perform were he choosing it under that description ('ϕ-ing') alone. This definition explains Abelard's use of *uelle/uoluntas* both in the simpler cases, where he is described as willing to perform the sinful action to which he does not consent, and in the more complex ones, where he is said not to will the sinful action to which he does consent. The man who resists the temptation, say, to eat a piece of delicious fruit which is not his (cf. *Sc.* 14: 4–13) would choose to perform that act under the description of 'eating a piece of delicious fruit' alone. Therefore, in Abelard's terms, he wills to eat the delicious fruit. But this is not the choice which actually faces him: he can only choose to perform the act under (at least) the two descriptions, 'eating a piece of delicious fruit' and 'committing the sin of theft'; and, under those two descriptions, he makes the choice not to perform it. The man pursued by his lord would not choose to perform an act under only the description 'killing my lord', nor would the adulterer choose to perform an act under only the description 'committing adultery'; and so neither of them can be said to will to perform those actions. In each case, however,

[35] Saarinen (*Weakness of the will*, pp. 51–60) has recently suggested a different (but not incompatible) reconstruction. He posits a three-place relation between the agent (x), the thing consented to (p) and the ultimate goal (q). Abelard wishes to argue, he says, that if x wills q, and if q implies p (because p is a means to q, or an unintended by-product of q, or because it is part of q), then x consents to p.

[36] What Abelard describes as 'venial sins' are an exception, however: see below, pp. 277–8.

they do choose to perform the actions under the multiple descriptions under which they in fact cannot but regard them: 'killing my lord', 'saving my life', 'committing the sin of murder'; 'sleeping with a married woman', 'sleeping with the woman I desire', 'committing the sin of adultery'. Abelard's central point is that in any case where one of the descriptions under which I act is 'committing the sin of . . .', it should outweigh in my choosing all the other descriptions under which I would choose to perform the action were I performing it under each of those descriptions alone.

By examining the different meanings of *uoluntas* and their relation to his idea of *consensus*, Abelard develops a view of human action which acts as a basis for his ethical theory. In order to construct the theory itself, however, he needs to explain what it is that makes one consent a sin, and another not. Abelard's answer to this question, the subject of the next chapter, involves three central concepts: contempt of God, conscience and law.

Chapter 12

Contempt, law and conscience

When writers say that Abelard proposed a 'morality of intention', they sometimes have in mind a meaning quite different from that which has just been discussed. They take 'intention' to refer, not just to the object of ethical judgement, but also to the basis of judgement. Moralities of intention are, on this interpretation, ones where the agent's own evaluation of his moral choice is preferred to any external criterion as the basis for moral judgement. Such moralities are – to use another description which has sometimes been applied to Abelard's ethics – subjective rather than objective. According to such a moral position, I do wrong if and only if I do what I believe I should not do or I do not do what I believe I should do. Abelard's theory of sin (which is formulated in the context of a supreme God) would be subjective, therefore, if (for instance) it held that someone sins if and only if, in performing an action or failing to perform one, he is not doing what he believes he should do for God.

Abelard's views about action and intention, as presented in the last chapter, do not themselves give any reason to think that Abelard's theory of sin was subjective in this sense. But Abelard adds to them another idea, which does seem to favour this interpretation. This is his view that sin (which is an act of willing or consent) consists in 'contempt' (*contemptus*) of God. Near the beginning of *Scito teipsum* (4: 31–2), Abelard asks rhetorically: 'For what is this consent but contempt of God and offence against him?' By saying that sinful consent 'is' contempt of God, Abelard indicates that showing contempt for God is not an extra mental act, beyond the mental act of sinful consent, but another, correct description of that mental act.[1] Every such consent is also an act of contempt (whether there are also other ways to show contempt for God Abelard does not say). The equation of

[1] Cf. Blomme, *Doctrine du péché*, pp. 154–8.

sin, consent and contempt for God reappears throughout the work.[2] Nor is the idea that sin is contempt of God a new development for Abelard: it is found, for instance, in his commentaries on the Hexaemeron and on Romans and in the *Sententie*, where sin, guilt (*culpa*) and contempt of God are all equated.[3]

The most obvious way to understand 'showing contempt for God' is as a relation between what an agent does and his *beliefs* about God's wishes. If I believe that what I should do for God is to write about Peter Abelard, but I write about Duns Scotus instead, then I am presumably showing contempt for God, whether or not I am right in my belief. So, if sin is contempt, must not Abelard's view of sinning be subjective?

Yet Abelard himself writes in ways which sometimes bear out this subjective view, and sometimes contradict it. The problem can be seen very clearly by juxtaposing two comments which occur within a few lines of each other in *Scito teipsum*. We sin, says Abelard (4: 27–8), 'when we incline to consenting to that which is not fitting (*ei quod non conuenit*)'; and then, equating sin with contempt of God, he adds (6: 3–6) that this takes place 'when we do not at all do on his account what we believe we should do on his account or when we do not on his account draw back from doing what we believe we should not do'.[4] In the first remark, sinful intent appears to be judged by an external measure (*quod non conuenit*); in the second, it appears to be based on the gap between what I believe I should do for God and what I in fact choose to do or not do.[5] Again, a little later in the same work, sin is described (14: 15–17) as consisting in consent to that which is not allowed

[2] A few examples (from *Sc.*): 16: 6–8: 'peccatum . . . hoc est, contemptum Dei siue consensum in eo quod credimus propter Deum dimittendum'; 32: 17–18: 'peccatum quod in consensu mali uel contemptu Dei statuimus . . .'; 90: 20–1: ' uno peccato, id est, uno Dei contemptu'.

[3] *Sententie* §269; Bu. 151: 50–3: 'Peccatum igitur nichil est aliud quam ipsa culpa . . . Est autem culpa nichil aliud quam contemptus creatoris'; cf. for instance, *Exp. Hex.* (767 D; Avranches, 135, f. 86r): 'Nemo itaque inobedientiae est arguendus . . . ubicumque offensa Dei cauetur, quae sola quemlibet reum constituit.'

[4] *Sc.* 4: 31 – 6: 6: 'Quid est enim iste consensus nisi Dei contemptus et offensa ipsius? Non enim Deus ex dampno sed ex contemptu offendi potest. Ipse quippe est summa illa potestas quae dampno aliquo non minuitur, sed contemptum sui ulciscitur. Peccatum itaque nostrum contemptus creatoris est, et peccare est creatorem contempnere, hoc est, id nequaquam facere propter ipsum quod credimus propter ipsum a nobis esse faciendum, vel non dimittere propter ipsum quod credimus esse dimittendum.'

[5] Abelard here talks of actions themselves rather than consent, not because he has changed his view but because he takes this point as already established and is concentrating on a different question. There is, however, a difficulty about Abelard's formulation which he does not explore: by including failure to act as well as positive action, he raises the question of what is consent *not* to do something.

(*quod non licet*) and, a few lines afterwards (16: 6–8, quoted below), as consent 'to what we believe we should draw back from on God's account'. Abelard seems, from these examples, sometimes to treat sin as if it were entirely a matter of the gap between the sinner's own belief about what he should do for God and the action to which he consents, but at other times as consent to an action which is objectively wrong.

Yet, despite appearances, Abelard is not confused. Abelard moves so nonchalantly between subjective and objective formulations about sin because he thought that a person always knows, in the circumstances where he might commit a sin, what he should or should not do for God. The only exceptions are children and the mentally deficient; and they, Abelard considers, are incapable of sinning.[6] For normal adults, then, about to give or withhold a sinful consent to action, there is no gap between what they should do for God and what they believe they should do for God.[7] Abelard was able to hold this position because of his view that, through natural or revealed laws, everyone knows God's general precepts, and because of his idea of 'conscience', which applies general laws to particular circumstances.[8]

LAW

Abelard, like most of his contemporaries, envisaged (on the basis of what he regarded as solid, historical evidence) just three, closely related types of general, God-given law: natural law, the Old Law and the New Law.[9] The 'Old Law' was the name for the law given to the Jews (and still followed by them) which is contained in the Old Testament; the 'New Law' was the law of Christ, revealed in the New Testament. It had been usual, from the early days of Christianity, to add to these two revealed laws a third law: natural law. Quite clearly, those who lived before Christianity was preached, and who were not Jews, were not without a law. St Paul spoke

[6] *Comm.Rom.* 164: 372–5; cf. 76: 8–9, and *Sc.* 56: 20–2: 'paruuli . . . et naturaliter stulti qui . . . ratione carentes nichil eis ad peccatum inputatur'; and cf. Blomme, *Doctrine du péché*, pp. 149–50.

[7] For a problem connected with the notion of withholding consent, see below, pp. 293–4.

[8] Abelard is at the opposite extreme from holding the voluntarist view of God attributed to him by De Siano ('God and man', esp. p. 648); cf. de Gandillac's pertinent criticism ('Intention et loi', p. 595).

[9] I have already discussed Abelard and the three types of law, rather more briefly than here, in 'Abelard's concept of natural law' in A. Zimmermann (ed.), *Miscellanea Mediaevalia* 21, 2: *Mensch und Natur im Mittelalter* (Berlin/New York, 1992), pp. 609–21. A rich and perceptive discussion of the area is given by M. de Gandillac in 'Intention et loi', esp. at pp. 596–604.

of a law written in the hearts of Gentiles, which enables them naturally to do the things which the written law commands.[10] The Apostle wished to make a negative point: the pagans had *not* followed this natural law and so deserved damnation. But the Fathers, who drew out the implications of Paul's words, also pointed to the positive value of natural law. For instance, commenting on the passage, Origen listed a set of commands (do not kill, steal, commit adultery or bear false witness; honour your father and mother) which could be known naturally.[11] Jerome spoke of a 'natural law which tells us in our hearts that good things are to be done and bad things avoided', whilst Ambrose remarked that 'if men had been able to preserve the natural law which God the creator instilled in the breasts of all men', the written law would have been unnecessary.[12]

Early twelfth-century scholars fitted these ideas about natural law into a scheme of salvation history.[13] They needed to explain how it was that, from the biblical account, many of the patriarchs of the early chapters of Genesis lived apparently excellent lives, although there was not yet a written law. The idea of natural law, innately in all men, solved their problem. The period of natural law lasted from the Fall until God gave the Jews a written law; after the period of the Old Law, which then began, there followed the period of the New Law.[14] But the scheme was not rigidly chronological

[10] Romans 2: 14–15: 'Cum enim Gentes, quae legem non habent, naturaliter ea, quae legis sunt, faciunt, eiusmodi legem non habentes, ipsi sibi sunt lex: qui ostendunt opus legis scriptum in cordibus suis, testimonium reddente illis conscientia ipsorum.'

[11] *In epistolam B. Pauli ad Romanos*, in J.-P. Migne, *Patrologia Graeca* 14, 890B.

[12] Jerome, *Commentarium in epistolam ad Galatas* I, 3, *Patrologia Latina* 26, 348–9; Ambrose, Epistola 73, *MPL* 16, 1251 BC; cf. *De paradiso* 8, in C. Schenkl (ed.), *Sancti Ambrosii opera* I, (Prague/Vienna/Leipzig, 1896) (CSEL 32, 1), 296: 18.

[13] General accounts of natural law in the early twelfth century include: O. Lottin, 'Le droit naturel chez Saint Thomas et ses prédécesseurs', Part I, *Ephemerides theologicae lovanienses* 1 (1924) 369–88 (a second edition of this article and the two succeeding parts was published under the same title in book-form (Bruges, 1931)); F. Flückiger, *Geschichte des Naturrechts* (Zollikon/Zurich, 1954), pp. 415–22; O. Lottin, *Psychologie et morale aux XIIe et XIIIe siècles* II, 1 (Louvain/Gembloux, 1949), pp. 71–3.

[14] The scheme is very clearly put in *Principium et causa omnium* (*c.* 1137) (pp. 78–9): 'Modus vero fuit lex; prius naturalis; postea vero, ea sopita, lex per Moysen scripta; tempore autem gratie spiritus scribens in corde, id est, fides operans ex dilectione'; and it underlies Anselm of Laon's comments (*Lottin* §§49 and 51) and William's (*Lottin* §261). See also among writings roughly contemporary with Abelard: *Lottin* §112, *Sententie diuine pagine* (ed. J. Bliemetzrieder, *Anselms von Laon systematische Sentenzen*, Münster, 1919) p. 37) – cf. *Dubitatur a quibusdam*, p. 337. Some writers suggest that the period of the Old Law began, not with Moses, but Abraham, who received the commandment to circumcise male children: cf. Anselm of Laon (*Lottin* §49): 'circumcisionem et ceteras obseruantias legales'; William of Champeaux (*Lottin* §261, p. 212: 47ff.).

because, as Anselm of Laon and many others observed, unlike the New Law, the Old Law was not universal. Whilst it contained some 'natural precepts', shared by natural law and the New Law, other parts of the Old Law consisted of promises, commands which applied only to the Jews and sacraments which had only a figural meaning and would be replaced by the real sacraments of the New Law.[15] In the period before the coming of Christ, therefore, men could live well, by following natural law, even after the Old Law had been revealed – a favourite example was Job.[16] The special precepts of the New Law, such as that requiring children to be baptized, were different: once they had been revealed, they applied to everyone.

Abelard used this scheme of the three laws, and he went along with Anselm and William in stressing that the precepts of the Old Law, such as circumcision, were not universal.[17] In the *Problemata* (no. 15) Abelard sets out very clearly the division between the figural precepts of the Old Law, which applied only to that particular period, and its moral precepts, such as loving God and one's neighbour, not killing, committing adultery or lying. These, he says, were always supposed to be followed by everyone naturally, even before the written law was given.[18] The main way in which Abelard's idea of the three laws differed from that of his contemporaries is that he shifted the emphasis in discussing natural law away from Adam's immediate progeny to the philosophers of ancient Greece and Rome. Although Job does provide one example of how a man could live well by natural law, he shares the position with an array of figures from classical antiquity.[19] Indeed Abelard's reconstruction of the lives and cities of the Greek philosophers provided him, in his thought of the mid-1120s, with a

[15] *Lottin* §§49, 51; William of Champeaux (*Lottin*, §261, p. 212: 53–6); cf. *Lottin* §§112 and 113; and *Sententie diuine pagine* (Bliemetzrieder, *Anselms Sentenzen*, p. 38).

[16] William of Champeaux (*Lottin* §261, p. 212: 53–4); cf. *Enarrationes in Matthaeum* (*c.* 1140–50), *MPL* 162, 1461D and Gregory the Great, *Moralia in Iob*, pp. 10–11.

[17] On circumcision, see *TChr* 124: 327–30, *Serm.* 3, *Coll.* 52: 296–300; 54: 364 – 55: 394; 58: 474 – 59: 484; 66: 692 – 67: 715; 76: 958 – 77: 988 and *Comm.Rom.* 87: 375 – 90: 458; 127: 165 – 143: 674.

[18] 703AB; Paris, BN, lat. 14511, f. 31ra: 'Moralia quidem precepta sunt agende uite . . . Et moralia quidem que naturaliter ab omnibus semper complenda furerunt, etiam antequam lex scripta daretur. Mores hominum ita necessario componunt ut nisi compleatur quod in eis precipitur, nemo unquam saluari meruerit: qualia sunt diligere Deum et proximum, non occidere, non moecari, non mentiri, et similia, sine impletione quorum nemo unquam iustificari potest.' On the question of salvation by natural law, see below, pp. 327–30.

[19] On Job, see e.g. *TChr* 142: 353–5; on Abelard's treatment of classical philosophers and other related figures (such as Solomon and John the Baptist), see J. Jolivet, 'Doctrines'.

moral ideal.[20] What is important, however, for Abelard's theory of the ethical act is not the degree of excellence he attributes to the followers of natural law, but the way in which Abelard makes clear the universality of that law. Where his contemporaries were usually content to look merely at the world of biblical history, Abelard extends the scope of his investigation to the other area of ancient history familiar to scholars in his period. No longer is it merely an assertion (albeit one based on scriptural and patristic authority) that there is natural law written in the hearts of men: historical investigation confirms the idea. And, although Abelard provides no evidence for this further step, he suggests, through the fictional figure of the Philosopher of the *Collationes*, that natural law is followed even in his own day, by those who accept neither the Old nor the New Testament.

Moreover, for Abelard, natural law is not just an inner impulsion to act rightly or to recognize certain types of behaviour as wrong. Although unwritten, it has the same structure as the Old and New Laws. Certain explicit commands and prohibitions are recognized and they are acknowledged as coming from God. Both the philosophers of antiquity and the Philosopher of the *Collationes* are considered to have an accurate knowledge of God and are represented as thinking of their efforts to live well and avoid sin as stemming from love for God and hope for eternal reward.[21]

According to Abelard, then, every moral agent (all normal adults) in all periods of history has known natural law. 'Know' here has the sense of habitual knowledge: as will become clear, Abelard thought that we might not bring a precept to mind, even when contemplating a course of action which would infringe it.[22] We all in this sense know a set of general divine precepts, such as: Do not murder! Do not steal! Do not commit adultery! But, although natural law is the most important of the three laws for Abelard's ethical theory, because it provides all moral agents in all periods with habitual knowledge of divine precepts, the Old Law and the New Law also have their roles, because they provide further knowledge of divine precepts for some agents in some periods. This further knowledge is of two quite different kinds, one of which is unproblematic. To a considerable extent, as has been explained, in the view of Abelard and his contemporaries, the Old Law and the New Law overlap with each other and with natural law. The basic moral prohibitions of murder, stealing and so on which are known as part of natural law are also revealed in the Bible. Jews or Christi-

[20] See below, pp. 305–7.

[21] See below, p. 306.

[22] See below, p. 277.

ans therefore know both naturally and from the law they accept as revealed that, for instance, they will be breaking a divine prohibition if they murder someone. But the Old Law and the New Law also contain precepts which are not part of natural law: for example, the Old Law's command that male children be circumcised and its dietary laws, prohibiting the eating of certain foods, or the New Law's command that everyone be baptized. These extra precepts present certain special problems for Abelard: those arising from the Old Law are due to its particularity of application, those arising from the New Law to its universality.

Abelard and his contemporaries, as mentioned above, were all certain that, even before the coming of Christ, the extra precepts of the Old Law did not apply universally, but only to the Jews. An Old Testament Jew would be wrong if he believed that anyone who eats pork sins, since God had not issued a general prohibition against eating pork – the Philistines were free to enjoy it to their hearts' content.[23] But the Jew would be right to believe that *he* would sin if he ate pork. Abelard also makes clear that the same would be true even if the Jew were living in Abelard's own time. He says, speaking generally, in the *Rule* (268): 'When we eat those foods which ... we exclude and separate as being unclean according to the law, then we judge and condemn ourselves through the law which we approve and accept.' But there is a difficulty. The Old Testament Jew was, according to Abelard's view, correct in his belief that God forbade him to eat pork: the dietary laws really did represent God's precepts for Old Testament Jews. But Abelard would certainly have considered that the twelfth-century Jew was wrong in his belief that he should follow the dietary laws. Taken in their literal sense these laws, Abelard thought along with other Christians of his time, no longer represented God's precepts for anyone, Jew or Christian. Abelard shows explicitly that this was how he thought when, in the commentary on Romans (306: 313–14), he describes someone as sinning in such a situation (because he believes he is doing what God forbids him), even though he is eating food which it is lawful to eat.

Does the gap which opens here between knowledge and belief about the law threaten the whole of Abelard's theory? Not as Abelard himself saw matters. The only example he considers of a law wrongly taken by its adherents to be divine is the Old Law still followed by Jews after it has been replaced by the New Law. Adherents of this law – wrongly in his view – regard certain actions as commanded or forbidden them by God.

[23] On the question of forbidden foods, see *Comm.Rom.* 306: 311–25; *Rule* 268–9; *Problemata* 710D–711A.

The Jews of his day can, therefore, show contempt for God, and so sin, by acting in ways which, if their beliefs were correct, they would recognize as licit for them. Why need Abelard worry that Jews have opportunities to sin which Christians lack? But if Abelard had thought about the more general application of the principle he appears to admit, he could hardly have remained complacent. Abelard accepts that a Jew sins by contravening what he believes, wrongly, is a revealed divine precept which applies to him. Applying the principle generally: I sin if I contravene what I believe, wrongly, is a revealed precept which applies to me. But I might believe wrongly that any precept is a revealed precept which applies to me, including ones which contradict precepts of natural law (for instance, supposedly revealed precepts commanding human sacrifice). I may even believe that my revealed precept includes the command to follow it, not natural law. Abelard does indeed recognize that there can be cases where someone is given a direct divine command to perform some particular action which contravenes natural law: he presents Samson's decision to pull the temple down on himself and the Philistines in this way.[24] Here, however, Samson's belief about a revealed precept is presumed to be correct. Abelard does not see the difficulty which wrongly believed revealed precepts (whether general or particular) present for his theory.

The problem raised by the New Law for Abelard's theory is quite different. Abelard's Philosopher, in the *Collationes*, treats the special precepts of the New Law – those not in natural law – as instances of 'positive law', like the law of a certain city or people.[25] Abelard himself could not treat them in this way. Along with the whole tradition of Christian theology he followed, he accepted that the New Law is universal in application. For instance, it requires *everyone* to be baptized. Would someone, then, living remote from Christian lands who had not heard of the New Law be guilty of sinning by not having himself baptized? But he cannot be showing contempt for God by not following a precept of which he is ignorant. Abelard does not deal with this problem directly. In discussing the salvation of pagans, however, he tends to treat their failures to perform what is enjoined by the New Law not as sins, but merely as omissions which must be made good if they are to be saved.[26]

[24] *TChr* 166: 1123 – 167: 1156. Here Abelard follows Augustine's view in *De ciuitate Dei*, which he quotes explicitly.

[25] See below, pp. 307–10 on the distinction between the Philosopher's views and Abelard's.

[26] See below, pp. 327–30.

CONSCIENCE

Besides 'consent' (or, earlier, *uoluntas*) and 'contempt', there is another term which Abelard uses frequently when he is distinguishing what is and what is not a sin: *conscientia*. The links between sin and conscience are very close. In *Scito teipsum* Abelard insists that sin, properly speaking, must involve going against one's conscience;[27] whilst in the *Rule* (267) he says that 'in everything which we do against our conscience and against that which we believe, we sin' (although, as it turns out, there are exceptions to this principle).

Abelard never pauses to explain exactly what he means by conscience, and it is very easy for modern readers to mistake him here. 'Conscience' is used nowadays to refer to an individual's own moral sense. We accept that the moral sense of one person may differ from that of another – indeed, this is often the occasion of an appeal to conscience. If I say that 'I did it' or 'I refused to do it' because my conscience dictated, I am appealing to my intuitive grasp of what is right and wrong. I cannot be asked to justify myself, since my appeal to conscience is itself my justification. (This is not to deny that someone who does not accept such ethical intuitionism might be dissatisfied with my reply.)

Abelard treats conscience very differently. For him, conscience refers primarily to a particular type of mental operation, which can be associated with purely intellectual judgements as well as moral ones. Take, for instance, the two occasions when the Philosopher of the *Collationes* uses the term (44: 98; 61: 546–7). In each case, he says, of an argument he has put, that the conscience of any man of judgement (*discreti hominis*) could not but accept it: one time he is referring to the view that people tend to adopt the religion into which they are born; the other, to the idea that the Old Law brought sin. The Philosopher's point, in each case, is that the conclusion he urges is absolutely obvious to anyone who considers the matter: to deny it would be deliberately to turn a blind eye. The same sense emerges in a passage from the *Theologia Christiana* (353: 239–42) repeated verbatim in the *Theologia Scholarium* (506: 223–6): there is no one, says Abelard, for whom 'the reason of his own conscience' (*ratio propriae conscientiae*) will not suggest how fitting it is that there should be only one God. Here too, acting according to conscience is a matter of *intellectual* honesty, of not pretending that something obviously true is false; and so it is when Abelard

[27] 56: 6–8: 'ubi contra conscientiam nostram non presumimus, frustra nos apud Deum de culpa reos statui formidamus'; cf. Blomme, *Doctrine du péché*, p. 147.

introduces the term in discussing the sin against the Holy Spirit.[28] To blaspheme against the Holy Spirit is for someone to say that the benefits which derive from God's *manifest* goodness – and which he is certain derive from it – are the work of the devil: that is, knowingly to slander God's work. Such a claim, Abelard explains, is made against conscience. The blasphemer denies the obvious truth, of which he is fully aware, that the benefits are indeed God's.

In the light of this underlying meaning of 'conscience', it is possible to make sense of a passage in the Commentary on Romans which would otherwise be very puzzling.[29] Suppose I am a judge who knows that a certain man is innocent, but cannot disprove the testimony against him given by false witnesses. I am compelled 'against conscience' to punish the innocent man. But, Abelard makes clear, I am not acting wrongly by doing so: I am justly punishing him although he is not justly punished. Were I to spare him, I would harm many (presumably by undermining the authority of the law). How, then, am I acting 'against conscience' when I am doing what is right? Abelard's assertion, which makes little sense according to a modern or a post-medieval idea of conscience, is entirely consistent with his own idea of it. There is an evident incongruity between the man's innocence, which I know, and the verdict of guilty which I pass. I am deliberately turning a blind eye to the truth, and so going against my conscience, although in this exceptional instance I am acting rightly in doing so.

Abelard, then, thought of conscience most generally as our power to recognize obvious truths. He does not say whether these include demonstrative arguments – though since he never uses the idea of conscience in this connection it may be that he considered that their truth, once understood, is simply indubitable and conscience is unnecessary for grasping it. They do certainly include the results of what Abelard takes to be obvious inductions. Usually, however, he uses the term in the context of sinning, which he says involves 'going against our conscience'. This usage fits easily into the general pattern. Where sinning is concerned, the obvious truth recognized by con-

[28] This is treated in much the same way in *Comm.Rom.* 108: 393–408; *Problemata* (no. 13; 695AB) and in *Sc.* (96: 6–17). Blomme (*Doctrine du péché*, p. 145) cites the passage from *Sc.* as an instance where acting against conscience is 'simplement aller à l'encontre des connaissances que l'on a ou de la persuasion intime qui en découle'. But according to Blomme this is an exception to Abelard's usual moral sense of conscience, not – as argued here – an illustration of the underlying sense the term had for him.

[29] 172: 622–30. Abelard discusses the same situation at *Sc.* 38: 22–40: 3, though he does not use the term *conscientia* here.

science is that a certain course of action falls under a general prohibition. Since Abelard very often talks of consenting to *act* against conscience, he seems to think of it as issuing, as it were, a command following such a recognition. So, granted that there is, for instance, a general prohibition against killing people, and one of the choices of actions facing me is to kill someone, my conscience recognizes the obvious truth that this choice would fall under the general prohibition and consequently it issues the command: 'Do not kill this person!' If I do choose to kill him, then I act against conscience.[30]

The idea of conscience helps, therefore, to explain why Abelard thinks that agents not only know God's general precepts, but also how they apply to particular circumstances: so that if they believe that for God they should not consent to something, this belief will in fact be true. Conscience will recognize the obvious truth that the action they are contemplating falls under the general prohibition they grasp through natural or revealed law. But what if the proposed action does not fall *clearly* under a prohibition, but uncertainly so? Abelard seems not to have considered this possibility. Or what if the proposed action, under one description, falls under a divine prohibition, and under another description it falls under a divine command? The story of Jephtha, who must sacrifice his daughter if he is to keep an oath made to God, is a case in point; but here Abelard just blames Jephtha for making the original promise.[31] Or there is the example of the judge, mentioned above, who must condemn a man he knows to be innocent. Here Abelard merely assumes (perhaps under the influence of his general view about earthly justice) that the judge's decision is right and not sinful.[32] It is certainly a weakness of Abelard's ethics that, despite his awareness in more practical discussions of moral unclarity and conflict, in his theoretical

[30] Abelard has been almost entirely neglected in discussions and analyses of the idea of conscience in medieval thought, which is usually considered to have begun with Peter the Lombard (*c*. 1155) but only seriously to have been developed from the 1230s onwards (see O. Lottin, *Psychologie et morale aux XIIe et XIIIe siècles* II (Gembloux, 1948) and T. Potts, *Conscience in medieval philosophy* (Cambridge, 1980) and 'Conscience' in A. Kenny, N. Kretzmann, J. Pinborg (eds.), *The Cambridge history of later medieval philosophy* (Cambridge, 1982), pp. 687–704). In fact, by treating conscience as the ability to apply general rules to particular situations, Abelard anticipated the later medieval discussion, although the later thinkers regarded the workings of conscience as a process of reasoning which could err, and they contrasted it with the infallibility of our grasp of the fundamental principles of natural law (they called this grasp *synderesis*).

[31] See below, pp. 319–20.

[32] For Abelard's discussion of earthly justice, see below, pp. 313–14.

account he thinks of sinning almost exclusively as the breaking of clear prohibitions which are either exceptionless or have only clear exceptions.

Despite these limitations, by linking together his ideas of law, conscience and contempt, Abelard has arrived at a clear theory about what makes a given volition or consent to act a sin. The definition of sin in the *Sententie* puts it succinctly. Sin is guilt, and 'guilt is nothing other than contempt of the creator, which is when either we will, against conscience, what we know displeases him and is prohibited (*prohibitum*) by him, or when we do not will what we know pleases him and is ordered (*preceptum*) by him'.[33] Here the various elements of Abelard's analysis are brought together. There are divine laws which prohibit certain sorts of actions and command certain sorts of actions. When we choose to act in a particular way which contravenes these general laws, our conscience recognizes this incongruity and we are said to act against conscience. Since the laws are God's laws, we know that it pleases him when we follow them and displeases him when we break them. Hence Abelard's tendency to equate contempt of God with consenting to act against conscience. Each is a different way of looking at the breaking of what one accepts as God's law. It is against conscience, because it is conscience which recognizes the clear disparity between the divine precept or prohibition and the intended action which infringes it. It is contempt of God, because it involves knowingly doing what displeases him.[34]

SIN AND IGNORANCE

Matters are not always so simple. Despite the narrowness which has been mentioned, Abelard realized this. As he puts it in *Scito teipsum* (26: 6–8): 'It is not a sin to kill a man or to sleep with someone else's wife. These things can sometimes be done without sin.' These apparent paradoxes can arise in the simple case where an action is performed under physical com-

[33] §269; Bu. 151: 52–6 (= *Sent.Par.* 55: 29 – 56: 4): 'Est autem culpa nichil aliud quam contemptus creatoris, quod est dum uel uolumus contra conscientiam quod ei displicere scimus et ab eo esse prohibitum, uel nolumus quod ei scimus placere et ab eo esse preceptum.'

[34] Abelard does recognize exceptional instances where someone might knowingly disobey a divine command without contempt for God. His example (*Sc.* 28: 26 – 30: 13) is the gospel story of Christ forbidding those who saw his miracles of healing to reveal them. They disobeyed this injunction and told of Christ's miracles in order to honour him, but they should not be judged guilty of sin. The circumstances of this example are very special – it is a personal and particular command (given by Christ from humility) which is broken for a reason which unmistakeably has to do with honouring God. It is difficult to see how these conditions could be reproduced outside the time of Christ's life on earth.

pulsion (as in the case of a woman who engages in sexual intercourse outside marriage when she is raped),[35] or in the far more difficult cases where some form of ignorance excuses the agent.

There are two obvious forms of such ignorance – moral ignorance or factual ignorance. In the case of moral ignorance, the agent has full knowledge of the nature of his action to which he consents, but less than full knowledge of the fact that it is forbidden by God. In the case of factual ignorance, the agent has less than full knowledge of the nature of the act to which he consents. Abelard does not leave much room for moral ignorance. His view of law and conscience, along with his tendency to overlook cases where laws conflict or cannot be clearly applied, led him to regard normal adults as never being fully ignorant that the sort of act they are about to perform is forbidden by God, if this is the case. None the less, Abelard does envisage cases of partial moral ignorance, where the agent temporarily fails to use knowledge he habitually possesses.

Abelard points out that there are many things which we know (habitually) even when we do not actually remember them or when we are not exercising our mind at all, as in sleep.[36] Sometimes, Abelard believes, we may consent to a sinful act without having in mind the fact that it 'displeases God'. Such actions he describes as venial sins, by contrast with mortal ones.[37] The examples Abelard gives are boasting and excessive eating or drinking. These are all sins which would usually be regarded as relatively slight. It is not their slightness, however, but the fact that they are committed without its being in mind that they displease God which makes them merely venial.[38] Abelard makes this clear in the *Sententie* when he says that even apparently slight sins are mortal if committed deliberately.[39] Probably

[35] Cf. *Sc.* 24: 11–12: 'Veluti si qua uim passa cum uiro alterius concubuerit' – which is an instance of something done *per uim*.

[36] *Sc.* 70: 1–2: 'Multa quippe scimus etiam dormientes uel quando eorum non recordamur.'

[37] *Sc.* 68: 31–70: 1: 'Venialia quidem uel leuia peccata sunt, quando in eo consentimus cui non consentiendum esse scimus, sed tunc tamen non occurrit memoriae illud quod scimus': cf. *Sc.* 70: 7–20; *Sententie* §271; Bu. 151: 61–73 = *Sent.Par.* 56: 9–20.

[38] Blomme (*Doctrine du péché*, pp. 123–8) argues that Abelard was never completely clear about this distinction.

[39] §271; Bu. 151: 69–73: 'Quantcumque igitur, ut ait Augustinus, in se leue sit peccatum, dum placet et ex industria perpetratur, mortale est; quantumcumque autem sit graue, dum displiceat et ex animi deliberatione non fiat, ueniale est' (= *Sent.Par.* 56: 17–20). Blomme (*Doctrine du péché*, p. 234, n. 1) quotes this passage, but considers that it (like the rest of the *Sententie*) is not the work of Abelard. From the *Reportatio* (f. 106r) it seems that the position is also confirmed by Abelard's oral teaching at the time of *Sc.* The passage as it stands reads: 'Notandum est quod nemo sine criminali (!) peccato damnari potest. Criminale est, si aliquis nimis rideat uel bibat ita etiam quod ei in mentem et in memoriam ueniat

Abelard chose the examples he did because he thought it more plausible that someone should be unaware that his act was displeasing to God when, in the heat of conversation or the enjoyment of a feast, he engages in boasting or indulgence, than if he commits murder or adultery.

Still, Abelard's theory of venial sins does leave two questions unanswered. First, what exactly is it that the agent temporarily fails to bring to mind when he does not realize that his intended act is 'displeasing to God'? Abelard does not present venial sins as a failure of conscience (which, indeed, he sees as working retrospectively in such cases),[40] so it seems that it is the general law forbidding such acts which he envisages as being temporarily out of mind. The phrasing of the *Sententie*, however suggests a rather more plausible idea: that the act itself is not deliberated on – it is performed mindlessly, without consideration about whether it pleases God or not.[41] But, if so, many questions – unexplored by Abelard – arise about our responsibility for particular acts which are neither compelled nor automatic, but nor are the direct result of any conscious moral choice. (For example, I colour my account of an incident to put myself in a better light than a rival; or I arrange my timetable without thinking about how it will affect my colleagues.)[42] Second, it is hard to see why, according to Abelard's view of sin, such choices to act are sins at all. Sin, he argues, is contempt of God, when we choose to act in a way we know displeases him. In the case of venial sins as he defines them, we do not make this sort of choice. Presumably Abelard wanted to include such acts as sins because there seems to be an obvious blameworthiness about the temporary ignorance in which they are performed. But his theory offers no way of explaining this blameworthiness itself.

Abelard places greater emphasis on sins excused by factual ignorance.

creatoris sui contemtus de illo opere. [Criminale est] Set si uel necessitate aliqua uel obliuione uel casu aliquo hoc faciat, ueniale est.' The reason why Abelard here is reported as saying *criminale* rather than *mortale* is probably that the question being answered is whether it is better to abstain from venial sins than from criminal ones. Whether it was Abelard himself or his student who was confused is not clear, but the distinction he is making must be between venial and mortal sin, since mortal sin (not criminal sin) is the prerequisite for being damned.

40 *Sent.* §271; Bu. 151: 64–7: 'Nec tamen potest dici quod contra conscientiam non sit. Etsi enim tunc a memoria seiunctum sit, tamen dum ad memoriam reducimus ex conscientia improbamus' (= *Sent. Par.* 56: 12–14).

41 See passage quoted in n. 39, especially: *ex animi deliberatione non fiat*.

42 Such an unthinking sin of omission can be distinguished from ordinary sins of omission (e.g. I am fully aware that I should visit my sick relative quickly, but a fortnight passes and I still have not done so), although these too present difficulties for Abelard's theory and are generally ignored by him: see above, p. 266.

Unlike venial sins, these he considers not to be really sins at all; no blame attaches to their perpetrators. The examples Abelard gives are a huntsman's accidental killing of someone with his arrow,[43] or a man sleeping with another woman believing her to be his wife (*Sc.* 24: 11–13) or marrying a woman who, unbeknown to anyone, is his own sister (*Sc.* 26: 14–20). In all these, it seems fair to take it that the ignorance which excuses the agent is taken by Abelard to have been impossible for the agent to avoid or, in his word, 'invincible'.[44] This is brought out especially clearly by Abelard's most notorious example of a sin committed in, and excused by, ignorance: the crucifixion of Jesus.[45] To their executioners, Christ and the early Christian martyrs were guilty of seducing the souls of the people, a crime which deserved the death penalty.[46] Only if they had known that Christ was really the Son of God would they have realized that he and his followers were not leading men away from true religion but towards it. Yet this, according to Abelard, they could not have known except through a divine revelation which was not granted them.[47] Had they *spared* Christ, his executioners would have acted against their conscience – their clear perception that Jesus was breaking God's law and deserved punishment – and so have been sinning.

Abelard has been accused by modern commentators of failing properly to distinguish between culpable and excusable ignorance.[48] For Abelard, they complain, factual ignorance excuses the agent from sin, even if the

[43] *Sc.* 66: 19–21; cf. *Comm.Rom.* 206: 639–42 (here the accident is caused by a stone).

[44] Abelard uses the term *ignorantia inuincibilis* at *Sc.* 66: 18–21 to apply to the case of the hunter who accidentally kills a man with an arrow, at *Problemata* (no. 13) 695A and 696A to apply to those who do not know Christ is God because this has not been revealed to them and at *TSch* 547: 1555–6 to apply to a case where a laudable effort to help the poor is in fact frustrated by circumstances and so is wasted. Blomme (*Doctrine du péché*, pp. 153–4) considers some of these examples unconvincing as illustrations of an ignorance which could not be prevented. So, all allowances made for the 'unrefined' behaviour and deficient record-keeping of the time, he finds the idea that one might marry one's own sister in ignorance sophistical. But few men, however refined the times, can be absolutely sure that the girl they are marrying is not their own father's illegitimate child, the product of a clandestine affair.

[45] See *Comm.Rom.* 306: 326–31; *Sc.* 58: 34 – 60: 12, 62: 5–10, 66: 31–4; cf. Blomme, *Doctrine du péché*, pp. 145–52. One of the heresies of which Abelard was accused at Sens was precisely that 'they did not sin who crucified Christ through ignorance'; and Abelard was made to recant this position in *Conf. Fid. 'Uniuersis'*, 136 (§IX). On the background to Abelard's position, and its influence, see Luscombe, *Peter Abelard's 'Ethics'*, p. 62, n. 1.

[46] Cf. *Comm.Rom.* 306: 329–31: 'Si enim credebant eos seductores animarum et ideo dignos morte, quomodo contra conscientiam suam eis parcere debebant?'

[47] This is brought out most clearly at *Problemata* (no. 13) 694D–695A.

[48] Blomme, *Doctrine du péché*, pp. 152–4; Luscombe, *Peter Abelard's 'Ethics'*, p. 62, n. 1.

ignorance might have been prevented by him. They are right to say that this is the case, so far as the particular act in question is concerned. Indeed, given that for Abelard sin properly speaking is contempt of God through knowingly breaking his law, he could not possibly suggest otherwise. If, however foolish it might be, my ignorance about the nature of the act I am committing leads me to believe that it is not an illicit act, I cannot, in performing that very act, be showing contempt for God. Yet Abelard's point of view does leave a place for what we would call culpable ignorance: not at the moment of performing the sin of ignorance, but at the moment when we perform the action, or make the omission, which will put us in the position of committing the sin of ignorance. Following this line of thought, we might say that if, in a drunken stupor, I slept with another man's wife under the impression that she was my own, I would not be guilty of adultery, but I would be guilty of drunkenness. Abelard does not himself develop his theory in this way, but it would be a natural extension of it; and in the *Carmen ad Astralabium* he moves in this direction by suggesting that there are cases where a person is guilty through putting himself into a position where he sins in ignorance.[49]

There are, however, many instances where a sinful act is performed out of ignorance which, although preventable, is the result of intellectual or practical deficiency rather than any moral failing. Take the case which Abelard uses in one of his best-known moral illustrations.[50] A poor woman takes her infant into her own bed, because she lacks the blankets to keep him warm in a cradle. She tries to stay awake but, eventually, falls asleep, and in her sleep she accidentally smothers him. Abelard insists that there is no sin here: the woman is entirely innocent. Yet he argues that it is right for her to be severely punished, 'so that in future she and other women should be made more careful in managing such things'. Here, then, is an instance of an act (killing a child) which, if performed knowingly, could hardly be without sin. Given that it is performed in ignorance – the mother is asleep – there is no sin connected with the act itself. Nor is there any prior *sin* which brought about the fatal circumstances: in bringing the infant to her bed, the woman acts from pity towards the child (*miseratione itaque infantuli commota*) whom 'she embraces with the greatest love'. Even her falling asleep is not her choice, but – as Abelard stresses by his phrasing

[49] 127: 370–1: 'non est contemptor qui nescit quid sit agendum/si non hoc culpa nesciat ipse sua'. Blomme (*Doctrine du péché*, p. 152) mentions these lines, but dismisses them as an isolated instance, and perhaps not the result of Abelard's own, spontaneous thought.

[50] *Sc.* 38: 13–22; *Reportatio*, f. 107r: for the text, see above, p. 68, n. 52.

(*tandem infirmitate eius ui naturae superata*) a physical necessity. Yet Abelard also makes it clear, from his comment about the purpose of the punishment, that the child's death might have been prevented, had the mother acted with more practical good sense, resisting the urge to keep him warm in so dangerous a way. Abelard's utilitarian theory of punishment allows him to mark out, and penalize, such prior practical and intellectual failings, without confusing either them, or the unfortunate actions in ignorance which ensue from them, with sin.[51]

To summarize Abelard's intricate theory of sin and ignorance. Let A be an agent, L be a law accepted by A as being instituted by God and applying to him, *s* an act of a sort prohibited by L, *m* an act of a sort not prohibited by L, *c* any one or group of the many acts by which A puts himself into the position where he performs *s*. Abelard would then envisage these cases:

(1) A chooses to do *s* whilst having it in mind that *s* is forbidden by L (mortal sin; blame).
(2) A performs *s*, but was not intending to perform *s* but *m* ; nor is *c* prohibited by L ('sin of ignorance' – i.e. not really sin; no blame).
(3) A performs *s*, but was not intending to perform *s* but *m*; and *c* is prohibited by L, and A had it in mind that *c* is prohibited by L (blame, as deserved for *c*).
(4) A performs *s*, but was not intending to perform *s* but *m*; and *c*, although not prohibited by L, results from practical or intellectual failings (no blame, but A should be punished).
(5) A chooses to do *s* but does not have in mind that *s* is forbidden by L, although he does habitually know that L forbids *s* ('venial sin' – Interpretation (i): reduced blame).
(6) A performs *s* voluntarily but without thinking about it, and he habitually know that L forbids *s* ('venial sin' – Interpretation (ii): reduced blame).

This is a sophisticated theory. Its greatest weakness has already been suggested – the unsuitability of the traditional idea of venial sin for the very different use Abelard makes of it, and the vagueness with which (6), especially, is developed. By so firmly identifying sin with a mental act in which we choose to go against what we believe divine law commands us to do or not do and so to scorn God, Abelard makes it impossible for himself to give any satisfactory place in his account to actions which we do not think about but for which it is reasonable to think we are fully responsible.

[51] On this theory of punishment, see below, pp. 313–14.

Chapter 13

Virtue, love and merit

Abelard's treatment of acting well is less homogeneous than his theory of sin. It involves three distinct facets: a theory of the virtues, a theory of love and an account of merit. The virtues and love are both dispositions to act well, whereas the (less fully developed) discussion of merit concerns particular acts. The classification of the virtues is derived mainly from classical sources; the theory of love combines Christian notions of charity with classical ideas of *amicitia*; and merit is a distinctively Christian notion. Yet Abelard, though not always explicit about the links he has constructed, succeeds in binding these disparate elements together into an account which coheres with his analysis of sin.

THE VIRTUES

Abelard turned to ancient discussions of the virtues because of the context in which he first began to discuss ethics. Although he touched on ethical questions in his logical works, when occasionally they were raised by a remark in his text, they were of merely passing concern there.[1] It is the *Theologia Christiana* which contains his first extended treatment of ethical matters. One of Abelard's main aims in revising the *Theologia Summi Boni* into the *Theologia Christiana* was to justify his use of testimonies to the Trinity by classical philosophers. Some say, remarks Abelard, that the philosophers cannot be authorities in matters to do with the faith since they are all damned (139: 236–40). The task of the second book of the *Theologia Christiana* is to answer this charge. Most of it (139: 241 – 184: 1771) is devoted to showing the moral excellence of the ancient Greeks and Romans – philosophers especially, but also other men and women. Although

[1] See *Cat.frag.* 59: 42–60: 5, *sup.Pred.* 163: 39–164: 9; and also (on virtues) see below, pp. 284–5.

Abelard is here particularly concerned, therefore, to show the ancients' virtues in practice, he naturally turns to their theoretical classification of virtues to provide supporting evidence for his case. The ancient philosophers, he says (*TChr* 143: 383–4), would never have been able to describe the virtues so well, if they did not know them through their own experience. In the *Collationes*, written a few years later, Abelard gives a fuller, analytical account of the nature and divisions of virtue, which he bases on the ancient classification and puts into the Philosopher's mouth.

The Christian in the dialogue accepts this part of the Philosopher's doctrine without question. As Abelard himself had remarked in *Theologia Christiana* (143: 384–8), the Church Fathers were willing to take over the ancient philosophers' descriptions as their own. There was, indeed, a long tradition of Christian writers who had adopted this classical division of the virtues.[2] But there was a very important difference between the way in which Abelard's predecessors and contemporaries treated the ancient classification of the virtues and Abelard's own approach. Writers such as Augustine and Alcuin had quoted, with apparent approval, Cicero's description of the virtues. But they did not attempt to integrate it into their moral theology. Abelard's immediate theological predecessors and contemporaries all but ignored the ancient description of the virtues in their treatment of sin and merit. By contrast, during Abelard's lifetime and in the decades afterwards, a whole series of works were produced which discussed the virtues and the virtuous life in classical terms (often through direct quotation and abbreviation of ancient texts), with little or no reference to any specifically Christian doctrine. They taught ethics as part of the trivium, linked both to grammar (through the moralizing reading of classical poetry) and to rhetoric. For Abelard, the theory of the virtues was linked to his defence of the ancient philosophers and their authority, but – precisely for this reason – it could not remain a self-contained subject, isolated from questions of Christian doctrine. Abelard had looked to the philosophers as witnesses to the doctrine of the Trinity and he had sought, when first expounding their virtues, to argue not just that they lived well, but that they were

[2] Some writers used the passage from *De inventione* directly – most importantly, Augustine, Chapter 31 of whose *De diuersis quaestionibus lxxxiii* is a quotation of it (*Sententia Ciceronis quemadmodum uirtutes animi ab illo diuisae ac definitae sint*), and Alcuin, in *De rhetorica et uirtutibus* (*MPL* 101, 950); others based themselves on the *De officiis* – especially Ambrose in his own *De officiis* (ed. J. Krabinger (Tübingen, 1867), and – in progress – M. Testard, *Saint Ambroise: Les Devoirs* (Paris, 1984–)). Martin of Braga's *Formula vitae honestae* (in C. Barlow, *Martini episcopi Bracarensis opera omnia* (New Haven, 1950), pp. 236–50, cf. pp. 204–34) may have taken its account of the four virtues from Seneca's lost *De officiis*.

saved. Abelard therefore puts into his Philosopher's mouth, not a simple recapitulation of the Ciceronian account, but an adaptation of it, subtle – subtle enough to have passed almost all commentators unnoticed[3] – but radical, which transforms it in line with his own ethical views and will enable it to fit the other elements of his ethical theory.[4]

Abelard begins to transform his sources even before the description of the four virtues, when he is defining what a virtue is in general. 'Virtue', says Abelard's Philosopher (115: 1986–7), 'is the best habit of the mind (*habitus animi optimus*) and, by contrast, vice is the worst.' This definition itself is taken from Boethius' *De divisione*,[5] but the Philosopher immediately turns to Aristotle's *Categories* to explain what is meant by a 'habit'. Or, rather, he turns to Abelard's interpretation of what Aristotle says there. According to Aristotle (8b26–9a13; *AL* 63: 18 – 64: 13), the virtues are examples of 'settled states'. Settled states are one of the two types of the first of four varieties of quality; the other type consists of 'conditions'.[6] Settled states, such as the virtues, are distinguished from conditions because they are hard to change once acquired, giving an impression of permanence although some serious cause, such as illness, might lead to their loss. Aristotle explains the distinction between settled states and conditions in some detail, but he is far sketchier about how settled states and conditions together differ from the other three varieties of quality. From the examples he gives of settled states (the branches of knowledge, as well as the virtues), and of conditions (heat, cold, sickness and health), it seems that he has in mind qualities which are not innate; but it is not clear whether a condition might not also be a quality of the third variety – affective qualities (*passibiles qualitates*) and affections (*passiones*): those qualities which produce an affection of the senses or are themselves produced by such an affection.[7] Abelard

[3] See e.g. Thomas, *Erkenntnisweg*, pp. 107–12; G. d'Anna, 'Abelardo e Cicerone', *Studi medievali* 3a serie, 10, 1 (1969), 333–419, esp. pp. 406–18; Mews, 'On dating', p. 114, n. 45. R. Gauthier (*Magnanimité* (Paris, 1951), pp. 257–62) does, however, show the originality and importance of Abelard's treatment of one of the subdivisions of the virtues – magnanimity.

[4] This view is argued in my 'Abelard's ethical theory', pp. 303–6.

[5] 885B: 'virtus est mentis habitus optimus'; in later works (*Sent.* and *Sc.*, though not *Sent.Par.*) Abelard adds a further definition from Boethius' *De topicis differentiis*.

[6] 'settled state' = Gr. *hexis* = Lat. *habitus*; 'condition' = Gr. *diathesis* = Boethius' translation *affectio*; composite translation and Abelard's usage: *dispositio*.

[7] 9a36–9b12; *AL* 64: 31 – 65: 7. Abelard definitely thought the same qualities, such as heat, could belong to the first and third varieties (*sup.Pred.* 226: 7–10) and he insists in both *Dial.* (101: 5 – 103: 18) and *sup.Pred.* (225: 21 – 227: 2) that the four varieties (*maneriae*) of quality are not its species (although he does refer to settled states and conditions as a species of quality at *Coll.* 116: 1989–90 and *Sc.* 128: 21–2 – perhaps as the result of looseness rather than a change of view).

tries to be clearer. In both the *Dialectica* (91: 21–5) and *Logica*, he introduces as the distinguishing feature of both settled states and conditions that they are a result of 'application':

> The qualities which belong to this variety are all those which are not naturally in their subjects, but come through some act of application (*applicatio*) by their subjects – such as the branches of knowledge (in order to gain which we have applied ourselves), and whichever other qualities arise from what we have done. (*sup.Pred.* 225: 6–9)

The Philosopher of *Collationes* takes Abelard's development of Aristotle's doctrine a stage further. A settled state, he announces (116: 1990–2), is not merely a quality which is not naturally innate and is not easily lost, it must be 'gained through care and deliberation' (*studio ac deliberatione conquisita*). He contrasts this with an example of a natural, innate potency.

In the classification itself (116: 2013 – 127: 2289), Abelard takes his definitions of prudence, justice, courage and temperance from Cicero's *De inventione*. Prudence is defined as 'the knowledge of good things and of evil things'. Justice is 'the virtue which, whilst preserving the common good, attributes to every one his intrinsic worth (*dignitas*). It is the virtue by which we will each person to have that for which he is worthy (*dignus*), so long as this does not damage the common good.' Courage is 'the considered ... enduring of hardships and undertaking of dangers'; and temperance is 'the firm and moderate control by reason of lust and other improper impulses of the soul'.[8] But Abelard's Philosopher relates these virtues to each other quite differently from Cicero. Cicero, like Aristotle, thought of the virtues as each being an aspect of the excellence of a good man. Whilst he might place more emphasis on justice than on the others, he did not consider the four main virtues hierarchically: each contributed (although not perhaps each to the same degree) to the worth of the man who possessed them. By contrast, Abelard's Philosopher, though using Cicero's words, relates the virtues in a hierarchic way, which develops the ethical conceptions he has already advanced when defining virtue in general.

For a start, prudence is no longer to be considered one of the virtues at all. This is a view which Abelard had already proposed in the *Logica* (*sup.Pred.* 227: 24–31). His starting point there is a remark in Boethius' commentary (242C), that 'Aristotle did not, like Socrates, consider the virtues to be sorts of knowledge (*scientiae*) but settled states.' Boethius' remark

[8] 117: 2019–21 cf. *De inventione* II, 159 (*prudentia*); 118: 2065–6 cf. *De inventione* II, 160 (*iustitia*); 120: 2108–9 cf. *De inventione* II, 163 (*fortitudo*); 120: 2113–15 cf. *De inventione* II, 164 (*temperantia*); cf. d'Anna, 'Abelardo', pp. 409–10.

is an accurate report of the Greek philosopher's position: Aristotle rejected Socrates' identification of virtue with knowledge, although he believed that knowledge was required for virtue and was itself a virtue. But Abelard reads Boethius as if he had said that, according to Aristotle, knowledge is not one of the virtues at all. Aristotle, he says, was right to distinguish virtue from knowledge, since knowledge consists in discerning what should or should not be done, virtue in doing 'what knowledge perceives and reason persuades'. Often a man knows what he should do, but does not do it because he is lacking in virtue. Similarly, Abelard's Philosopher (who refers to the passage from Boethius' commentary) believes that he is following Aristotle in regarding prudence as the 'mother or origin' of virtues, a precondition for being virtuous rather than a virtue itself, since evil men as well as good ones can have prudence (117: 2018 – 118: 2061). Indeed, the Philosopher adds, knowledge can even make a person more guilty, if he knows that he should do something or not do it, and yet acts otherwise: ignorance might to some extent have excused him.

As for courage and temperance, Abelard's Philosopher does accept that they are virtues, but he sees them as mere auxiliaries to justice. A just person is led to act unjustly, when fear of what he does not want, or desire (*cupiditas*) for what he does want, overcomes his good purpose. He therefore needs courage as his shield against fear and temperance to rein his desires. These two virtues enable him to fulfil what, through justice, he already wishes to do (119: 2094 – 120: 2104). The system of four cardinal virtues is thus transformed into a hierarchy, in which justice requires prudence (not itself a virtue) and is strengthened by courage and temperance.[9]

The Philosopher cannot always be taken as a mouthpiece for Abelard

[9] A similar analysis of the relation between the cardinal virtues is found in the *Ysagoge in Theologiam* (ed. in A. Landgraf *Ecrits théologiques de l'école d'Abélard* (Louvain, 1934)), at p. 75: 20–35 and in the *Moralium dogma philosophorum* (ed. J. Holmberg under attribution to William of Conches (Paris/Cambridge/Uppsala/Leipzig/The Hague, 1929)), p. 8: 7–19. The influence of Abelard on the *Ysagoge* is generally acknowledged. But there has been considerable dispute about the relationship between the *Moralium dogma* and the *Ysagoge in theologiam*. It has been urged (P. Delhaye, 'Une adaptation du "De officiis" au XIIe siècle, le "Moralium dogma philosophorum" ', *RTAM* 16 (1949), 227–58; *Gauthier de Chatillon est-il l'auteur des Moralium dogma?* (Namur/Lille, 1953)) that the *Ysagoge* uses the *Moralium dogma* as its source, not vice versa. This would raise the possibility that this analysis is not Abelard's but borrowed by him and the *Ysagoge* from the *Moralium dogma* (or from the source used by that work). But it has been shown beyond all doubt that at least in the passage concerned here (p. 8: 7–19), the *Moralium dogma* must be using either the *Ysagoge* or some other source from Abelard or based on his teaching: see R. Gauthier, 'Les deux récensions des *Moralium Dogma Philosophorum*', *Revue du moyen âge latin* 9 (1953), 171–260 at pp. 234–5.

himself: he is a speaker in a dialogue and, as will be seen below, sometimes a fallible one. But in his account of the relations between prudence, justice, temperance and courage, there is no reason to doubt that he is putting forward Abelard's own view. *Scito teipsum* breaks off before it comes to classify the virtues; but in the *Carmen ad Astralabium* (111: 85–92) Abelard explains the position of temperance and courage as aids to justice. In both the *Sententie* (§§255–61; Bu. 145: 106 – 147: 171) and *Sententie Parisienses* (51: 4 – 52: 14) an explanation, very close to the Philosopher's, that prudence is not itself a virtue, is followed by a presentation of the scheme in which temperance and courage support justice: they are described as its props or its wings. This language suggests that, whilst these two virtues are merely auxiliary to justice, their help is necessary: without courage and temperance, a person cannot succeed in being just at all. The example given by the *Sententie* of how courage and temperance support justice backs up this suggestion (§259; Bu. 146: 153–9). Suppose that there is someone whom I ought to honour and to whom I should give money, because he is wise and is such a man that I owe him this from justice, and suppose someone tells me *not* to do so, because he is the king's enemy, and that if I help him I will incur the king's enmity, then courage is needed to stop me from turning away out of fear from doing what I owe to him in justice.

The two works also describe the difference between justice and the other two main virtues in a more theoretical way. Justice, they say (*Sententie* §261; Bu. 147: 167–71; *Sent.Par.* 52: 10–14), is a *uoluntas*; but courage and temperance are potencies (*potentie*), as can be seen from their contraries, timidity and intemperance, which are weaknesses. What does Abelard mean here by *uoluntas*? He must have in mind a sense connected to that he gave *uoluntas* in his discussion of sin in the *Sententie* and the Commentary on Romans, which was then taken over by *consensus*: a mental act preceding the physical action which is willed. But since he is clear that all the virtues are settled states – dispositions, not acts – he cannot here be using *uoluntas* to mean a single such volition, but rather what might be translated as 'will': the disposition to have such volitions under the appropriate circumstances. The fact that justice is a will, in this sense, turns out to provide one of the most important links between Abelard's theory of the virtues and his theory of love.

LOVE

Abelard developed his own ideas about love against a background of contemporary discussion. His complicated links with it – which also involved his own intellectual relationship with Heloise – will be discussed in detail in the excursus at the end of the chapter. The central idea of the contemporary discussion was that love for God (usually described as 'charity', *caritas*) must be selfless. Someone who obeys God's laws because he hopes to be rewarded in heaven for doing so cannot be said to love God, because he is concerned with his own good. Abelard enthusiastically took up this line of thought, but he changed its emphasis. Rather than stressing merely that those who look for reward from God do not love him, he turned his attention to what it is they are missing: the understanding that God, and God alone, should be the final object of our love. In his own theory of love, Abelard develops this idea.

Abelard's theory of love is designed, like that of his contemporaries, to explain the nature of charity. Abelard considered charity to be a disposition, not a particular act. His theory of love is therefore concerned with the nature of the disposition to love God in the right way. He studies the nature of the particular volitions through which love of God is manifested in his treatment of merit. The first version of Abelard's own theory of love as a disposition is already found in the earliest drafts of what would become the *Theologia Scholarium*, and with a few minor additions it is taken into the *Sententie* (*Sent.* §§3–5; Bu. 25: 14 – 26: 34; cf. *Sent.Flor.* 1: 20 – 2: 9).

Charity is defined as 'right love' (*amor honestus*), love which is directed towards that to which it ought to be: love of God for his own sake or of one's neighbour for the sake of God.[10] In the *Theologia Scholarium* itself (319: 17 – 321: 89), Abelard adds to the definition of charity given in the drafts another definition, of love (*amor*). Love, he says (319: 19–20), 'is a good will (*uoluntas*) towards another for his own sake (*bona erga alterum propter ipsum uoluntas*)'. Since the context is the discussion of love as a disposition, *uoluntas* here must mean – as in the case of justice – not a particular act of willing, but the disposition to such acts. The definition itself is based on Cicero's definition of friendship (*amicitia*) in *De inventione*, and a few lines later Abelard makes an explicit quotation. But even this verbatim reference contains an important omission (of which Abelard must have been aware, because he had used the definition unshortened in *Sic et non*). Cicero had said that friendship is a will for good things for someone whom one loves, for his own sake, *with the same will on his part [towards*

[10] *tsch* 405: 124–6: 'Caritas uero est amor honestus, qui ad hoc uidelicet refertur ad quod debet,(*) ut si Deum ipsum propter se uel proximum diligam propter Deum' = (with minor changes) *Sent.* §3; Bu. 25: 14–16; cf. *Sent.Flor.* 1: 20–1, which is similar up to (*).

oneself].[11] Whereas Cicero, thinking in a tradition which goes back to Aristotle's *Nicomachean Ethics* VIII–IX, wished to emphasize the reciprocity in a relationship between two men, by his shortening Abelard makes the definition refer, rather, to an ideal of altruism. He spells this out in the explanation he adds: the will which constitutes love is one 'by which we choose [to act] so that what happens to [another] is what we believe is for his good, and we desire this for his sake rather than for our own'.[12]

Abelard uses this concept of *amor* to make a very general division of types of love: true love (*amor*), on the one hand, which is altruistic in intention, and false love, on the other hand, which is selfish. *Caritas*, which Abelard continues to define as he had done in the drafts, is a species of true love – true love which is *honestus*, 'that is to say (*uidelicet*), which is directed to the end which is fitting'. Altruism is, then, a necessary but not a sufficient condition for charity; and Abelard would in theory distinguish between altruistic but wrongly directed love (for which he has no name) and selfish love (which he calls 'false friendship' or 'cupidity').[13] From the point of view of defining charity, the Ciceronian definition of *amor* which Abelard introduces in the *Theologia Scholarium* is strictly speaking superfluous, since if love is directed fittingly, that is, to God, it will thereby be altruistic.[14] But, by adding the Ciceronian definition, Abelard is able to recapitulate the concerns about selflessness which he shared with his contemporaries, whilst at the same time putting them into their subsidiary place within his own theory of love and stressing that altruism is not, in itself, confined to Christian charity but is a condition of any love worthy of the name.

In what does Abelard think that rightly directed love – to God and to one's neighbour for the sake of God – consists?[15] First, it involves loving

11 *De inventione* II, 55, 166; p. 150: 22–4: 'Amicitia uoluntas erga aliquem rerum bonarum illius ipsius causa, quem diligit, *cum eius pari uoluntate*' (= *SN* 473: 84–6). At *TSch* 319: 31–2, Abelard quotes the definition, but without the italicized final phrase.

12 319: 20–2: 'uoluntas, qua uidelicet optamus ut eo modo se habeat quo se habere bonum ei esse credimus, et hoc eius potius quam nostri causa desideramus'.

13 When Abelard remarks (*TSch* 319: 38–40) that those who love selfishly are demonstrating *cupiditas* rather than *caritas*, he should not be taken as implying that merely by being selfless our love is *caritas* but rather that, if it is not selfless, it cannot be *caritas*.

14 In *Sent.Par.* (48: 20–6), the only one of the *Sententie* collections to use the Ciceronian definition, this becomes very clear, when the argument (which may well be a very condensed or even garbled version of what Abelard said) moves directly from the fact that I wish someone to go to heaven for my sake, not for his own, to the fact that my love is not therefore *tendens in ipsum finem in quem oportet, id est in ipsum Deum*.

15 See *Sententie* §§247–9; Bu. 142: 18 – 143: 53; *Sent.Par.* 48: 27 – 49: 15, 49: 26 – 50: 6 has similar material to the *Sententie*; cf. also *Comm.Rom.* 290: 163–291: 175.

God 'with one's whole heart' – a biblical phrase Abelard glosses as meaning without measure. Such love, Abelard explains, is shown by someone 'who is ready to obey God in so far as he is able'. In most of his work, Abelard tends to think of obedience to God in negative terms: not going against his precepts. But in his presentation of his theory of love as a disposition, Abelard also gives a more positive account.[16] If whatever is loved rightly, is loved for the sake of God, it follows, in Abelard's view, that we should do nothing except for God's sake. God must be set up as the final cause of one's actions. We should not eat, sleep, marry or do anything whatsoever except for the sake of God. So, for instance, when we eat or sleep, we should do so because these are physical necessities for us, if we are to continue with our living service of God. It is not, however, clear exactly how these general injunctions should be translated into practice under given circumstances.

By contrast with love for God, love of one's neighbour should be measured (*Sent.* §§248–9; Bu. 142: 25 – 143: 53). We are commanded to love our neighbour 'as we love ourselves' – that is, as Abelard explains, not 'to the same extent as' (*quantum*), but 'in the same way as'. Our charity should, therefore, be 'ordered' (*ordinata*) according to the relative excellence of its objects: God should be loved beyond all other things, because he is good beyond all other things; then 'the mother of God', because she is better than all others except him; and then others according to their worth – so that if someone else is worthy (*dignus*) of greater good than I am, then I should desire it for him rather than for myself. Abelard even adapts the Golden Rule ('Do to others as you would have them do to you'/'Do not do to others what you would not have them do to you'), which would seem to provide a principle of action in which everyone is treated equally, so as to take account of the differences in worth among people. It must be understood to mean, he says, 'we should do all those things to others which we would wish them to do to us if we were of the same status (*gradus*) and of the same worth (*dignitas*) as they'.[17] Exactly how Abelard's 'ordering of

[16] *TSch* 320: 67 – 321: 84; *Sent.* §4; Bu. 25: 16 – 26: 29; *Sent.Flor.* 1: 21 – 2: 4.

[17] See Tobiah 4: 16 (negative version); Matthew 7: 2 (positive version). On the history of this rule, see A. Dihle, *Die goldene Regel* (Göttingen, 1962) (Studienhefte zur Altertumswissenschaft 7). The Rule was often quoted by the Fathers, especially Augustine (see e.g. *Enarratio in Psalmum* 57, 1 (ed. Dekkers and Fraipont, pp. 708: 23 – 709: 55). For use by Abelard's contemporaries, see e.g. *Principium et causa omnium*, p. 79 and *Sententiae Atrebatenses* (*Lottin*, p. 417: 5–6). For a fuller discussion of Abelard's use of the Rule, see Marenbon, 'Abelard's concept of natural law', pp. 612–14, and cf. *Comm.Rom.* 291: 176–203, *Sent.Par.* 50: 1–6 and *Problemata* XX (on which, see above, p. 77). Abelard's and Heloise's doubts

charity' might work out in practice is as hazy as the practical implications of the injunction to do everything for the sake of God. Indeed, Abelard seems to shy away from suggesting that the order of charity should have a direct effect on practice. Whilst, if someone is more devout than my father, I should love him more, I should direct the practical activity which stems from love (*exhibitio caritatis*) to my father rather than the devouter man if I cannot extend it to them both.[18]

Abelard's theory of love and his theory of the virtues both concern acting well as a disposition. How do the two theories relate to each other? The answer is provided by the *Sententie*. The opening of the section about the virtues there (§251; Bu. 143: 68 – 144: 78) repeats and discusses Augustine's statement that 'every virtue is charity'. By this statement, Augustine meant to stress the difference between the pagan virtues – sham virtues, in his view – and the true virtues which a person has only once he has charity. The discussion in the *Sententie* does not explicitly contradict this view: indeed, Abelard talks in a rather Augustinian way of charity *making* a person virtuous, and he even mentions, besides the virtue of courage, the distinctly Christian virtues of patience and humility. But the *Sententie* then continue by giving an account of the Ciceronian virtues, with no suggestion that these are not the virtues linked to charity. At the end of the discussion (§261; Bu. 157: 171–5), these links are made explicit and it becomes obvious that Abelard's view is very different from Augustine's. Abelard distinguishes justice, which is a will, from courage and temperance which are potencies. He goes on to explain that Augustine's 'every virtue is charity' means that 'all the virtues which consist in the will are charity, and whichever are potencies are its effects'. Since Abelard has explained that, of virtues, justice alone is a will, he has in effect identified justice with charity, though with one difference: whereas in his account of the Ciceronian virtues courage and temperance are the props of justice, they are considered to be the effects of charity.[19]

The identification of justice, one of the Ciceronian virtues, with Christian

about the Golden Rule may have been suggested to them initially by Augustine: see *De libero arbitrio* I, iii, 6; p. 214: 23–30.

[18] Peter Dronke, who saved me from seriously misinterpreting this passage, suggests that it is psychologically implausible that Abelard should have used his own father (who ended his life as a monk) as an example of someone lacking in devoutness. Perhaps here the *Sententie* do not recount Abelard's own words.

[19] The *Sententie* (§261; Bu. 147: 183–6) do raise the possibility that – contrary to Abelard's normal position – temperance and courage are also wills, like justice: in this case, he says, charity would simply be the genus of the three virtues.

charity may seem shocking, but in fact it follows easily from the way Abelard adapts the classical scheme of virtues and modifies current ideas about charity into his own theory of love. The Ciceronian virtue of justice, taken over by Abelard in the *Collationes* and *Sententie*, is that of giving to everyone according to his worth.[20] Abelard insists that charity is distinguished from other sorts of love by being rightly directed, and that rightly directed love involves an 'ordering' of charity, in which love is given to everyone according to his worth. And, by describing justice, alone of the virtues, as a will, and suggesting that it is necessarily accompanied by temperance and courage, Abelard made it, like charity, a supreme virtue. But there might still seem to remain two fundamental differences between charity and justice. First, the ordering of charity recognizes God as supremely worthy, whereas justice seems to order only human worth. But, in fact, for Cicero himself worship of God comes under the general heading of justice, and Abelard everywhere stresses that the philosophers, who described justice and the other virtues, regarded God as supreme and directed their love to him. Second, it might be objected that the just person is one who gives to others according to their due, whereas the charitable person is one who loves them according to their due. But this distinction can hardly be made, since 'giving to others' is understood by Abelard to cover behaviour to others in general, while usually Abelard considers charity also in terms of behaviour.[21]

For Abelard, then, someone who has the acquired disposition to will justly, supported (as it needs to be) by the dispositions of courage and temperance, will thereby be someone with the disposition of charity. Faced by the temptation to disobey what he believes to be God's command, he will be strongly disposed to resist; faced with the opportunity to do what he believes is pleasing to God, he will be strongly disposed to do it. What about the particular volitions to act well which manifest these dispositions? Abelard studied them by looking at the idea of merit; but, as will appear, he did not tackle nearly all the problems which it raised.

MERIT

'Merit' is the word Abelard uses, in accord with the theological language of the time, for the reward we receive when we act well. Abelard explains

[20] On Abelard's treatment of the other aspect of justice, preservation of the common good, see below, pp. 306–8.

[21] The love owed to the devout man in the passage discussed above would be a counter-example.

(*Sententie* §274; Bu. 153: 5–9) that this reward is 'eternal life' but that 'because we merit it [eternal life] by various good *uoluntates*, so we talk of many, diverse merits'. Merit, then, in this sense, is the particular reward for a particular volition to act well, just as a sin is a particular volition or consent to act wrongly. The mirror-image analogy with sin is made even closer by Abelard's comment (*Sententie* §274; Bu. 153: 9–10) that 'merit' can also be used to mean the good volition itself, rather than the reward it brings. With this alternative meaning in mind, Abelard also equates merit with loving God. The *Sententie Parisienses* declare that 'Man's merit is in love alone. To merit is to love God with your heart, soul and might for himself.'[22] In his discussion of love, Abelard explains that 'loving God with all your heart' means being ready to obey God so far as one can.[23] So, just as the consent to do what the agent believes is disobedient to God is an act of contempt for God, so the volition to do what the agent believes is obedient to God is an act of love for God.

Abelard usually thinks about merit in direct connection with an instance of temptation to sin. When the agent, though tempted, does not consent to perform the sinful action, Abelard considers that he does not merely not sin: he gains merit. The more difficult it is for him to resist, the more merit is earned. To give just two examples. In the *Sententie*, after it has been argued that innate vices make people prone to sin, Abelard goes on to say that they can 'restrain their desire' and, by being victorious in the struggle, they gain more merit.[24] In *Scito teipsum*, after describing (10: 31 – 12: 25) someone who fights successfully against the temptation to sin by sleeping with a woman he lusts for, Abelard explains that the person 'puts God's will before his own' and that by doing this 'we obtain great merit'. In neither these examples nor the many other instances where Abelard mentions merit in the context of temptation resisted, does he enquire about the good volition which earns the merit. Had he done so, he would have faced the problem (also posed, but left untackled, by sins of omission)[25] that it is often difficult to identify a particular mental act of *not* consenting to a sin, analogous to the mental act Abelard calls volition or consent and identifies with sin. I am tempted by the delicious fruit in another's garden but continue on my path through it, doing nothing which I would not do if there were there

[22] 59: 23–5; cf. *Sent.* §274: 154: 32–3.

[23] See above, p. 290.

[24] §267; Bu. 150: 38–40: 'Multi siquidem sunt qui, cum proni sunt ad hoc, uoluntatem tamen cohibent. Vnde et maioris meriti in tantum esse deprehenduntur quod uictores in lucta efficiuntur.'

[25] See above, p. 278.

no fruit there. What exactly was my mental act of willing not to eat the fruit? Could there be such a volition?

Abelard did not think that the only way to earn merit was in resisting temptation to sin. He thought that people could act (or intend to act) well under circumstances where they would not be sinning if they failed to act in that way. His only extended account of merit, in the *Sententie* (§§275–7; Bu. 153: 1 – 155: 60), is devoted to such cases. The examples include fasting, giving money for the poor and suffering torture and death in the case of the martyrs and Christ. Abelard makes the same point with regard to them all: the merit does not depend on the action itself, but on the agent's *uoluntas* (presumably, 'act of willing', though the locating of this might present difficulties).

One consequence of this position is that a good volition to perform an action which is in fact thwarted earns as much merit as if the action had been performed. If someone decides to build a hostel for the poor but the money for it is stolen before the building is put up, his merit is no less than that of another person who decides on the same plan and executes it successfully.[26] Abelard also wants to insist that, even where the action is not thwarted, it does not in itself supply the basis for judgement. So, for instance, Abelard observes that the poor widow's gift of a penny earns her more merit than the rich man's pound, and that a hypocrite may fast even more strictly than a saint but will not gain merit for it. What counts for merit is that someone should be acting out of love for God. It seems that, just as an agent shows contempt for God by performing an act he believes God forbids him, whether or not the belief is correct, so an agent will be acting out of love for God if he performs an act which he believes is pleasing to God, whether or not his belief is correct. In the case of contempt, Abelard uses the apparatus of law (natural and revealed) and conscience to avoid the subjectivism which threatens to follow from this position. There is little such apparatus to help him in the case of earning merit. True, besides observing divine prohibitions, love for God as a disposition involves, in Abelard's account, performing every action 'for the sake of God' and observing an 'order of charity' in choosing whom to help. But it was observed above that neither of these requirements translates into any clear set of directives about what someone should do. Abelard seems simply not to have envisaged the many foolish, bizarre and destructive actions people might believe are pleasing to God.

Perhaps, however, it was out of concern for the extreme subjectivist

[26] See also *Sc.* 48: 13–18.

consequences of his view that Abelard, on a couple of occasions in his latest writing, apparently qualifies his position. In one of the passages added to the *Theologia Scholarium* in its final revision (547: 1536–54), Abelard takes the example of the person whose project to build a hostel for the poor is thwarted. But here he says that in such a case, although his ignorance is 'invincible' (547: 1555) – he could not have known his plan was going to fail – his intention cannot be said to be right. But then he goes on to reiterate his general view by saying that the person will still be rewarded by God 'who counts the volition for the performance of the action (*uoluntatem pro opere facti*)'. In *Scito teipsum* (54: 1–25) Abelard considers those who put martyrs to death in the belief that they are doing what is pleasing to God. Abelard is sure that such men do not sin (54: 26 – 56: 1), but (using the scriptural idea of the unclean eye of the intention, as he does also in the *Theologia Scholarium* passage) he insists that their intention is not 'good or right'. Abelard does not actually say here that the persecutors would actually be rewarded by God for their acts (it caused enough scandal for him to insist that they did not sin!), though he does not rule out this position, which is what the consistency of his thought would require.[27] As with some other facets of his discussion of merit, Abelard does not seem here to have worked out his thoughts very clearly.

PAGAN RIGOUR AND CHRISTIAN SALVATION

The preceding sections have illustrated how fully Abelard unites classical with Christian moral thought. Yet there is one, remarkable way in which he very deliberately draws a distinction between the ancient point of view and that of Christianity.

For Abelard, there is charity apart from the virtue of charity. Charity,

[27] His comment (*Sc.* 54: 23–5), 'Alioquin ipsi etiam infideles sicut et nos bona opera haberent, cum ipsi etiam non minus quam nos per opera sua se saluari uel Deo placere credant' merely states that (1) infidels' actions cannot be called 'good' because they do not stem from what can be called a 'good intention', given the infidels' ignorance and that (2) their ignorance consists in thinking that their actions please God and that, as infidels, they can be saved. This is not inconsistent with holding that God rewards them for their good will: see below, pp. 329–30. In *Comm.Cant.* (179–180), Abelard is reported as discussing the same problem in the same terms. Abelard there says explicitly that an act which proceeds from an intention which, because of ignorance, is not right, but is done for God, should be considered an example of *amor honestus*. He is then asked whether someone gains merit from such an act, but the reply is unenlightening, because it deals merely with the form of the question: not at all, because merit comes from the will to act, not from the acts themselves.

he considers, can be perfect or imperfect. If it is perfect, then it is a virtue, that is to say, a settled state (equivalent to justice, with courage and temperance as necessary concomitants). But there is also imperfect charity, intense love of God which is not a settled state because it is a disposition which can be shifted without great difficulty.[28] What is needed for salvation, according to Abelard, is *not* perfect charity, but merely imperfect charity. A person who dies intensely loving God dies in a state of charity and will be saved – even though he lacks the virtue, the settled state, of charity. Charity, as has been explained, consists for Abelard in setting God as the end of everything we do, in making choices not to fulfil our own desired aims but from love of him. It follows that, if we have charity, we must be willing, if necessary, to die for God. But this willingness might or might not be a settled state. There are, as Abelard remarks in *Scito teipsum* 'many of the faithful who lack the constancy to bear the sufferings of the martyrs'. But, if when they die they are at that time in a state of charity (imperfect charity, because their willingness to obey God to death is not a settled state), they will be saved.[29] In the lectures on the Pauline Epistles reported in the Cambridge Commentary, a passage reporting the Philosophus (Abelard) makes the position very clear indeed.[30] If someone dies with it in his mind that he would not show contempt for God, whatever the danger, then he will be saved even if, as a matter of fact, he does not know his own weakness and would have denied God under torture.[31]

Through the idea of imperfect charity, Abelard is able to use the Chris-

[28] In the *Sententie* (§261; Bu. 147: 178–9) Abelard describes charity which is a virtue (a settled state) as 'perfect charity' (*caritas perfecta*); in *Comm.Cant.* (827), the Philosophus uses the term 'rooted (*radicata*) charity' in the same context.

[29] *Sc.* 128: 26 – 130: 6. In order to make this passage fully clear, it should be read in conjunction with *Sent.* §261; Bu. 147: 179–83: 'multi sine perfecta caritate saluantur, quia cum tunc, quando moriuntur, hanc uoluntatem habeant quod, si optio eis daretur, pro Christo morerentur, non tamen habent illam uoluntatem difficile mobilem, quia, si uiuerent, mutaretur illa uoluntas'.

[30] 826–7: 'In quibus nichil refert dum solummodo in propositio habeant quod pro nullo periculo Deum contempnent, licet illi suam non cognoscant fragilitatem, quod videlicet ad tormenta applicati Deum denegarent.'

[31] Abelard also considers the converse of this type of case – where someone (his example is King David) does 'have Christ as his foundation' because he would choose to die rather than deny him, but none the less 'overcome by some sickness' has fallen into sin (see *Sent.* §250; Bu. 145: 53–4). The obvious way to interpret this is as a comment about perfect charity – an example of the way in which one can have a settled state but not act according to it in every instance. In *Sent.Par.* (51: 20–1), however, David is given as an example of someone who had a settled disposition of virtue, but lost it, but he is not cited there as an example of the case of the man who sins but still has Christ as his foundation (50: 21–8).

tian and the pagan moral traditions on which he draws to balance and qualify one another. Abelard happily adopts the classical ideal of the virtuous man and fits it to the idea of perfect charity. The person who has perfect charity has a settled disposition to act justly – to set up God as the end of his action, and its being settled must involve the courage and temperance to perform these acts despite the temptations of fear or pleasure. But Abelard also has a place in his moral scheme for the person whose charity is imperfect, who acts meritoriously but does not do so as a settled state, since there are many circumstances under which he would not maintain his love for God above all things. Christianity recognizes the ancient ideal through the concept of perfect charity, but it is through imperfect charity that we are saved. In his thought about practical ethics Abelard explored more thoroughly this very contrast between a heroic ideal, linked to antiquity, and a less ambitious measure which caters for human weakness.

Excursus II

Love, selflessness and Heloise

Love (*dilectio*) of God is a very important idea for Abelard in his first mainly ethical work, the *Collationes*, but it appears almost exclusively in an eschatological context. The Christian surprises the Philosopher by concluding (132: 2347 – 133: 2461) that the greatest evil for men is not the punishment of Hell but the ever-increasing hate they will feel there for God, and their greatest good the highest love for God. The discussion of good earthly behaviour, however, is conducted in terms of the pagan virtues: the concept of charity appears, but only in connection with the Philosopher's argument, shown to be mistaken, that no one can have one virtue without having them all.[1] A little earlier, in the *Theologia Christiana*, Abelard had used the notion of charity rather as one which he adopted without giving much thought of his own to its definition, or giving it an important place in his analysis. He mentions charity particularly in the context of the Trinity.[2] But he also makes passing references to it in connection with human action which show that he seemed to take it for granted that charity, in the sense of love for God, is necessary for salvation, and that, in general, charity – man's or God's – is love for someone else, in which his desired ends and not one's own are sought.[3]

Yet, a little before Abelard wrote his *Theologia Christiana*, one of his contemporaries – very probably Walter of Mortagne – had subjected the idea of charity to careful scrutiny in his brief *De caritate* and radicalized

[1] 109: 1803 – 190: 1823; there is also a brief reference (130: 2374–5) by the Philosopher to the view that, once gained, charity can never be lost.

[2] See *TChr* 323: 1858–62 (cf. *TSum* 195: 1195 – 196: 1197; *TSch* 469: 1832–7), 323: 1866 – 324: 1868 (cf. *TSum* 196: 1201–2; *TSch* 470: 1845–7), 369: 711 – 370: 736.

[3] 152: 707–8: 'Alioquin non est in proximum caritas perfecta quae non quaerit quae sua sunt, sed amici sui commoda'; cf. 150: 637, 646; 151: 676; 152: 700–1 and also 143: 394–5 (linking love of virtue, love of God and merit, although not using the word *caritas*).

Augustine's definition of it.[4] The main contention of *De caritate* is that charity consists in entirely selfless love of God and, for his sake, of our neighbour. If we love God because we wish to enjoy the beatific vision and be in paradise, we are like hired servants, seeking our own ends. In consequence, we will not be rewarded with salvation. We ought to desire the heavenly kingdom merely so that we can serve Christ more perfectly there.[5] In support of this view, the author silently alters the definition of charity given by Augustine in *De doctrina christiana*. Augustine had written, 'Charity is the movement of the soul to *enjoy* God for his own sake and oneself and one's neighbour for the sake of God'; *De caritate* states, rather, that 'Charity is the movement of the soul to *love* God for the sake of God, and oneself and one's neighbour for the sake of God.'[6]

When he wrote the *Theologia Christiana*, Abelard picked up some of these ideas from the *De caritate* without, it seems, paying any attention to their implications. At one point (149: 596–600), he mentions our being 'called in grace according to the liberty of charity, not in the servile manner of the Jews, from fear of punishment and ambition for earthly things, nor *from the desire of eternal things*'. Later (369: 717–18), Abelard quotes Augustine's definition of charity with the *De caritate*'s substitution of 'loving' (*diligendum*) for 'enjoying' – but not in a context where the substitution makes any significant difference. By contrast, six or seven years later, when Abelard wrote his commentary on Romans, charity – and especially the

[4] Ed. and discussed in R. Wielockx, 'La Sentence *De caritate* et la discussion scolastique sur l'amour', *Ephemerides theologicae lovanienses* 58 (1982), 50–86, 334–56; 59 (1988), 26–45 (edition at 1982, pp. 69–73); cf. Luscombe, 'The School revisited', p. 132. Wielockx shows that three elements (*Lottin* §§420, 71/2, 73) which previous scholars had taken as separate *sententiae* belong together as a single piece. Wielockx's dating of *De caritate* to *c.* 1133–6 must be corrected because: (1) as he shows, it is used in *TChr*: this establishes a *terminus ante quem* of *c.* 1126 (Wielockx is misled by Buytaert's views on the dating and recensions of *TChr*: see above, p. 58, n. 9); (2) the *De caritate* is found in the *Liber pancrisis*, a collection probably put together in the 1120s. (See O. Lottin, *Psychologie et morale* VI, pp. 479–88 = 'A propos de la date de deux florilèges concernant Anselme de Laon', *RTAM* 26 (1959), 307–14. Wielockx does not take account of Lottin's arguments and dates the *Liber Pancrisis* to the 1150s.)

[5] Pp. 72: 4 – 73: 11: 'Qui autem mercenarii, alii quaerunt commodum temporale, alii aeternum. Qui vero quaerunt aeternum, hi sunt qui propter propriam delectationem Christum videre desiderant et in paradiso esse optant. Hi ergo quaerunt quae sua sunt, non quae Iesu Christi. Propterea nec illud habebunt. Non ergo propter delectationem nostram aut aliquod nostrum commodum regnum Christi desiderare debemus, sed ut ei melius et perfectius servire possimus.'

[6] *De doctrina christiana* (CC 32, p. 87: 32–3): 'Caritatem voco motum animi ad fruendum deo propter ipsum, et se atque proximo propter deum'; cf. *De caritate*, p. 69: 1–2: 'Caritas est motus animi ad diligendum Deum propter Deum, et se et proximum propter Deum.'

concerns raised by *De caritate* – is a subject of great importance to him, calling for separate, detailed treatment. It is most probable that Abelard's attention was drawn towards the idea of selfless love not by any of the other masters of his time, but by a writer whom he could not ignore: Heloise.

In her first letter to Abelard, Heloise describes her love for Abelard in precisely the terms in which charity is conceived in *De caritate*. She sought for nothing in Abelard save himself, desiring him only not anything of his. So far was her love free from any selfish desire for its own fulfilment that, in order to obey Abelard's wish, she was willing to give up what her love alone desired, Abelard himself, and become a nun.[7] Etienne Gilson was led by this passage to suggest that Heloise was mainly responsible for inventing the theory of selfless love which Abelard then applied to man's love for God.[8] It seems, rather, that Heloise herself is borrowing a current theological doctrine and (encouraged perhaps by similar ideas in pagan texts, such as Cicero's *De amicitia*) transforming it into a theory of human love – rather as love poets of the time did not hesitate to use the themes and images of the Song of Songs.

Abelard did not respond to Heloise's views about selfless love until his reply to her second letter (Letter 5). He wished to turn her devotion from himself towards God (he could hardly, either as her spiritual adviser or as a man who still loved her, have done otherwise). But he did not simply insist that the selfless love which Heloise directed towards him should be given, rather, to God: he found an emotionally and rhetorically more powerful form in which to counter Heloise's view, personalizing God's love as Christ's love and presenting Christ, not himself, as Heloise's true lover.[9]

In the Commentary on Romans, written perhaps a year or two after this letter, Abelard looks in detail at charity, especially in one much-discussed passage (201: 479 – 204: 577).[10] This discussion marks the high-point of the

[7] 70–1: 'Nihil umquam, Deus scit, in te nisi te requisivi, te pure non tua concupiscens. Non matrimonii foedera, non dotes aliquas expectavi, non denique meas voluptates aut voluntates sed tuas, sicut ipse nosti, adimplere studui'; 70: 'Et quod maius est dictuque mirabile, in tantam versus est amor insaniam ut quod solum appetebat, hoc ipse sibi sine spe recuperationis auferret, cum ad tuam statim iussionem tam habitum ipsa quam animum immutarem ut te tam corporis mei quam animi unicum possessorem ostenderem.'

[8] *La théologie mystique de Saint Bernard* (Paris, 1934) (Etudes de philosophie médiévale 20), pp. 183–9, appendix II, 'Abélard'.

[9] For further discussion of this passage, see below, p. 321.

[10] See e.g. Gilson, *Saint Bernard*, pp. 183–9; Z. Alszeghy, *Grundforme der Liebe* (Rome, 1941) (Analecta Gregoriana 38), pp. 200–3; R. Weingart, *The logic of divine love: a critical analysis*

conscious influence on Abelard of the views expressed in *De caritate*. But, even so, he modifies them, elaborating their presentation and, in an important respect, altering their emphasis. For a start, Abelard spells out in far greater detail than *De caritate* what is meant by mercenary love and why it deserves no reward. He turns to a passage from Augustine:

If you praise God because he might give you something, then you do not love God freely (*gratis*). You would blush if your wife loved you because of your wealth and if it happened that you became poor would think of adultery. Since, then, you wish to be loved freely by your wife, will you love God for something else? What reward will you gain from God, you miser?[11]

Abelard explains:

If I love God because he loves me, and not, rather, because whatever he might do with me, he is such as should be loved above all things, then these words of Truth speak against me: 'For if you love those who love you, what repayment will you have?' No repayment indeed according to justice (*aequitas*), because my concern is not for the justice of the beloved thing but my own desired ends (*utilitas*). And I would love another equally much or more, were he to profit me equally or more; nor would I love him now, did I not hope in him for my own desired ends. (202: 518–26)

In this comment, Abelard contrasts selfish love of God (loving God because he loves me) and a love of God which is characterized not merely negatively as selfless, but also positively: 'because ... he is such as should be loved above all things'. He also introduces the idea that true love is characterized by not being even hypothetically inconstant, and that unless I love someone for his own sake (X for X), there is always the danger of inconstancy. If I love X for the sake of Y, then there is always the possibility that X might be without Y, in which case my love would cease.

By using the example of the love a man might expect of his wife, Augustine had raised the idea that the true love we should give to God is not, in its nature, something strange and untoward, but rather an attitude encountered in the usual run of human life. Abelard takes up this idea at the end of his discussion. The selfless love which we should show towards God is, he says, like a father's love towards his son or a chaste wife's to her husband.

of the soteriology of Peter Abelard, (Oxford 1970), pp. 171–4; Anna, 'Abelardo', pp. 368–73; Peppermüller, *Abaelards Auslegung*, pp. 159 – 61; Moos, 'Cornelia und Heloise', pp. 1033–8.

11 202: 503–8. The whole quotation runs from 202: 498 to 202: 515 = Augustine, *Enarratio in Psalmos* 53, 10; pp. 653–4. Abelard also introduces a quote from another of Augustine's works at 202: 496–7 = *De diuersis quaestionibus lxxxiii* 35, 1; p. 50: 9–10.

Even if the object of their love is of no use to them, they love him more greatly than whatever they could have which would serve their desired ends, nor 'if because of him they suffer hardships (*incommoda*) can their love be diminished, because the whole cause of their love remains in him whom they love, so long as they have *him*, not in any benefits which they might have *through* him' (204: 564–6). And Abelard thinks (as he had done in his letter to Heloise) of Lucan's *Pharsalia*, recalling Pompey's words to Cornelia, in tears when she meets him, alive but defeated: *Quod defles, id amasti*. If Cornelia loved him truly, why should she weep, when she still had him?

The clearest indication of the way in which Abelard has changed the emphasis of the ideas in *De caritate* comes in the passage immediately before this (203: 542–59). Abelard cites a possible objection to his view – one which he explicitly links to Augustine and which, indeed, does represent Augustine's view. Since the reward which God gives us is nothing other than God himself, to serve him because of the eternal beatitude one hopes from him is to act for his sake and so 'purely and sincerely'. Abelard then remarks:

> And we would indeed then be loving God sincerely and purely, if we did this only for him, not for own desired ends; and if we were not considering what he might give us but what he is in himself. But if we make him alone the cause of our loving, then (as has been said) we will love him equally whatever he does, to us or to others, because we will always find in him the cause of our whole love – he who remains always and in the same way entirely good in himself and worthy of love. (203: 552–9)

Abelard does not reject the idea that, if we act from love of God we are, in fact, acting from love of what will be our final reward. But he distinguishes this from acting from love of our reward, which is in fact God. His implicit premise is, again, that pure love must not be even hypothetically inconstant. Since God is always good and worthy of love and whatever he does is for the best, so long as we love him for himself, our love must remain; but if we love him for the reward we hope from him – even if that reward is God himself – then we may not love him 'whatever he does to us or to others'.

It is hard to know how much, if at all, Abelard has distorted Augustine's thought about loving God. After the passage Abelard quotes from the *Enarratio in Psalmos* on selfless love, Augustine goes on to exhort his listener to 'seek now what will profit you afterwards, seek what will help you in eternity'; and when Augustine warns his audience not to love God as a giver of gifts, he seems to have earthly rewards in mind: gold and silver, wealth and honours. Yet the distinction he draws here is the same as Abelard's: love God not for anything he gives (though Abelard thinks of spiritual gifts), but *because he is good*.[12] Whilst some scholars argue that Augustine's ideas about love were, in general, far removed from twelfth-century notions of selflessness, others do attribute to him a notion of selfless love, but one which involves the reward of God himself.[13] Abelard made this idea more subtle but did not reject it, attaching it to his view of God as the ordainer of a best possible universe which, however, may appear wretchedly imperfect from the point of view of the individual human being.

At much the same time as he wrote up the commentary on Romans, Abelard was developing his own theory of love (examined in the preceding chapter) in his oral teaching and in the early drafts of the *Theologia Scholarium*. In doing so, he turned to the very statement in Augustine's *De doctrina christiana* which was at issue in the dispute over selfless love: 'Love is the motion of the soul towards enjoying God for his own sake, and oneself and one's neighbour for the sake of God.' Abelard's own definition of love states that charity is 'right love' (*amor honestus*), love which is directed towards that to which it ought to be: love of God for his own sake or of one's neighbour for the sake of God.[14] But, where in the dispute the emphasis fell on the attitude towards God (must the love involve the enjoyment of God?), Abelard transfers attention to the object of the love. What matters is that the love be rightly referred or, as he puts it even more clearly in the *Theologia Scholarium* itself, 'directed'. Like the author of *De caritate*, Abelard has eliminated the idea of enjoyment from the definition of love, but he has not done so ostentatiously, as a direct contrast to Augustine. It is enough for him to make clear that, to have charity, we must act in a way which makes God the final cause of all we do.

[12] *Enarratio in Psalmos*, 654: 58–62: 'Numquid ait: Confitebor nomini tuo, Domine, quia das mihi fructuosa praedia, quia das mihi aurum et argentum, quia das mihi latas diuitias, amplam pecuniam, excellentissimam dignitatem? Non. Sed quid? *'Quoniam bonus est.'*

[13] O. O'Donovan, *The problem of self-love in Augustine* (New Haven/London, 1980), pp. 148–9.

[14] See above, p. 288, n. 10 for text and references.

Chapter 14

Ethics, society and practice

The best moral philosophers are not content merely to develop a theory of ethics at a high level of abstraction. They wish, in addition, to give some idea of the practical implications of their theories: how they measure up to the complexities of the real world, and what sort of life is the best for man, individually and in society. Abelard is no exception. To his theoretical ethics is linked a practical examination of morality, itself conducted at a number of different levels: his social and political thought; his practical ethics and his examination of ethics in practice. As a political thinker, Abelard changes, over a decade, from being the proponent of a bold, but naively optimistic, vision of a perfect community to accepting human weakness as the basis for his thought about human communities. His *Rule* and the *Carmen ad Astralabium* are largely devoted to considering individual matters of practical ethics. And, in a wide variety of works, including sermons, his *planctus* and the *Historia Calamitatum*, Abelard uses examples (usually biblical stories and characters) to explore the workings and dilemmas of morality in practice.

SOCIETY AND THE CLASSICAL IDEAL

In Book II of his *Theologia Christiana* Abelard develops, in connection with his defence of the ancient philosophers, a remarkable political theory. His fundamental text is one which has been central to the whole history of political thought: Plato's *Republic*. The *Republic* is a work which neither Abelard, nor any western scholar of his century or the two following centuries, had read. But Abelard knew about it – and the vague, inaccurate impression he gained provided a core around which he could formulate his own ideas. At the opening of the *Timaeus* – the one work of Plato's which was well known both to Abelard and his contemporaries – Socrates recalls the conversation of the previous day, which turns out to be the dialogue we know as the *Republic*. Taking little notice of the details of the account, Abelard derived from it the idea that Plato had advocated a form of rule where all was done for the common good, where property was held in common and where the rulers lived austere lives.[1] He was particularly struck by the remark that wives and children would be in common. It could not be, he reasoned, that Plato advocated adultery. What he must have had in mind, Abelard concluded, was not that the use of women should be common, but their offspring. Children would belong, not to their parents, but to the whole city – a reassuring metaphor of community.[2] Abelard did not present this city, as Plato had done, as an impossible ideal: he takes Plato's recommendations as a set of practical guidelines, which the ancient philosophers exemplified in their own manner of living (150: 623–8).

In *De civitate Dei*, Augustine had rejected the idea that there could ever be a true republic, according to Cicero's definition, among pagans. Cicero had explained that a republic (*respublica*) means the 'affair' (*res*) of the people (*populus*), and that a people is 'a gathering of many, united by consent to law (*ius*) and common utility'.[3] Augustine argues that, when the true God is not known and false Gods are worshipped, there cannot be true justice (*iustitia*), and so neither law (*ius*), nor utility. Abelard knew the *De civitate Dei* and drew on it, selectively, for his eulogistic account of the behaviour of the ancient philosophers and the excellence of Platonism. But

[1] On Abelard's attitude to the ancient city states and its background, see D. Luscombe, 'City and politics before the coming of the *Politics*: some illustrations', in D. Abulafia, M. Franklin and M. Rubin (eds.), *Church and city 1000–1500. Essays in honour of Christopher Brooke* (Cambridge, 1992), pp. 41–55, at pp. 47–8.

[2] *TChr* 150: 648–151: 679, esp. p. 151: 670–9: 'Cum itaque Socrates uxores quoque publicandas esse instituerit, de communitate quarum nihil omnino tenendum esse uidebatur, profecto nihil penitus reliquit proprium, quod uidelicet ad communitatem non reduceret. Vxores itaque uult communes esse secundum fructum, non secundum usum . . . ut uidelicet tanta sit in omnibus caritas propagata, ut unusquisque omnia quae habet, tam filios quam quaecumque alia, nonnisi ad communem omnium utilitatem possidere appetat.' This interpretation of Plato seems not to have been original to Abelard. In the glosses on the *Timaeus* very probably by Bernard of Chartres, and dating probably from between 1100 and 1115, much the same idea is put forward in similar terms: the common marriages must not be understood 'as a carnal matter' but just with regard to 'affection'; everyone would regard every son and every parent as his own, and thus they would all be joined to one another in common affection. See P. Dutton (ed.), *The 'Glosae super Platonem' of Bernard of Chartres* (Toronto, 1991) (Studies and texts 107), p. 148: 75–92. I am grateful to David Luscombe for having alerted me to the importance of Bernard's *Glosae*; for a more detailed discussion, see my 'The Platonisms of Peter Abelard'.

[3] *De civitate Dei* XIX, 21; II 389: 27–8): 'Populum enim esse definivit coetum multitudinis iuris consensu et utilitatis communione sociatum.'

he is willing to imply very clearly that the city-states outlined by Plato and even Rome, under virtuous rulers, were true republics, in which the people were indeed a community united under law and through common utility. Abelard takes up the three cardinal virtues defined by Cicero and concentrates on an extreme form of each of them.[4] Cicero had said that justice is giving each man his own, provided that the common good is preserved. Abelard emphasizes the common good, taking it in a very strong sense: everything should be dispensed with one end in view – the common safety of the city (152: 694–701). Rather than mere temperance, Abelard concentrates on the abstinence (*abstinentia*) and sexual self-denial (*continentia*) of the ancient philosophers. Even the most exhibitionistic of philosophical ascetics finds his place and his praise: Diogenes in his tub, asking the Emperor Alexander to step out of his light, or discarding his beaker when he realizes that he can drink from his cupped hands (162: 1008–163: 1040). Similarly, Abelard says little about ordinary courage, preferring to talk about the extraordinary virtue of magnanimity. And the community of goods and interest advocated by the philosophers is presented, not as a scheme for the maximal fulfilment of individuals' ends, but in terms of selfless love, as the achievement of Christian charity: loving one's neighbour as oneself and seeking, not one's own desired ends, but those of one's friend (150: 643–7, 152: 699–701, 707–8).

The austere and perfectly communal life advocated by the ancient philosophers is not just a lost ideal for Abelard. The ancient philosophers and their states have (at least in theory) a modern counterpart: monks and their monasteries:

> [The philosophers] set up (in the way commended by the Gospels) a life of sexual self-denial, both for married couples and for the rulers, when they set out a plan for life in cities as if they were convents for married couples, and when they defined how the rulers of those republics should behave, and when they exemplified in themselves the life of sexual self-denial and abstinence which now is followed by clerics and monks. (150: 630–6)

Abelard goes on to emphasize his point, saying that the community of goods and brotherhood of the ancient philosophers' republics prefigured the apostolic way of life of the early Church, now followed in monasteries; or, rather, which should now be followed there – for he goes on to draw a highly unflattering comparison between the truly monastic life lived by the ancients and the laxity of Christian monks in his own time.

[4] For Cicero's definitions (in the *De inventione*), see above, pp. 285–6.

Abelard most probably wrote the *Theologia Christiana* (or at least this part of it) when he was living at the Paraclete, directing his monastic and scholarly community under conditions of perhaps not entirely voluntary austerity. He had begun to think seriously about monasticism and, surrounded by eager students who had abandoned every comfort in order to follow their master, he may have felt himself close to realizing an ideal communal and philosophical way of life. These circumstances help to explain the enthusiasm with which, at this stage, Abelard advocates his ascetic, perfectionist model of social life; and also why, in the middle of his account, he changes direction and, although he has been commending the justice of the philosophers in their role as rulers of cities, he now (following Jerome) praises the same ancient philosophers as men who, sacrificing the comforts of urban life, sought solitude in the wilderness.[5] He refers to Plotinus' distinction of the virtues, as recounted by Macrobius: characteristic of the philosopher are, not the political virtues, but the purificatory ones (*uirtutes purgatoriae*), according to which it is prudent to despise all that is in the world and devote oneself to contemplating the divine, and temperate to give up everything, so far as the body allows (157: 878–90). Where, earlier in the account, Abelard had drawn the parallel between the communal life of the ancient philosophers' cities and that of a monastery, now (160: 949–64) he likens the philosophers' life of solitude to that of anchorites.

Abelard wrote his *Collationes* after he finished the *Theologia Christiana*, probably during the time, then, when he was in charge not of the idealistic students who had flocked to the Paraclete but of the unreformed and rebellious monks of a remote Breton monastery. The Philosopher, who is one of the speakers in this work, represents just the sort of wise pagan, enlightened through natural law, that Abelard had praised in the *Theologia Christiana*. In his description of justice, the Philosopher sets out a model of government explicitly modelled on that which Abelard believed was advocated in Plato's *Republic*. Glossing Cicero's definition in the *De inventione*, 'Justice is the virtue by which each person is given his due, so long as the common utility is preserved', the Philosopher emphasizes the qualifying phrase.[6] He stresses that someone should *not* be given his due if this would lead to the harm of the whole community:

[5] 156: 857 – 157: 877. In *HC* (93: 1053–83; cf. 92: 1038 – 93: 1053) Abelard makes the parallel explicit by using the same passage from Jerome's *Contra Jovinianum* to describe his disciple at the Paraclete. On Abelard's use of Jerome, see C. Mews, 'Un lecteur de Jérome au XIIe siècle: Pierre Abélard' in Y.-M. Duval (ed.), *Jérome entre l'occident et l'orient* (Paris, 1988), pp. 429–44.

[6] For Cicero's definitions of justice and the other virtues, see above, pp. 285–6.

For it often happens that, when we give someone what is his due on account of his merits, what we do for one individual brings common harm. Therefore, in order to prevent the part being put before the whole, the individual before the community, to the definition [of justice] there is added 'provided that the common utility is preserved'. We should do all things so that we each seek not our own, but the common good, and provide for the public welfare rather than that of our families and live not for ourselves but our fatherland. (118: 2068 – 119: 2075)

Abelard's Philosopher follows this statement with the examples from antiquity cited in the *Theologia Christiana*: the community of children in Plato's ideal state, and the patriotic zeal of Aulus Fulvius, who executed his own son when he betrayed his fatherland.

It seems, then, as if Abelard wishes to repeat, with added emphasis, his earlier views about the ideal community. These remarks are not, however, Abelard's, although he wrote them: they are those of a fictional character in a dialogue.[7] The other speaker, the Christian, does not contest them, and most of the Philosopher's discussion of virtues can indeed be shown, from parallel passages in other works, to be an expression of views Abelard himself held. But not everything. Before he begins to classify them, the Philosopher has already been made to give an example of his proneness to error about the virtues, when he argues that no man is good if he lacks any of the virtues and that all good men are equally good, all evil men equally wicked (107: 1765 – 110: 1823). Here the Christian argues firmly and directly against a position which he describes as 'insane' (109: 1795–6), and the Philosopher capitulates.[8] On other occasions, the Philosopher's limitations emerge only after careful comparison between his remarks and those of Abelard himself. Consider the Philosopher's views on clemency. The Philosopher sharply distinguishes mercy (*misericordia*) from clemency (*clementia*). Clemency, he says, is a part of justice, because it consists in bringing help to those who are *unjustly* afflicted; whereas mercy, which is a merely natural feeling of compassion through which we help people simply because they are being afflicted, whether they are guilty or not, is a weakness of the mind rather than a virtue (122: 2156–70). Abelard, in his own person, discusses mercy and clemency in the *Problemata* (700A). There

[7] The following discussion of the Philosopher's fallibility draws on, and modifies, my 'Abelard's ethical theory', pp. 306–9.

[8] For the Christian's arguments, Abelard drew on the very author whose reasoning he makes the Philosopher misuse – Augustine: see his Letter 167 ('De sententia Iacobi Apostoli', ed. A. Goldbacher (Vienna/Leipzig, 1904) (CSEL 44), pp. 586–609) which is quoted extensively in *Sic et non*, q. 137 (467ff.). In *Sc.* (74: 9) Abelard described the view that all sins are equal as *manifesta stulticia*.

too he draws a distinction between mercy, which is seen as a weakness, and the virtue of clemency (even though the word *misericordia* is used for both). But he has a different and broader notion of what clemency involves: not, like the Philosopher, a strict accord with justice, but a tempering of justice, so that the guilty do not receive the full punishment they deserve. Whereas for the Philosopher 'retribution' (*vindicatio*), inflicting due punishment for evils performed, is part of the virtue of justice, Abelard would write in the *Problemata* that 'whoever has justice without mercy (*misericordia*), so that he wishes to exact retribution (*vindicare velit*) and not to make the punishment less severe, is cruel'.[9] Again, the Philosopher's view about tranquillity of mind contradicts some of what Abelard says. The Philosopher argues that

> whatever happens, it is a weakness rather than a virtue to submit the soul to pain – it belongs to wretchedness not happiness, to a disturbed not a tranquil mind. For since God, who ordains all things for the best, may do nothing without a cause, what is there that can happen which should make a just man sad or pained and thus go against God's supremely good ordering of things ... as if he judged that it needed putting right? (122: 2170 – 123: 2176)

The *Sententie* describe such grief as irrational, but they do not condemn it, recognizing in it, rather, the measurelessness of charity.[10] And, even in the *Collationes* themselves, the Christian later on makes it clear that penitence for sins causes pain in the soul, but is necessary if the sinner is to be saved.[11] There is a discrepancy too between Abelard's understanding of charity and the purely civic altruism which the Philosopher makes his ideal – 'the end for which we should act ... is that each of us should seek not what benefits himself (*propria commoda*) but what benefits the whole of society, and that he should live, not for himself, but for everyone' (123: 2189–92) – and commends in the person of Cato 'who considered that he had been born, not for himself, but the whole world'. The *Sententie* and the *Theologia Scholarium* make very clear that we must set up God as the end of all things, and that love of our neighbour must be for the sake of God.[12]

Since these discrepancies are almost all with comments in works written later than the *Collationes*, they might be explained as instances where

[9] Cf. also *Comm.Rom.*167: 463–6: 'ut uidelicet notet non id Deum ex iustitia permittere, quod tamen aliqua permittat dispensatione, aut ex abundantia caritatis potius fieri iubet quam ex aequitate iustitiae'.

[10] §§156–7; Bu. 94:149–95:181; cf. *Sent.Par.*, 25:4–26:4.

[11] 162: 3207–11; cf. *Sent.* §279; Bu. 156: 1–5.

[12] See above, pp. 288–90.

Abelard's thought developed. There is, however, at least one striking difference between what the Philosopher argues and an earlier work. The Philosopher calls on everyone to imitate God 'who, because he needs nothing, does not at all take care of himself but of all things and provides, not what is necessary for himself but for all things' (124: 2204–6). By contrast, in the *Theologia Christiana* (368: 65 – 370: 741) Abelard had argued that God acts for his own glory more than for any other reason, otherwise he would not act for the best possible end.

The most plausible view of Abelard's intentions is that he made the Philosopher neither into a simple mouthpiece for his own views, nor into the representative of a viewpoint clearly distinct from his own. Rather, Abelard is using the Philosopher as a way of exploring the ideas which flow from a certain set of assumptions, some of which he holds himself, some of which he rejects. Each aspect of his views was marked out for further scrutiny. By placing an exaggerated version of the social ideal of *Theologia Christiana* in his mouth, Abelard is not, then, issuing a disclaimer, but he is distancing himself a little from it.

This reading is strengthened by the evidence of the *Sententie* and *Sententie Parisienses*, which record Abelard's teaching in the period soon after he returned to Paris, a little time after writing the *Collationes*.[13] Abelard now considers that Cicero's definition of justice ('giving everybody what is his') can be taken in two ways: 'his' can apply either to the recipient of justice or to the giver of it. When it applies to the recipient, then the qualification 'so long as the common utility is preserved' must be added. To reward or punish someone too greatly, even though it is his due, might damage the republic as a whole. Just as God looks to the common utility in his punishments and rewards, so should civil and ecclesiastical judges. When, however, 'his' applies to the giver of justice, there is no need to add any qualification to the definition. The judge rewards or punishes as befits him (in his office of judge): that is to say, he avoids both cruelty and laxity, neither imposing the full penalty which is deserved nor remitting punishment altogether. In this way, Abelard integrates into his very understanding of justice a view of clemency which would have been foreign to the Philosopher of *Collationes*.

HELOISE AND THE IDEAL OF MODERATION

It was not just his own, developing thought about charity which led Abelard away from his earlier, perfectionist view about the possibilities of human

[13] *Sent.* §§256–8; Bu. 145: 125 – 146: 149. *Sent.Par.* (52: 15–26) gives a much briefer account of the same theory.

society. One of the themes running through all three of Heloise's letters to Abelard in the collected correspondence – both the personal Letters 2 and 4, and Letter 6, where she is making suggestions about the sort of Rule Abelard should write for her and her nuns – is the extreme difficulty, perhaps impossibility, of living a perfect life in a religious community; and the need, therefore – if utter failure is to be avoided – to adopt some more achievable, less than perfect aim. In Letters 2 and 4 she gives a vivid portrait of herself, one which has lived through the centuries, as a nun and abbess unable, as her vocation demands, to put earthly love for Abelard behind her and devote herself entirely to God. She cannot even regret her past pleasures. Outwardly she may be irreproachable, but this is mere hypocrisy when her thoughts are anything but pure.[14] Heloise is not, however, as a modern reader might be inclined to imagine, making a protest against the life of religion she chose in obedience to Abelard's command, or trying to justify her authentic, unconverted self. The letters are a plea for help: for advice, consolation, prayer – and for Abelard not to ask too much of her or think her stronger than she is. Similarly, but less personally, Letter 6 points out the weaknesses of her sex and asks for a Rule which takes them into account. Heloise puts her view most directly in the plea which ends Letter 4:

> Do not, I beg you, exhort me to virtue and encourage me to the fight, saying 'Virtue is perfected in weakness' and 'No one receives the crown who has not properly struggled.' I do not seek the victor's crown. It is enough for me to avoid danger. It is safer to avoid danger, than to engage in war. I shall be satisfied with whatever corner of heaven God places me in.[15]

Such sentiments could hardly be further from those which Abelard himself had expressed in the *Theologia Christiana*, where he portrayed an ideal of life in which human endurance was tested to the limits in the victorious struggle to live a fully ascetic life. Yet now Abelard, Heloise's mentor, was willing to learn from her experience. In the *Rule* for the Paraclete which he wrote at Heloise's request, he echoes her very words, advising (274) that 'it is sufficient for weak people if they avoid sins even if they cannot reach the summit of perfection. It is enough to reside in a corner of paradise, if you are not able to be placed along with the martyrs.' (He also repeats the

[14] *Ep.* 4, 81: 'Quae cum ingemiscere debeam de commissis, suspiro potius de amissis ... Castam me praedicant qui non deprehendunt hypocritam ... Aliquid laudis apud homines habens, nihil apud Deum mereor, qui cordis et renum probator est, et in abscondito videt.'

[15] 82; on this passage in the context of Heloise's thought, see L. Georgianna, 'Any corner of heaven: Heloise's critique of monasticism', *Mediaeval Studies* 49 (1987), 221–53 at pp. 250–2.

point in his *Carmen ad Astralabium*.[16]) Nor is this an isolated comment: the theme raised is central to the *Rule*. Consider carefully, Abelard advises, before binding yourself to the rule of religious life. Only take on the vows you can keep. Better to marry, if you cannot remain a virgin.[17] Better, for those who have chosen their life as nuns, to pursue moderation in food and drink, rather than commit themselves to a degree of abstinence beyond their powers.[18] Abelard, who had earlier turned to the ancient philosophers for examples of extreme self-denial, now quotes with approval Seneca's proposal to live 'according to nature'. It is against nature, Seneca says, to torture one's body, to seek squalor and eat food which is not merely poor but disgusting. Frugality, but not uncouthness, is what should be sought.[19] Eating food and drinking wine, like marriage, are 'intermediate between good and evil, that is, they are considered indifferent'. And so, laying down his Rule for the nuns, 'taking into account both the fortune and the nature of men', he forbids 'nothing in the way of food, except what is superfluous' (278–9). The avoidance of superfluity, rather than the pursuit of asceticism, has become the aim. Although some of Abelard's prescriptions are influenced by the sex of those for whom he is writing, much of what he writes implies a rethinking of his ideas about monasticism in general. No longer is it seen in terms of perfectionism, but those of moderation. The perfect communities – once set up by the ancient philosophers, now to be imitated by monasteries – have been replaced in Abelard's thought by communities which must adjust their ideals in accord with human weakness.

This new-found moderation is found in other aspects of Abelard's social thinking in the 1130s. Abelard retained, it seems to the end of his life, his admiration for much in ancient civilization and behaviour. And he firmly held that many of the ancient philosophers are among the saved. But, in his Letter 7 – the history of female monasticism he wrote, also at Heloise's request, probably at much the same time as the *Rule* – he is willing (without retracting his earlier idealized view of the ancients) to depict ancient society in a more balanced fashion. Instead of focusing firmly, as he had done

[16] 295–6: 'ne maiore petas paradisi sede locari:/sufficit ut quiuis angulus hic tibi sit'.

[17] 275: 'Attendat hoc cum tremore quisquis se jugo alicujus regulae quasi novae legis professioni vult alligare. Eligat quod possit, timeat quod non possit. Nemo legis efficitur reus nisi qui eam fuerit ante professus. Antequam profitearis, delibera. Cum professus fueris, observa.'

[18] 274: 'Huic vero diligentiae sic omnium virtutum mater discretio praesit ut quae quibus imponat onera sollicite videat, unicuique scilicet secundum propriam virtutem et naturam sequens potius quam trahens nequaquam usum saturitatis sed abusum superfluitatis, et sic extirpentur vitia ne laedatur natura.'

[19] Epistola 5; 10: 17 – 11: 2, quoted at 277–8.

before, on the period before the coming of Christ and reproducing his earlier picture of philosophers and rulers who were Christians in all but name, and lived the ascetic lives which monks should live, he now evokes a later period in antiquity, describing its mixture of good with evil, and arguing that the goodness retains its value, even within a far from perfect whole:

who can deny that the power of pagan rulers – even if it is used by them perversely – is a gift from God, or the love of justice and mercifulness which they have, taught by natural law, or the other qualities which befit rulers? Who can deny that they are goods, because they are mixed with evils, especially since, as St Augustine asserts, and reason clearly testifies, there cannot be evils except in natures which are good? Who will not approve the poet's saying, that 'the good hate to sin from love of virtue'? Who will not accept, rather than deny, the miracle which Suetonius recounts, performed by Vespasian before he became Emperor, when he cured a blind man and a lame one, so that rulers will wish to emulate his virtue, or what Gregory is said to have done with regard to the soul of Trajan? Men can discover a pearl amongst the dirt and separate the wheat from the chaff; and God cannot but know his gifts in those who lack the faith, nor can he hate any of those things which he has made. (277)

Abelard's new way of thinking seems to be reflected, too, in his theory of punishment, which he develops fully only in *Scito teipsum* written late in the 1130s (and the oral teaching on which it is based).[20] Judges should not, he argues, try to discern whether the accused person has really sinned – shown contempt for God by knowingly acting against his law. That judgement is for God alone, who can examine our hidden thoughts. Men must judge according to the external deeds and, even where it is obvious that there was no sin, Abelard condones punishment if it serves the good of the community by warning others against practically unwise conduct. So, in his example, the woman who accidentally smothers her baby in her sleep is punished so as to warn other mothers against the dangers of taking their babies into their own beds, even though they may have the laudable intention of keeping them warm. As in Abelard's earlier social theory, the community is put before the individual. But now it is the negative aspects of this position which are emphasized. Such unjust justice is seen as congruent with human limitations and contrasted with God 'who examines guilt with true judgement'.[21]

[20] See *Sc.* 38: 13 – 40: 19; *Reportatio*, f. 107r.

[21] *Sc.* 40: 9–11: 'Deus uero solus qui non tam quae fiunt, quam quo animo fiant adtendit, ueraciter in intentione nostra reatum pensat et uero iudicio culpam examinat.' Luscombe's

In this passage of *Scito teipsum*, Abelard also raises (38: 22 – 40: 5) the example of the judge who knows the accused man brought before him to be innocent but must punish him all the same, because he is unable to discredit the testimony of false witnesses. He had raised the same example in the Commentary on Romans.[22] There, however, the purpose of the illustration is to provide a parallel in human affairs to God's apparent injustice in damning unbaptized infants who have done no wrong. Now, by contrast, Abelard wishes to distinguish sharply between the imperfect justice of humans and perfect divine judgement. In a passage from *De civitate Dei* which may have inspired this whole discussion, Augustine shows the pitiable position of judges, required by the needs of society to give judgement and mete out punishments, yet constrained by necessary human ignorance often to torture or execute the innocent.[23] By the last years of his life Abelard, too, seemed to have reached a view of society not far from the one implicit in these remarks: necessarily imperfect because of human imperfection.

PRACTICAL ETHICS

The dividing line between social thought of Abelard's generalized kind and practical ethics is not rigid or even always very clear. The doctrines in Abelard's *Rule* which have just been discussed in the context of his developing thought about communal life – moderation, avoidance of excess rather than asceticism, aiming at an attainable ideal – can also be taken as providing practical guidance for each individual's behaviour. The *Rule* also illustrates, in its prescriptions, another – connected but distinct – important doctrine in practical ethics. It embraces a relativism, not of moral values or aims, but of ways of life. In order to accommodate the particular needs, strengths and weaknesses of women, Abelard is willing to depart markedly from St Benedict's detailed prescriptions for the monastic way of life, just as he is willing to adjust Jerome's ideal of a scholarly eremitic life in order to fit the exigencies of communal life. Here, however, the credit for original thinking must go, not to Abelard, but Heloise.

Heloise's final letter to Abelard in the collected correspondence (Letter

translation of *uero iudicio* as 'in a true trial' brings out nicely the contrast Abelard is drawing with the correct, but necessarily false, trial carried out by earthly judges.

[22] 172: 622–30; see above, p. 274. In *TSch* (522: 710–22) a similar example is used, but the purpose here is to make a logical, rather than an ethical point – that it is not contradictory to hold both that the judge should punish *x*, and that *x* should not be punished by the judge.

[23] XIX, 6. See esp. p. 365: 20–3; 'non enim haec facit sapiens iudex nocendi voluntate, sed necessitate nesciendi, et tamen, quia cogit humana societas, necessitate etiam iudicandi'.

6) is a remarkable document and, even if her very famous, personal letters (2 and 4) had never survived, it alone would show her to have been an outstanding thinker and writer. As Peter Dronke has pointed out, Heloise uses a gentle mockery to show how Benedict's *Rule*, although followed by both male and female religious, is quite unsuitable for women in many of its prescriptions, taking no account of their physical differences from male monks, their special needs and perils: 'And it is quite clear that, not only did those who wrote monastic rules say nothing at all about women, but they also laid down rules which they knew were completely inappropriate for them' (243).[24] Different rules about manual work, about food and about receiving guests are needed for women. She goes on, without offering any very detailed prescriptions, to advocate an unexhibitionistic, moderate rule of life, based on the moderate austerity of Augustinian canons rather than a Benedictine ideal of asceticism, and more concerned with inner goodness than a show of self-denial. Abelard was willing to learn from Heloise. But whereas he took up her ideas here (and in Letter 4) on moderation, developed them and integrated them into his own thought, he seems to have borrowed her ideas about the relativity of practical ethics passively, not so much absorbing or thinking about them, but using them to guide him in his precepts, somewhat unimaginatively – and, it must be said, impractically, for it seems that the *Rule* was never actually followed![25]

Abelard's main work of practical ethics is his *Carmen ad Astralabium*. To describe this poem as a contribution to moral philosophy, even practical moral philosophy, may seem wishful thinking. In the longer version, which is almost certainly authentic, the *Carmen* is rambling in structure and contains many distichs of Polonius-like, conventional moralizing. Some of these lines may be interpolations, but it would be a very shaky editorial principle indeed which deleted material merely because it seemed unworthy of Abelard. It would also miss Abelard's point. The *Carmen* is supposed to be a didactic work, in the tradition of the *Disticha Catonis*: as such, it provides a series of apophthegms, which the young Astralabius, and other readers, can use to guide their conduct. But to the brief statements of traditional worldly wisdom, Abelard adds more: not only a summary of ideas from Cicero's *De amicitia* – the most extended use of this treatise anywhere in his work[26] – but also an epitome, concise but accurate, of the whole of his

[24] See *Women writers*, pp. 130–4; on Letter 6, see also Bourgain, 'Héloïse', pp. 211–37, esp. p. 235, and M. McLaughlin, 'Peter Abelard and the dignity of women: twelfth century "feminism" in theory and practice' in *Pierre Abélard,* pp. 287–333.

[25] See Bourgain, 'Héloïse', pp. 218–23 and Waddell (ed.), *The Paraclete Statutes*, pp. 31–6.

[26] Lines 115–64, 719–22.

ethical thought. Each of its main themes is treated: selfless love of God (lines 41–52), the difference between vice and sin (lines 77–80), the relationship between prudence, justice, courage and temperance (lines 85–94), the avoidance of unachievably high moral aims (lines 293–6), sin as contempt of God (lines 369–72), penitence (lines 373–84), God's good ordering of all things, which is not inconsistent with a wise man's feeling grief at evils (lines 529–36; lines 845–58), guilt as bad will and merit as requiring deliberate effort (lines 741–6). As this list makes clear, the order in which the topics are treated is arbitrary, and these characteristically Abelardian thoughts are interrupted by long passages of often commonplace observations. This, however, does not detract from the importance of Abelard's decision to include his own ethical system within this didactic poem. For the implication is that he believed that his moral theory could provide a practical guide to living. It could be grasped not merely in its abstract complexity, but as a series of simple, memorable maxims, rather like the biblical and classical *sententiae* which appear so frequently in the *Carmen*.

The *Carmen*, therefore, shows that Abelard thought of himself as a practical moralist as well as an investigator into the theory of ethics. Nor was Abelard deceiving himself. The *Carmen* was among his most popular works in the Middle Ages, and extracts from it are found in florilegia and other writings, although it is true that some of the characteristically Abelardian material is dropped from two of the three recensions in which it circulated.[27] And Abelard's ethical ideas also reached a wide medieval audience interested in practical morality through another, indirect route: by way of the *Ysagoge in Theologiam* and the extremely popular *Moralium dogmata philosophorum*, which it influenced.[28] But it is one thing for ideas to have a practical moral application, another for a thinker to engage in the question of how his theories do in fact connect with particular, real ethical problems. Abelard does not do this in the *Rule* or the *Carmen*. In a series of other works, however, he approaches the same problem from a different direction, examining not so much practical ethics as ethics in practice through his treatment of particular examples of moral life.

ETHICS IN PRACTICE

It was a very common homiletic technique to use an example – a story, perhaps from scripture – in order to explain an idea or give emphasis to

[27] See Rubingh-Bosscher, *Carmen ad Astralabium*, pp. 19–65, on the manuscripts and the three recensions.

[28] See above, p. 286, n. 9.

an injunction. In some of his sermons, however, Abelard goes far beyond this merely illustrative use of examples. The homily is centred on a character and his story and, although scripture and other sources may provide a starting point, there is a depth of psychological insight, allied to ethical enquiry, which is entirely Abelard's own.

There is no better example of these qualities than the very first sermon in the collection as it survives (379–88), which is on the Annunciation. Mary is described in the Gospel as 'a betrothed virgin' (Luke 1: 26): does this mean that she had already consented to the sexual ties of marriage and merely happened still to be a virgin at the time when Gabriel visited her? Abelard emphatically rejects the idea: 'What dignity', he asks, 'is there in being a virgin in the flesh, if her mind had already lost its virginity through consent?' (381C). Mary, Abelard insists, had vowed herself to perpetual virginity. Her parents, compelled by the Old Law, which condemned those who left no progeny, forced her into marriage.[29] But Joseph, whose love of chastity Mary already knew, was willing to enter into a marriage with her based on mutual consent, not to sexual ties but, rather, to chastity (582BC). By marrying Joseph, Mary was able to avoid being compelled to marry someone else, who might have forced her to break her vow of chastity. She still, however, faced the legal curse on those who bore no children.

Against this background, Abelard describes and analyses in minute detail the Annunciation itself. Gabriel finds Mary, not out in public with worldly women, not preparing herself for her wedding, but inside, alone, in prayer, begging God that she and her husband will be able to keep their vow (382D–383A). When the angel greeted her and called her 'blessed among women', according to the gospel Mary was disturbed and asked herself what the greeting can mean. Abelard explains that Mary did not look at Gabriel: her eyes were fixed on her reading, or downcast in prayer; her mind entirely absorbed. She was perturbed both because she had fled from the company of men and because of the intensity of the praying or reading which Gabriel had interrupted. But Gabriel did not merely say, 'Do not be perturbed' but 'Do not fear', meaning – as he would go on to explain – that she would be able both to fulfil her vow and escape the curse which the law laid on those without children (384A–C).

The individual elements in this sermon are not new. Jerome, to whom Abelard refers explicitly, had strongly defended the perpetual virginity of both Mary and Joseph.[30] Augustine had reasoned, as Abelard would, that

[29] 382C: 'Videbat quippe se a parentibus ad nuptias cogi, ex ipsa maxime legis sanctione, quae sub maledicto ponebat omnes qui non relinquerent semen in Israel.'

[30] *De perpetua virginitate S. Mariae adversus Helvidium*, *MPL* 23, esp. 185A–186C.

Mary must have vowed herself to chastity and married Joseph because he would allow her to fulfil the vow.[31] It may have been Abelard who first formulated Mary and Joseph's relationship precisely in terms of consent, but the nature of their marriage was a subject over which other scholars of the time were engaged in debate.[32] Even the Old Law's curse on the childless had already been linked to Mary's state of mind.[33] Where Abelard is completely original is in linking all these considerations into a vivid and coherent plot, which has its climax in the moment of the Annunciation itself, analysed with a psychological complexity which suggests how Mary's moral choice – her inner consent to chastity – is reflected in the tiniest details of her thought and behaviour.

In the sermon on Susanna and the elders (29), Abelard shows a similar sensitivity towards the complexities of thought and feeling which colour moral problems. Susanna is a good woman, falsely accused. She herself is not afraid of death, but she does not endure her mistrial with stoic detachment. Abelard explores her mixture of disgust at physical contact with her accusers, when they place their hands on her head and, despite her indifference to her own fate, her concern for the shame which her family will endure, because she knows that many will believe the false testimony against her.[34]

[31] *De sancta virginitate* IV (ed. J. Zycha (Prague/Vienna/Leipzig, 1900) (CSEL 41), p. 238: 5–8: 'Quod [*sc.* "uirum non cognoui"] profecto non diceret, nisi Deo uirginem se ante uouisset. Sed quia hoc Israhelitarum mores adhuc recusabant, desponsata est uiro iusto, non uiolenter ablaturo, sed potius contra uiolentes custodituro quod illa iam uouerat.'

[32] In his *De beatae Mariae virginitate* (*MPL* 176, 857–76), Hugh of St Victor discusses Mary's marriage at length, in terms of consent. He defends the genuineness of the marriage, despite her vow of chastity by distinguishing two types of marital consent: (1) that by which each partner promises himself to the other as a debtor; (2) that to sexual intercourse. (2) he argues is merely an accompaniment to (1), which is sufficient alone to make a marriage. Hugh must have written the treatise between 1131 and *c.* 1137 (see D. van den Eynde, *Essai sur la succession et la date des écrits de Hugues de Saint-Victor* (Rome, 1960) (Spicilegium Pontificii Athenaei Antoniani 13), pp. 92–5 – that is to say, probably at much the same time as Abelard composed his sermon. It seems unlikely that Abelard knew Hugh's discussion, since he simply takes it for granted that Mary and Joseph's marriage is a proper one, whereas Hugh considers that this is a problem which needs detailed discussion. From Hugh's work, however, it is clear that the whole question of Mary's virginity was being discussed widely in the 1130s. Abelard may have been led to talk about 'consent' (*consensus*) in this context by Augustine's *De nuptiis et concupiscentia* I, ii (*MPL* 44, 420–1); the use of the notion of consent is not the same as that which is found in *Scito teipsum* above, pp. 259–62.

[33] Eadmer, *De excellentia Virginis Mariae*, *MPL* 159, cols. 557–80 at col. 563 A–C.

[34] See especially 560C: 'Flebat utique de praesente, et si diligentius attendimus, non solum corporis contactum, set et famae futurum flebat detrimentum, cum illi scilicet ad testifican-

Better known than the ethical examples of the sermons are those which are developed in each of the six *Planctus*, or songs of lamentation, which Abelard wrote, probably for Heloise in the mid-1130s. Peter Dronke has shown how Abelard rethinks the biblical stories, influenced but not bounded by earlier interpretative traditions.[35] There is also a wider, philosophical purpose which informs the collection. The tradition of *planctus* is an ancient one, which remained strong throughout the Middle Ages. Yet Abelard's choice, not merely to write in this genre, but to write a whole set of *planctus*, and to base them on stories from the Bible, has a special meaning within the context of his thought. Abelard held, in an even stronger sense than Christians in general have always believed, that God has ordained the world in the best possible way. How then should we react to the miseries and disasters of human life? For the Philosopher of the *Collationes*, the only wise course of action is to adopt a stoic impassivity: to be sad, to submit the soul to pain, is tantamount to judging that God's supremely good ordering of things is deficient.[36] Abelard's distancing of himself from this approach, already discussed, goes a stage further with his composition of poems of lamentation.

Yet they are not purely laments. At least in the *Planctus* for Samson and for Jephtha's daughter, the events they commemorate are at once lamentable disasters and, in some sense, victories – most obviously for Samson, when he takes revenge on the Israelites' captors; but for Jephtha's daughter too, when by accepting execution she at once enables her father to fulfil his hasty vow (to sacrifice to God the first person he meets on his return from defeating the Ammonites) and shows an exemplary calm and constancy in the face of death. Abelard talks of Jephtha's daughter elsewhere, in the *Hymnarius Paraclitensis* and in his Letter 7.[37] In both places Jephtha's daughter is presented as an heroic woman, an example of constancy and greatness of mind. She, 'the greatest lover of truth', accepted death, says Abelard, of her own free will, encouraging rather than fearing it.[38] If she was so zealous in fulfilling someone else's (foolish) vow, how firm she would have been in fulfilling her own. Consider, Abelard asks, just how she would

dum prorumperent, quorum testimonio plurimum credi providebat.' On this sermon, see Jaeger, 'Peter Abelard's silence'.

35 See above, p. 80.

36 See 122: 2170 – 123: 2176, quoted above, p. 309.

37 *Hymn.Par.* 125, verse 4; 126, verses 1–2 (259–61); *Ep.* 7, 270.

38 *Ep.* 7, 270: 'Sponte morti se ingerit et eam magis provocat quam veretur. Stultum patris plectitur votum, et paternum redimit mendacium amatrix maxima veritatis'; cf. *Hymn. Par.* 125, verse 4.

have borne up had she been a Christian faced with martyrdom unless she denied Christ – a rhetorical question Abelard also uses in connection with another example of stoic resolution, the pagan Diogenes.[39] In the *Planctus*, the daughter's resolution is also emphasized – indeed, exaggerated: she eagerly accepts death in fulfilment of her father's vow, pointing out to him how it will make her an honour to her sex and begging him not to stand in the way of his own or her glory. In this version (as Peter Dronke has observed) Abelard presents the girl's death in terms of a marriage ceremony – an idea he took from a first-century work called the *Liber antiquitatum biblicarum*.[40] The moment before she hands the sword, by which she will die, to her father, Abelard's heroine pulls off the bridal finery in which she has been decked, saying (lines 137–8): *Que nupture satis sunt/periture nimis sunt*. For Dronke, at this moment 'Abelard's stoic heroine shows her naked anguish.'[41] Yet perhaps *her* stoic serenity remains untroubled. It is hard to be sure of the tone of the remark, but the girl's words and manner until now would suggest one of haughty sarcasm. If so, the comment would bring to its climax a contrast which Abelard has developed throughout the poem, between the calm resolution of the victim on the one hand and, on the other, the horror of her situation, underlined by the mock wedding ceremony, and the folly which lies behind this unnecessary execution of an innocent, openly berated in the final verse. Magnanimous acceptance of what, ultimately, God has ordained for the best, or lamentation which, though irrational, stems from charity: both are in order, and neither is fully adequate to bridge the gap between the perfection of providence and the cruel twists of individuals' destinies.

No crueller twists, Abelard would have said, than those which shaped his own life and made it (even before the final blow of Sens) an *historia calamitatum* – a story not, as some translators would have it, of 'misfortunes', but of 'disasters'. One of the purposes of the autobiographical account to which Abelard gave this name was to make himself into an ethical example. At first, this may seem contrived, a mere excuse for complaint and self-

[39] *Ep*. 7, 270: 'Quid haec, quaeso, in agone martyrum factura esset, si forte ab infidelibus negando Deum apostatare cogeretur'; cf. *Hymn.Par*. 126, verse 2. For Diogenes, see *TChr* 165: 1104–10 (noted in J. Szövérffy, *Peter Abelard's Hymnarius Paraclitensis* II (Brookline, Mass., 1975) (Medieval classics: texts and studies 3), pp. 259–60); in his case Abelard's emphasis is rather on contempt of death than keeping vows.

[40] 'The lament of Jephtha's daughter: themes, traditions, originality' in *Intellecuals and poets*, pp. 345–88: see pp. 345–51 for pseudo-Philo's *Liber antiquitatum biblicarum*, and pp. 378–82 for Abelard's use of this source.

[41] 'The lament', p. 382.

justification: Abelard says that he will console the friend to whom he is writing by showing that, whatever his tribulations, they are minor compared to Abelard's own (63: 1–7). But, at the end of the letter (107: 1564–109: 1609), Abelard adds a further element to this theme which complicates and deepens it. He draws on another common consolatory *topos*: that all which happens takes place by God's will, that whatever happens 'perversely' is fitted by God into his best of all dispositions.[42] The argument gains its special force by the fact that, despite all the disasters which have befallen him, it is Abelard himself who proposes it, and who ends the *Historia* by declaring the necessity of putting God's will before his own and by saying (109: 1602–3), in the words of Proverbs (12: 21): 'The just man is not saddened whatever happens to him.' In this way, Abelard shows in his own life, not just an example of calamity which will put his friend's misfortunes into perspective, but an attitude which his friend (and others) should follow.

Abelard also uses himself and his own life as an ethical example of a far less self-flattering kind. In her second letter to him (*Ep.* 4), Heloise had told of her continuing love for Abelard, which made her outward holiness of life hypocrisy, since she loves him rather than God. In his reply, Abelard counters her view by personalizing God as Christ. He describes a type of love-triangle, involving Heloise, Christ and himself (91–2). Heloise should love not him, Abelard, but Christ; for it is Christ who has suffered for her. Christ has shown to her exactly the selfless love which she professes for Abelard. Christ is her true friend 'who desires herself only, not anything of hers' and who gave his life for her.[43] By contrast, Abelard's own love was mere desire (*concupiscentia*): 'I fulfilled my wretched pleasures in you, and that was all which I loved.'

Here, and elsewhere, Christ – 'seized by wicked men, stripped, beaten, blindfolded and beaten, spat at, crowned with thorns and hung on the cross . . . among thieves to die by so fearful and abominable a death' – is Abelard's central ethical example.[44] There is no hint of triumphalism in Abelard's portrayal of the crucifixion. Christ died with suffering far greater than anyone's – such suffering that, by comparison, those of the martyrs would

[42] *HC* 108: 1592–8. On God's will as a consolatory *topos*, see P. von Moos, *Consolatio* (Munich, 1972) (Münstersche Mittelalter-Schriften 3/1–4), III, pp. 137–51. The reading given here of *HC* would suggest that von Moos is wrong when he argues (I, p. 43) that apart from its opening and conclusion *HC* does not belong to the genre of *consolatio*.

[43] 92: 'Quid in te, inquam, quaerit nisi teipsam? Verus est amicus qui teipsam non tua desiderat. Verus est amicus qui pro te moriturus dicebat: "Maiorem hac dilectionem nemo habet ut animam suam ponat quis pro amicis suis." Amabat te ille veraciter, non ego.'

[44] (*Ep.* 5) 91; a very similar description is found in *Sententie* §172; Bu. 104: 66–8.

seem to be 'as nothing' (*Sent.* §173; Bu. 105: 71–6). The punishments which were inflicted on Christ were far more terrible and unbearable even than death itself (*Serm.* 12, 481B). Christ's divinity did not at all diminish his suffering, but rather increased it. For, as Abelard noted, following St Ambrose, Christ through his supernatural knowledge knew, as no ordinary man could, the pain involved in the separation of soul from body. Whereas the martyrs went to their deaths rejoicing, Christ was filled with fear, because he knew what he faced. His self-sacrifice was all the greater because he persisted, despite this fear, remaining obedient to God's will (*Serm.* 11, 468C–469C; cf. *Serm.* 12, 481B).

The view of Christ's death as an ethical example has often been seen as one of Abelard's most controversial – indeed, heretical – teachings. Not, of course, that any Christian would doubt the value of imitating the behaviour of Jesus. But, in a famous passage in the Commentary on Romans (113: 124 – 118: 269), where he raises the *quaestio* 'what is our redemption through Christ's death', Abelard seems to reject any objective explanation of Christ's work in favour of a purely exemplary one:

> Our redemption is <brought about> by the very great love <instilled> in us through the passion of Christ which not only liberates us from the slavery of sin, but acquires for us the true liberty of sons of God, so that we may fulfil everything not by fear but rather through love of him – he who showed us such beneficence that, as he says, no greater can be found. 'No one has greater love', he said, 'than to lay down his soul for his friends.' (118: 256–62)

Recent scholars have shown that this interpretation of Abelard's thought is a misleading one, although this particular *quaestio* in the Commentary on Romans, taken in isolation, seems to support it.[45] In fact, even this passage, read carefully and taken in the context of Abelard's ideas, does not support a pure exemplarism. Unless the offering up of his life had been objectively necessary, there would have been no sacrifice through which Christ could show his love: his suffering and death would have been pointless. The way in which Christ died, however, allowed him not merely objectively to redeem mankind but to spread, in the best way possible, the example of love. Since for Abelard God always chooses only the course of action which is best, this way of redeeming mankind, which also involved giving the best example of love, was the way God could not but choose, although it would (purely as regards the process of redemption) have been

[45] See especially Weingart, *The logic of divine love* – although this book must be read with caution, since the author's desire to make Abelard's thought conform with what he takes to be orthodoxy sometimes leads him to distort it.

possible for him to redeem man in many other ways.[46] It remains true, however, that Abelard's emphasis falls on Christ's ethical example, and the brute fact of redemptive death falls into the background. And Christ's death also has another exemplary role in Abelard's thought – as an example not merely to follow but to contemplate. For what better example could he have chosen to capture the perplexities of divine providence, its justice in seeming injustice, than the figure of an all-powerful God humbled and tortured for the sake of his sinful creation?

[46] Both these points are made very clearly in the *Sententie* (§§171–2; Bu. 103: 37 – 104: 44): 'Venit ergo Filius Dei non ut hominem de potestate diaboli redimeret – cum nec ipse diabolus pretium aliquod inde reciperet, immo hominem reconciliatum Deo numquam esse uellet – sed ut eum a seruitute peccati dilectionem suam ei infundens redimeret, se ipsum precium et hostiam puram Patri offerendo et persoluendo. Hoc multis denique aliis modis sed nullo tam conuenienti facere potuit.'

Conclusion

Abelard's theological doctrines and his philosophical ethics

The preceding chapters describe the systematic analysis of ethics which Abelard developed within his theology. Specifically Christian doctrines have been mentioned only where necessary to set the context for Abelard's treatment of ethical issues. But is not this attempt to separate a moral philosophy from its wider doctrinal setting misleading? Abelard was a Christian. Did he not accept, on authority, certain teachings which, if not incompatible with any type of philosophical ethics, are certainly inconsistent with Abelard's moral philosophy as it has been represented here? In particular, Abelard's ethics places its emphasis on the individual's free choice to sin or refrain from sinning. But Christian doctrine holds that all men inherit original sin and that, as a result, they cannot live in a way which is meritorious and leads to salvation without the help of entirely unmerited grace from God. Moreover, Abelard saw ethics as universal to mankind. Starting from the view that the Trinity of power, wisdom and love is to a great extent graspable by men through reason and observation, Abelard turns to antique as much as to Christian sources for his understanding of morality and holds not merely that the ancients could lead good lives, but that the Greek philosophers have set a standard of conduct which Christians need to emulate. But these virtuous pagans did not merely lack baptism – the remedy instituted by Christ for original sin: whatever they knew about the Trinity, they could not, by reason alone, acquire the faith in Christ's incarnation and work which is necessary for salvation. Abelard thus seems to be led to the extraordinary position that those who, according to him, have led the best lives are condemned to eternal damnation.

In fact, Abelard had anticipated exactly these questions and, in each case, he proposed an understanding of Christian doctrine which left his ethical theory intact. Abelard did not hesitate to put forward views on original sin, grace and salvation which would fit in with his philosophical ethics and, although he intended them to fit within the limits of doctrinal orthodoxy, some of them were counted by his opponents among his heresies. Whilst a full analysis of these discussions would involve an extended study of Abelard's theology, the main positions can be sketched quite briefly.

With regard to original sin, Abelard insists that the sin which we all inherit should be understood as the *punishment* (*poena*) for sin, rather than the *guilt* (*culpa*) of sin.[1] Properly speaking, sin is guilt – contempt of God, the evil will which makes us guilty before God.[2] Sin in the sense of guilt cannot be passed on from parents to their children, since newborn children, lacking reason and so free will, cannot incur guilt. In this way, Abelard preserves his central notion of sin as something freely chosen by the individual. But he raises a further doctrinal problem for himself. The medieval church, with Augustine's authority, held that babies who died before baptism would be sent hell as a result of original sin. How could God be just in damning them if, as Abelard held, they had *not* inherited the guilt of Adam's sin? 'Would we not regard it among men as the greatest of evils if someone handed over an innocent son on account of his father's sin to transitory earthly flames, not to speak of perpetual ones?' (*Comm.Rom.* 168: 486–8). Abelard answers by claiming that, in principle, whatever God decides is for the best, even if we cannot understand why; but, in any case, it is possible to show how the damnation of unbaptized babies is for the good. Their damnation, Abelard suggests, merely consists in deprivation of the beatific vision; and, he claims, God allows to die unbaptized only those babies who he has foreseen would have been very wicked had they lived and merited severer punishments (*Comm.Rom.* 169: 536 – 170: 554).

Like the idea of original sin, the doctrine of grace poses an apparent threat to an ethics based on the free decisions of individuals by suggesting that we cannot each simply choose to act well. As Abelard himself puts it,[3] although God cannot be blamed for not giving his grace to some, how can those to whom he does not give it be damned because of their guilt (*culpa*),

[1] *Comm.Rom.* 164: 368–72: 'Cum ... dicimus homines cum originali peccato procreari et nasci atque hoc ipsum originale peccatum ex primo parente contrahere, magis hoc ad poenam peccati, cui uidelicet poenae obnoxii tenentur, quam ad culpam animi et contemptum Dei referendum uidetur.' Abelard's fullest exposition of this whole position is at *Comm.Rom.* 164: 354 – 166: 440. See Peppermüller, *Abaelards Auslegung*, pp. 105–6. This position ('Quod non contraximus culpam ex Adam, sed poenam tantum') is in Bernard's list of nineteen heresies (no. 9): see Mews, 'Lists of heresies', p. 109.

[2] See above, pp. 265–7.

[3] *Comm.Rom.* 240: 78 – 242: 363; *Sent.* §278; Bu. 155: 60–81; *Sent.Flor.* 13: 3–25; *Sent.Par.* 59: 26 – 60: 26; Peppermüller, *Abaelards Auslegung*, pp. 53–9. Abelard seems to have been thinking about grace in this general way even early in the 1120s: see *TSum* 103: 491–2: 'pulchre designat gratiam dei omnibus communiter oblatam'.

since without grace they cannot but be damned? If they are not guilty, how can God, who repays people according to what they do, damn them? Some might answer that God offers his grace to the good and the wicked alike, but the wicked are guilty because they do not choose to take it. But, Abelard replies initially – citing the Augustinian view of grace which was generally accepted – even to be able to accept God's gift of grace, grace is needed.[4] How then can there be any guilt in someone who is damned because he does not accept a gift of grace which he lacks the grace to accept? Abelard was fond of using the case of a sick man and his medicine as an analogy. Suppose a doctor brings a sick man medicine that can cure him, but the sick man is too weak to reach out and take the medicine and the doctor does not hand it to him: what blame can be ascribed to the invalid, or what praise to the doctor?

Abelard's answer to this problem is radical. He does not deny that we need grace to act well, but he considers that we do not need fresh grace in order to act well each time we do so. In itself, this position might not seem so different from the view Abelard has rejected. But Abelard makes it clear that what he has in mind is a single gift of grace, offered to all men, which they are free to accept or reject: 'So God every day offers us the kingdom of heaven, and one person inflamed with desire for that kingdom perseveres in good works, whilst another remains lazily in idleness' (*Comm.Rom.* 241: 351–3). Moreover, this gift of grace which inflames us to seek the kingdom of heaven is nothing other than 'that the happiness of heaven to which he invites us, and the way by which we can reach it, is expounded and believed' (*Comm.Rom.* 242: 345–6) – that is to say, it is simply faith. To perform our individual good works we have need of no grace other than that brought by 'the faith by which we believe that we shall be rewarded only for what we do'. In his oral teaching Abelard apparently made completely explicit that this theory depends on accepting man's innate ability to choose unaided to love God and follow him. The *Sententie Parisienses* (60: 18–21), after giving the analogy of the doctor, continue: 'I do not see how I could solve this problem, unless I said that the sick man had something from himself (*aliquid ex se habuit*) which enabled him to get up <and reach the medicine>. And we say that, in the same way, all men have from themselves

[4] An indication of the general acceptance of this view is the fact that among Abelard's heresies listed in the *Capitula Haeresum XIV* is (no. 6) 'Quod Deus non plus faciat ei qui salvatur, antequam cohaereat gratiae, quam ei qui non salvatur'; St Bernard's version of this – (no. 6) 'Quod liberum arbitrium per se sufficiat ad aliquod bonum' – reflects Abelard's theory as he apparently put it, more provocatively, in his oral teaching; cf. Mews, 'Lists of heresies', p. 109.

that which enables them to get up <and accept the grace they are offered>.' And, in the *Sententie* (§278; Bu. 155: 71–4), it is stated, with a reference to the full discussion in the commentary on Romans, that 'unless we say that man from himself through free will from his nature has the ability to love God and cleave to him, we shall not be able to avoid the conclusion that our merits are prearranged through grace (*gratia meritis nostris praeiudicare probetur*)'. Whilst insisting on fallen man's need for grace, and maintaining that it is a free gift from God, in no way owed to man, Abelard's theory completely removes the element of *moral* arbitrariness in the granting of grace: indeed, grace has been transformed into faith – freely made available to all – in the absence of arbitrariness in God's moral dealings with us.

The problem of the salvation of good pagans who lived before Christ had two aspects for Abelard. One was easy to resolve. The mere fact that those who lived before Christ were not baptized might seem to make salvation for them impossible, since they had no way of removing the stain of Original Sin. Abelard was by no means unusual in his time in rejecting this position.[5] Anselm of Laon and William of Champeaux, systematizing and adapting patristic teaching, argued that, just as baptism is the remedy for Original Sin under the New Law, so the Old Law has its remedy – circumcision (though enjoined only on Jewish males), and so did natural law – gifts and sacrifices. Although when they thought of good men living under natural law, they had in mind especially the patriarchs of the early chapters of Genesis, William of Champeaux was willing to envisage Job as a good man, uncircumcised but saved by natural law, although he lived after the time when the Jews had been given the Old Law. Abelard merely had to extend this way of thinking to the world of ancient Greece and Rome. The Philosopher of *Collationes* goes even further, describing circumcision and baptism as stipulations of 'positive justice', thus relegating them to the level of merely local requirements; but here he probably does not speak for Abelard himself.[6]

A far more serious obstacle to the salvation of pagans, from Abelard's point of view, is their lack of faith.[7] It was a central (perhaps *the* central) feature of Abelard's theology to insist that not merely the existence of God, but also his nature as a trinity of power, wisdom and love, is and has been

[5] See Marenbon, 'Abelard's concept of natural law', pp. 610–11 and cf. above, pp. 268–9.

[6] 121: 2234–40; cf. Marenbon, 'Abelard's concept of natural law', pp. 617–18. For Abelard's views on circumcision and baptism, see esp. *Serm.* 3 and *Comm.Rom.* 126: 142 – 143: 674; cf. Peppermüller, *Abaelards Auslegung*, pp. 105–113.

[7] See Peppermüller, *Abaelards Auslegung*, pp. 67–74 and Marenbon, 'Abelard's concept of natural law', pp. 611–12, 620.

knowable to all through reason and through the testimony of the created universe. Yet, far though it goes, this naturally available knowledge of God has a limit. Abelard did not believe that we can know about the incarnation except through revelation, and he distinguished this knowledge sharply from the knowledge of Christ's divinity, which reason naturally teaches. But it is in the 'mystery of the incarnation that the whole sum of human salvation resides; without belief in it all other belief is in vain'.[8] There is, however, no doubt that Abelard did believe that many good pagans, who lived before the coming of Christ, were saved. Abelard makes many explicit statements to this effect. To give just two examples: he writes in the *Theologia Christiana* (141: 285–7) that 'there seems . . . to be no reason forcing us to doubt the salvation of those Gentiles who lived before the coming of the Redeemer and had no written law to instruct them'; and in the *Theologia Scholarium* (359: 1158–61), 'Should anyone despair of the salvation of all the philosophers . . . let him hear St Jerome', and there follows a passage of Jerome's commentary on St Matthew's Gospel which is taken by Abelard to support the salvation of some of the ancient philosophers (the fact that this passage is a new addition in the *Theologia Scholarium* shows that Abelard maintained, and even wished to strengthen, his view about the salvation of good pagans).

Abelard had available to him an easy explanation of how ancient philosophers could be said to have the faith necessary for their salvation. William of Champeaux had clearly enunciated a doctrine of what later theologians would call implicit faith:

> those who were saved before the coming of Christ believed that there was a just and pious judge who would repay good with good and evil with evil. There were also some who believed that someone would come for God who would redeem the people; but they did not know how. And there were also a very few to whom the way in which the redemption would take place was known.[9]

This type of view was common among the theologians of the 1130s and 1140s. As one of them remarked: 'It may have been that both before and after the time of Abraham the incarnation was revealed to certain good

[8] *TSum* 201: 1343–51: 'Quod et nos quidem concedimus sequentes apostolum qui ait: *Quod notum est dei manifestum est illis*, ac si diceret: quod ad diunitatem pertinet, ratione perceperunt, quia hec de deo naturaliter ratio unumquemque edocet. Vnde et superius cum platonicorum sententias de uerbo dei Augustinus presentaret, solum quod ad diunitatem pertinet uerbi se in eis repperisse confirmauit at nichil de incarnationis misterio, in quo totam humane salutis summam consistere certum est, sine quo frustra cetera creduntur' = *TChr* 345: 2539–48 = *TSch* 497: 2671–9.

[9] *Lottin* §261: 38–42.

men. But all good men had faith in Christ, even if for some it was closed in mystery.'[10] Abelard, however, rejected this idea that salvation might be possible without explicit faith in Christ. He talks very clearly of the necessity of faith in the incarnation for salvation (as above). No hint of a notion of implicit faith appears in his writing, and in the *Theologia Christiana* he sharply criticizes a master for holding that 'many of those who lived before God's incarnation have been saved and redeemed by his passion when they never believed in his incarnation or his passion'.[11]

Abelard must, then, show how good pagans who lived before Christ could have had *explicit* faith. He does so in two complementary ways. First, he places great emphasis on the fact that the incarnation was prophesied, not just by the prophets of the Old Testament (who were commonly acknowledged to have had explicit faith in Christ) but also in ancient Greece and Rome, by the Sibyl, by poets and philosophers.[12] These prophecies are the result of supernatural revelation, not the discoveries of reason – indeed, in some cases those who give the prophecies do not themselves understand them. But no one can say, in the light of them, that faith in the incarnation was not available for the ancients to follow, if they chose. In the *Theologia Christiana* (140: 257–65) Abelard goes so far as to interpret a passage in Plato's description in the *Timaeus* of how the World Soul is formed as an allegory of Christ's passion. In the *Theologia Scholarium* (361: 1211–15) he argues more generally against those who consider that the ancient philosophers must be damned because they lacked faith in Christ who was to come: 'how can they show that they did not believe in him – he who, they might see, had been prophesied even by a Gentile woman, the Sibyl, much more explicitly than through all the prophets of the Old Testament?' Second, Abelard anticipates the idea which would be popular in the fourteenth century that God does not deny grace to those who live as well as they can by natural law.[13] As he puts it, most clearly, in the *Problemata Heloissae*:

[10] *Principium et causa omnium*, p. 80; cf. pp. 79–80 and *Sententiae Atrebatenses*, p. 417: 19–36.

[11] *TChr* 302: 1139–42; cf. *TSch* 440: 1003–5.

[12] See *TSum* 107: 592 – 110: 668; *TChr* 124: 1644 – 129: 1765; 140: 250–65; *TSch* 397: 2235 – 401: 2351; cf. *TSum* 110: 671–5: 'Cum itaque dominus et per prophetas iudeis et per prestantes philosophos seu uates gentibus catholice fidei tenorem annunciauerit, inexcusabiles redduntur tam iudei quam gentes si, cum hos in ceteris doctores habeant, in salutem anime, cuius fundamentum est fides, ipsos non audiant' = *TChr* 130: 1843–8; *TSch* 405: 2455–9.

[13] Cf. A. Landgraf, *Dogmengeschichte der frühen Scholastik* I (Regensburg, 1952), p. 251 and Peppermüller, *Abaelards Auslegung*, p. 72: Abelard does not actually use the wording which became standard – *facientibus quod in se est Deus non denegat gratiam.*

It accords with both piety and reason for us to consider that whoever, recognizing from natural law God as the creator and repayer of all things, cling to him with such zeal that they strive never to offend him through consent (which is properly sin), will in no way be damned, and that those things which it is necessary for them to learn for their salvation will be revealed to them before they die by God, either through inward inspiration or through someone sent to them to instruct them, as we read in the case of Cornelius's baptism and faith in Christ.[14]

This view does not, as it might seem at first, go against Abelard's emphasis on Christ's work as setting an example of love which man needs in order to be able love God sufficiently and follow him closely enough to deserve salvation.[15] Man's natural knowledge of God (which does not include faith in the incarnation) is enough to make him follow God and lead a good life, though he will still not love God sufficiently to merit salvation: the faith which is revealed to him, inwardly or by a prophet, as a reward for this good life according to natural reason, increases his love for God and obedience to him to the degree where he can be saved.

Abelard, then, removes the various obstacles which Christian doctrine might seem to put in the way of his ethical theory by interpreting Christian doctrine so that it no longer provides these obstacles. It is important to stress the limits of this claim. The claim is *not* that, as a theologian, Abelard is consistent in proposing a new, rationally appealing and very probably heterodox set of views about some of the central dogmas of Christianity: original sin, Christ's work and grace. In a hundred years of careful and dispassionate investigation of Abelard's theology, it has become clear that to describe him – whether in praise or blame – as straightforwardly and unreservedly innovative and unorthodox in these areas is a misleading over-simplification. Alongside the characteristically Abelardian doctrines there appear, though usually with less prominence, passages which propose or imply the traditional ideas which they replace. For instance, talking of babies who are damned because they die unbaptized, Abelard explains that it is no wonder that they should be punished whilst their parents are pardoned since the sin is transferred to them through the wicked carnal desire in their conception;[16] and he seems to consider that it was only after Christ descended to Hell that good pagans were freed and allowed to enter heaven.[17] Most strikingly, a large dossier can be assembled of references to

[14] *Problemata* 696A; see also *Comm.Rom.* 200: 446–50.

[15] Peppermüller, *Abaelards Auslegung*, p. 68.

[16] *Comm.Rom.* 173: 664–6, cited by Peppermüller, *Abaelards Auslegung*, p. 117.

[17] *Comm.Rom.* 250: 72–7; cf. 130: 251–4 and the other references assembled by Peppermüller, *Abaelards Auslegung*, p. 112, n. 611.

Christ's passion, not merely as providing the supreme and necessary example of love, but as objectively redeeming mankind.[18] From the point of view of Abelard's theology, these inconsistencies are evidence either of a strange carelessness or hesitancy, or perhaps of an anxiety to qualify a line of thinking which might be judged heretical – even a vain attempt by Abelard to safeguard himself against the consequences of his doctrinal radicalism. From the point of view of Abelard's ethics, however, they are of little relevance, because they do not imply any positions incompatible with his moral theory. What would make Abelard's ethical theories untenable would be an admission that God allows *moral* arbitrariness: that a man can except through his own free choice be morally blameworthy. Abelard's theology is entirely consistent in excluding this possibility.

[18] See above, p. 323, n. 46 and cf. Peppermüller's judicious summary (*Abaelards Auslegung*, pp. 118–21).

General conclusion

In the Introduction, it was promised that this book would offer, not merely a survey of Abelard's philosophy, but a re-evaluation of it. It is time now to look back over this new picture and ask how it differs from the old one.

Although Part 1 is mainly devoted to clarifying the individual details of Abelard's life and *oeuvre*, some important general ideas for the understanding of his thought emerge there. His work can be grouped into two roughly chronological phases, divided at the year 1120 or thereabouts. In the first phase, which therefore stretches from Abelard's earliest teaching until about 1120, shortly after his entry into St Denis, Abelard's interest was predominantly in logic and in the philosophical problems raised by the ancient logical texts. In the second phase, which stretches from when he began to compose the first version of his *Theologia* up to the end of his working life, his main interest was in an ethically based theology. The distinction is not, it must be stressed, clear-cut. Abelard's theological interests stretch back to 1113 or earlier, whilst he continued to teach logic as late as 1136. He produced important logical work in the mid-1120s and the *Theologia Christiana*, written *c.* 1126 to 1127, contains both some of his most developed thinking about the philosophical subjects connected with his logical work, and an early exposition of his ethical ideas. Yet the change in emphasis is hard to deny. After the *Theologia Christiana*, Abelard went on to clarify and extend his ethical theory in the *Collationes*; and when he revised his *Theologia* to make the *Theologia Scholarium*, he eliminated much of the logical and ontological material so as to concentrate on his presentation of the Trinity as power, wisdom and love – the basis of his ethics. All the surviving evidence suggests that, during the extraordinarily productive period from *c.* 1133 to 1139, Abelard's concern was almost entirely with developing the different aspects of his ethics and closely related theology.

Such a view of how Abelard's thought developed depends in part on questions of attribution and chronology. Following, though to some extent modifying, the work of Mews, it is argued that the *Dialectica* must be dated quite early in Abelard's career, and that the *Sententie* collections provide fairly accurate accounts of Abelard's teaching in the early and mid-1130s. If, as earlier scholars have held, Abelard wrote or substantially revised the *Dialectica* in the 1130s or later, then a rather different pattern of development in his interests would be implied; whilst the *Sententie* provide some of the best material for showing how Abelard elaborated his ethically based theological system. An even more controversial question of authorship concerns the famous correspondence between Abelard and Heloise. Here, on the basis especially of the work of Bautier, Dronke and Luscombe, the case is made strongly for regarding the correspondence as authentic. This has an important bearing on understanding how Abelard's thought about morality took shape, since it is suggested that Heloise influenced Abelard's ideas about love of God and about moderation in practical ethics.

Part 2 shows how, as a logician, Abelard was led into areas of philosophy such as ontology, semantics and epistemology by the ancient logical texts and commentaries themselves. He attempts nothing less than a rethinking, in accord with his fundamental presumption that there are no universal things, of the ontology inherited from Aristotle's *Categories* and Porphyry's *Isagoge*, according to which the fundamental building-blocks of reality are substances belonging to natural kinds and structured according to necessary patterns.

Abelard is remarkably successful in adapting the scheme of genera, species and *differentiae* to a world of particulars. He accepts, at first, the extraordinarily crowded ontology which results – a world crammed with particular accidents in every category. But then, gradually, he rethinks his ontological commitments and eliminates altogether real accidents in most categories (without, however, providing a completely satisfactory alternative interpretation). His account of cognition, too, is one which develops: Abelard uses the Aristotelian material he knew through Boethius with increasing sophistication and independence. Abelard's changing theory of cognition provides a basis for his sophisticated analysis of the semantics of universal words. He shows how it makes sense to say that a universal word signifies, without there being a universal thing which it signifies. And he draws a subtle distinction between what universal words would mean, if we had a perfect and complete view of the nature of things, and what they do mean, given that the original impositor of words for natural kinds intended to name them according to their real nature and properties, although he may not fully have grasped or distinguished this nature or these properties.

Yet Abelard by no means resolves all the problems which he is set by the assumptions from which he begins. He provides two unreconciled accounts of how a particular substance, its *differentiae* and its attached accidents should be analysed: one envisages it as a bundle, the other insists on the primacy of substance. He explores this problem further through his innovative distinctions between difference by essence, number, definition and property. Here, although Abelard certainly avoids a naive confusion between language and reality, he shows a tendency – probably linked to the use of the distinctions for considering the Trinity – to think of the same thing variously described as if it were in some sense a number of different things. His treatment of the ontological problem raised by universal words is less sustained than his analysis of their semantics. With his idea of *status* – that men, for instance, 'come together' in that they are men or in the *status* of man – Abelard takes the first step towards an explanation which might reconcile his nominalism with his view about natural kinds, since he also claims that *status* are not things. But he seems to think of shared *status* in terms of identical structures of *differentiae*: every man has his particular rationality, his particular mortality and so on. And, when Abelard asks himself by virtue of what my rationality and your rationality are both rationalities, he does not, as he might have done, advocate some type of resemblance nominalism, but eventually allows himself to talk of a rationality which is essential to a man, as opposed to the particular rationality by which he is in fact rational, which is accidental to him. This seems to concede the existence of real universal properties in some sense, although Abelard also insists that the essential rationality is numerically identical to the particular, accidental rationality, differing from it only 'by definition'. When Abelard considers the meaning, not of individual words, but of statements, he provides strong arguments to show that what is said by a statement, its *dictum*, cannot be a thought nor can it be identified with the things about which the statement is being made. But when he describes *dicta*, like *status*, as non-things, it is hard to see how (without a sophisticated semantics of possible worlds, which Abelard does not employ) the requisite further explanation to show what is meant by this claim is possible. *Dicta*, Abelard insists, remain true or false irrespective of whether any of the things or thoughts associated with them continue to exist. In terms of what, then, could Abelard explain the meaning of his statements about *dicta*?

None of these comments is intended to belittle Abelard as a logician. On the contrary, they show that in addition to his achievements in the more technical areas of logic (such as his theory of entailment, and his analysis of impersonal statements), Abelard ventured much further into epistemology and what would later be called metaphysics than has usually been acknowledged. It is true, too, that given the nature of Abelard's fundamental ontological assumptions, some degree of failure in putting them together was probably inevitable, unless he had been able to elaborate a complex theory of God's knowing and willing (in the manner of late thirteenth and fourteenth-century theologians). But this remark itself points to the limitations of the Abelard's philosophical enterprise in the first phase of his work. As a commentator – despite the freedom with which he exercised this function – Abelard had to take many of the starting points for his thought from the texts he commented, whether or not they fitted with his own presumptions. Moreover, although Abelard was able to digress in order to explore particular problems, the form of commentary (which he followed in effect even in his independent textbook, the *Dialectica*) did not encourage him to bring his ideas together in a way which would allow him best to notice and resolve contradictions and discrepancies.

Part 3 offers an analysis of the ethical theory which Abelard developed in the second phase of his work. Abelard, it argues, approaches ethics on three levels: in terms of God and his providential ordering of the universe, of human ethical acts in general and of practical ethics.

For Abelard, to regard God as a Trinity is to recognize his power, his wisdom and his love. By considering these three attributes Abelard presents his God's eye view of ethics. He adopts what he recognizes as a highly controversial view of divine power: that God cannot do other than he does, because as supremely good, wise and powerful, he cannot but choose the best course for providence. At the root of this view is the presumption that there exists some common measure of God's goodness and that of his creation. Abelard treats God's wisdom mainly by considering the well-known problem of reconciling divine prescience and human free will. He had already examined this problem in his logical writings and now he repeated and elaborated his earlier solutions. In his discussion of God's goodness, however, Abelard breaks new ground with a careful analysis of how the word 'good' is used and of the difference between the goodness of things, intentions and *dicta*. His analysis allows him to hold, unlike almost all his contemporaries, that there do indeed exist evil things, and yet at the same time to maintain that God is wholly good and omnipotent.

Abelard's theory of the ethical act is based on the simple idea that we act well in so far as we act out of love for God, and badly in so far as we put anything before our love for God. Around this notion, Abelard brings in elements from both the Christian (especially Augustinian) tradition and from the moralists of pagan antiquity. He considers that all people in all periods have had knowledge of divine commands and prohibitions through natural law, and that through their intellectual power of conscience they can recognize when a given act is divinely commanded or prohibited. The act itself is not, however, of ethical importance, but only the love for God which is manifest in obedience, or the contempt in disobedience, of his commands and prohibitions. Such a view will tend to make almost any sort of ignorance a reason for excuse from blame, and a modern reader will be struck by Abelard's failure to consider the variety of sincere beliefs different people from different cultures might have about what God commands, even if it is granted that everyone shares in knowledge of the natural law. None the less, Abelard does explore the problem of sins committed in ignorance carefully and arrives at a finely nuanced position, though one which fits rather uncomfortably with the traditional vocabulary of venial and mortal sins which he uses.

As has long been recognized, Abelard devotes great energy to analysing the relation between willing and acting in relation to sin. He separates himself from his contemporaries by his insistence that people can sin only by willing (or, as he later says, 'consenting') to act sinfully. Although (external) acts themselves are, he claims, morally indifferent, it is only through the volition or consent to act – which may turn out to be thwarted – that someone sins. Thinking about a possible sinful act with pleasure and longing is not, he considers, itself sinful; indeed, the greater temptation such thoughts provide to disobey God's will, as manifested in his laws, the greater merit a person gains by resisting them, if he does so successfully. In refining this view, Abelard provides a penetrating, if not fully worked out, analysis of the different senses of 'will' which takes into account the idea that when we will to act, we will to act under a certain description. Whereas Abelard's treatment of sinning concentrates on the particular sinful act, he examines acting well mainly through dispositions to act well, which he identifies with the classical virtues of justice, courage and temperance. Abelard adapts this scheme to his own purposes and ends by making it clear that the disposition of charity – loving God in the right way – is another way of describing the virtue of justice, when supported by courage and temperance. Christian and classical moral schemes are seen to coincide, although Christianity tempers the rigour of the ancients' approach.

Abelard's discussions of practical ethics show him intensely aware of the difficult contrast between the moral dilemmas faced by men and a God's eye view of events, according to which whatever happens is not only good, but part of the best possible providence. In his earliest ethical writings, he is unstinted in his admiration for the ascetic perfectionism he attributes to the ancient philosophers. Although he never recants this praise, as he develops his moral theory Abelard comes to advocate a doctrine of moderation in practical ethics. Moreover, moral judgement, in the proper sense, is left to God who, Abelard believes, alone knows man's inward intentions. Abelard asks earthly judges to restrict themselves to considering external acts, even though this means that they will often condemn people who have not sinned. Abelard's practical ethics also extends to the study of ethics in practice – that is, to examples of individual moral problems. Drawing usually on the Bible (though he also makes his own life a moral example), Abelard uses his imagination to evoke complex ethical situations, which bear out his theoretical analyses, but without minimizing the human suffering which takes place even in a universe ordered according to God's best providence.

Abelard worked out his ethics in the course of expounding a theological system. Yet he treated Christian doctrine with remarkable flexibility, adapting traditional teaching on areas such as original sin, grace and the salvation of pagans so as to accord with his own ethical ideas. He strove, however, to be orthodox as a theologian, and he is happy at times to espouse doctrines which he might in consistency have been expected to reject, so long as they do not undermine his ethical theory.

As will be evident from this summary, the second phase of Abelard's work marks in many respect a fresh start. Certainly, Abelard uses some concepts and arguments in it which he formulated in the first phase of his work (for instance, *dicta* and the logical analysis of statements about divine prescience), but his ethical theory is developed in considerable independence from the ontology and epistemology associated with the logical works. Whether this is to some extent the result of a consciousness of the unresolved problems in his ontology, it is hard to say. At all events, although Abelard looks back to the creation when he discusses the relation of substance to forms, his ontology otherwise excludes God. Abelard appears to have abandoned, without putting anything else into their place, the broadly Neoplatonic positions held, not only by Augustine and Boethius, but also by thinkers near his time such as Anselm, which see in God a constant source of all being. It is not surprising, then, that whilst concepts and arguments from his ontology reappear incidentally, the philosophy which runs through and shapes Abelard's theology rests, not on a view of what or how God is, but on how he acts, ethically, towards his creation.

How, then, does this picture of Abelard's thought differ from the accepted one? As the appendix illustrates in detail, Abelard has long been regarded primarily as a critical, rather than a constructive thinker, powerful and innovative as a logician, but otherwise, though often brilliant, lacking in profundity and not philosophically an inventor. In line with this view, Abelard's work as a theologian is usually said to be characterized by the application of logic (or 'dialectic') to Christian doctrine. By contrast, the preceding pages have presented Abelard as not only a critical but also a constructive thinker, profound at times in his understanding of moral problems (especially when he turns to individual examples) and highly inventive – though sometimes careless, technically ill equipped, naive or confused – as a philosopher in the fields of ontology, epistemology and ethics. By contrast too, Abelard's theology is not seen here as *characterized* by the use it makes of logic. Abelard did, indeed, make abundant use of logic as a theologian, but in doing so he differed from many of his contemporaries only by his greater acuteness as a logician. What characterizes his theology, it has been argued, is rather that it is dominated by a single-minded effort to construct a coherent ethical scheme.

The picture of Abelard offered here is, therefore, a new one. But, in scholarship, 'new' is a relative term, and much of what has been argued in the preceding pages should be seen as a development of the work and ideas of many who have studied Abelard over the past decades and centuries. It is fitting to conclude this conclusion by noting two particular ways in which this is so.

In the nineteenth century, especially, Abelard came to be seen by many as a 'rationalist', an iconoclastic thinker who developed his ideas with scant regard for religious orthodoxy. More recent scholars have dealt severely with this view, pointing rightly to Abelard's wish to avoid heresy and to the many themes and positions which he takes from the Church Fathers or shares with his contemporaries. Yet, if the argument of this book is not entirely misdirected, there remains an important core of truth in the image of Abelard the rationalist, if his rationalism can be seen, not as a critical effort directed at Christian doctrine from the outside, but rather as an audacious attempt to rethink many traditional positions in the light of what Abelard himself would have regarded as at once a rationally coherent and profoundly Christian moral theory.

Over the past forty years, some of the most interesting interpretative study on Abelard has followed two main directions. Some scholars (such as Jolivet, de Rijk, Tweedale, Jacobi, Knuuttila, de Libera and Martin) have used their expertise to show the complexity and sophistication of Abelard's work in logic and semantics. Others (such as Gregory, von Moos, Engels, Zerbi, Dronke and Luscombe) have looked at Abelard more broadly in the context of the twelfth-century culture, showing his individuality in his reading and use of the classics and his range and subtlety as a writer. The picture of Abelard offered here builds on the work of both groups of scholars. But, by rejecting the view of Abelard as a critical thinker, characterized by his application of logic to theology, and seeing him as a constructive philosopher, both in ontology and epistemology, and more boldly and successfully in ethics, this book provides a new framework in which the insights of both approaches can be combined and developed; turning two, rather disparate profiles – Abelard the logician and Abelard the humanist – into a fuller (though still of course, partial) portrait of Abelard the Philosopher.

Appendix

Abelard as a 'critical thinker'

How did the common view of Abelard as a critical rather than a constructive thinker emerge?[1]

The first place to look is at the manuscripts (surviving or known from references in catalogues and elsewhere) of his works. Thanks to the *Checklist*, it is possible to find out at a glance which works by or about Abelard were widely copied in the Middle Ages, and which were almost unknown. The result is instructive. Abelard was most famous in his time as a logician and, at every period of his life, he devoted a great part of his energies to this subject. Yet between them, just two manuscripts (Milan, Ambrosiana, M 63 sup.; Paris, BN, lat. 14614: both from the twelfth century) contain the only copies of the greater part of Abelard's logical work; six further manuscripts (all from the twelfth or early thirteenth centuries) complete the total of those which contain logical works by, or possibly by, Abelard.[2] None of his logical writings survives in more than two medieval copies. The *Collationes* contains some of Abelard's most wide-ranging discussion about good and evil and about religious faith. It is preserved in just three medieval manuscripts, one of them a large fourteenth-century collection of Abelard's work (Oxford, Balliol College, 296). The commentary on St Paul's Letter to the Romans, which includes Abelard's most detailed discussions of topics such as grace, redemption and love, also survives in only three manuscripts, one of which is the Balliol manuscript. Even the most widely

[1] For (rather different) accounts of the history of Abelardian scholarship from that given here, see M. Fumagalli Beonio-Brocchieri, *Introduzione a Abelardo* (2nd edn, Rome/Bari, 1988), pp. 103–16, and J. Jolivet, 'Abélard entre chien et loup', *Cahiers de civilisation médiévale* 20 (1971), pp. 307–22, esp. 307–8 (reprinted in *Aspects*, pp. 169–84).

[2] See above, pp. 36–53. This figure includes Munich, clm 14779 (not in *Checklist*); it excludes manuscripts which contain works which mention here and there opinions of Abelard on logical questions (see below, pp. 51–2) – although even these would add only another handful of manuscripts to the total.

copied of Abelard's major works, the *Theologia Scholarium*, survives in no more than eleven medieval manuscripts. Far more widely copied is the brief and inaccurate presentation of Abelard's views, which he himself thoroughly repudiated: the list of nineteen heresies appended to some copies of St Bernard's Letter 190, extant in thirty-seven manuscripts.[3] But the letter itself, a rhetorically accomplished denunciation to the Pope of what Bernard took to be Abelard's teachings, was much more popular still, throughout the Middle Ages, and survives in 117 manuscripts from the twelfth to the fifteenth centuries.[4]

The conclusion to be drawn is not, of course, that Abelard's logical or theological teaching lacked an audience. There is excellent evidence of Abelard's fame and influence as a teacher.[5] But it is clear from these figures that, once the generation of those who had known or been taught by him personally had died out, Abelard's reputation in the Middle Ages was not based to any great extent on his logical or theological works; and that the thirteenth, fourteenth or fifteenth century was most likely to come across Abelard's name as the object of vituperation by a highly respected (and canonized) author. The chronicles by and large bear out this view. In the late Middle Ages there does seem to have been a very limited revival of interest in Abelard's thought (especially on ethics), witnessed by the compilation of Oxford, Balliol College, 296 in the mid-fourteenth century, two fifteenth-century manuscripts of the *Scito teipsum* and two of the *Theologia Scholarium*. But Abelard's few, though weighty, supporters in the later Middle Ages were largely ignorant of his theology and philosophy. They had been drawn to Abelard by a different route. Abelard's correspondence with Heloise began to circulate from the middle of the thirteenth century onwards. Jean de Meun translated it into French[6] and mentioned Heloise in his very widely read *Roman de la Rose*. Some of the ten surviving medieval manuscripts of these letters contain all or part of the collection alone or with non-Abelardian material. But the contents of others show that an interest in the story of Abelard and Heloise often went along with a wider interest in Abelard as a controversial figure: two include letters by St

3 See above, pp. 28–9.

4 See Leclercq, 'Formes successives de la lettre-traité de Saint Bernard contre Abélard', *RB* 78 (1969), 87–105 and Leclerq and Rochais, *Sancti Bernardi opera* VIII, pp. xi: 31 (s. xii), 34 (s. xiii), 17 (s. xiv) and 35 (s. xv).

5 See Luscombe, *The school*, pp. 1–9.

6 This translation has now been newly edited by E. Hicks, *La vie et les epistres Pierres Abaelart et Heloys sa fame* I (Geneva, 1991); and cf. *Checklist*, p. 245, for details of other partial or unpublished editions).

Bernard against Abelard, two include pieces which view the dispute from Abelard's side: the satirical *Apologia* written by his disciple, Berengar of Poitiers 'against St Bernard . . . and those who have condemned Peter Abelard' and Abelard's own response to Bernard's accusations, the *Confessio fidei 'Universis'*. A manuscript of this second type (Paris, BN, lat. 2923) was owned and annotated by Petrarch. Not only do his marginal comments show him sympathetic to both Abelard and Heloise as lovers.[7] Petrarch was also willing to take Abelard's side against St Bernard: there is no doubt, Petrarch wrote, that today Bernard is a saint; but perhaps when he wrote to the Pope against Abelard he was not yet one![8] Other humanists – including Coluccio Salutati, Pico della Mirandola, Gautier Col and perhaps Boccaccio – were also interested by Abelard.[9] And, in the late sixteenth century, Papire Masson gave a full and sympathetic account of Abelard's life, in which he told of a reconciliation with St Bernard and quoted from Peter the Venerable's eulogistic letter to Heloise about her husband's last days and death.[10]

François d'Amboise who, with the help of the young scholar André Duchesne, produced the first edition of Abelard's works in 1616,[11] was in most respects a typical representative of this humanist interest. He came to Abelard through the correspondence; delighted by it, he set out to find other writings of his.[12] D'Amboise's admiration for Abelard, and his conviction that he could not justly be regarded as a heretic, are evident throughout

[7] Printed in P. de Nolhac, *Pétrarque et l'humanisme* (Paris, 19072) (Bibliothèque littéraire de la renaissance, 1), pp. 220–2, supplemented by Burnett, 'Peter Abelard "Soliloquium" ' (= *Soliloquium*), p. 861; cf. Dronke, *Abelard and Heloise in medieval testimonies*, pp. 56–8 = *Intellectuals and poets*, pp. 289–91.

[8] 'sed illud dico, quod licet hodie procul dubio sanctus sit, fieri potest ut, dum ad Eugenium scripsit, nondum forsitan sanctus esset', *Apologia contra Gallum*, quoted in Nolhac, *Pétrarque*, p. 223, n. 3.

[9] See C. Bozzolo, 'L'Humaniste Gautier Col et la traduction française des *Lettres d'Abélard et d'Héloïse*', *Romania* 95 (1974), 199–215, esp. pp. 209–13; Dronke, *Abelard and Heloise in medieval testimonies*, pp. 55–60; Burnett in *Soliloquium*, pp. 869–72.

[10] *Annalium libri quatuor* (Paris, 1577), pp. 255–61; for Peter the Venerable's letter, see above, pp. 34–5.

[11] F. d'Amboise, *Petri Abaelardi Filosofi et theologi, abbatis ruyensis, et Heloisae conjugis ejus, Primae paracletensis abbatissae opera* (Paris); on the production of this edition, the roles of d'Amboise and Duchesne and the existence of some copies with a different cover-sheet, naming Duchesne as editor, see Monfrin (ed.), *Abélard: Historia calamitatum* (= *HC*), pp. 31–9, and (for some important revisions of Monfrin's conclusions) L. Engels and J. Kingma, ' "Hos ego versiculos". De editio princeps van werken van Abaelard' in L. Engels, G. Huisman, J. Kingma, et al. (eds.), *Bibliotheek, Wetenschap en Cultur* (Groningen, 1990), pp. 238–61.

[12] *Apologetica praefatio* in *Petri Abaelardi . . . opera* = *MPL* 178, col. 71–104, at col. 72C–73A.

the long *Praefatio Apologetica* with which he prefixed his edition. Yet, in issuing a volume of Abelard, d'Amboise found himself in a very delicate position: Abelard's works were on the Vatican's *Index* of prohibited writings; and Abelard's chief antagonist, St Bernard, was a venerated figure whose judgement could hardly be called publicly into question. D'Amboise's strategy was, on the one hand, to assemble in his preface whatever eulogies of Abelard he could find or invent (and insinuate that St Bernard's zeal for the faith might have made him ready to accept and condemn inaccurate accounts of Abelard's views);[13] and, on the other hand, to include among the opening material a *Censure by the doctors of Paris*,[14] which protected readers by warning them of any erroneous doctrines they would encounter, and both of Abelard's own 'confessions of faith' (although these could also be found in the body of the volume): the *Confessio fidei 'Universis'*, which made clear that, whatever heresies he might have perpetrated, he did not stand by them, but professed himself a son of the Church, ready to accept all that it accepts, and reject all it rejects; and the *Confessio fidei ad Heloissam*, where Abelard declares his adherence to the faith in the most personal and emphatic of terms.[15]

D'Amboise was successful in opening Abelard's way to a wider public, both by making the writings available and by bringing about a softening in the ecclesiastical prohibition on them.[16] But the dossier of praise, criticism and apology he had assembled ensured that Abelard would be approached, not through a balanced reading of what he wrote, but in an adversarial spirit: a figure to be admired, or condemned. As lover and husband of Heloise, Abelard became famous in the eighteenth century, and the personal letters were much translated and adapted.[17] By contrast, those responsible for putting into print some of the texts omitted by d'Amboise tended to take an antagonistic view of their author. Bernard Pez, introducing the first edition of *Scito teipsum* in 1721 used the *Confessio fidei 'Universis'* not only to show that Abelard did not persist in heresy, but also as evidence of the intellectual vices he had previously perpetrated.[18] Martène and Durand, the first editors of the *Theologia Christiana* and the Hexaemeron (1717),

[13] *MPL* 178, 85B–87B.

[14] *MPL* 178, cols. 109–12.

[15] Ff. *r–**v (the *Conf. fid. 'Universis'* is also printed at pp. 330–3, and the *Conf. fid. Hel.* is found in Berengar's *Apologia* (pp. 302–26) at pp. 308–9); cf. above, p. 70.

[16] Cf. Engels and Kingma, ' "Hos ego versiculos" ', pp. 256–7 (correcting Monfrin *Historia* (= *HC*), p. 39).

[17] Cf. Jolivet, 'Abélard entre chien et loup', pp. 307–8.

[18] *Thesaurus anecdotorum novissimus* (Augsburg, 1721), pp. XIX–XXII.

ridiculed those who tried to show that the contentious passages in Abelard's works were not heretical and remarked with irony of the man who wrote *Sic et non:* 'anyone who has once discovered Peter Abelard's cast of mind will recognize a man so put together by nature that, without the slightest difficulty, he could teach propositions which were opposite to one another'.[19] The extensive article on Abelard in the *Histoire littéraire de la France* echoed and extended these views. Its author had read the works of Abelard in print, and some available only in manuscript; but he hardly approached them with an open mind. His opening sentences make clear that he set out with the opposing judgements of Abelard firmly in his sights; whilst in his discussion of Abelard's 'doctrine', he is willing to take St Bernard's starting point as his own. The well-known conclusion puts a judgement no less harsh than that of St Bernard and his followers; but, in order to take account of the evidence brought by Abelard's supporters of his learning and intelligence, it adds to the characterization the idea of intellectual superficiality – a good brain put to bad use:

> Abelard was a highly intelligent man who could have gone far in the world of learning, had he been more submissive to the advice of the wise and enlightened people of his time, had he applied himself more fully to the subjects he treated, and had he been less of an enthusiast for novelty. Lacking these qualities, he became merely a vainglorious sophist, a bad reasoner, a mediocre poet, an unconvincing orator, a superficial scholar and a theologian condemned by the Church.[20]

The view of Abelard as a clever but shallow thinker, who tended to mislead rather than to enlighten, received support from scholars engaged in a more systematic account of the history of thought. To it they added another element. It derived, not from a reading of Abelard's works, but from the comments of chroniclers. Abelard's contemporary, Otto of Freising, had remarked in his history of the Emperor Frederick I that Abelard 'incautiously mixed into <his> theology the vocalism or nominalism which he followed when dealing with the natural world'.[21] Very possibly influenced by these words, in the fifteenth century Trithemius remarked that from Abelard's time 'secular philosophy began to foul theology with its

[19] *Thesaurus novus anecdotorum* V (Paris, 1717), preface to *Theologia Christiana*, cols. 1140–56 and general preface to the volume (which is reprinted in *MPL* 178, cols. 67–70: see esp. col. 69C).

[20] *Histoire littéraire* XII, p. 148 (= *MPL* 178, cols. 51–2).

[21] *Gesta Friderici I Imperatoris*, p. 69: 19–20: 'sententiam ergo vocum seu nominum in naturali tenens facultate non caute theologiae admiscuit'.

vain curiosity' – a comment quoted by d'Amboise in his preface.[22] This idea is used by Brucker in his *Historia critica philosophiae* (1743) to help explain how it was that, despite his intellectual aptitude, Abelard fell into heresy.[23] He considered that Abelard had a very subtle mind, and was the best philosopher of his day; but he was 'a dialectician and scholastic' – a type of thinker who exercised his subtlety disputing about empty things and the meanings of words. 'It is no wonder', Brucker went on, 'that when he turned to theology and defined the divine mysteries with dialectical axioms, he should have fallen into various errors or, rather, that he should have obscured clear and simple truths by his useless and irksome curiosity and subtlety.'[24] In similar vein, Cramer entitled the chapter on Abelard in his continuation of Bossuet (1785), 'On Peter Abelard's attempt to elucidate and demonstrate by dialectic the system of religion of his time'. He did not think much of the results: 'not a system but just a bit of one, full of errors ... an attempt to defend and honour incomprehensible and obscure pieces of ecclesiastical jargon, rather than to enlighten the minds of men about any truths'.[25]

As intellectual fashions changed, Abelard's reputation as an innovator, impatient of authority, and confident in the power of his reasoning, began to be turned to his credit. Both Buhle and Tennemann, in their histories of philosophy (1800, 1810), praised Abelard as a thinker who aided the development of reason.[26] For Frerichs (1827), he was a Herderian hero of the free mind, a rationalist who insisted (by contrast with earlier thinkers, such as Anselm) that nothing was to be believed unless it was first understood.[27] Michelet went further and, in his *Histoire de France* (1833), described Abelard as the 'daring young man' who 'brought religion back to

[22] Johannes de Trittenheim abbas, *De scriptoribus ecclesiasticis* (Paris, 1512), f. 87r; quoted in d'Amboise, *Petri Abaelardi ... opera*, *MPL* 178, 83B).

[23] Cf. Beonio-Brocchieri, *Introduzione*, p. 112.

[24] Abelard is treated in volume III (Leipzig, 1743), pp. 675–80 and 734–764; see esp. p. 764.

[25] *J.B. Bossuet: Einleitung*, pp. 309–441, esp. p. 439.

[26] Buhle, *Geschichte der neueren Philosophie* I, pp. 839–43, esp. p. 841; Tennemann, *Geschichte der Philosophie* VIII, pp. 170–204, esp. p. 202.

[27] Frerichs, *Commentatio theologico-critica*, see esp. pp. 15 and 27; similarly, X. Rousselot (*Etudes sur la philosophie dans le moyen âge* II (Paris, 1841), pp. 93–4) presents Abelard as a 'free thinker' – though not the first in the Middle Ages, whilst for C. Wilken (*Peter Abälard* (Bremen, 1855), p. 20) Abelard's by-word is *intelligo ut credam*. On approaches to Abelard in this period, see M. Lemoine, 'Un philosophe médiévale au temps des Lumières: Abélard avant Victor Cousin' in A. Cazenave, J. Lyotard, H. Gouhier (eds.), *L'art des confins: Mélanges offerts à Maurice de Gandillac* (Paris, 1985), pp. 581–4.

philosophy, morality and humanity'; 'he handled Christianity gently, but it melted in his hands'.[28]

Yet these historians, despite their eulogies, did not contradict the view of Abelard which had developed in the previous century: they merely re-evaluated it. Abelard was admired, because he refused to accept dogma blindly and insisted rather on treating Christian doctrine rationally and critically: he was seen as a champion of reason, not because of any system of thought he established, but because of what he rejected or even (for Michelet) destroyed. In the writings of the two mid-nineteenth-century French scholars who best knew Abelard's thought, this negative side to the picture of Abelard the rationalist became explicit. Introducing his collection of previously unedited works by Abelard (1836), Victor Cousin coupled him with Descartes as 'without question the two greatest philosophers which France has produced'; but he also remarked that both men's opinions were distinguished 'more by their importance than their solidity, by their perspicacity than by their range' and that their 'minds and character were stamped by vigour rather than by elevation or profundity of thought'.[29] Charles de Rémusat (1845) presented an even more carefully balanced assessment. Abelard, he said, 'is one of the noble liberators of the human spirit'. But he continued:

> He was not, however, a great man. He was not even a great philosopher, but a man of exceptional intelligence, ingenious and subtle, inventive in reasoning, a penetrating critic who grasped points and expounded them marvellously.[30]

[28] *Oeuvres complétes* IV, ed. P. Viallaneix (Paris, 1974), pp. 452–8, see esp. p. 453. The view of Abelard is not significantly altered by any of the revisions Michelet made to his original edition of 1833: see pp. 648–51. On Michelet's view of Abelard, see M. de Gandillac, 'Sur quelques figures d'Abélard au temps du Roi Louis-Philippe' in *Abélard en son temps*, pp. 197–209 at pp. 197–9.

[29] *Ouvrages inédits*, p. V. On Cousin's approach to Abelard and its relation to his general views on the history of philosophy, see my forthcoming article 'Victor Cousin' for the *Dictionary of Medieval Scholarship*, Gandillac, 'Sur quelques figures', pp. 199–204 and J. Jolivet, 'Les études de philosophie médiévale en France de Victor Cousin à Étienne Gilson' in *Gli studi di filosofia medievale fra otto e novecento* (Rome, 1991), pp. 1–20.

[30] *Abélard* (Paris, 1845) I, p. 273; cf. II, p. 547 (cited above, in the introduction, p. 2): 'Subtil et pénétrant, il excelle par l'exactitude et il ne manque pas d'étendue ni d'abondance; il est fécond en détails, en remarques, en arguments, mais peu riches en grandes vues ... Encyclopédique pour le temps, critique de premier ordre, c'est un inventeur médiocre.' A similar assessment, though linked to a harsher evaluation, was proffered a little later by H. Hayd (*Abälard und seine Lehre* (Regensburg, 1863), pp. 423–33, esp. p. 424): 'er war stärker im Widerlegen und im Verneinen, als im Begründen und Bauen, und im Grunde hat er der Wissenschaft doch keine neue Bahn gebrochen'.

By the end of the nineteenth century, specialists had begun to reject the description of Abelard as a rationalist. In a thorough and detailed study (1883), Deutsch argued that Abelard's theology was characterized by the central position which it gave to Christ: Abelard could be seen as the precocious precursor, not of Locke, Rousseau and Kant, but of the seventeenth-century theologians. His thought adumbrated a type of theology which, unlike scholasticism – 'a magnificent construction which rested on untenable foundations'[31] – would investigate the bases of the Church's teaching. Deutsch believed, however, that Abelard's actual achievement fell very far short of this promise. His thought does not merely fail to form a system: it contains internal discrepancies and contradictions. This lack of unity, argued Deutsch, was the result of an approach which examined and altered received teaching, without even doing so from a fixed point of view; an approach in which the negatively critical aspect predominated.[32]

Deutsch's successors in the early part of the twentieth century were even more emphatic in dismissing the description of Abelard as a 'rationalist'; and they tried to see him, not as a forerunner of any later development, but as a twelfth-century Christian.[33] Yet, in general, their characterizations of Abelard share the strand which unites Deutsch, de Rémusat, Cousin and almost all the eighteenth and nineteenth-century accounts, favourable or adverse. Abelard is presented as an exceptionally talented, innovative thinker, who brought powerful logical tools to his study of theology, who produced (but did not fully develop) individual ideas of value, but who failed to construct a solid, coherent and profound body of thought. So Sikes concluded his book on Abelard (1932) by stressing that his subject was 'no rationalist in the Voltairian sense of the word'.[34] He considered that Abelard was 'a great ethical thinker' because of his theory of intention, and that ethics had shaped his christology. But he went on to contrast Abelard with Anselm and Hugh of St Victor. For them 'doctrine was, consciously or unconsciously, expressive of religious feeling. Abailard's preoccupation with logic made him negligent of these matters . . . [H]is training as a dialectician brought him . . . to regard each doctrine separately, neglecting its religious

[31] *Peter Abälard*, p. 424.

[32] *Ibid.*, pp. 415–16, cf. p. 432.

[33] None the less, the image of Abelard the rationalist lingered among some scholars: see, for instance, R. Poole, *Illustrations of the history of medieval thought and learning* (2nd edn, London, 1920), p. 116. Nor has this image entirely disappeared from some more recent work: see de Gandillac's comments in 'Sur quelques interprétations récentes d'Abélard', *Cahiers de civilisation médiévale* 4 (1961), pp. 293–301, esp. 293–6.

[34] *Peter Abailard*, p. 252.

signification and concentrating upon its intrinsic truth.'[35] In a series of articles published in the same year, 1932, Cottiaux reached a similar, but more nuanced conclusion.[36] For much of his career, he argued, Abelard's conception of theology was 'dialectical': he set out to examine according to the rules of logic, not (as his contemporary and modern critics had mistakenly imagined) the contents of faith, but merely their verbal expression. In his last works, however, Abelard had become interested in discussing supernatural realities rather than written formulas; but he had been careful, Cottiaux added, to insist on the limitations of these reasonings.

This survey began by noting the rapid disappearance from circulation of Abelard's logical works, and the effect which this had on later perceptions of his thought. In the period since 1933 historians have increasingly been able to appreciate his logic. Previously, they had been forced to rely on Cousin's edition (1836) of part of the *Dialectica* and some of the early, short logical glosses. In 1933, Bernhard Geyer completed his edition of Abelard's detailed commentaries on Porphyry and Aristotle; and in the 1950s almost all of Abelard's other logical glosses, and the complete text of the *Dialectica* became available. Moreover, a new-found enthusiasm among philosophers and historians of philosophy for logic and semantics meant that these often highly technical texts began to receive the attentive commentary needed to make them comprehensible. Although these developments have provided substance to the view (long accepted, even by anatagonistic historians) of Abelard as a brilliant logician, they have not altered the general terms in which his thought as a whole is regarded. Indeed, fuller understanding and appreciation of Abelard's logic has tended to reinforce the idea, which goes back at least to Trithemius, that Abelard's non-logical writings are primarily attempts to apply the tools of logic to religious teaching. For example (in a widely read textbook on medieval thought), David Knowles explains that, whilst Abelard did not intend to formulate, establish or invalidate the doctrines of the faith in terms of dialectic,

> besides having his full share of the contemporary trust in dialectic as the mistress of all truth, [he] had a far greater acquaintance with, and trust in, the current *Sprachlogik*, the conviction that just as words and terms and methods could be found to express truth with absolute fidelity, so all speculation and indeed the nature and modes of acting of things in themselves, must follow and in a sense be modified by, the words and terms used by the skilled logician . . . The dogmas of the faith are not for him wells of infinite depth . . . Rather, they are so many

[35] Ibid., p. 253.
[36] 'La conception'.

propositions or facts thrown, so to say, to the Christian philosopher, upon which he may exercise his ingenuity and to which he can apply no laws but those of logic and grammar.[37]

Similarly, in a study of Abelard's soteriology aimed principally at establishing Abelard's orthodoxy, Richard Weingart comments: 'As is appropriate for a master logician, Abailard displays a certain consistency of methodology throughout his theological work; dialectics interprets the revealed truths of the Catholic faith.'[38] And Leif Grane, remarking that '[i]t is as a linguistic logician that Abelard occupies an outstanding place in history', proceeds to present his thought in terms of dialectic applied to theology and thereby to judge its limitations: 'Abelard's discussion of the doctrine of the Trinity reveals none of that wider interest that might have tempted him to reproduce Augustine's metaphysical thought. His tool is dialectic alone and his material is Church dogma alone.'[39]

Despite a wealth of specialized studies analysing this or that aspect of Abelard's thought, these views represent what has become a widely accepted – indeed hardly questioned – overall assessment of Abelard. Abelard's work is seen to be unified by common motifs[40] – or even, as Jolivet has argued, by a pervasive tendency to de-reification.[41] Yet, despite this sort of coherence, it is not seen as constructive. Abelard's writings, Jolivet remarks, like their author, are products of a time of transition between two eras, reflecting its instability without surpassing it. He was not (to repeat Jolivet's comment reported at the very beginning of this book) 'an inventor'.[42] The preceding chapters have attempted to give some reasons for doubting this judgement.

[37] *The evolution of medieval thought* (London, 1962), pp. 123–4. The editors of the second edition (London and New York, 1988), David Luscombe and Christopher Brooke, do add a comment qualifying this judgement (introduction, p. xvii). A similar approach predominates in Blackwell's recent study, *Non-ontological constructs*: see e.g. p. 29: 'By constantly resorting to *Sprachlogik*, Abaelard's method was thought to belittle the mysteries of the faith by directing them into a discipline apart from their traditional identification with metaphysics.'

[38] *The logic of divine love*, p. 31; cf. p. 117.

[39] *Peter Abelard*, trsl. F. and C. Crowley (London, 1970).

[40] See the articles by M. Beonio-Brocchieri cited in p. 94, n. 1, above.

[41] See especially *Arts du langage*, pp. 353–63.

[42] *Arts du langage*, p. 363; *Abélard ou la philosophie dans le langage*, p. 96 (see above, p. 2).

Select bibliography

This bibliography has three sections:

(1) An *Index of manuscripts*, which lists all manuscripts mentioned and records the page number of each reference to them.

(2) A list of *Primary sources*, which is intended to include all the works written before 1400 mentioned in the text or notes, citing the edition or manuscript(s) used, except for the works of Abelard himself which are listed in the Note on the reference system (pp. xvi–xx).

(3) A list of *Secondary works*. This is *not* a complete list of the secondary works mentioned in the book, but is confined to those which are mentioned more than once (and a few others which are of importance for the argument of a whole section). For a bibliography of writing on Abelard since 1958, see C. Mews and J. Jolivet, 'Peter Abelard and his influence', in G. Fløistad (ed.), *Contemporary philosophy, A new survey*, VI/1 (The Hague, 1990), pp. 105–40, which can be supplemented, for recent publications, by C. Mews, *Peter Abelard*, pp. 65–88.

Where cross-references to a collection containing the work cited are made by author (where applicable) and short-title alone, the full details are listed at the appropriate point in the bibliography. Where a cross-reference is to a work listed only in the list of abbreviations or note on the reference system, this is indicated.

INDEX OF MANUSCRIPTS

Einsiedeln, Stiftsbibliothek,
300: 78
Florence, Biblioteca Medicea Laurenziana,
S. Marco 113: 135 (cf. 352)
London, British Library,
Cotton Faustina A X: 68–9, 260–1, 277–8, 313
Royal XI: 66
Lunel, Bibliothèque municipale,
6: 48
Milan, Biblioteca Ambrosiana,
M 63 sup.: 46, 48, 340
Monte Cassino, Archivio della Bada,
174: 59
Munich, Bayerische Staatsbibliothek,
clm 14160: 8
clm 14779: 38–9, 340
Orléans, Bibliothèque municipale,
266: 45, 48–9
Oxford, Balliol College,
296: 60, 66, 68, 71, 220, 242, 340–1
Oxford, Bodleian Library,
laud. lat. 67: 125, 128
Padua, Biblioteca universitaria,
2087: 51
Paris, Bibliothèque nationale,
lat. 2923: 342
lat. 7094A: 108
lat. 7493: 47
lat. 13368: 38–40, 110, 125, 128, 130, 140
lat. 14511: 77, 269
lat. 14614: 340
lat. 15015: 51
lat. 15141: 52
lat. 17813: 110, 128, 130, 145–6
Tours, Bibliothèque municipale,
85: 59, 157
Troyes Bibliothèque municipale,
802: 72
Vatican, Biblioteca apostolica,
lat. 567: 135
Reg. lat. 159: 58
Reg. lat. 230: 110, 134, 140, 177
Vienna, Österreichische Nationalbibliothek,
cvp 819: 66
cvp 2486: 51, 242

PRIMARY SOURCES

Alcuin: *De rhetorica et uirtutibus*, *MPL* 101, 919–50

Ambrose: *De officiis*, ed. J. Krabinger (Tübingen, 1867); ed. M. Testard (Paris, 1984–in progress)

Ambrose: *De paradiso*, ed. C. Schenkl (Prague/Vienna/Leipzig, 1896) (CSEL 32, 1), pp. 265–336

Ambrose: Epistolae *MPL* 16, 876–1280.

Anon.: *Beati Goswini vita . . . a duobus diversis eiusdem coenobij Monachis separatim exarata* (Douai, 1620), ed. R. Gibbon

Anon.: *Carmina Burana*, ed. A. Hilka, O. Schumann, B. Bischoff (Heidelberg, 1930–70)

Anon.: Chronicle of the Abbey of Morigny, ed. L. Mirot, *La Chronique de Morigny (1095–1152)* (Paris, 1909)

Anon.: commentary on Aristotle's *Categories* (C7), Paris, BN, lat. 17813, ff. 19bis/r–54v

Anon.: commentary on Aristotle's *Categories* (C8) (longer version) in Vatican Reg. lat. 230, ff. 41r–71r

Anon.: commentary on Aristotle's *Categories* (C12), in Paris, BN, lat. 7094A, ff. 74r–79r

Anon.: (Abelard?): commentary on Aristotle's *De interpretatione* (H5), in Munich, clm 14779, ff. 44r–66r

Anon.: (Abelard?): commentary on Porphyry's *Isagoge* (P7), ed. Iwakuma, 'Vocales', appendix II, pp. 74–100

Anon.: (William of Champeaux or a follower?): commentary on Porphyry's *Isagoge* (P14): in Paris, BN, lat. 17813, ff. 1r–16v.

Anon.: commentary on Porphyry's *Isagoge* (P4a/b), ed. Iwakuma, 'Vocales', appendix III–1, 2, pp. 103–10

Anon.: commentary on Porphyry's *Isagoge* (P3), in Oxford, Bodleian, Laud. lat. 67, ff. 9v–14v; Assisi, Biblioteca conv. franc. 573, ff. 4r–15v; Paris, BN, lat. 13368, ff. 215r–223r

Anon.: commentary on Porphyry's *Isagoge* (P9), in Paris, BN, lat. 13368, ff. 177v–179r

Anon.: commentary on pseudo-Augustine's *Categoriae Decem* (C18), in Florence, Biblioteca Medicea Laurenziana, S. Marco 113, ff. 26r–28v

Anon.: *Dubitatur a quibusdam* in H. Weisweler, *Das Schrifttum der Schule Anselms von Laon und Wilhelms von Champeaux in Deutschen Bibliotheken* (Münster, 1936) (BGPMA 33, 2), pp. 314–58

Anon.: *Enarrationes in Matthaeum*, *MPL* 162, 1227–550

Anon.: *Glosule* to Priscian's *Institutiones Grammaticae*, in Philippus Pincius' Venice, 1500 edition of the *Institutiones*; extracts in Mews, 'Nominalism and theology'; section on *voces* ed. in I. Rosier, 'Le commentaire des Glosulae et des Glosae de Guillaume de Conches sur le chapitre De Voce des Institutiones Grammaticae de Priscien', *CIMAGL* 63 (1993), at pp. 119–30

Anon.: *Institutiones nostrae*, ed. C. Waddell, *The Paraclete Statutes: Institutiones nostrae: introduction, edition, commentary* (Gethsemani Abbey, Trappist, Kentucky, 1987) (Cistercian liturgy series 20)

Anon.: *Introductiones montane maiores*, Paris, BN, lat. 15141, ff. 47r –104r

Anon.: *Moralium dogma philosophorum*, ed. J. Holmberg (Paris/Cambridge/Uppsala/Leipzig/The Hague, 1929) under attribution to William of Conches

Anon.: *Principium et causa omnium*, ed. in J. Bliemetzrieder, *Anselms von Laon systematische Sentenzen* (Münster, 1919) (BGPMA 18), pp. 47–153

Anon.: *Sententiae Atrebatenses*, ed. in *Lottin*, pp. 403–40

Anon.: *Sententie diuine pagine*, ed. Bliemetzrieder, *Anselms von Laon Sentenzen* (see above: Anon.: *Principium et causa omnium*), pp. 3–46

Anon.: *Summa Sophisticorum elenchorum*, ed. de Rijk, *Logica modernorum* I, pp. 257–458

Anon.: *Tractatus de Dissimilitudine argumentorum*, ed. de Rijk, *Logica modernorum* I, pp. 459–89

Anon.: *Ysagoge in Theologiam*, ed. in A. Landgraf, *Ecrits théologiques de l'école d'Abélard* (Louvain, 1934), pp. 63–285

Anselm of Canterbury: Works, in F. Schmitt, *Anselmi opera* I and II (Edinburgh, 1946 – reissue)

Anselm of Laon: Sentences, in *Lottin*, pp. 19–81

Aquinas, Thomas: *Summa Theologiae*, I (Madrid, 1978)

Archbishop of Rheims: Letter to Pope Innocent II, printed with letters of St Bernard as no. 191 in Leclercq and Rochais, *S. Bernardi opera* VIII (see Bernard of Clairvaux)

Aristotle: *Categories* (in 'composite' Boethian translation) in L. Minio-Paluello (ed.), *AL* I, 1–5, *Categoriae vel Praedicamenta* (Bruges/Paris, 1961), pp. 47–79 (see also Ackrill, in the list of secondary works)

De interpretatione (in Boethius' Latin translation) in L. Minio-Paluello, ed., *AL* II, 1–2, *De interpretatione vel Periermenias* (Bruges/Paris, 1965), pp. 5–38 (see also Ackrill, in the list of secondary works)

Metaphysics Books Z and *H*, ed. and transl. D. Bostock (Oxford, 1994)

Augustine: *Contra Secundinum Manichaeum*, ed. J. Zycha (Prague/Vienna/Leipzig, 1892) (CSEL 25), pp. 905–47

De ciuitate dei, ed. B. Dombart and A. Kalb, (4th edn, Leipzig, 1928)

De continentia, ed. J. Zycha (Prague/Vienna/Leipzig, 1900) (CSEL 41), pp. 141–83

De diuersis quaestionibus lxxxiii, ed. A. Mutzenbecher, (Turnhout, 1975) (CC 44A), pp. 1–249

De doctrina christiana, ed. J. Martin (Turnhout, 1972) (CC 32), pp. 1–167

De libero arbitrio, ed. W. Green (Turnhout, 1970) (CC 29), pp. 211–321

De nuptiis et concupiscentia, ed. C. Urba and J. Zycha (Prague/Vienna/Leipzig, 1902) (CSEL 42), pp. 209–319

De sancta virginitate, ed. J. Zycha (Prague/Vienna/Leipzig, 1900) (CSEL 41), pp. 235–302

De sermone domini in Monte, ed. A. Mutzenbecher (Turnhout, 1967) (CC 35)

Enarrationes in Psalmos, ed. E. Dekkers and J. Fraipont (Turnhout, 1956) (CC 39–40)

Enchiridion, (Turnhout, 1969) (CC 46), pp. 23–114

Epistolae 124–184A, ed. A. Goldbacher (Vienna/Leipzig, 1904) (CSEL 44)

Expositio quarundam propositionum ex ep. ad Romanos, *MPL* 35, 2063–88

Bede: *In Genesim*, ed. C. Jones (Turnhout, 1967) (CC 118a)

Berengar of Poitiers: *Apologia*, ed. R. Thomson, in 'The satirical works of Berengar of Poitiers: an edition with introduction', *Mediaeval Studies* 42 (1980) 89–138

Bernard of Clairvaux: Letters, in J. Leclercq and H. Rochais (eds.), *Sancti Bernardi opera* VIII (Rome, 1977)

Bishops of France: Letter to Pope Innocent II, ed. J. Leclercq, 'Autour de la correspondance de S. Bernard' in *Sapientiae doctrina. Mélanges de théologie et de littérature médiévales offerts à Dom Hildebrand Bascour O.S.B.* (Louvain, 1980) (RTAM numéro spécial, 1), pp. 185–98

Boethius: Commentary on Aristotle's *Categories*, in *MPL* 64, 159–294

Commentaries on Aristotle's *De interpretatione*, ed. C. Meiser, 2 vols. (Leipzig, 1877, 1880)

Commentaries on Porphyry's *Isagoge*, ed. S. Brandt (Vienna/Leipzig, 1906) (CSEL 48)

De differentiis topicis, in *MPL* 64, 1173–216

De divisione, in *MPL* 64, 875–92

Cicero: *De inventione*, ed. G. Stroebel (Leipzig, 1915)
Eadmer: *De excellentia Virginis Mariae*, *MPL* 159, 557–80
Fulk of Deuil: *Letter to Abelard*, in *MPL* 178, 371B–376B; a missing section is edited in D. van den Eynde, 'Détails biographiques sur Pierre Abélard', *Antonianum* 38 (1963) 217–23
Garlandus (of Besançon): *Dialectica*, ed. L. de Rijk (Assen, 1959) (Wijsgerige teksten en studies 3)
Geoffrey of Auxerre: *S. Bernardi vita prima*, *MPL* 185, 225–466
Gregory the Great: *Moralia in Iob*, ed. M. Adriaen (Turnhout, 1979) (CC 143, 143A, 143B)
Hugh of St Victor: *De baptismo*, *MPL* 182, 1031–46
De beatae Mariae virginitate, *MPL* 176, 857–76
De sacramentis, *MPL* 176, 173–618
Jean de Meun: *La vie et les epistres Pierres Abaelart et sa fame* I (Geneva, 1991)
Jerome: *Commentarium in epistolam ad Galatas*, *MPL* 26, 307–438
De perpetua virginitate S. Mariae adversus Helvidium, *MPL* 23, 183–206
John of Salisbury: *Historia Pontificalis*, ed. and transl. M. Chibnall (London etc., 1956)
Metalogicon, ed. J. Hall (assisted by K. Keats-Rohan) (Turnhout, 1991) (CC [cm] 98)
Martin of Braga: *Formula vitae honestae*, ed. in C. Barlow, *Martini episcopi Bracarensis opera omnia* (New Haven, 1950), pp. 236–50
Masson, Papire: *Annalium, libri quattuor* (Paris, 1577)
Origen: *In epistolam B. Pauli ad Romanos*, J.-P. Migne, *Patrologia Graeca* 14 (trans. Rufinus), 833–1292
Otto of Freising: ed. G. Waitz and B. von Simson, *Gesta Friderici I Imperatoris* (3rd edn, Hanover/Leipzig, 1912) (*MGH* Scripta rerum germanicarum in usu scholarum)
Peter the Venerable: *The letters of Peter the Venerable*, ed. G. Constable, 2 vols. (Harvard, 1967) (Harvard historical studies 78)
Plato: *Timaeus* (in Calcidius' Latin translation), ed. J. Waszink (London/Leiden, 1975) (Corpus philosophorum medii aevi: Corpus Platonicum. Plato Latinus IV)
Porphyry: *Isagoge*, in Greek original in *Busse*; in Boethius' Latin translation, in L. Minio-Paluello and B. Dodd (eds.), *AL* I, 6–7 *Categoriarum supplementa* (Bruges/Paris, 1966), pp. 5–31
Priscian *Institutiones Grammaticae*, ed. M. Hertz in H. Keil, *Grammatici Latini*, II–III (Leipzig, 1855–9)
Richard of Poitiers: *Chronicon*, extracts in MGH *Scriptores* XXVI (Hanover, 1882), pp. 74–86
Roscelin: *Epistola ad Abaelardum* in Reiners, *Nominalismus*, pp. 63–80
Seneca: *Epistolae morales ad Lucilium*, ed. O. Hense (Leipzig, 1914)
Thomas of Morigny: *Disputatio catholicorum patrum*, ed. M. Carra de Vaux St Cyr, *Revue des sciences philosophiques et théologiques* 47 (1963), 205–20
Walter of Mortagne (?): *De caritate*, ed. in Wielockx, 'La Sentence' (1982) pp. 69–73
Letter to Abelard, in H. Ostlender (ed.), *Sententiae Florianenses* (Bonn, 1929) (Florilegium patristicum 19), pp. 34–40

William of Champeaux: *Sententiae* in *Lottin*, pp. 189–227

William of Conches, *Glosae super Platonem* ed. Edouard Jeauneau (Paris, 1965) (Textes philosophiques du moyen âge 15)

William of Lucca, *Summa dialetice artis*, ed. L. Pozzi (Padua, 1975) (Testi e saggi 7)

William of St Thierry: Letter to St Bernard and Geoffrey of Chartres in J. Leclercq (ed.), 'Les lettres de Guillaume de Saint-Thierry – Saint Bernard', *Revue Bénédictine* 79 (1969), 375–91 at pp. 377–8

SECONDARY WORKS

'ABÉLARD' in *Histoire littéraire de la France* XII, (Paris, 1763), pp. 86–152 = *MPL* 178, cols. 9–54

Abélard. Le 'Dialogus', la philosophie de la logique (Geneva/Lausanne/Neuchâtel, 1981) (Cahiers de la revue de théologie et de philosophie 6)

Ackrill, J., ed., *Aristotle's 'Categories' and 'De interpretatione'* (Oxford, 1963)

Anna, G. d', 'Abelardo e Cicerone', *Studi Medievali* 3a serie, 10.1 (1969), pp. 333–419

Armstrong, D., *Nominalism and realism: universals and scientific realism* I (Cambridge, 1978)

Benton, J., 'A reconsideration of the authenticity of the correspondence of Abelard and Heloise' in *Petrus Abaelardus* (see abbreviations), pp. 41–52

'Fraud, fiction and borrowing in the correspondence of Abelard and Heloise', in *Pierre Abélard* (see abbreviations), pp. 469–511

'Suger's life and personality' in P. Gerson, (ed.), *Abbot Suger and Saint-Denis* (New York, 1986), pp. 3–15

Beonio-Brocchieri, M. Fumagalli, *Introduzione a Abelardo* (2nd edn, Rome/Bari, 1988)

Blackwell, D., *Non-ontological constructs. The effects of Abaelard's logical and ethical theories on his theology: a study in meaning and verification* (Berne/Frankfurt/New York/Paris, 1988)

Blomme, R., *La doctrine du péché dans les écoles théologiques de la premiére moitié du XIIe siècle* (Louvain/Gembloux, 1958) (Universitas catholica Lovaniensis. Dissertationes ad gradum magistri ... consequendum conscriptae, series III, 6)

Borst, A., 'Abälard und Bernhard', *Historische Zeitschrift* 186 (1958), 497–526

Bourgain, P., 'Héloïse' in *Abélard en son temps* (see abbreviations), pp. 211–37

Brooke, C., *The medieval idea of marriage* (Oxford, 1989)

Buhle, J., *Geschichte der neueren Philosophie* I (Göttingen, 1800)

Buytaert, E., 'Abelard's Collationes', *Antonianum* 44 (1969), 18–39

'Abelard's Expositio in Hexaemeron', *Antonianum* 43 (1968), 163–94

Campbell, K., *Abstract particulars* (Oxford, 1986)

Châtillon, J., 'De Guillaume de Champeaux à Thomas Gallus', *Revue du moyen âge latin* 8 (1952) 139–62, 247–72

Constable, G., 'Suger's monastic administration' in P. Gerson, (ed.), *Abbot Suger and Saint-Denis* (New York, 1986), pp. 17–32

Cottiaux, J., 'La conception de la théologie chez Abélard', *Revue d'histoire ecclésiastique* 28 (1932), 247–95, 533–51, 788–828

Cramer, J., *J.B. Bossuet: Einleitung in die Geschichte der Welt und der Religion fortgesetzt* VI (Leipzig, 1785)

de Rijk, L. 'Abelard's semantic views and later developments' in H. Braakhuis, C. Kneepkens and L. de Rijk, (eds.), *English logic and semantics* (Nijmegen, 1981) (Artistarium supplementa 1), pp. 1–58

'La signification de la proposition (dictum propositionis) chez Abélard' in *Pierre Abélard* (see abbreviations), pp. 547–55

'Martin M. Tweedale on Abailard. Some criticisms of a fascinating venture', *Vivarium* 23 (1985), 81–97

'Peter Abelard's semantics and his doctrine of being', *Vivarium* 24 (1986), 85–128

Postscript to Tweedale, 'Reply', *Vivarium* 25 (1987), 23

'Some new evidence on twelfth century logic: Alberic and the School of Mont Ste Geneviève (Montani)', *Vivarium* 4 (1966), 1–57

'The semantical impact of Abailard's solution of the problem of universals' in *Petrus Abaelardus* (see abbreviations), pp. 139–50

Logica modernorum I, (Assen, 1962); *Logica modernorum* II, 1 (Assen, 1967)

De Siano, F., 'Of God and man: consequences of Abelard's ethic', *The Thomist* 35 (1971), 631–60

Denifle, H., 'Die Sentenzen Abaelards und die Bearbeitungen seiner Theologia vor Mitte des 12. Jhs.', *Archiv f. Litteratur- und Kirchengeschichte* 1 (1885) 402–69, 584–624

Deutsch, S., *Peter Abälard. Ein kritischer Theologe des zwölften Jahrhunderts* (Leipzig, 1883)

Dronke, P., 'Heloise, Abelard and some recent discussions' in *Intellectuals and poets*, pp. 323–42

'Heloise's *Problemata* and *Letters*: some questions of form and content' in *Petrus Abaelardus* (see abbreviations), pp. 53–73 (reprinted in Dronke, *Intellectuals and poets*, pp. 247–94).

'The lament of Jephtha's daughter: themes, traditions, originality' in *Intellectuals and poets*, pp. 345–88

A history of twelfth-century western philosophy (Cambridge, 1988)

Abelard and Heloise in medieval testimonies (Glasgow, 1976)

Intellectuals and poets in medieval Europe (Rome, 1992) (Storia e letteratura: Raccolta di studi e testi 183)

Poetic Individuality in the Middle Ages (Oxford, 1970)

Women writers of the Middle Ages (Cambridge, 1984)

Ebbesen, S., 'Porphyry's legacy to logic: a reconstruction' in Sorabji, *Aristotle transformed*, pp. 141–171 = S. Ebbesen, *Commentators and commentaries on Aristotle's Sophistici Elenchi* I (Leiden, 1981) (Corpus latinum commentariorum in Aristotelem graecorum 7, 1), pp. 133–70

Engels, L. and J. Kingma, '"Hos ego versiculos". De editio princeps van werken van Abaelard' in L. Engels, G. Huisman, J. Kingma, et al., (eds.), *Bibliotheek, Wetenschap en Cultuur* (Groningen, 1990), pp. 238–61

Evangeliou, C., *Aristotle's Categories and Porphyry* (Philosophia antiqua 48) (Leiden/New York/Copenhagen/Cologne, 1988)

Frede, M., *Essays in ancient philosophy* (Oxford, 1987)

Frerichs, J., *Commentatio theologico-critica de Petri Abaelardi doctrina dogmatica et morali* (Jena, 1827)

Gale, C., 'From dialogue to disputation: St Anselm and his students on disbelief', *Tjurunga* 44 (1993), 71–86

Gandillac, M. de, 'Intention et loi dans l'éthique d'Abélard' in *Pierre Abélard* (see abbreviations), pp. 585–608

'Sur quelques figures d'Abélard au temps du Roi Louis-Philippe' in *Abélard en son temps* (see abbreviations), pp. 197–209

Gilson, E., *Héloïse et Abélard* (Paris, 1938)

La théologie mystique de Saint Bernard (Paris, 1934) (Etudes de philosophie médiévale 20)

Gracia, J., *Introduction to the problem of individuation in the early Middle Ages* (Munich/Vienna, 1984)

Graham, M., *Aristotle's two systems* (Oxford, 1987)

Henry, D., *Commentary on De grammatico: the historico-logical dimensions of a dialogue of St Anselm's* (Dordrecht/Boston, 1974)

Medieval mereology (Amsterdam/Philadelphia, 1991) (Bochumer Studien zur Philosophie 16)

The logic of St Anselm (Oxford, 1967)

Iwakuma, Y., '"Vocales", or early nominalists', *Traditio* 47 (1992), 37–111

'William of Champeaux and the *Introductiones*' (forthcoming in the *Acts of the 10th European Symposium on medieval semantics*, ed. H. Braakhuis and C. Kneepkens)

Jacobi, K., 'Statements about events: modal and tense analysis in medieval logic', *Vivarium* 21 (1983), 85–107

Jaeger, C., 'Peter Abelard's silence at the Council of Sens', *Res publica litterarum* 3 (1980), 31–54

Janson, T., 'Schools of cursus in the twelfth century and the *Letters* of Heloise and Abelard' in C. Leonardi and E. Menestò (eds.), *Retorica e poetica tra i secoli XII e XIV* (Florence, 1988)

Jolivet, J., 'Abélard entre chien et loup', *Cahiers de civilisation médiévale* 20 (1971), 307–22 (reprinted in Jolivet, *Aspects*, pp. 169–84)

'Doctrines et figures de philosophes chez Abélard', in *Petrus Abaelardus* (see abbreviations), pp. 103–20

'Eléments du concept de nature chez Abélard' in *La filosofia della natura nel medioevo*, pp. 297–304

'Non-réalisme et platonisme chez Abélard. Essai d'interprétation' in *Abélard et son temps* (see abbreviations), pp. 175–195

'Trois variations médiévales sur l'universel et l'individu: Roscelin, Abélard, Gilbert de la Porrée, *Revue du Métaphysique et de morale* 1 (1992), 111–55

'Vues médiévales sur les paronymes', *Revue internationale de philosophie* 113 (1975), 222–42 reprinted in Jolivet, *Aspects* pp. 138–58

Abélard ou la philosophie dans le langage (Paris, 1969)

Arts du langage et théologie chez Abélard (2nd edn, Paris, 1982) (Etudes de philosophie médiévale 57)

Aspects de la pensée médiévale: Abélard. Doctrines du langage (Paris, 1987)

Jolivet, J. and Libera, A. de (eds.), *Gilbert de Poitiers et ses contemporains* (Naples, 1987) (History of Logic 5)

Jolivet, J., *Le probléme du mal d'après Saint Augustin* (2nd edn, Paris, 1936)

Kenny, A., *The God of the philosophers* (Oxford, 1979)

Kirwan, C., *Augustine* (London/New York, 1989)

Klibansky, R., 'Peter Abailard and Bernard of Clairvaux', *Mediaeval and Renaissance Studies* 5 (1961), 1–27

Knuuttila, S., 'Time and modality in scholasticism' in S. Knuuttila (ed.), *Reforging the great chain of being* (Dordrecht/Boston/London, 1981), pp. 163–257

Modalities in medieval philosophy (London, 1993)

Kolmer, L., 'Abaelard und Bernhard von Clairvaux in Sens', *Zeitschrift der Savigny-Stiftung für Rechtsgeschichte*, kanonistische Abt. 67 (1981), 121–47

La filosofia della natura nel medioevo (Atti del terzo congresso internazionale di filosofia medioevale) (Milan, 1964)

Leclercq, J., 'Autour de la correspondance de S. Bernard' in *Sapientiae doctrina. Mélanges de théologie et de littérature médiévales offerts à Dom Hildebrand Bascour O.S.B.* (Louvain, 1980) (RTAM numéro spécial, 1), pp. 185–98

'Les formes successives de la lettre-traité de Saint Bernard contre Abélard', *RB* 78 (1968), 87–105

'Les lettres de Guillaume de Saint-Thierry à Saint Bernard', *RB* 79 (1969), 375–91

Lewis, N., 'Determinate truth in Abelard', *Vivarium* 25 (1987), 81–109

Libera, A. de, 'Abélard et le dictisme' in *Abélard. Le 'Dialogus'*, pp. 59–92

Little, E., 'Relations between St Bernard and Abelard before 1139' in M. Pennington, (ed.), *Saint Bernard of Clairvaux* (Kalamazoo, 1977), pp. 155–68

Luchaire, A., *Etudes sur les actes de Louis VII* (Paris, 1885)

Luscombe, D., 'From Paris to the Paraclete: the correspondence of Abelard and Heloise', *Proceedings of the British Academy* 74 (1988), 247–83

'Nature in the thought of Peter Abelard', in *La filosofia della natura nel medioevo*, pp. 314–19

'The school of Peter Abelard revisited', *Vivarium* 30 (1992), 127–38

'Peter Abelard and his school' (King's College, Cambridge Fellowship dissertation, 1962)

Peter Abelard's 'Ethics' (Oxford, 1971)

The school of Peter Abelard (Cambridge, 1969) (Cambridge studies in medieval life and thought, 2nd series 14)

Marenbon, J., 'Abelard, *ens* and unity', *Topoi* 11 (1992), 149–58

'Abelard's concept of natural law' in A. Zimmermann, (ed.), *Miscellanea Mediaevalia* 21, 2: *Mensch und Natur im Mittelalter* (Berlin/New York, 1992), pp. 609–21

'Abelard's concept of possibility' in B. Mojsisch and O. Pluta, (eds.), *Historia philosophiae medii aevi* (Amsterdam/Philadelphia, 1991), pp. 595–609

'Abelard's ethical theory: two definitions from the *Collationes*' in H. Westra, (ed.), *From Athens to Chartres* (Leiden/New York/Cologne, 1992), pp. 301–14

'Glosses and commentaries on the *Categories* and *De interpretatione* before Abelard', J. Fried (ed.), *Dialektik und Rhetorik im früheren und hohen Mittelalter* (Munich, 1996), pp. 21–49

'The Platonisms of Peter Abelard' in L. Benakis (ed.), *Neoplatonism in medieval philosophy* (forthcoming)

'Vocalism, nominalism and the commentaries on the *Categories* from the earlier twelfth century', *Vivarium* 30 (1992), 51–61

Martin, C., 'Embarrassing arguments and surprising conclusions in the development of theories of the conditional in the twelfth century' in Jolivet and de Libera, *Gilbert de Poitiers*, pp. 377–400

'The logic of the Nominales', *Vivarium* 30 (1992), 110–26

'William's machine', *Journal of Philosophy* 83 (1986), 562–72

Mews, C., 'A neglected gloss on the "Isagoge" by Peter Abelard', *Freiburger Zeitschrift für Philosophie und Theologie* 31 (1984), 35–550

'Aspects of the evolution of Peter Abaelard's thought on signification and predication' in Jolivet and de Libera, *Gilbert de Poitiers*, pp. 15–41

'In search of a name and its significance: a twelfth century anecdote about Thierry and Peter Abaelard', *Traditio* 44 (1988), 171–200

'La bibliothèque du Paraclet du XIIIe siècle à la Révolution', *Studia monastica* 27 (1985), 31–67

'Nominalism and theology before Peter Abaelard: new light on Roscelin of Compiègne', *Vivarium* 30 (1992), 5–37

'On dating the works of Peter Abelard', *AHDLMA* 52 (1985), 73–134

'Peter Abelard's (Theologia Christiana) and (Theologia 'Scholarium') re-examined', *RTAM* 52 (1985), 109–158

'The lists of heresies imputed to Peter Abelard', *RB* 95 (1985), 73–110

'The *Sententie* of Peter Abelard', *RTAM* 53 (1986), 130–83

Peter Abelard (Aldershot, 1995) (Authors of the Middle Ages II, 5 – Historical and religious writers of the Latin West)

Miethke, J., 'Abaelards Stellung zur Kirchenreform. Eine biographische Studie', *Francia* 1 (1973), 158–92

Moos, P. von, 'Cornelia und Heloise', *Latomus* 34 (1975), 1024–59

'Lucan und Abelard' in G. Cambier, (ed.), *Hommages à André Boutemy* (Collection Latomus 145) (Brussels, 1976), pp. 413–43

Mittelalterforschung und Ideologiekritik (Munich, 1974) (Kritische Information 15)

Morris, T., ed., *The concept of God* (Oxford, 1987)

Nicolau d'Olwer, L., 'Sur la date de la *dialectica* d'Abélard', *Revue du moyen âge latin* 1 (1945), 375–90

Nolhac, P. de, *Pétrarque et l'humanisme* (2nd edn, Paris, 1907) (Bibliothèque littéraire de la renaissance 1)

Nuchelmans, G., *Theories of the proposition* (Amsterdam/London, 1973)

Oehler, K., (ed.), *Aristoteles: Kategorien* (Berlin, 1984) (Aristoteles Werke in deutscher Übersetzung I, I)

Orlandi, G., 'Per una nuova edizione del *Dialogus* di Abelardo', *Rivista critica di storia della filosofia* 24 (1979), 474–94

Ostlender, H. [Introduction to ed.], *Peter Abaelards Theologia 'Summi Boni'* (Münster, 1939) (BGPMA 35, 2/3)

Ott, L., *Untersuchungen zur theologischen Briefliteratur der Frühscholastik* (Münster, 1937) (BGPMA 34).

Peppermüller, R., *Abaelards Auslegung des Römerbriefes* (Münster, 1972) (BGPMA n.f. 10)

Picavet, F., *Roscelin philosophe et théologien d'après la légende et d'après l'histoire* (Paris, 1911)

Reiners, J., *Der Nominalismus in der Frühscholastik* (Münster, 1910) (BGPMA 8, 5)

Rémusat, C. de, *Abélard* (Paris, 1845)

Robertson, D. W., *Abelard and Heloise* (New York, 1972)

Rohmer, J., *La finalité morale chez les théologiens* (Paris, 1939) (Etudes de philosophie médiévale XXVII), 31–40

Saarinen, R., *Weakness of the will in medieval thought. From Augustine to Buridan* (Leiden/New York/Cologne, 1994) (Studien und Texte zur Geistesgeschichte des Mittelalters 44)

Schmeidler, H., 'Abaelard und Heloise: eine geschichtlich-psychologische Studie', *Die Welt als Geschichte* 6 (1940), 93–123

'Der Briefwechsel zwischen Abälard und Heloise eine Fälschung', *Archiv für Kulturgeschichte* 11 (1913), 1–30

Shimizu, T., 'From vocalism to nominalism: progression in Abaelard's theory of signification', *Didascalia* 1 (1995), 15–46

Sikes, P., *Peter Abailard* (Cambridge, 1932)

Silvestre, H., 'Die Liebesgeschichte zwischen Abaelard und Heloise: der Anteil des Romans', in *Fälschungen im Mittelalter* V (MGH Schriften 33, 5) (Hanover, 1988), pp. 121–65 = an extended version, in translation of 'L'idylle d'Abélard et Héloïse: la part du roman', *Académie royale de Belgique, Bulletin de la classe des lettres et des sciences morales et politiques*, 5e série, 71 (1985), 157–200

Simonis, W., *Trinität und Vernunft* (Frankfurt, 1972) (Frankfurter Theologische Studien 12)

Sorabji, R. (ed.), *Aristotle transformed: the ancient commentators and their influence* (London, 1990)

Tennemann, W., *Geschichte der Philosophie* VIII (Leipzig, 1810)

Thomas, R., *Der philosophische-theologische Erkenntnisweg Peter Abaelards im Dialogus inter Philosophum, Iudaeum et Christianum* (Bonn, 1966) (Untersuchungen zur allgemeinen Religionsgeschichte n.f. 6)

Tweedale, M., 'Logic: to the time of Abelard' in Dronke, *Twelfth-century western philosophy*, pp. 196–226

'Reply to Prof. de Rijk', *Vivarium* 25 (1987), 3–22

Abailard on universals (Amsterdam/New York/Oxford, 1976)

Verger, J., 'Abélard et les milieux sociaux de son temps' in *Abélard en son temps* (see abbreviations), pp. 107–31

Waddell, C. 'Peter Abelard as creator of liturgical texts', in *Petrus Abaelardus* (see abbreviations)

The Paraclete statutes: Institutiones nostrae: introduction, edition, commentary (Gethsemani Abbey, Trappist, Kentucky, 1987) (Cisterian liturgy series 20)

Weidemann, H., 'Zur Semantik der Modalbegriffe bei Peter Abelard', *Medioevo* 7 (1981), 1–40

'Modalität und Konsequenz. Zur logischen Struktur eines theologischen Arguments in Peter Abaelards *Dialectica*,' in K. Jacobi, (ed.), *Argumentationstheorie. Scholastische Forschungen zu den logischen und semantischen Regeln korrekten Folgerns* (Leiden/Cologne, 1993) (Studien und Texte zur Geistesgeschichte des Mittelalters 38), pp. 695–705

Weingart, R., *The logic of divine love: a critical analysis of the soteriology of Peter Abelard* (Oxford, 1970)

Wenin, C., 'La signification des universaux chez Abélard', *Revue philosophique de Louvain* 80 (1982), 414–47

Wielockx, R., 'La Sentence *De caritate* et la discussion scolastique sur l'amour', *Ephemerides theologicae lovanienses* 58 (1982), 50–86, 334–56; 59 (1988), 26–45

Williams, J., 'The cathedral school of Reims in the time of Master Alberic, 1118–1136', *Traditio* 20 (1964), 93–114

Zerbi, P., 'Abelardo ed Eloisa: il problema di un amore e di una corrispondenza' in W. van Hoecke and A. Welkenhuysen, eds, *Love and marriage in the twelfth century* (Mediaevalia Lovaniensia Series 1, 8) (Louvain, 1981), pp. 130–61

'Remarques sur l'epistola 98 de Pierre le Vénérable', in *Pierre Abélard* (see abbreviations), pp. 215–32

'San Bernardo di Chiaravalle e il concilio di Sens' in *Studi su S. Bernardo di Chiaravalle nell'otto centenario della canonizzazione* (Rome, 1975) (Bibliotheca Cisterciensis 6), pp. 49–73

Index